The publisher gratefully acknowledges the generous contribution to this book provided by the Classical Literature Endowment Fund of the University of California Press Associates, which is supported by a major gift from Joan Palevsky.

The Rhetoric of Manhood

The Rhetoric of Manhood

Masculinity in the Attic Orators

Joseph Roisman

UNIVERSITY OF CALIFORNIA PRESS
Berkeley · Los Angeles · London

University of California Press
Berkeley and Los Angeles, California

University of California Press, Ltd.
London, England

© 2005 by the Regents of the University of California

Library of Congress Cataloging-in-Publication Data

Roisman, Joseph, 1946–.
    The rhetoric of manhood : masculinity in the Attic
orators / Joseph Roisman.
        p.   cm.
    Includes bibliographical references and index.
    ISBN 0–520–24192–4 (cloth : alk. paper)
        1. Masculinity—Greece—Athens—History.
2. Rhetoric, Ancient.   3. Athens (Greece)—Civilization.   I. Title.

DF275.R65   2005
305.31'0938'5—dc22
                        2004013433

Manufactured in the United States of America
14   13   12   11   10   09   08   07   06   05
10   9   8   7   6   5   4   3   2   1

Printed on Ecobook 50 containing a minimum 50%
post-consumer waste, processed chlorine free. The balance contains virgin pulp, including 25% Forest Stew-
ardship Council Certified for no old growth tree cut-
ting, processed either TCF or ECF. The sheet is acid-free
and meets the minimum requirements of ANSI/NISO
Z39.48–1992 (R 1997) (Permanence of Paper).♾

To Hanna, Elad, and Shalev

Contents

Preface

This book has been several years in the making. Its writing evoked excitement, joy of discovery, disappointment, tedium, hate, love, pride, disillusionment, an intense feeling of good riddance, and gentle satisfaction. I could not have endured these mood swings without the kindness of others. I discussed this project with too many scholars to be able to mention their names here, and I hope that they will accept this collective expression of recognition and gratitude. I thank Karen Gillum, Toby Mostysser, and Jane Dieckmann for their patient review of the work, and the University of California Press's anonymous readers for their helpful comments. In a selfless act of friendship, Glenn Altschuler scrutinized the manuscript, and his incisive suggestions greatly improved it. Professor Andrew Stewart kindly suggested the idea for the book cover. Kate Toll, Laura Cerruti, Cindy Fulton, and Lynne Withey were both helpful and encouraging in facilitating the publication process. Lastly, I owe a debt of gratitude to my wife Hanna and my children, Elad and Shalev.

The book is intended for both knowledgeable students of Athenian culture and the imaginary "general reader." Hence, I have deliberately avoided the use of jargon or noting every piece and nuance of the ancient evidence and its modern treatment. To promote accessibility, there is a conscious bias toward recent studies in the English language. Considerations of space have led me in many cases to avoid discussing points of disagreement with other scholars or triumphantly exposing what I have considered to be missing evidence or mistaken and unproven assessments.

Transliteration of Greek names and words is at present an open field, which invites taking advantage of the situation. Latin spellings are used for proper names, but the transliteration of other Greek words is close to the original. The translations from the Greek texts, unless otherwise indicated, are my own. The abbreviations of the ancient sources not included in the Abbreviations list, and of titles of periodicals and other modern work, follow the conventions of the *Oxford Classical Dictionary* and the bibliographical journal *L'Année philologique*. For the order of Hyperides' speeches, as well as for collections of fragments, preference is given to the accessible Loeb Classical Library.

Abbreviations

Ancient works and authors frequently cited have been identified by the following abbreviations:

Aes.	Aeschines
And.	Andocides
Ant.	Antiphon
Arist.	Aristotle
Ath. Pol.	[Aristotle's] *Athēnaiōn Politeia (Constitution of Athens)*
Dem.	Demosthenes
Din.	Dinarchus
Dion. Hal.	Dionysius of Halicarnassus
EN	Aristotle's *Nicomachean Ethics*
Eur.	Euripides
fr.	fragment
Hell.	Xenophon's *Hellenica*
Hyp.	Hyperides
Is.	Isaeus
Isoc.	Isocrates

Lyc.	Lycurgus
Lys.	Lysias
Mem.	Xenophon's *Memorabilia*
Oec.	Xenophon's *Oeconomicus*
Plut.	Plutarch
Pol.	Aristotle's *Politics*
Pr.	Demosthenes' *Prooimia (Preambles)*
Rep.	Plato's *Republic*
Rhet.	Aristotle's *Rhetoric*
Thuc.	Thucydides
Xen.	Xenophon

Introduction

This book is about perceptions of manhood as they are recorded in the works of Athenian orators. The corpus of works commonly known as "The Attic Orators" consists of speeches, the majority of them addressed Athenians who sat in political assemblies and institutions and the law courts roughly from the two last decades of the fifth century to the 320s B.C.E. It was thus Athenian citizens whom the orators were seeking to win over, and the French scholar Nicole Loraux has aptly remarked that "the true name of the citizen is really *anēr* [man], meaning that the sexual identity comes first."[1] Indeed, only adult male citizens were empowered to make decisions in the Assembly, Council, or the courts, and none of these public institutions suffered any active female presence in its space.[2] Speakers therefore appealed to values that were shared by most Athenian men, including ideas about manhood.

1. Loraux 1993, 16; cf. Christ 1998, 4. Even though women may have been considered citizens (Patterson 1986), their citizenship lacked many of the powers and rights to which their male counterparts were entitled. Unless otherwise noted, all dates in this study are B.C.E. See Dover 1974, 30; Ober 1989, 37; and Hunter 1994, 6–7, in justification of using the Attic orations synchronically.

2. Women's attendance in the courts is attested in the orations only when they appear as defendants (Ant. 1; [Dem.] 59), or when male defendants bring their female relatives to strengthen pleas for pity: Rubinstein 2000, 154–55, and see also Foxhall 1996, 141–42. For the perception of the polis as a men's club: Ferrari 2002, 113–14.

Manhood in this book concerns primarily the privileged citizens of the city, as they fulfilled the exclusively male roles of political leaders and followers, soldiers, lovers, heads of households, kinsmen, chief guardians of communal morals, and other functions.[3] Manhood, then, is viewed here as a cultural construct that embraces roles, practices, and beliefs that put man at its center. I find this inclusive perspective useful for two main reasons. In the first place, manhood, which I use as a synonym for masculinity, was an all-encompassing perception that the Athenians were happy to leave ill defined. Second, sociologists, anthropologists, and even gender scholars have been unable to produce an authoritative definition of masculinity that satisfies the theoretical expectations of students of manhood.[4] The concept is too complex and full of contradictions, most likely because the "practitioners of masculinity"—the investigator's human subjects—often fail to agree about what it entails, or what makes a manly man.

Rather than striving to present a comprehensive picture of Athenian manhood, I limit myself here to illuminating it in one genre. By restricting this investigation to the orators, the uniqueness of this source and its particular properties are less likely to get lost, as they might in a larger endeavor. Although aspects of Greek manhood have been discussed by scholars, no publication focuses on masculine perceptions, activities, and discourse in a specific locale, time, and genre.[5] I aim to describe the concepts of masculinity presented in the orators, as well as to improve our understanding of the orations through an exploration of the rhetoric of manhood.

Nonoratorical sources are of course useful in reconstructing Athenian manhood. Yet such sources, be they literary or material, have special properties that cannot be ignored or dissociated from the information they convey, and including them would make this a work of immense proportions. Moreover, the orations have an advantage over historical and philosophical works, because they are richer in information on our subject and were addressed to a wider and more diversified audience than the readerships of history and philosophy.[6]

---

3. The sources tend to deal with masculine perceptions chiefly in relation to citizens. On noncitizens in Athens, see E. E. Cohen 2000.

4. See, e.g., Brittan 1989, 1–18; Gilmore 1990, 9–29; Brod and Kaufman 1994.

5. This statement remains valid despite the publication of three anthologies on ancient manhood: Foxhall and Salmon 1998a, 1998b; Rosen and Sluiter 2003.

6. On philosophical works as a source and the merits of the oratorical evidence: Dover 1974, 1–2, 58–61; Hanson 1990, 313; Whitehead 1993, 38; Thornton 1997, xii–xiii. On gender in philosophical and medical writings: Föllinger 1996. Similarly, speeches found in

Athenian drama, to be sure, appealed to a large audience, which included non-Athenians and perhaps even women.[7] Yet the heroic world of tragedy and the playwrights' wish to problematize fundamental political and social ideas remove the discourse somewhat from the world of everyday life in Athens. In addition, fourth-century tragedy is practically lost to us, while the extant fifth-century drama to a large extent preceded the period covered by the speeches. Comedy is no less problematic because of the difficulty of ascertaining, much more so than in the oratorical works, when the author is mocking, exaggerating, or faithfully depicting social ideas or reality.[8]

Contemporary and near contemporary evidence outside of the oratorical corpus has not been ignored, although I use it more often than not for comparative or supplementary purposes. Of course, orators, like playwrights, could and did fictionalize reality.[9] The speaker's wish to depict himself as one of the audience or as a close follower of his audience's ideals, however, while characterizing his rival as disreputable, makes the rhetorical accounts of Athens an invaluable source of information about popular masculine discourse and images. Indeed, because the orations are especially informative about what was expected of Athenian men, but less reliable when it comes the actual fulfillment of these ideals, I deal chiefly with concepts of manhood rather than with its practices. I have adopted a similar approach to Athenian law, dealing mainly with the way the ancients interpreted the law.[10]

THE ORATIONS

The corpus of the "The Attic Orators" includes orations delivered in person or given to others to deliver, often in court and for a fee. These orations are commonly divided into private and public speeches, that is, speeches dealing with personal or communal affairs, respectively. The di-

---

Thucydides, Xenophon, Plato, and Isocrates (except for Isoc. 18–21) freed their creators from the constraints of addressing a live audience: cf. Yunis 1996, esp. 61–63, 136, 237.

7. For women's presence in the theater: Podlecki 1990; Jeffrey Henderson 1991b. Denial of their presence: Goldhill 1994, 360–69. On masculinity in Athenian drama, see, e.g. Zeitlin 1996, Index s.v. "Masculinity," "Men"; Hawley 1998; Wohl 1998.

8. Heath 1997, 236–38; 242–43; Rubinstein 1993, 4–5. *Contra*: Jeffrey Henderson 1998, though see his comments in 268–70. Males and females in Aristophanes: Rosen 1997; Bobrick 1997. Aspects of masculinity in Menander: Sommerstein 1998; Heap 1998; Pierce 1998.

9. On differences between literary and oratorical fiction: Schmitz 2000, 52–59.

10. For an approach similar to the one taken here, see Saller 1997.

vision is misleading, because in Athens the line separating the private from the public sphere was easily crossed. Public issues were frequently linked to personal feuds, and legal actions involving disputed inheritances or unpaid debts, for example, often make references to issues concerning the state.[11]

The Athenian Assembly *(ekklēsia),* which normally met on the hill of the Pnyx, next to the Agora, heard speeches on public affairs. The audience here consisted of registered male citizens in possession of their political rights who were no younger than eighteen years old. According to Mogens Hansen, who has long studied Athenian political institutions, attendance was normally about 6,000 men out of about 30,000 adult citizens.[12] The social composition of the Assembly is a subject of controversy, but most scholars agree that it was sufficiently inclusive to force speakers to appeal to more than one social group.[13]

Speakers also appeared in Athenian courts, where the decision was given to a judicial board of *dikastai* (singular *dikastēs).* These men were expected to interpret the law, and in some cases, they decided on the punishment. Even though some of these powers correspond to those of a modern judge, I choose, with many other scholars, to translate *dikastai* as "jurors," to take note of the process of their selection, their lack of legal expertise, and their status as a group. The jurors came from a roster of 6,000 male citizens no younger than thirty years old, who took an oath allowing them to undertake this duty, and who volunteered for judicial service on the day the court met. A lottery assigned them to one of the jury courts *(dikastēria).* The jury panels ranged from 200 to 400 men in certain private cases, and reached 500 or more in others. Some trials took place in institutions such as the Council or the Areopagos (chiefly a homicide court), and decisions in all institutions were made by majority vote.[14] Except for the age difference, the speakers' audience in the Athenian courts was not very different from that in the Assembly. In fact, speakers occasionally spoke to both audiences as if they were

---

11. Humphreys 1985c, 318–19; Osborne 1985b; D. Cohen 1991c, 1995.

12. Hansen 1987; 1991, 125–60, esp. 129–32, but see Sinclair 1988, 114–19. The participants' age: Sinclair 1988, 55, 118: eighteen; Hansen 1987, 7: twenty.

13. Dyck 1985; Hansen 1987, 5–11; Sinclair 1988, 119–27, 133–34; Yunis 1996, 4–12.

14. This general description ignores changes in judicial procedures over time. On Athenian courts see, e.g., Harrison 1971; Todd 1993, 77–97; Boegehold 1995, 1–9, 21–42. Age of jurors: *Ath Pol.* 63.3; Hansen 1991, 181; cf. Hansen 1985, 11–13.

one and the same group of people.[15] The jurors represented no special interest group and obliged the speakers to present themselves and their cases as conforming to popular and common perceptions and ideas.[16] Thus the speeches can inform us of contemporary popular ideologies of masculinity.

Notwithstanding all the advantages of the oratorical sources, however, they present problems. Attic orators preferred to present their cases without referring to a written text. Lapses of memory, improvisations, and revisions make it impossible to assess accurately how faithful the publication of a given text was to its original delivery.[17] Nevertheless, the genre of published speeches allowed only a limited suspension of disbelief, and even if the written speeches differed from their oral presentations, they were not sufficiently removed from the realities of pleading in the Athenian popular assemblies and courts to be classified as sheer fiction. I thus assume that the extant written orations resemble the actual delivery and proceed accordingly.

To what extent were the oratorical documents colored by the elitist concerns of men who could afford expert advice or risk financial loss in court? I argue that they neither ignored nor suppressed popular perceptions and values. The speeches in fact show the coexistence (albeit far from peaceful) of elitist and commoner perspectives on manhood.

Does the inauthenticity of some speeches cast doubt on the reliability of the picture they give of Athenian masculinity? At least six speeches in Demosthenes' collection of orations, for example, were the work of another speechwriter, Apollodorus, son of Pasion. Others may have been composed by students of oratory from different periods as rhetorical exercises or for other purposes.[18] With the search for cultural clues, the

---

15. E.g., Is. 5.38; Dem. 21.215–16; Ober 1989, 145–46.

16. For the value of speeches as evidence for popular concepts, see, e.g., Dover 1968, esp. 148–96; 1974, esp. 8–14; Todd 1990c; Herman 1998, 207, 216–17.

17. On memorization and improvisation: esp. Alcidamas *Sophists* 9–13, 20. For the controversy over the authenticity of written speeches, see Adams 1912; Kennedy 1963, 206; Lavency 1964; Dover 1968, 148–74; Usher 1976; Lentz 1983; Cole 1991, 115–38; Worthington 1991; 1992, 27–39; Yunis 1996, 175, 242–47; Gagarin 1999; and for the case of Dem. 19 and Aes. 2, Paulsen 1999, 420–45, and MacDowell 2000, 24–26.

18. Apollodorus's speeches: [Dem.] 46, 49, 50, 52, 53, 59; Trevett 1992, 50–76. For claims of lack of authenticity regarding, e.g., [And.] 4, see Cobetto Ghiggia 1995, 13–45, 69–121; Edwards 1995, 131–36; Gribble 1997, 367–73, and Gazzano 1999, xx–xxviii; contra: Raubitschek 1948 and Furley 1989. A fourth-century date for the composition will not draw heavy fire; cf. Gribble 1997, 386–89. See also the highly critical approach of Dover 1968 to the Lysian corpus. In this study I restrict indications of inauthenticity (usually marked by the author name given in square brackets) to a minimum.

identity of the author of a given speech takes second place to its contents. Even a poor forger strove to conform to common perceptions.[19]

Finally, deliberative and forensic orations have a propensity to focus on crises and the irregular rather than the normal and routine.[20] In addition, the speeches are partisan pleadings, full of rhetorical devices, one-sided observations, and biased or false presentations, all problems that complicate the task of the historian. Fortunately, however, a judicious examination of the sources allows one to extract the normal and the normative from the irregular and the hyperbolic. Similarly, the veracity of speakers' statements is not of great concern here, because it is not necessary to reconstruct the "truth of the matter" to locate representations of masculinity and its ideals. When one is aware of the circumstances of each individual speech, its purpose as well as its rhetorical nature, a circumspect use of the evidence may overcome its limitations.[21]

Thus, the Attic orations can yield significant information about manhood and other social concepts of fourth-century Athens. To be sure, reliance on the orations restricts the investigation to those aspects of manhood that the speeches privilege (e.g., honor or power), as opposed to those about which they say little, including the role of rituals and religion.[22] The orations also privilege speech over viewing in the study of manhood, which may result in underestimating the significance of the body and bodily images, including sport and sexuality, to Athenian manhood.[23] Fortunately, manhood as expressed through or associated with male *erōs* and male physique has been adequately discussed elsewhere.[24] The extant orations have the merit of going beyond physical representations and manifestations of virility into contexts of masculinity that are no less, and at times even more, important aspects of manhood, such as group solidarity and dutiful citizenship.[25]

---

19. Hence, my identification of speakers in this study as Demosthenean or Lysian is no confirmation of their authorship.

20. Cf. Lefkowitz 1986, 28; Scafuro 1997, 32–33.

21. See Harris 1995, 7–16.

22. See the bibliography in Cartledge 1998a, 8.

23. On the body in the orators: Biraud 1991. On the male body in the arts, see, e.g, Stewart 1997; Ferrari 2002,112–61.

24. On sport: Poliakoff 1987; Golden 1998; and T. F. Scanlon, *Eros and Greek Athletics* (Oxford, 2002), which came out too late to be consulted here. On Athenian sexuality, see the sample literature in chapter 3, n. 22.

25. I cannot agree, therefore, with Goldhill's privileging the visual in democratic Athens: Goldhill 1998, esp. 108–9, 115. cf. Hawley 1998. Athens was as much a "culture of speaking" as a "culture of viewing"; cf. Osborne 1998b, 30.

THE IDEOLOGY OF MANHOOD

When Athenians feuded before the Assembly or the court, they emphasized their differences and rarely drew attention to gray areas. In many speeches, the speaker is a model of normative conduct and excellence, while his opponent is a picture of deviancy and villainy. It was believed that a pleader could not afford to allow the audience to entertain doubts about the merit of his case (cf. Arist. *Rhet.* 3.19.1 1419b13–22).

Out of these circumstances emerged the opposing images of the good and the bad man,[26] of what constituted desirable and undesirable male conduct and characteristics. I shall identify these images as products of the ideology of Athenian masculinity. By "ideology," I mean a set of beliefs, attitudes, and assumptions held by members of the society that guides, justifies, or helps to explain conduct and social environment.[27] Like other social ideals, this ideology was not fully coherent or free of contradictions or competition from other models; nor did it exercise unlimited power over its adherents.[28]

The Athenians' ideology of manhood often corresponded to their moral ideology.[29] The typical positive male image in the speeches is that of an adult man *(anēr)*, a loyal and useful citizen or leader of his *polis* (city-state), free in origin and way of life, willing to rank public interest over personal needs, courageous in war and politics, competitive within approved boundaries, helpful to friends and community, zealous of honor, considerate in use of power, fulfilling familial duties, truthful, hardworking, careful, practical, intelligent, guided by reason, and able to control his appetites. The bad or wicked Athenian was disgraceful and treated others hubristically (insolently), aggressively, and inconsiderately. He gave way to pleasures or any desires that a man was supposed to control, which often led to sexual misconduct, wasting of resources, violence, or other forms of wrongdoing. He was self-centered in his re-

---

26. Cf. Hunter 1994, 109–11; Christ 1998, 69.

27. For more elaborate definitions, see, e.g., Ober 1989, 38–40, with bibliography.

28. I follow here the line taken by different authors in Cornwell and Lindisfarne 1994, as well as Herzfeld 1986, 215–16; Conway-Long 1994, 64–65; Kimmel 1994, 120; Foxhall 1998b, 6–8.

29. On Athenian moral values, see, esp., Pearson 1962; Dover 1974; Fisher 1992; Cairns 1993. The correspondence between morality and manliness is evident also in gender terms used by Roman writers and orators, who seem, however, to have paid greater attention than the Athenians to one's social class: Santoro L'Hoir 1992, 1–2, 12.

lations with family, friends, or the city, or even a destroyer of his *oikos* (household) and the state. He was slavish in origin or character, and cowardly or rash on the battlefield, in the political arena, or in his inter-action with other men.[30]

Some features defining the good and the bad man crossed boundaries of age, social status, role, and even gender. A woman, like a man, could be praised for living properly and displaying *sōphrosunē* (broadly speak-ing, self-control or moderation) and, when the context permitted, for her manly courage (*andreia:* Dem. 60.29). But feminine and masculine courage or restraint often carried different meanings, and the dominant consensus that articulated this ideology was male-oriented or male-dominated, as were the contexts in which it was situated.

This point is not self-evident. Despite its biological roots, manhood is, in the final analysis, a cultural construct, a gender. Gender, we are told, is defined relationally, that is, society views manhood in relation to the feminine and vice versa.[31] Such a definition may have been ap-proved by many Greeks, who tended to look at their world and its human environment in antithetical terms (Lloyd 1966). Greek philoso-phers and medical writers discuss male and female in opposition to each other, and, as we shall see, one can find this outlook in the ora-torical corpus as well. Yet it is more common to find speakers assess-ing men, not so much by comparing them to women, as by observing how they measured up to masculine standards in relation to other men.[32]

The evaluation of manly character and performance in relation to men rather than women will be demonstrated throughout the book, but the following examples may suffice to illustrate this point here. Even though speakers in the Assembly or the courthouse did not enjoy the li-cense enjoyed by comic poets to abuse others, we would expect the Athe-nians, if they viewed men principally in contrast to women, to denigrate and insult a rival by feminizing him. Most orators, however, depict ri-vals as deficient in the performance of such masculine roles as family

30. For similar catalogs of typical masculine traits, especially in opposition to female attributes, see Dover 1974, 98–102; Just 1989, 153–54.
31. E.g., Loraux 1993, 19, 115–16; Foxhall and Salmon 1998a, 1998b; Gilmore 1990, 22–23.
32. See MacCormack 1980; Blok 1987; and cf. Laqueur 1990, 1–62; Zeitlin 1992, 212; Loraux 1993, 17; Hearn and Collinson 1994, 111; Gleason 1994, 161; Stewart 1997, 11; Humphreys 1995, 106; Osborne 1998b, 34; Pierce 1998, 130.

member, friend, soldier, citizen, or leader.[33] Similarly, there is not much feminization of opponents even in name-calling in the orations.[34] Although we do find an *androgunos* (womanish man) and charges of *malakia* (literally, softness, but mainly cowardice), *anandreia* (unmanliness, cowardice), and male prostitution, opponents are much more often described as "bad," "wicked," "shameless," or more specifically as "*sukophantēs*" (victimizing litigant), "insolent" *(hubristes),* "polluted" *(miaros),* and so forth.[35] It may be argued that the number of female comparisons is relatively limited because of the speeches' political and legal interest in male actors. Men were rarely compared or contrasted with women, however, even in incidental remarks or in efforts at character assassination, which were less constrained by relevance.

For Athenians, being the opposite of a woman was an insufficient criterion for manhood, although a necessary prerequisite. To be admitted into the discriminating group of Athenian men (naturalization excepted), one had to be of free birth, an adult, and a member of the Athenian citizen body and one of its subgroups. But acceptance into this male group did not mean the end of the quest for manhood. As we shall see, other members of the group, by means of formal and informal supervision, comparison, and ranking, assessed how well one had followed or deviated from the desired standards of manhood.

Such assessment was easy for the observer but challenging for the observed, because standards of manhood were demanding and encompassed almost all aspects of behavior. To show the extensive range of the Athenian masculine ideology, as well as the difficulties men met in complying with it, I identify features of manhood in different domains and contexts, rather than highlighting their commonality. Such an approach will help us see how Athenian men fulfilled, or deviated from, masculine norms and values, and, no less important, how they presented and articulated manly conduct in different contexts. The standards of masculinity could be stringent or lax, depending on the individual, the observers, the circumstances that framed the manly conduct or attitude, and the

33. Aes. 1 seems to be an exception. On the etiquette of language in public addresses: Isoc. 1.15; [Aristotle] *Rhetoric to Alexander* 35 1441b20–23; Halliwell 1991a, 67–68; 1991b, 289, 292–94; Carey 1994a, c; Fisher 2001, 166–68.

34. Süss 1910, 245–56; Burke 1972; and Hunter 1994, 96–119, 221 nn. 13–14; Harding 1987, 27–31; 1994, 198–99.

35. *Androgunos:* Aes. 2.127; *malakia:* e.g., Lys. 10.11; Dem. 8.68; 18.245; Aes. 2.106; male prostitution: e.g., Dem. 22.58, 61, 73; 24.181; Aes. 1 passim. For the other charges, see Burke 1972.

perceived legitimacy of those standards. Such a complex of factors often produced vague rules of behavior, conflicting demands, and confusion. They also encouraged men to manipulate masculine ideology to gain approval or repel attacks. Hence the focus here on rhetorical depictions of men and how they affect our understanding of Athenian manhood.

CHAPTER I

Manly Youth

From the age of thirty on, free adult males stood at the pinnacle of the social and political hierarchy of Athens; younger adults ranked lower, as did older men. Yet the precise age that separated young from mature adults (in the singular, both may be called *anēr*), as well as the ages that separated various categories of youth, are difficult to pin down. The rituals by which the Athenians marked the incorporation of a male baby into the household *(amphidromia)* and the young man's coming of age are of little help here.[1]

Broadly speaking, an Athenian male was considered a boy (usually called a *pais*) until puberty; a *hebē* until the age of fourteen; a youngster (usually, *meirakion*) until about age twenty-one; an *ephēbos* from roughly eighteen to nineteen or twenty, a period that corresponded to military service in the *ephēbeia*; a young man (usually *neos* or *neaniskos*) until he reached mature adulthood around thirty; and an old man *(gerōn)* from approximately sixty years old on. The separations were imprecise, however. Xenophon writes that Socrates was ordered by one of the Thirty (a group of oligarchs who ruled Athens in a tyrannical fash-

---

1. For ages and their loosely defined terms, see Nash 1978, esp. 4–5; Garland 1990, passim, esp. 1–16, 242–43; Golden 1990, 14–16; and Strauss 1993, 89–97; cf. Dover 1974, 102–6 (esp. on youth). The division of Athenian males into age classes for the purpose of conscription is a special case: *Ath. Pol.* 53.4, 7. *Amphidromia:* Garland 1990, 93–96; Strauss 1993, 1–2. For the ritual of admission into the phratry: Lambert 1993, 163–68; and generally, Rudhardt 1962.

ion in 404–403) not to converse with the young. The philosopher retorted with a typically subversive question: what age is considered young?[2]

In ancient Athens, as in the modern world, age was not only a biological but also a culturally constructed social category. In the speeches, as elsewhere in Greek literature, age is characterized not so much in terms of chronology as of physical appearance, mental development, and behavior.[3]

This chapter discusses the Athenians' perceptions of youth and the orators' use of those perceptions with the same chronological ambiguity and behavioral emphasis that the Greeks bought to this age group.

NEGATIVE STEREOTYPES AND REALISTIC EXPECTATIONS

Aristotle's *Rhetoric* offers a concise depiction of youth that conveys the mixed feelings with which the ancient Greeks evidently regarded this age group. He describes youths *(neoi)* as young men who cannot master their appetites and emotions; they are impulsive and prone to excess, although also competitive, courageous, and sensitive to honor. Owing to their lack of experience, they are also naïve, optimistic, friendly, magnanimous, and uncalculating (Arist. *Rhet.* 2.12.3–16 1389a3–1389b12). The orators' attributions are similar, only in a different mix. Although they occasionally describe a young man as brave or magnanimous, public-spirited, and free of pettiness and self-interest, more often they measure the young against the ideal of the mature adult male and find them lacking.[4]

The ideal youth was a young man with adult qualities. This ideal was embedded in an oath taken by those enrolled in the institution of the *ephēbeia*. Young Athenian men, eighteen through nineteen years old, of various classes, although probably not the poor, enrolled in a group of *ephēbeioi* as part of state-sponsored education toward becoming soldiers, citizens, and men.[5] They took an oath that emphasized the virtues

2. Xen. *Mem.* 1.2.35. For the ill-defined age category of *neaniskos*, see Golden 1990, 14–15; Kleijwegt 1991, 56, with bibliography; Cantarella 2002, 29–32. For the links between the systems of age groups and male power: Bernardi 1985, esp. 132–42.

3. See Lys. 10.29; Dem. 21.18; Aristoxenus fr. 35 (Wehrli); Robertson 2000.

4. Kind or bold young men: [Dem.] 53.12; Lys. 2.51–52; Arist. *Rhet.* 2.12.12 1389a30–35, 13.15 1389b18–20. Public-spirited and self-restrained: Dem. 54 (passim and pp. 17–21 below); cf. Xen. *Mem.* 1.2.26; Golden 1984, 313.

5. *Ath. Pol.* 42.2–5; Tod 1947, 2, no. 204. I share the scholarly view that the *ephēbeia* existed in Athens throughout the fourth century in one form or another. For the institution, see Pélékidis 1962; Reinmuth 1971, esp. 123–38; Vidal-Naquet 1986a, 106–28; 1986b; Winkler 1990b, esp. 20–22, 50 with n. 91. For reservations on interpreting the

of conformity, competitiveness, cooperation, discipline, and obedience in the military, civic, and religious spheres—all traits that the Athenians wished to see in adult males.[6]

Few of the young men referred to in the orations seem to have possessed these qualities. It is indicative of the speakers' largely unfavorable attitude toward the young that the positive attributes of a youth are most fully described not in the public addresses or court speeches but in an erotic work attributed to Demosthenes (Dem. 61). In contrast to most of the orations, this erotic composition—an address by an *erastēs* (male lover) to a prospective male beloved *(erōmenos)*, probably in his teens— is full of praise for its youthful subject.[7]

The speaker lauds the youth for exhibiting traits that go beyond his age. He praises his caution in entertaining propositions for love affairs, his graceful and dignified speech, his *sōphrosunē* (moderation) and mature prudence. To be sure, the speaker also praises his courage and athletic skills, which the Athenians found meritorious in the young. In the main, however, the young man's excellence is depicted as consisting of his rare ability to overcome the faults of youth.[8]

In the orations, the ideal is present in the negative. A clear example can be found in a Lysian speech against Alcibiades the Younger, the son of the Athenian general and politician, whose unruly, debauched conduct had become notorious. The speaker describes Alcibiades the Younger as a child *(pais)* who had lived in the home of a discredited politician, drinking and sharing his host's cloak—a probable allusion to indecent intimacy. Although still beardless *(anēbos)*, he reveled and had a *hetaira* (courtesan; Lys. 14.25). As a young man, he had surrendered an Athenian stronghold to his father's enemy, who abused him in the bloom of his youth *(hubrizen auton hōraion onta)* and held him for ransom. Alcibiades then went on to gamble away his fortune (Lys. 14.26–27). This depiction of a man who was disloyal to his father and polis, sexually incontinent, stupid, reckless, profligate, and unproductive was the antithesis of the ideal youth.[9]

---

ephēbeia as a rite of passage from boyhood to adulthood, see Kleijwegt 1991, 44; Burckhardt 1996, esp. 53–57; Hesk 2000, 29–30, 86–89. *Thētes* (poor) and the *ephēbeia*: Rhodes 1993, esp. 502–10, 768; Hansen 1991, 108–9; cf. Raaflaub 1994, 140–41.

6. Tod 1948, vol. 2, no. 204; Lyc. 1.76–77. The ephebic oath: Siewert 1977; cf. Humphreys 1985b, 206–9; Kleijwegt 1991, 50; p. 107 below.

7. Dem. 61 and its author: pp. 85–87 below with n. 3.

8. Dem. 61.5, 8, 13, 17, 21, 27–28, passim.

9. Gribble 1999, 94 for this portrait, and see pp. 165–66 for the negative portrait of young Timarchus (Aes. 1.39–71).

Speakers often describe young men as aggressive, haughty, disre-
spectful of their betters, full of bravado, and preoccupied with drinking,
gambling, and sex.[10] The young use their physical strength to bully and
insult innocent people (Lys. fr. 75 [Thalheim]); they squander their resources in the pursuit of honor and bodily satisfaction and are rash,
thoughtless, and overly ambitious to make a name for themselves; they
lack self-control and often cannot tell right from wrong. Like Aristotle's
youth, they are dominated by their passions, but, unlike Aristotle, the orators fail to give equal place to redeeming qualities. They emphasize the
danger of such youthful behavior to the youths themselves, their families, friends, innocent third parties, and the polis. Even when young persons did no wrong, the assumption was that they were impressionable
and easily corruptible.[11]

Terms frequently applied to the young include *hubris:* insult, attack,
or brutish, insolent behavior (depending on the context); *aselgeia:* aggressiveness or licentiousness; *anoia:* thoughtlessness; *akrētos:* lacking
control; *akolasia:* lacking discipline; lack of *sōphrosunē:* self-restraint
and proper conduct, or moderation; lack of *aiskhunē:* respect (especially
for one's elders); *neanieuomai* or *neanikos:* when used in the negative
sense, acting like a juvenile or brutally; *thrasus:* fresh or rash; *iskhuein:*
having physical strength; and *philotimia:* ambition for honor (in both
positive and negative senses).[12]

This criticism implies that Athenians measured young men by high
standards. The attitude is expressed in the erotic composition discussed
above, which follows elaborate praise with the assertion that the best
that the young man's peers could wish for was that they do no wrong
(Dem. 61.22).

---

10. Youthful characteristics: Dover 1974, 102–5; Fisher 1992, esp. 97–99; MacDowell 1990, 18–23; Murray 1990d, 139–40, 142; Halliwell 1991a, 284–86; Sommerstein
1998, 109–10; Ferrari 2002, esp. 87–93, 121–26. Pierce 1998, 130–36 has distinguished
between pre- and post-matrimonial young masculinities, a distinction that the extant orators seem to have ignored.
11. Harmful young men: Ant. 4.3.2; Aes. 1.94–95; cf. Dem. 19.229; 38.27; Aes. 1.65.
Rash, insolent, and excessively ambitious: Lys. 20.3; Is. fr. 6 (Forster); Hyp. 4.27; cf. Din.
fr. 14.2 (Burtt). Lacking in control, thoughtless, and indiscriminate: Is. 3.16–17; Isoc. 7.43;
cf. [Aristotle] *Rhetoric to Alexander* 35 1441a16–18. Impressionable youth: Aes.
3.245–46; cf. Arist. *Rhet.* 2.12.7 1389a16–18.
12. The following references are just a sample. *Hubris:* Dem. 54.4; *aselgeia:* [And.]
4.21, 39; Dem. 40.57; *anoia* and *akrētos:* n. 11 above; *akolasia:* Ant. 3.3.6; 4.1.6; Isoc.
7.50; lacking *sōphrosunē:* Dem. 61.3; *neanieuomai* or *neanikos:* Dem. 19.242; 21.201;
Isoc. 20.17; *philotimia:* Dem. 42.24; *thrasus:* cf. Dem. 51.19; *iskhuein:* Dem. 21.223; cf.
59.40; Theophrastus *Characters* 27. For the young as busy with the pursuit of ephemeral
pleasures see pp. 171–72 below.

Yet the Athenians also seem to have been ready to recognize that boys will be boys.[13] Moreover, the high place that Athenians accorded honor, which Aristotle defines as a key motive of young men (Arist. *Rhet.* 2.12.5–6 1389a9–16), did not always sit well with the values of moderation and self-control. Honor was closely associated in Greek thought with besting one's rivals, often through competitive displays of wealth and strength. And honor often required one to respond to an inimical action by inflicting harm. Failure to do so was perceived as cowardly and unmanly. The result was ambivalence about violence in general and youthful aggression in particular. Youthful aggression was intimidating because of young men's physical strength and because of the challenge that every new generation posed to the norms of the previous one. On the other hand, aggressiveness could be confused with a claim to superior manhood, and the community tolerated (although not officially condoning) acts of violence by youths forcibly defending their personal honor, as they often did.[14] Thus, while speakers often disapproved of youthful spending, luxury, and violence, there was a tendency to mitigate disapproval of these vices when they were committed by the young.

EDUCATING AND SUPERVISING THE YOUNG

Even so, the descriptions of youth in the orations suggest that ancient Athenians viewed young men as a potential threat to the social order, and took pains to ensure that they did not put the city at risk (Lyc. fr. 1 [Burtt]) or undermine adult supremacy. They barred males under eighteen (or twenty) from admission to the *ekklēsia* (Assembly), and men under thirty from other decision-making bodies and public offices.[15]

The Athenians also placed a great deal of emphasis on the socialization of the young through education. They used education to keep the volatility of youth in check by inculcating the ideals of civic and personal behavior, teaching deference and obedience to adults, protecting the young from bad influences, and, especially, ensuring that the young were closely supervised and controlled. They sought as well to produce men of excellence *(aretē),* pinning on youths their hopes for a better future for Athens, and expecting them to continue the legacy of their elders and

13. Lys. 24.17; And. 2.7; cf. [Arist.] *Rhetoric to Alexander* 7 1428b38; Pierce 1998, 131. Cf. Dover 1974, 102–3. Cantarella 2002, 32.
14. Cf. Forrest 1975, 46–48; Cantarella 1990; Strauss 1993, 98–99, 148–53, cf. 186.
15. Roussel 1951, 133–40, 153; Hansen 1991, esp. 88–90. Restrictions on youth participation in sports events might have served a similar purpose: Golden 1998, esp. 139–40.

even to improve upon it.[16] To these two ends, the Athenians tried to shape the behavior of young men through schools, *ephēbeia,* and gymnasia, and they closely supervised the functions of these institutions through laws and regulations (cf. Hyp. 6.8; Aes. 1.6–7).

Formal education was supplemented with informal education. Adults were expected to serve as positive role models for the young. Socrates' trial is perhaps the most famous example of the prevalent ideology that stressed the need to protect the city's youth from corrupting influences. A similar concern informs the aforementioned erotic address, which discusses at length how the older partner in a homosexual relationship should supervise the conduct of the young *erōmenos* (Dem. 61; cf. Aes. 1.138–39). Speakers in forensic orations often claimed that they were prosecuting someone in order to teach the young moderation, or warned juries that acquitting a defendant would set a bad example for youths.[17]

The education of the young through precept and example was the concern of the entire city. Adults took it upon themselves to watch over the young in order to curb their excesses (Lys. 20.3; cf. Dem. 54.22–23; Isoc. 7.47–49). The educational ideal was used by a Demosthenean speaker to illustrate how harmony was attained in Athens (Dem. 25.87–89). The ideal, illustrated in a three-generational household, was predicated on the understanding that "the young are different from the old in word and deed." The young, if they behaved properly (literally, were *metrioi:* modest or moderate); they did not call attention to their actions or, if that was impossible, indicated their intention. The old pretended not to see them wasting money, drinking, or amusing themselves to excess—that is, they refrained from the heavy-handed exercise of their superior status and power to shame.[18]

Behind the elders' tact, however, were the expectation that the young would not flaunt their excesses, on the one hand, and an unequal relationship, tight social control, and the assumption that adults were always in the right, on the other. In Athens, men were constantly watched, and

16. On schooling children in excellence: Plato *Protagoras* 325c–326d. For similar attitudes in early modern England, cf. Ben-Amos 1994, 36–37.

17. E.g., Dem. 19.285; Isoc. 16.4; 20.21; Lyc. 1.10; cf. [And.] 4.21; Hyp. 5.21–22. See Ober 1989, 170–71, on the didactic value of popular resolutions.

18. Cf. Dem. 10.39–40; Thuc. 2.37; Strauss 1993, 47–48; D. Cohen 1991c, 93; Bailey 1991, 33. The city as an imaginary family or kinship group: Plato *Menexenus* 249b–c; Isoc. 4.24; Goldhill 1990, 112–13; Loraux 1993, 65, 119–20. The question of who authored Dem. 25 is not very relevant to the issue at hand; see Hansen 1976, 144–52 (Demosthenes or a contemporary); Sealey 1993, 237–39, argues for a later rhetorician, but this is disputed by Rubinstein 2000, 30–32.

verbal or nonverbal signs were perceived as meaningful comments on other people's conduct.

YOUNG MEN IN COURT

To a large extent, the perceptions of youth that emerge from the orations are stereotypes, and some ancient Greeks recognized them as such. A series of speeches written by Antiphon in the last quarter of the fifth century for a hypothetical case in which an old man is killed by a younger man following a drunken brawl is revealing in this respect (Ant. 4).[19] The young defendant argues that it is wrong to make an indisputable law of nature out of the commonly held opinion that the young commit hubris and the old behave with restraint and moderation. Such a law, he points out, obviates the need to render judgment, because the young are convicted by their age alone. There are many temperate young men and many drunk old men, he observes (Ant. 4.4.2; cf. Isoc. 6.4; Eurip. *Electra* 367–90).

The defendant's logic is impeccable, but the need to make the point suggests that the stereotype had power. Clearly, the orators related to it, whether because they felt that it would be useful to do so or because they had to. In several speeches, it plays a significant role.

Ariston against Conon (Dem. 54)

Of all of the speeches in the orators' corpus, the oration *Against Conon*, written by Demosthenes for Ariston (Dem. 54), makes the most extensive use of images of youth. The case involved a charge of assault by the young claimant Ariston against Conon and his sons.[20] Ariston charged that when he was doing garrison duty, Conon's sons had set about abusing the slaves attached to his company and then attacked him and his companions.[21] After they returned to the city, Conon and his sons fell upon him as he was taking a walk, stripped him, and beat him to within an inch of his life. Ariston was therefore suing.

---

19. Regarding the *Tetralogies,* I agree with Michael Gagarin that they are Antiphon's work or of a contemporary: Gagarin 1997, 8–9; 2002, 52–62, citing earlier bibliography for and against their authenticity. Carawan 1998, 171–77, opts for a later generation.

20. The speech has been commented on by Gernet *Démosthène* III (1959); Carey and Reid (1985) 69–105, and D. Cohen (1995a) 119–130.

21. Dem. 54.3. Against the assumption that they were ephebes at the time (Carlier 1990, 50), see Carey and Reid 1985, 69, 78; Burckhardt 1996, 244 n. 329.

The claimant labored under two handicaps. He himself was a young man, by definition suspected of engaging in the same excesses as his adversaries. He suffered as well from the Athenians' tolerance of youthful excess in general and of youthful violence in particular. In anticipation of the defense that he expected Conon to make, Ariston suggested to the jury that Conon would trivialize the matter by presenting the fight as an affair over a woman and claim that "things of this sort are typical of young men" and quite common among the sons of Athens's social elite—*kaloi k'agathoi* (literally, the beautiful and the good; Dem. 54.14).[22] In addition, Ariston said, Conon would charge him and his friends with being "drunken and insolent fellows," as well as "unreasonable and vindictive" *(agnōmonas de kai pikrous)* in bringing the matter to court (Dem. 54.14; cf. 54.16; Aes. 1.58–62). Ariston's suit was constructed not only to refute these claims but more broadly to overcome the liabilities of his youth.

The claim was lodged against Conon, the father, rather than Ctesias, the son. The reason Ariston gave was that Conon had struck him first (Dem. 54.8, 33). This argument was based on the Athenian law of battery, which punished the man who initiated hostilities. But in his description, Ariston indicated that the three attackers had worked in concert, and he described Ctesias, Conon's son, as the most active of the assailants. Had Ariston so wished, he could have charged Ctesias with the assault and produced witnesses to prove it.[23]

The probable motive for not charging Ctesias, suggested in the text of the speech, was that youth could be a mitigating circumstance in the jury's decision. Ariston himself pointed out that youth was the only legitimate ground for pleading for a reduced sentence (Dem. 54.21). At over fifty, Conon was doubly guilty because, as a mature male, he should have avoided participating in the crime and prevented it (Dem. 54.22). Ariston's argument, like the legal and rhetorical strategies he pursued, reflected the Athenians' expectation that men act their age (Lys. 24.17–18; cf. Dem. 21.18).

22. For the commonality of such conflicts in Athens, see Dem. 21.36, 38; Lys. 3.43. The remark about the youth's social position attributed to Conon might have been designed to prejudice the audience against him: Ober 1989, 258–59; Millett 1998a, 227–28. Conon's defense: 54.22–23; Halliwell 1991a.

23. For striking first as a proof of guilt of assault: Dem. 23.50; 47.47; cf. Lys. 4.11; Isoc. 20.1; Menander *Samia* 576; Scafuro 1997, 101–2. Ctesias's involvement: Dem. 54.8, cf. 54.35; *contra*: Davidson 1997, 224. Cf. D. Cohen 1995a, 128–30. Testimonies in the service of a litigant: Humphreys 1985c, esp. 322–27, 344, 346; 1986, 59, 65; Todd 1990b; 1993, 96–97, 261–62; cf. Thür 1995, 325–31, but also Eder 1995b, 332–33.

The speechwriter uses the positive and negative stereotypes of youth to present Ariston as the innocent victim of an unprovoked hubristic attack by drunken, violent, and dangerous assailants. Ariston consistently depicts himself as a *metrios* young man—temperate, moderate, and self-controlled—and his attackers as the antithesis.[24]

Ariston presents himself as a young man of limited capacities who had been advised by friends and relatives that he should avoid appearing too ambitious for his age. He is suing only for battery, a lesser charge than was warranted by the seriousness of his injuries.[25] To dispel any notion that he may be looking for a confrontation, as young men are wont to do, or taking up the court's time with a trivial matter, he repeats several times that he pressed charges only after his assailants had almost killed him.[26]

At camp, according to Ariston, Conon's sons had spent their days drinking; he and his fellow servicemen had not. Conon's sons had "behaved with every sort of licentious brutality *[aselgeia]* and hubris": they had struck the slaves, emptied their chamber pots on them, and urinated on them (Dem. 54.4); and they had then gone on to attack Ariston and his men under the cover of night. He and his men had never raised a hand against them, but had rather "expostulated" with them to stop their abusive conduct and complained to the general. Although Ariston admitted that the abuse had produced anger and hate, he stressed that on his return home, he had not sought revenge or pressed charges, but had simply resolved to keep his distance from "people of this sort" (Dem. 54.6).

The account of the events at camp was not material to the case. Its aim was to contrast Ariston's conduct and character with the conduct and character of his assailants for the jury. To overcome the suspicion that he too might be a hothead, Ariston depicted himself as a self-controlled young man who had tried to avoid escalating the conflict. But because Athenians expected young men not to accept insults passively, he had to justify his failure to defend himself.[27] He thus showed his effort to curb

---

24. On *metrios* as a valued attribute, see pp. 171–79 below. See Carey and Reid 1985, 73–74, for the speaker's effort to present a consistent character.

25. The choice of a lesser charge could have been motivated by practical considerations: Carey and Reid 1985, 74–76. D. Cohen 1995a, 122, has suggested that Ariston picked a suit befitting his self-proclaimed identity as a man hesitant to initiate a heavy legal battle; cf. Is. fr. 6 (Forster); Dem. 44.1

26. Dem. 54.6, 12–13, 24. The case was a private action of injury *(aikeias dikē)*, but Ariston refers constantly to the graver charge and public action of *hubris (hubreōs graphē)*: MacDowell 1978, 131–32; Carey and Reid 1985, 69–72.

27. D. Cohen 1995a, 123–24.

Ctsesias and his friends and pointed out that his superiors had stopped
the attack before he had to put up his fists. In other words, he presented
himself as an innocent victim but not a passive one, and as a mature and
self-controlled young man, yet mindful of his honor.[28]

The description of the attack in the city was the key to Ariston's case.
He sought to show that the attackers' conduct greatly exceeded youthful boisterousness or harmless masculine aggression. Ariston framed his
account so as to persuade the jury that his attackers were not only badly
behaved and abusive but also posed a danger to the social order.

It was not enough to charge that Conon, his son Ctesias, and another
young man had attacked him on their way home from a *sumposion* (banquet), where they had been drinking.[29] There is evidence that the phe-
nomenon of young men leaving a *sumposion* drunk and picking a fight
was neither rare nor unequivocally condemned in ancient Athens.
Drunken violence could be depicted as either deviant or excusable behavior, depending on the circumstances and the speaker's needs.

To present the assault as an unmanly conflict, Ariston stressed that it
was totally unprovoked and had occurred as he was strolling along
peaceably minding his own business; that it was an unequal attack of
three against one; and, by implication, that his adversaries' conduct had
been dishonorable. He described in vivid detail how Conon, Ctesias, and
another young man had pulled off his clothing, pushed him into the mud,
jumped on him, and so pummeled him that he had to be carried home
on a litter and barely recovered. He drew a picture of himself at the scene
of the attack lying helpless, injured, and humiliatingly exposed in the
mud of the *agora*, unable to move or utter a sound, while his assailants
cursed and Conon mimicked a cock that had won a fight and was encouraged by his companions to flap his elbows like wings against his
sides (Dem. 54.9). Conon's crowing act, set against his victim's unwarranted humiliation, revealed a degraded, swaggering, and immature
masculinity. It was an undignified gesture, more characteristic of a cal-
low youth, and certainly unbecoming in an older man.[30]

In his characterization of Conon's sons, Ariston plays on the Atheni-

    28. *Pace* Herman 1993; 1994; 1995, esp. 45.
    29. Dem. 54.7. For the rhetorical use of topography in Dem. 54: Millett 1998a, 203–4,
227–28.
    30. On the cock as symbol: Csapo 1993, esp. 20–21. D. Cohen 1995a, 125–26, de-
tects in Conon's conduct an attempt to humiliate Ariston sexually; cf. Winkler 1990a, 48,
224 n. 3; Halperin 1990, 96. The description alludes as well to military disgrace: Jackson
1991, 242; cf. Carey and Reid 1985, 83–84. For the humiliation of forced (semi-) nakedness, cf. Osborne 1997, 506–7; Geddes 1987; Bassi 1995.

ans' fears of unbridled young men who defied the polis's social and religious norms. He claims that Conon's sons belong to two mysterious groups called *ithuphalloi* and *autolēkuthoi* (Dem. 54.14, 16–17)—respectively "erect phalluses" and "carrying their own oil flask."[31] Ariston leaves it to the jury to conjure up what took place at the meetings of these groups, but his accusation reminds jurors that youthful gangs, which were not uncommon in ancient Athens, evoked trepidation in ordinary citizens.[32]

A little later in the speech, Ariston mentioned Conon's misbehavior as a youngster *(meirakion),* when he and his friends had called themselves "Triballians"—a name denoting a wild, lawless people—and that they committed such outrages as eating food left as sacrifice at Hekate's altars and pigs' testicles used for purification rituals.[33] These deeds were adduced to show Conon's current contempt for all that was sacred and to convince the jury that there was thus no lie or perjury to which he would not stoop.

Scholars have questioned the veracity of Ariston's version of events and his characterization of his attackers.[34] What is important to this discussion, however, is the use of stereotypes of youth to try to win the jury over to his side. Ariston presents himself as a mature, civic-minded adult, young only in years, who is seeking to benefit the city by bringing criminals to justice, and who, despite his youth, has performed many services for the city (Dem. 54.42–44). Ctesias, in contrast, is presented as an unbridled youth, and Conon as adult with all the vices of the young.

Epichares against Theocrines (Dem. 58)

The stereotypes of youth, which played a central role in Ariston's claim against Conon, are not as well-developed in other orations. But young

---

31. *Ithuphalloi:* Dover 1989, 38; Carey and Reid 1985, 86–87; N. Jones 1999, 225–26. *Autolēkuthoi:* Carey and Reid 1985, 87; Borthwick 1993. The oil flask distinguishes males from females in Aristophanes' *Women at the Thesmophoria* 139–40; Golden 1998, 124.

32. Cf. Dover 1989, 38. Earlier associations of similar nature: And. 1.61, and cf. Lys. fr. 53 (Thalheim) about the poet Cinesias's membership in a group called the *kakodaimonistoi* (evil-spirit men); Cf. Peristiany 1992, 124. For comparable social activity in modern Greece, which the actors described as *kefi* (party-spirit), see Papataxiarchis1991, 172.

33. *Triballoi:* Dover 1989, 38; Carey and Reid 1985, 101. Their actions bring to mind the notorious Hermai and Mysteries affairs, on which see, e.g., MacDowell 1962.

34. Reid and Carey 1985, 80–81; Humphreys 1985c, 331–32.

plaintiffs did contend with and manipulate Athenians' perceptions of youth.

The speechwriter for Epichares (Dem. 58) turned the supposed weakness of youth to his client's advantage. At his father's behest, young Epichares had brought a case against Theocrines, his senior, who had won a case against Epichares' father for making an illegal proposal. The defendant was heavily fined and partially deprived of his rights as a citizen (i.e., suffered partial *atimia*), including the right to speak for himself in court. Epichares' case was a legal procedure called an *endeixis*, in which the plaintiff charged the defendant with criminal activity for the purpose of having him tried or arrested. Its aim, Epichares informed the jury, was to make Theocrines liable to legal punishment and thereby to avenge the former's father.[35]

Most of the case consisted of highly detailed proofs of the various criminal acts with which Epichares charged Theocrines. Several times, however, Epichares drew the jury's attention to his youth in order to win their sympathy. While Ariston presented himself as mature for his years, Epichares highlighted those aspects of youth—vulnerability, naïveté, guilelessness, inexperience, and inferiority to adults—that might evoke the sympathy and protective urges of the mature men who made up the jury.

He placed himself where Athenians liked their young men to stand: respectful, unthreatening, and in need of adult help (cf. Dem. 44.1–3). He portrayed himself as a dutiful son pressed by his father and the exigencies of time into this action. In fact, his motives included a good dose of self-interest. According to Athenian law, should the father die, the fine and deprivation of the right to speak would fall upon the son. Epichares briefly referred to his sharing his father's misfortune (Dem. 58.59) but stressed his filial piety. As he told it, his father had exhorted him to press charges while he was still living and Epichares could still "take vengeance" (Dem. 58.1–2, 52, 58).

Before proceeding to Theocrines' criminal acts, Epichares referred to his own youth three times: he claimed that he must take it upon himself to lodge a legal complaint, "without taking into account my youth"; that his father regarded it important that he, Epichares, did not "make an excuse of my inexperience and my young age" to let Theocrines get

---

35. Dem. 58.1–3. For *atimia*, see Hansen 1976, 55–90; MacDowell 1978, 73–74; Todd 1993, 142–43. For the political background of the speech: Osborne 1985b, 49.

away with criminal acts; and that the jury should extend its goodwill to someone who was "both young and inexperienced" (Dem. 58.1–3). These references efface the image of the litigating youth as brash, aspiring, and overweening. Later in his speech (58.40–43), he played on the Athenian association of youth with candor and naïveté and essentially told the jury that, faced with a young claimant, they needed not be suspicious.[36]

When Epichares asked the jury for justice, he observed that there were some who might criticize his suit as inappropriate to his age (Dem. 58.57–59; cf. Lys. 13.42). He did not spell out the criticisms, but one may assume that they included the suspicion that the suit was motivated by a typically excessive agonistic drive, attendant on youth, or by an improper search for notoriety at the expense of an elder and better.

To refute these suspicions, Epichares referred to his youthful vulnerability to reinforce his argument that the contest was uneven (Dem. 58.61) and might require the jury to level the playing field. He also reemphasized his filial duty to avenge his father, hoping that the jury would approve his efforts as the proper behavior for a young man with a sense of masculine honor. Bidding for sympathy, he reminded the jurors that his father could speak in court only through the voice of a male representative or guardian *(kurios)*.[37] He had to speak on his father's behalf, even though he was unequal to the task. While other men his age were aided and guided by their fathers, his father was dependent on him (Dem. 58.60; cf. 58.3, but also 58.5). The image of a vulnerable youth prematurely forced into a man's role made Theocrines an utter villain who had inverted the normal familial hierarchy. In addition, it invited the jurors to stand in for Epichares' father and become his protectors, and, by implication, to mete out the punishment that Theocrines deserved.

In Defense of Mantitheus at his Dokimasia (Lys. 16)

In the speech that he wrote for Mantitheus to present at a *dokimasia* (review) of his qualifications for membership in the Council of Five Hun-

---

36. In the corpus of Demosthenes' speeches, the claim of youth and inexperience is almost a commonplace: Dem. 21.78, 80; 27.2–3; 34.1; 53.12–13; 55.7; 59.14–15, and cf. Lys. fr. 16 (Thalheim); Arist. *Rhet.* 2.12.7 1389A17–18; Dion. Hal. *Isaeus* 10–11. If the speaker of Hyperides' *Against Athenogenes* (Hyp. 3) was a young man (his father was still alive), his youth strengthened his self-portrait as a naïve and inexperienced man.

37. Cf. Winkler 1990b, 27; Scafuro 1997, 28. For a similar rhetorical ploy: Ant. 5.79, and for silence in court: Dem. 21.95.

dred *(boulē)*, Lysias manipulated the positive stereotypes of both youth
and mature adulthood on his client's behalf (Lys. 16).[38]

Mantitheus's right to take office was challenged on basis of his service
in the cavalry in his youth, which exposed him to the charge of having
supported the tyrannical rule of the Thirty. Mantitheus also had to refute criticisms of his long hair, which supposedly made him look like a
young oligarch, and his address to the Assembly as a young man, which
marked him as overly greedy for honor and power.[39]

Although Mantitheus had to be over thirty to be elected to the Council, his exact age is not known. The speech suggests that his status as a
full adult was still in question. For at the close of his defense, he refers
to those who object to his speaking before the people "when he was too
young" (Lys. 16.20)[40] In the defense Lysias wrote, Mantitheus straddles
the world of the young man and the mature adult, adapting elements of
each role as it suits him.

Mantitheus denied that he had served in the cavalry and asserted that,
even if he had, it should not disqualify him from serving on the Council.
The bulk of the speech, however, consists of Mantitheus's account of his
life's history. Adopting a somewhat cocky manner, which was frowned
on in adults, but tolerated in young men, he extols his own virtues and
elaborates on his service to the polis.[41]

In relating his client's career, Lysias drew on the Athenian perception
of young men as fearless and courageous in battle (Aristotle *Rhet.* 2.12.9
1389a25–29; cf. Lys. 2.50–51). Mantitheus stressed that while fighting
in the military on behalf of democracy, he had always volunteered for the
most dangerous assignments, and that he was among the first to enter
every battle and the last to leave (Lys. 16.13–18).

Interspersed with his military record, Mantitheus told his hearers of
his virtues. He depicted himself as free of the vices of youth and then as
a mature manly adult. That he was slandered by younger men *(neōteroi)*

---

38. *Dokimasia*: see p. 141 below.

39. I am unconvinced by the objections of Craik 1999, 626–27, to the emendation of
tolma (boldness) to *komai* (having long hair) in Lys. 16.18, especially in view of Lys. 16.19,
which calls on the audience not to judge him by his appearance. *Pace* Craik, oratorical references to appearances are not general but refer to specific physical attributes: see chapter
4, n. 40.

40. Resentful reception of young speakers: [Aristotle] *Rhetoric to Alexander* 29 1437a
32–34. Councilor's age: Xen. *Mem.* 1.2.35; *Ath. Pol.* 4.3, 30.2, 31.1, and Rhodes 1985, 1,
172. Hansen 1985, 55–56, estimates that the average age of a councilor was forty.

41. See Lys. 16.2 and Edwards and Usher 1985, 253; Weissenberger 1987, esp. 76–79;
cf. 57–71; Craik 1999.

who spent their time drinking and gambling was evidence of his *epieikeia* (temperance or goodness) (Lys. 16.11).[42] The image of temperance that he tried to project was similar to that which we have seen in Ariston. He was profligate neither as a youth nor as an adult, and despite limited means, he had fulfilled his duties as a male guardian *(kurios)* and a dedicated patriot.[43] As a guardian, he had arranged marriages for his sisters (Lys. 16.10). As a patriot, he had initiated donations of money to impecunious soldiers of his deme (local community) and donated money himself (Lys. 16.14).

As for his long hair, Mantitheus argued that appearances could be deceiving, that what counted was conduct, and that he was a man of honor and orderliness *(philotimōs kai kosmiōs;* Lys. 16.18–19; cf. 16.3). He conceded that his political activity might have been somewhat too ambitious but claimed that such activity was required to protect his interests, was entirely in keeping with his family tradition of service to the city, and was generally deemed worthy by the people who were sitting in judgment on him (Lys. 16.19–21). In short, he told his hearers that the manly values they espoused were responsible for his conduct.

The orations reveal two largely antithetical images of youth. One is that of the self-controlled, obedient, mature young men, ready to learn from adults, in whom Athenian men placed their hopes for the future of their society. The other is that of young men who threaten adult power, institutions, and conventions. Such youths might turn their good looks, wealth, and strength against adults.

The inclusiveness of the images, and the contradictions and ambivalences that inhered in them, left a great deal of room for manipulation. As we have seen, skilled writers took advantage of that space in the service of their clients. With the help of a clever speechwriter, a young man in court could adopt the positive image of youth to contrast with the negative ones to win the sympathy of the jury and to support his claims.

42. Cf. Dover 1974, 61–63, 191; Cobetto Ghiggia 1995, 221–23.
43. On young men and wastefulness: Arist. *Rhet.* 2.12.6 1389A13–15; Dem. 42.4; Aes. 1.42.

CHAPTER 2

The Roles and Responsibilities of the Adult Male

Kurios, *Husband, Son, Kinsman, Friend, and Citizen*

Chapter 1 has dealt with orations written for Athenian youths. Most of the extant orations were, however, delivered by or on behalf of mature men. This chapter deals with what the orations tell us of the responsibilities—and the attendant apprehensions—of the adult man, aged roughly twenty to sixty, in his role as head of the household, or *kurios,* husband, son, kinsman, friend, and citizen. My focus is on the ideology and expectations of masculinity relevant to these roles. The chapter therefore includes an examination of the obligation to dower brides, the complex perceptions of marital and extramarital relationships, and the challenges that solidarity within the family, the kinship group, and among friends entailed for Athenian men.[1]

THE *KURIOS:* HEAD OF THE HOUSEHOLD

The term *kurios* is commonly translated as master, guardian, or steward.[2] By law and custom, the *kurios* was the head of the Athenian household, or *oikos,* a social, economic, and sometimes religious unit that, in

---

1. The literature on the Athenian *oikos* and its status in the polis is too vast. Among the more recent works on the subject are Pomeroy 1997, esp. 17–39; Patterson 1998; Cox 1998, esp. 132–35, which offers a revision of the view that focuses on the nuclear family in the household; Roy 1999; and E. E. Cohen 2000, 32–46.
2. See the previous note, as well as Todd 1993, 207–10, 216–27; and Hunter 1994, esp. 10–11.

addition to the nuclear family, might include relatives who lived in the house, unrelated dependents, and slaves, as well as the household possessions. The Athenian *kurios* was usually the *oikos*'s oldest male member with citizen's rights. He had authority over the property of the *oikos* and represented the household in its dealings with outside individuals, groups, and institutions. Responsibility for the prosperity and perpetuation of the *oikos,* and for the safety and well-being of its members, rested on his shoulders.

The *kurios* had considerable authority over women, minors, dependents, slaves, and wards in the *oikos*. His formal authority did not extend to his grown sons, who at eighteen became legally independent (Strauss 1993, 2, 8), although informally, they too were expected to comply with their father's wishes. Recent studies have shown that women exercised some formal and informal control within the household,[3] but the *kurios* remained the most powerful individual in the *oikos*.

The Responsibilities of the Kurios *for Perpetuating the* Oikos

It was the duty of the *kurios* was to make sure that the *oikos* survived him.[4] The prevailing notion was that the *oikos* and its assets did not really belong to its head, but were given to him as a trust to be transferred in due course to his legitimate heir, preferably a male, but, where none was available, a female (esp. Dem. 43.12). A childless *kurios* could adopt an heir, an exclusively male prerogative.[5]

The obligation to perpetuate the *oikos* was anchored in strong emotional, economic, and religious injunctions. Virginia Hunter has characterized it as a "deep, almost obsessive" concern.[6] Various speeches, especially those of Isaeus and Demosthenes, which deal extensively with conflicts over property and inheritance, refer to the obligation as a mat-

---

3. E.g., Schaps 1979; Humphreys 1993; Foxhall 1989, 1996; Hunter 1989a, 1989b, 1994; D. Cohen 1998; E. E. Cohen 1992; 2000, esp. 43–48. For various legal restraints on the *kurios*'s freedom of action vis-à-vis his *oikos,* see Is. 3.68; 10.9; Aes. 1.113–14; *Ath. Pol.* 56.6.
    4. Wyse 1904, 326; Asheri 1960; Hunter 1993, 108–9, 113–14.
    5. On Athenian adoptions, see Gernet 1955, 121–49, modified by Hunter 1993 and Rubinstein 1993, 125–28, 148–51; cf. Just 1989, 89–104. P. Cobetto Ghiggia's *L'adozione ad Athene in epoca classica* (Turin, 1999) has come to my attention too late to be consulted here.
    6. Hunter 1993, 112; and see also Carey 1992, 116. Rubinstein 1993, esp. 3, 69–76, 105–16, argues that continuing the *oikos* was not the state's concern, but the family's; cf. Cox 1998, 166–67. See, however, below, and Lys. 7.41; Is. 7.42; And. 1.144–46; Lyc. 1.25.

ter of course, confirming the centrality of the ideal among Athenian males (Is. 6.5; 7.30; Dem. 43.75).

The speeches present the obligation as consistent with the needs of the *kurios*.[7] The speaker in Isaeus 7 claimed that Apollodorus, son of Thrasyllus, whose son had died, had chosen to adopt him (the speaker) and make him his heir because he was trustworthy and was already a friend and benefactor (Is 7.33–36). Similarly, the speaker in Isaeus 2 implied that the childless old Menecles had adopted him to perpetuate his *oikos*. Menecles had chosen a wife for the speaker (Is. 2.15), who named his son after Menecles to perpetuate the name (Is. 2.35). The adoption also served Menecles' wish to preserve his long-standing friendship with the speaker's family and to have someone to take care of him in his old age, as well as his desire for a proper burial and funeral rites (Is. 2.4, 10, 13, 20, 22, 25–26, 46). Although not directly related to the perpetuation of the *oikos,* these reasons were part of the fabric of familial give-and-take in which the *oikos* functioned and its perpetuation occurred.

The injunction to perpetuate the household exemplified the Athenian view of the dominant male as a man whose power was circumscribed by his duties. A similar view existed in relation to the power of the *kurios* over the female members of his household and kinship group.

The Responsibilities of the Kurios *in Marriage and Dowry*

Among the various responsibilities of the *kurios* to the women in his *oikos* was the duty to marry off his daughters, sisters, and, in certain cases, other kinswomen. Whether as a father, brother, or other relative, he was expected to make sure that the women in his household and kinship group did not remain without an adult male's care and supervision, and that they would be able to fulfill themselves as wives and mothers. This responsibility was part of his larger duty to ensure the welfare and protect the honor of the women in his charge.[8]

The responsibility of the *kurios* for the marriage of his female charges rested on the Athenians' view that the principal purpose of marriage was the perpetuation of the *oikos* and the polis. Other purposes named by the orators include putting an end to conflicts (Is. 7.11–12), turning friends

---

7. Humphreys 1993, 22–32; Rubinstein 1993, esp. 13–14, 64–68, 105–12; Cf. Maffi 1991, 228–29, with Avramovic 1991, 237. Isoc. 19 is relevant here, but caution dictates excluding it from the discussion, because it deals with non-Athenians.

8. [Dem.] 59.114; cf. Just 1989, 126–28; D. Cohen 1991c, 161; Pomeroy 1994, 231.

into kin, and augmenting the intimacy of those who are already kin (Is. 2.5; Dem. 27.5; 30.12). Marriage was a practical matter, which involved economic distribution, group alliance, and social status. The Athenians' view of reason as a male property, which was deficient or even lacking in females, legitimized the arrangement of marriage as a male domain.[9]

The *kurios* was believed to be the best judge of the interests of the *oikos* and the couple. Women's wishes were secondary to the ambitions and interests of the males involved in a marriage, and the orations make few references to them. The notable exception was in a second marriage, where the woman's wishes were likely to be taken into consideration.[10]

Men had more say in choosing their spouses, but not total freedom. Several speakers tell of marrying a woman their father had selected for them or recommended to them (Is. 2.18; Lys. 19.16; Dem. 40.4, 12). Although fatherless and mature men seem to have been free to make their own marriage decisions, convention generally limited the choice to a relative. Men who married for money or passion or who chose non-Athenian women or courtesans came in for criticism (Aes. 3.172; Is. 6.22; Lys. 19.13, 17). Moreover, for most of the period under discussion in this book, the children of Athenians who married non-Athenian women were not entitled to citizenship.[11]

The *kurios* was expected to provide his female charges with an appropriate dowry, usually a sum of money or movable possessions. As distinct from the modern dowry, which the bride's parents give to the husband, the ancient Athenian dowry remained the property of the wife, serving as a safety net for her. It stayed with her if she divorced or was widowed and could be claimed only by her heirs. At the same time, the dowry became part of the husband's *oikos* through the couple's children, and the husband was entitled to manage and use the income from it. A good dowry improved a woman's prospects for marriage and enhanced

9. Reason and rationality as a masculine property that is lacking in women: Dover 1974, 98–102; Lloyd 1983, 62–86; 1984, 1–33; Just 1989, 164–65; 183–91; Cartledge 2002, 69–70; Thornton 1997, 70, 73–74. For masculine rationality as a means of exclusion and of legitimizing power relationships, see Brittan 1989, 199, and van Wees 1998a, 44.

10. Fathers marrying off their daughters: Lys. 32.4,8; Is. 8.7; 10.5; Dem. 28.15; 40.6; 41.4; 43.74; 44.10, 49; 45.66; 46.18; 57.43; 59.2, 13, 119; Hyp. 3.29; 4.31. Brothers marrying off their sisters: Lys. 16.10; Is. 3.18; 5.26; 7.9; 9.27, 29; Dem. 30.7; 40.7, 19; 43.24; 44.9, 17; 46.18; 57.41; Humphreys 1993, 62–64; Hunter 1994, 16–17. Husbands arranging a second marriage for their wives: Is. 2.7–10; Dem. 27.69; 36.28–30; 57.41; cf. Hyp. 1.7; Lacey 1968, 108; Pomeroy 1997, 169.

11. Independent marriage decisions: cf. And. 1.124, 128; Lys. 1.6. Marriage within the kinship group: Is. 7.11; 10.5; Dem. 43.74; 44.10; 45.75.

her status and power within the union; a meager dowry did the opposite.[12] A dowry was so important that Athenian law required the kinsman of a poor *epiklēros* (translated as "heiress," although her inheritance was not necessarily large) either to marry her himself or to provide
her with a dowry so that someone else would.[13]

Speakers tried to manipulate juries' sensitivity to the *kurios*'s obligation to provide his charges with dowries, as well as evoke pity for girls
without dowries and *kurioi* who could not fulfill their obligations. They
argued that punishing the latter would harm the women under their protection or destroy their chances of finding a husband.[14] One Athenian father asked for a favorable verdict in a property claim so that he could
give his daughter a dowry.[15]

The way in which a man handled the marriage and dowry of his
charges was one of the yardsticks used to measure his character. Greek
society expected the *kurios* to ensure that the bride and the *oikos* benefited from a marriage, even if it meant placing their interests above his
own. Demosthenes, for example, asserts that people celebrate marriage
banquets so that the guests can witness the dowry transaction and thus
attest to the care of the *kurios* for his sisters or daughters.[16] Apparently
expecting the jury to appreciate their behavior, some speakers detailed
in court the sacrifices they had made to ensure that female relatives
would have attractive dowries and enjoy security in their new homes.[17]
Conversely, speakers roundly censured *kurioi* who married off female
charges without due regard for their welfare.[18] In the orations, then, the
dowry often serves as an indication of how selflessly the *kurios* performed his task and of his affection for the women under his authority.

The written and unwritten rules that governed the conduct of the *kurios* seem also to have applied to his own marriage. Here, though, the

12. Is. 3.29, 36; [Dem.] 59.8, cf. 59.112–13; And. 1.119. Dowry practices: Harrison
1968, 1: 45–60; Lacey 1968, 109–10; Schaps 1979, 74–84; Lane-Fox 1985, 223–27; Just
1989, 72–75; Foxhall 1989, 32–33; Todd 1993, 215–16; Cox 1998, esp. 69–70, 103–20.
13. Dem. 43.54, 75; Is. 1.39; fr. 26 (Forster); *Ath. Pol.* 56.6. See Harrison 1968, 1:
48–49, 135–36, on thetic heiress; cf. Schaps 1979, 79; Cox 1998, 116–17.
14. E.g., Lys. 7.41; Dem. 27.66, 69; 28.21; 40.56; 45.85; 48.57; cf. Lys. 32.11; Carey
1989, 141; 1994, 33.
15. Dem. 40.4, 56–57, 60; cf. Dem. 27.55; 45.74; 59.8, 69; Lys. 12.21; 13.45.
16. Dem. 30.21. See also Is. 7.12; cf. Is. 1.39; Cox 1998, 116–20. For affections in an
unequal relationship, cf. Abu-Lughod 1986, 85.
17. Lys. 16.10; Is. 10.25; cf. Dem. 30.12; 45.54. Cf. Is. 3.28–29, 50–51, with Hunter
1994, 52; Dem. 40.25; 59.69; Hyp. 1.13, with Whitehead 2000, 132.
18. Is. 6.51; 10.19; [Dem.] 49.66. See Schaps 1979, 77–81; Just 1989, 40–43, 82–83;
Millett 1991, 62–68; Cox 1998, esp. ch. 4.

orations draw a different picture. While giving a daughter or sister a meager dowry is presented as meanness and dereliction of duty, willingly forfeiting a dowry is evidence of the man's embrace of virtue and honor over profit. A Lysian speaker, in denying allegations that his father had married a woman from a prominent family for money, attributed to him a consistent policy of declining large dowries in favor of marriage alliances based on virtue and prestige. He proudly declared, in clear expectation of the jury's approval, that his father had given up a rich bride for a dowryless marriage to a woman from a well-respected family. He had then refused to let his daughters marry rich men of lowly origin, even though the option of not paying their dowries was offered to him, and he had instructed his son to give up on a large dowry and marry into a poorer but more respectable family.[19] Such demanding standards seem to have been exceptional. The normative expectation appears to have been that a man of wealth and social status would not consider taking a dowryless wife (Is. 11.40).

The orations highlight an ambivalence regarding the financial arrangements in marriage. One Demosthenean speaker told the jury quite matter-of-factly that his mother's first husband, who had been poor, had divorced her to marry a rich heiress.[20] The speaker's citation of an economic motive and his failure to refer to the law requiring kin to marry unwed heiresses in the family suggests that his motive was acceptable. Yet when economic necessity was not an issue, marrying for money could be presented as reprehensible. The aforementioned Lysian speaker, for example, elaborated on his father's refusal to marry for money; and Demosthenes charged his opponent Aphobus with "shameful greed" (aiskhrokerdeia) for breaking his promise to marry Demosthenes' mother in order to marry a wealthier woman (Dem. 29.48). Another speaker suggested that greed had motivated the marriage of Alcibiades the Elder, who allegedly received ten talents for marrying his wife and ten more for producing a son from her.[21]

The kurios, especially if he was wealthy, had to tread a fine line in carrying out his marital responsibilities. He had to provide adequately for

19. Lys. 19.14–17. See Lacey 1968, 109; Davies 1984, 70.
20. Dem. 57.41. The case is complicated by the denouncement of the speaker as an illegitimate son: Gernet 1960, 4: 11; Humphreys 1986b, 62. It is possible that the son wished to free his mother from any responsibility for the divorce. Divorce in Athens: A. R. W. Harrison 1968, 1: 38–45; Rosivach 1984; Cohn-Haft 1995; Scafuro 1997, esp. 306–9; Cox 1998, 71–73.
21. [And.] 4.13 (probably a slander: Gazzano 1999, 66–68), and Aes. 3.172; cf. And. 1.119.

the women in his charge without exceeding the means of the *oikos* (Dem.
27.44). For himself, he had to be careful not to be seen as marrying solely
for money, and without regard to the status and character of the woman
and her family.

THE HUSBAND: MARITAL AND
EXTRAMARITAL RELATIONSHIPS

In marrying, the adult man assumed the responsibility for his wife that
had previously been borne by her father or brother. He was expected to
treat her with respect: not to bring home his *hetaira* (courtesan), if he had
one;[22] not to be miserly if his wife brought a substantial dowry; and not
to allow monetary considerations to disrupt his bond with her.[23] He was
also expected to provide her with a child. An Isaean speaker (Is. 2.7, 11)
went so far as to commend an elderly husband for divorcing his young
wife when he had realized that he would not be able to impregnate her,
so as to allow her to marry someone who could.[24]

In return, the man expected his wife to produce children, to keep his
house in good order and to manage it frugally, and to make his home a
warm and intimate place. Although the man and wife did not marry for
love, they could gratify each other emotionally and enjoy mutual concord (cf. Lyc. fr. C 11–12.3 [Burtt]; Arist. *Eudemian Ethics* 1242a26).
The farmer Euphiletus told the jury, for example, that after his first child
was born, he had let his guard down and achieved great intimacy with
his wife, implying that he expected affection, loyalty, comfort, and support.[25] A similar expectation is behind the story told by the speaker Apollodorus about Phrastor and Phano. When he learnt that Phano was not

22. [Dem.] 59.22; [And.] 4.14; cf. Dem. 40.8–9; 48.55; Arist. *Pol.* 1.5 1259a40–1259b2;
Ogden 1996a, 100–106. On philosophical censure of husbands' unfaithfulness: Thornton
1997, 173.
23. Miserly to wife: Theophrastus *Characters* 22.10; 28.4. Refusal to separate from
wife: Is. 10.19, but see Just 1989, 102, 128–30, whose interpretation is preferable to that
of Scafuro 1997, 292–93; cf. also Rubinstein 1993, 98–99. [And.] 4.13–14 implies that
physical violence against one's wife was an act of hubris; cf. Fisher 1992, 108; Cobetto
Ghiggia 1995, 210; Gazzano 1999, 74–75. Cox 1998, 69–77 discusses the husband-wife
relationship, especially in relation to property.
24. On the husband's "sacrifice," cf. Plut. *Solon* 20.2–3; Mossé 1995, 31–32.
25. Lys. 1.6–7. Lysias describes the woman as *oikeiotēta*, a term that elsewhere in his
corpus denotes the closest of friends: Lys. 29.2; 32.19. Cf. Xen. *Hiero* 3.4, 4.1; Just 1989,
128–30. Conjugal love and sex in philosophy and comedy: Raepsaet 1981; P. Brown 1993;
Thornton 1997, 163, 173–75, 178–79. Emotional relationship with the wife: D. Cohen
1991c, 168–69; Kapparis 1999, 19–20; Konstan 2000. Relationships within the household: Foxhall 1989; cf. MacDowell 1989; E. Cohen 1991, 243–45, 258.

an Athenian and, moreover, the daughter of a courtesan, Phrastor divorced her, only to take her back after she and her mother tended him when he was sick and alone. "And I suppose that you know yourselves," Apollodorus added, "how worthy a woman is in time of sickness, standing by a sick person."[26] Although this depiction of the man as being on the receiving end of services from women (be they wives or former wives) is not surprising, it would be a mistake to think that Greek males perceived the home merely as a place for the utilitarian exchange of services.

The orations suggest that the Athenian male envisioned his home as a safe place, free of the aggressiveness, strife, and stiff stratification that not infrequently typified his life outside. The idealized *oikos* was a place where each male member treated the others with kindness *(philanthrōpia)* and moderation, and where harmony *(homonoia)* reigned.[27] These images drawn from the orations contrast with the depiction in some Greek dramas, and by their modern interpreters, of the home as a female domain, where men, whose sphere lay outside, did not really belong, and where they were often in danger.[28] While these images do not contradict these negative conceptions, they balance them with indications that the Athenian man invested his yearning for security, trust, and freedom from menace in his *oikos* and its women.

To keep his home and his authority intact, the *kurios* had to protect both against the dangers that threatened them. Studies have shown that Athenian men feared the challenge that assertive women posed to male control, hierarchy, and order.[29] Scholars have also identified male fear of woman's supposedly unbridled sexuality, especially in Attic drama and myth, and argued that Greek men appreciated, depended on, and were affectionate toward women in their roles of mother and household manager, but feared and resented women's potential for subversion and adul-

26. [Dem.] 59.56. Cf. Patteson 1978, 89. For a husband tending his sick wife, see Dem. 30.34. Husband served and nurtured by the wife: cf. D. Cohen 1991c, 138. For the wife providing an audience to her husband's boasts of public reputation: Theophrastus *Characters* 21.11.

27. Dem. 25.87–89. Cf. pp. 16–17 above; D. Cohen 1991c, 93–94. Thwarted expectations in the *oikos:* Dem. 48.8; cf. Is. 5.30; Lys. 31.22–23; Ant. 1.1–2; Simonides 7.103–5 (Page).

28. See, e.g., Zeitlin 1996, 355; Heap 1998, 119–21. Feminine and indoors and masculine and the outdoors: Xen. *Oec.* 7.22–23; Hunter 1994, 35, 202 n. 55; Zeitlin 1996, 354–56. Even the *andrōn*, the "men's room," where the male host entertained his male friends, has been interpreted as designed to segregate men within the house: Nevett 1995a, 373, cf. Walker 1993.

29. Gould 1980, 57; Keuls 1985, e.g., 3–6; Carson 1990, esp. 153–164; cf. Van Nortwick 1998, 164–65. For a subconscious masculine fear of women, see Slater 1968; Zeitlin 1996, 87–119; *contra*, Lefkowitz 1986.

tery, and their presumed inability to control their sexual drive and other appetites.[30]

Although these apprehensions are evident in the orations, the emphasis in the speeches is on the masculine, not the feminine, danger to the *oikos*. In only one speech in the entire oratorical corpus, Antiphon 1, does the speaker treat a woman as a Clytemnestra—a wife who actively and independently harmed her husband. As the orations present it, it took unscrupulous male outsiders to activate the potential for harm that existed in wives. This harm or danger might come in the form of adultery or the possibility that a wife's loyalty to her husband's *oikos* might be undermined by her loyalty to her natal home.

Euphiletus's Defense (Lys. 1)

In Athenian law, an adulterous woman was compelled to divorce her husband and forbidden, under penalty of public humiliation, to adorn herself or to enter a public temple. The punishment for an adulterous man ranged from the mild—that he compensated the cuckolded *kurios*—to the most severe: the wronged *kurios* was permitted to kill the adulterer if he caught him in the act. The harshness of these punishments reflected the view that because women were less capable of self-control than men, they should be judged less harshly (cf. Aes. 1.185), but also that men posed the greater danger to the household. Nonetheless, killing the adulterer was apparently rare and not universally approved of.[31]

Lysias 1 was written in defense of the farmer Euphiletus, who killed his wife's lover after catching him in the act.[32] Euphilitus did not exonerate his wife. He related how she had won his trust by being a clever, frugal housekeeper, only to betray him with Eratosthenes. She had tricked him with the help of a servant girl and brought her lover into their home. She was able to do so after his mother had died and was no

30. Arthur 1973; Foley 1981b; Thornton 1997, 69–98, 166–69. Fear of women and Greeks' attitudes toward adultery: Gardner 1989, 51–53; Just 1989, 213–14, cf. 70; Carson 1990, 158; Foxhall 1991, 300–303.

31. I use "adultery" as a convenient translation for *moikheia* with full awareness of the problems of translation: Patterson 1998, 121–25. For adultery and other sexual offenses see Cole 1984; Harris 1990; P. Brown 1991; Carey 1995, 407–8; Kapparis 1995; Davidson 1997, 131–32, 337–38 nn. 28–29; Scafuro 1997, 195–206, 474–79; Deacy and Pierce 1997; Patterson 1998, 114–79. On D. Cohen's 1984; 1991, esp. 83–132, interpretation of adultery, see, e.g., Cantarella 1991; Foxhall 1991; Patterson 1998, 115–32.

32. Edwards and Usher 1985, 220–21; D. Cohen 1991c, 114–22, 129–32; Herman 1993, 412; 1995, esp. 51–54; Davidson 1997, 199–200; Scafuro 1997, 212–13.

longer there to keep an eye on her, and after he himself had let down his guard when their child was born. The account exploits masculine fears of the female's powers of deception and reflects the apparently commonplace assumption that a husband had to keep a close watch over his wife if he wanted her to be faithful.[33]

The bulk of Euphilitus's defense, however, focused on the lover, who, he stressed, had initiated the affair, corrupted his wife, shamed his children, and committed hubris by invading his *oikos*.[34] The law stipulated the death penalty for adulterers, he argued, because adulterers corrupted the souls of the women they slept with, transferred the women's attachment from their husbands to themselves, gained control over the *oikos*, and cast doubt on the paternity of the children (Lys. 1.32–33), which not only threatened the security of the *oikos* and the honor of its head but undermined the link between citizenship and identifiably Athenian parentage.[35]

The thrust of Euphiletus's defense was that his wife's lover deserved the punishment he had meted out to him, and that in killing him, he had acted legally, properly, and fulfilled his masculine duty to defend the household and polis. It is unlikely that all the men in the audience shared Euphiletus's views. Xenophon, for example, presents the adulterer as undermining the trust and friendship *(philia)* between wife and husband, but not as a danger to the *oikos* and the polis.[36] Even Lysias, who composed Euphiletus's defense speech, in another case depicted an adulterer as an object more of derision than of fear (Lys. fr. 1 [Thalheim]).

Nonetheless, Euphiletus's views of the male adulterer were not unique. A client of Hyperides' charged with adultery was accused of

33. Lys. 1.6; cf. Edwards and Usher 1985, 222–23 (preferable to Herman 1993, 414–17; 1995 53); Carey 1989, 61–62; Golden 1990, 164–65; D. Cohen 1991c, 160. Porter 1997 rightly points to comic elements in Euphiletus's self-portrait, but one should not lose sight of the presentation of the crime as most serious: Lys. 1.2. For the wife's deception, cf. Gardner 1989, 53. For Lys. 1.20, see Todd 1998, 165.

34. Lys. 1.1–2, 4, 30–31; Cf. Gorgias *Helen* 7; Fisher 1992, 104, with n. 125; Todd 1993, 202; Ogden 1996a, 144. Patterson has claimed that emphasizing the adulterer's role was a rhetorical trick, and that we should trust drama, which focuses on the adulteress, as a more faithful mirror of reality: 1998, 119–24, 163–76, 271 n. 76; cf. Johnstone 1999, 53–54. I cannot share her ranking of the evidence, especially because the case of Clytemnestra, on which she chiefly relies, is too special.

35. Men's fear of uncertain paternity: Lacey 1968, 115; Gardner 1989, 53, 55–56; D. Cohen 1991c, 107; Konstan 1994, esp. 226–29; Kapparis 1995, 117–19; but see Scafuro 1997, 197. For criticism of the speaker's contrasting rape with adultery: Harris 1990; cf. P. Brown 1991; but also Ogden 1996a, 146–50.

36. Xen. *Hiero* 3.3–4; cf. Arist. *Rhet.* 1.14.5 1375a8–12 with D. Cohen 1991c, 108 n. 29; Foxhall 1991. See Aristotle, ibid., for the rhetoric of multiplying offenses.

causing women to grow old unmarried, living with their male companions contrary to the law, and of wishing to topple Athens's democratic
regime (Hyp. 1.12; Lyc. frs. C11–12 [Burtt]). Demosthenes justified the
Athenian law that permitted a man to kill another man who had had sex
with his wife, mother, sister, daughter, or concubine intended for producing free children on the grounds that men were duty bound to protect women from unlawful acts that dishonored *(hubrizōsi)* or otherwise
harmed them (Dem. 23.55–56). In similar spirit, the speaker Apollodorus claimed that the law allowed a man wronged by a convicted
adulterer to do anything he pleased to him except shed his blood ([Dem.]
59.66).

Isaeus 8 and Isaeus 2

These two Isaean speeches convey the concern that the wife's natal kin
will draw her loyalty away from her husband. The public nature of wedding ceremonies and dowry transactions and the introduction of the wife
into her husband's family cult and kinship organizations proclaimed the
woman's transfer from her natal to her marital household. Yet Athenian
laws treated the wife as not fully integrated into her new *oikos*. They
gave a woman's close natal kinsman the right to demand that she divorce
her husband in order to marry a relative, and the kin of a married heiress
the right to claim an heir for her father's *oikos* if they had no heir of their
own; and they kept the wife's dowry separate from her husband's property. Together, the laws reinforced the perception that the wife was
something of an outsider.[37] This perception led to concern on the part of
the husband's kinsmen that marriage would give the wife's relatives an
opportunity to challenge their own claims on the household. Childless
wives were especially suspect, since the birth of a child was perceived as
cementing a marriage (Lys. 1.6; cf. 1.14).

    These apprehensions emerged in the dispute over the estate of Ciron
(Is. 8). Ciron had died without leaving a son, and his estate was disputed
by two contenders: the speaker, who claimed to be the son of Ciron's
daughter, and an unnamed opponent, who claimed to be the son of
Ciron's brother. The speaker contended that Diocles, the brother of

37. Wolff 1944, 47–53; Harrison 1968, 1: 30–32; Hunter 1993, 108–10; Scafuro
1997, 308–9. It is unclear whether the authority to ask the wife to divorce was legal or con-
ventional. On the rivalry between natal and conjugal households in drama: Visser 1986;
Seaford 1990.

Ciron's wife, had conspired with her to keep Ciron from naming the speaker as his heir. Diocles had allegedly persuaded his sister to tell her husband that she thought she was pregnant, and then, each time, that she had miscarried. Expecting an heir, Ciron did not therefore adopt his grandson (Is. 8.36). This extraordinary claim testified to the fear that a woman, even one who had been married for many years, would retain her primary loyalty to her natal family. It also suggested that the woman's male relatives instigated and fueled the trouble.

This last concern is also evident in Isaeus 2, which dealt with a dispute over an inheritance between the brother of the deceased, the childless Menecles, and the speaker, who claimed to be Menecles' adopted son. In addressing the legality of his adoption, he defended himself against the charge that Menecles had adopted him in a moment of insanity, under the influence of his wife, the speaker's sister (Is. 2.1, 19–20). The speaker depicted Menecles as having been in full possession of his wits, and his young wife as a loving, ingenuous, and loyal spouse, who in any case was already married to another man when Menecles chose his heir.[38] To the implication that the speaker had connived with his sister to harm the interests of her husband and his kin, he replied with evidence of his deep regard for Menecles, asserting that he had cared for and respected him just as a son should (Is. 2.18).

In contrast to Isaeus 8, which conveys Athenian male apprehensions about a wife's natal kin from the perspective of the accuser, Isaeus 2 conveys them from the perspective of the defendant. It also suggests that even if some women remain more loyal to their natal than their marital homes, others do not. This assumption can be identified in the speaker's argument that if his sister, whom Menecles had divorced when he realized that he would not be able to father a child, and who was remarried when Menecles adopted him, had, in fact, been instrumental in his choice of heir, she would have persuaded Menecles to adopt her son by her new husband, not her brother (Is. 2.19–20). This argument from probability reflects the jurors' perception that plenty of wives were loyal to their marital homes, even if they had scheming natal relatives.[39]

Although the danger to the *oikos* was perceived as coming mainly from men outside its walls, Athenian society offered husbands a variety

---

38. Is. 2.7–10. Menecles describes his childless status as "unlucky" *(atukhōn)*. I could find no orator who suggested that a child was a proof of a man's virility: Pierce 1998, 132.

39. This was especially true of mothers whose loyalty to their children tied them to their marital houses; cf. 32.11–18.

of defensive measures aimed at their wives. These measures included, among others, endogamous marriages, in the hope that the wife's premarital ties to the family would make her less likely to serve the interests of parties outside the *oikos* or to breach the protection of the house;[40] the often violated ideal of feminine seclusion; and monitoring and restricting wife's activities with the help of the man's mother or household slaves.[41] As in some traditional societies today, these measures, which were aimed at protecting the men of the house, were justified in the name of protecting the women of the house from other males (Dem. 23.56).

The emphasis on the male danger to the *oikos* had several possible sources, including the nature of the oratorical genre, which advanced claims of agonistic males in *fora* where women lacked an independent legal persona or voice; the ancient Greek view of women as passive and men as active; and the reality that men had a far greater capacity to harm *kurioi* and their households than women did. The primary reason for that emphasis, however, was the fact that Athenian men's frame of reference was male-focused, since men, and not women, stood at the center of men's experience in most situations in ancient Athens.

A Husband's Extramarital Liaisons

In addition to weak women and designing men, the *kurios* himself was a potential source of damage to the *oikos,* through unrestrained spending,[42] or a liaison with a *pallakē* (concubine) or a *hetaira* (courtesan). Such liaisons are frequently mentioned in the orations and have been extensively discussed in modern scholarship. What is relevant here is the threat these liaisons posed to the *oikos,* even when they were not extramarital affairs.

A *pallakē* was a woman who had a long-term relationship with a man without being legally married to him.[43] The term *hetaira* could designate

40. Cf. Hesiod *Works and Days* 700–701; Bourdieu 1966, 227–28; Di Bella 1992, 152–57. Endogamous marriages served other goals as well, such as retaining property within the kinship group, see, e.g., Davies 1981, 76–77; Garland 1990, 214–15, or reinforcing kinship solidarity, see, e.g., Thompson 1967, 281; Just 1989, 79–82.

41. Kapparis 1999, 217–20.

42. Is. 5.43; 7.32; 10.25; Lys. 19.45–49; Aes. 1.30, 95–96; Dem. 36.42; 38.25–27; 40.58; Foxhall 1989, and Cox 1998, 130–67. For the striking case of Callias, who allegedly reduced his family fortune from two hundred talents to two, see Davidson 1997, 184–86. Praiseworthy *kurioi* who preserved or enlarged the household: Is. 11.39; fr. 1 (Forster); cf. Lys. 7.32.

43. Sealey 1984; Just 1989, 50–54; Patterson 1990; 1991b, 54–55; Mossé 1991; Kapparis 1999, 8–13.

a mistress, a courtesan, a prostitute, or simply a woman who was hired to entertain one or more men at a banquet.[44]

Some of the danger posed by the *pallakē* and *hetaira* to the *oikos* was legal in origin. A *pallakē* or *hetaira* could be a free woman or a slave, an Athenian or foreigner.[45] The children of a free woman of Athenian descent, whether she was married to the father or not, were regarded as fully legitimate if he acknowledged them as his (Is. 3.30: [Dem.] 59.122). Such children had rights to inheritance and could make claims on the man's property. In Demosthenes 39 and 40 and Isaeus 6, the speakers argued that their rivals were the sons of concubines or kept women, and that their claims on an estate (Is. 6) or to legitimate sonship (Dem. 39–40) were based on false or unfair grounds. The two cases highlight the danger that a man's attachment to a concubine was seen to pose to the *oikos*, and to the *kurios*'s rightful children.[46]

Although there is little criticism in the orations of a man simply having a *pallakē* or *hetaira*, there is harsh condemnation of men whose extramarital affairs harmed their families. A Demosthenean speaker lambasted his adversary for freeing one of his *hetairai* (who may have been his mistress) and giving another in marriage while he had a wife of his own (Dem. 36.45; Hunter 1994, 88). Another Demosthenean speaker charged that his adversary's infatuation with a *hetaira* (probably a mistress) prevented him from marrying an Athenian woman and fathering Athenian children, and led to such prodigal spending on his *hetaira* that he deprived his sister and her daughter—the speaker's wife and daughter—of their fair share of the revenues of the disputed estate (Dem. 48.53–55; cf. 39.26; 40.9, 51).

The perception that a man's love for a *hetaira* threatened the *oikos* and the community is exploited in Apollodorus's speech against Neaera.[47] At the time of the trial, Athenian law recognized marriage only

44. Davidson 1998, esp. 73–136; Cox 1998, 170–89; Kapparis 1999. The terms are broad, and the orations are not always precise in telling the *pallakē* and *hetaira* apart: Wolff 1944, 73–74; Carey 1992, 148; Hunter 1994, 212 n. 8; Davidson 1997, 101–4, 333 n. 75; although now see Miner 2003. On various types of sexual liaisons: Dover 1989, 20–22; Halperin 1990, 102, 109–12.

45. Patterson 1991b; Ogden 1996, esp. 158–59; and Kapparis 1999, 9–10, regard concubinage as a servile institution, but the sources are imprecise about the civil status of concubines.

46. For Dem. 39–40, see Rudhardt 1962; Davies 1971, 364–68; Carey and Reid 1985, 160–67; Humphreys 1989; Hunter 1994, 29–30, 63–64, 224 n. 39; Ogden 1996a, 192–94; Cox 1998, 86–87, 181. For Is. 6, see Wyse 1904, 483–547; Hunter 1994, 52, 113–14. Is. 3 too describes a case where a father sowed seeds of contention in his family through his attachment to another woman.

47. [Dem.] 59. Patteson 1978; Carey 1992; and Kapparis 1999 provide useful English commentaries on the speech. Debra Hamel's *Trying Neaira: The True Story of a Courte-*

between Athenians. Apollodorus charges Neaera with living with Stephanus as his wife even though she was not an Athenian and, moreover, not deserving to become one because of the type of woman she was.

Toward the end of the speech, Apollodorus describes the havoc that will descend on the home and polity if Neaera is acquitted and is permitted to live with Stephanus as his wife.[48] Undiscerning women will interpret the verdict as permission to do as they please.[49] The distinction between decent and indecent women will be obliterated. Laws will lose their authority, parenthood will be established by whoring mothers instead of by male citizens, whores *(pornai)* will cohabit with whomever they pleased, and women of a *hetaira*'s lifestyle will become *kurioi,* with the power to do as they wish. The daughters of poor citizens will prostitute themselves in return for attractive dowries, and the *axiōma* (honor or rank) of free women will deteriorate to that of *hetairai,* who will be free to bear children to whomever they pleased ([Dem.] 59.112–113). It would be a nightmare, topsy-turvy world; masculine order would be replaced by feminine anarchy, and loose women would become masters but live like whores. The man's rule of the *oikos,* his supervision of female sexual conduct, and his monopoly in matters relating to marriage and parenthood would be lost to lusting women.[50]

Nonetheless, even where the orators cast aspersions on the *pallakē* or *hetaira,* it was the masculine danger with which they were concerned. As they saw it, women could not harm men without the voluntary or involuntary collaboration of other men. This can be illustrated in a case where the speaker charged that his rival for the estate of the Athenian Mantias was the son of a woman named Plangon, Mantias's concubine. Plangon had allegedly tricked Mantias into accepting the rival as his son (Dem. 39.3–5; 40.2, 10–11). Yet this claimant could not bring himself to say that Plangon alone had been responsible for Mantias's conduct: she

---

san's Scandalous Life in Ancient Greece (New Haven, Conn., 2003) came out after the manuscript of this book had been completed.

48. On the threat to the *oikos* in this speech: Patterson 1994. See also p. 195 below.

49. [Dem.] 59.110–111. For the Greeks' correlation of intelligence with morality: Dover 1974, 116–33; Carey 1992, 143. For the perception of women as the guardians of morality and the status quo as opposed as to novelty-fond men, cf. Aristophanes *Ekklesiazusai* 217–20; Plato *Rep.* 549c–d; Is. 12.5; Dover 1974, 96–97.

50. Cf. Aristophanes' *Ekklesiazusai;* Eur. *Bacchae* 217–23 with Segal 1982, 88. For Menander's comic manipulation of these motifs, see Konstan 1989; Reden 1998, esp. 269–75.

had tricked Mantias with the help of a male acquaintance, he said, and emphasized the role of Mantias's own passion for her in their relationship (Dem. 40.9–10, 51). In another case, the speaker argued that his rivals for an estate were the sons of a former slave and a prostitute named Alce. Alce too had allegedly tricked the estate's owner into recognizing her sons as his own (Is. 6.18–26). But this speaker added that the actions of his male opponents and the victim's old age and lack of mental acuity, as much as Alce's plotting, had caused the old man to liquidate his assets and acknowledge her sons as his own (Is. 6.29–34). Even the collapse of Athenian social institutions and values envisioned in Apollodorus's nightmare scenario would be caused not so much by the actions of women as agents of chaos, it is implied, as because men's lust, greed, and lack of control over their passions would allow it to happen.

FATHERS AND SONS

An adult male Athenian was expected not only to attend to his duties as a *kurios* and husband but simultaneously also to fulfill his paternal and filial obligations. Athenian law stressed the mutual responsibility of father and son.[51] A son who struck his father, failed to support him at his old age, or did not perform funeral rites for him could lose some of his citizen's rights. Fathers were supposed to raise their sons and try to ensure their economic future; a father who prostituted his son forfeited his right to care by the son in his old age (Is. 8.32; Aes. 1.13; cf. Lys. 10. 9–10; 13.91). The speeches are replete with references to the duties of fathers and sons. Speakers told of fathers' taking the legal steps to certify their sons' legitimacy and ensure their free status (e.g., Dem. 39.21; cf. Dem. 43.12; 57.24); of seeing to their sons' education and mentoring them (Dem. 40.8, 50, 54; cf. Dem. 54.22–23; 58.60); of planning their careers and arranging their marriages (Is. 2.18). They reflected the expectations that the son would continue the family line, show his father respect, comply with his wishes, and stand by him if he were attacked (Is. 2.36; Lys. 10.28; 19.55; Dem. 40.12–13, 34, 47; 58.2, 57–60). To defame opponents' characters, speakers cited offenses against fathers. Accusations ranged from patricide (Lys. 10.1–3; Dem. 24.7) and failure to

51. Golden 1990, 80–114; Millett 1991, 129–35; Rubinstein 1993, 64–68; Strauss 1993, esp. 96–97. According to Millett, the obligation to assist parents was strongest with sons and decreased beyond this relation.

support an elderly father and give him a proper burial (Dem. 24.107, 201; 25.54; Din. 2.8) to vague offenses such as being one's parent's "enemy" (Dem. *Lett.* 4.11; cf. And. 1.130–31). Even offenses committed as a youth were held against a man: a Lysian speaker condemned his adversary for betraying his father when he was a young man (Lys. 14.26), and Aeschines condemned an opponent for leaving home and squandering his father's fortune in his youth (Aes. 1.42). To be sure, there were also accusations that a son had acted violently against his mother (Dem. 25.55; cf. Lys. 10.8) and that a father had led a son to commit a crime (Dem. 54.22–23), but such accusations were relatively rare, while accusations that a son mistreated his father were hurled with some frequency, apparently because portraying a man as a bad son offended jurors' paternal expectations and raised doubts in their minds about his probity and integrity.

The ideal was of a close father-son bond, marked by hierarchy, amity, and solidarity, and concern for the reputation of the other.[52] A Lysian pleader told his audience that even as a thirty-year-old, he never contradicted his father (Lys. 19.55). Mantitheus asserted that he had complied with his father's wish that he take a bride of his father's choosing and made every effort to please him (Dem. 40.11–12).

This ideal made any public quarrels between fathers and sons potentially embarrassing. A man who spoke badly of his father in court or even admitted to a conflict with him violated injunctions against disgracing his family and risked incurring the displeasure of the jury, who could be expected to side with the older authority figure.[53]

Natural Son versus Legal Son (Dem. 39–40)

Speeches 39 and 40 in Demosthenes' corpus involve a conflict between Mantitheus and his half brother Boeotus.[54] Both men were Mantias's sons, Mantitheus by Mantias and his wife, Boeotus by Manthias and Plangon, a woman presented as his concubine, with whom Manthias had probably lived while married to Mantitheus's mother, and most certainly

---

52. Mutual care for reputation: Lys. 10.2–3; 26.21; Is. 2.42; Dem. 22.61; 40.5, 45–48; Cox 1998, 79–80.

53. For rivalry and conflicts between fathers and sons and within the household and among kin: Millett 1991, 135–36; Strauss 1993, esp. 100–129; Hunter 1994, 43–69, 118–19; Cox 1998, 68–129.

54. See n. 46 above on this case.

following her death.[55] Mantitheus was trying to stop Boeotus from changing his name to Mantitheus, which would, he contended, create personal, political, and administrative confusion and result in him having to account for his brother's misdeeds.

Mantitheus wished to confirm his legitimate status as Mantias's son and perhaps to claim seniority (and score a victory) over his half brother as well. To that end, he denied the legitimacy of Boeotus's sonship. He made much of Mantias's initial refusal to acknowledge that he was Boeotus's father and contended that his subsequent acceptance of Boeotus was the result a trick played on him by Boeotus, his mother, and their fellow conspirators (Dem. 39.2; 40.9–10). Yet much of Mantitheus's strategy in both speeches revolves around the distinction that he draws between a "true" son and one who is a son only in terms of the letter of the law.

As Mantitheus describes him, Boeotus was certainly not the former. He took Mantias to court, conspired to blackmail him, and tarnished his reputation. He repeatedly thwarted Mantias's wishes: by forcing him to register him as his own, trying to assume a name that Mantias had never given him, and, along with his mother, forcing him to divide his estate rather than bequeath it to his designated heir. Moreover, in violation of the rules of filial piety, he had quarreled with Mantias and tarnished his reputation, both when he was alive and posthumously (Dem. 39.2, 20; 40.5, 11, 13, 45, 47, 49).

Unlike Boeotus, Mantitheus said, he had striven to please his father, who had raised and loved him. He had always obeyed him, married in accordance with his wishes, and brought him pleasure by producing a child (Dem. 40.4, 8, 12–13). Indeed, his very claim to the exclusive use of name that his father had given him was an act of respect for his father's wishes (Dem. 39.20). Moreover, the model of a tactful son, he refused to discuss his father's financial losses or to specify his relationship with Plangon (Dem. 39.25; 40.8).

Although Mantitheus probably lost his suit (Todd 1993, 281), his strategy exploited the notion that a man who spoke badly of and openly against his father, or even admitted to a conflict with him, violated social norms. From a rhetorical perspective, however, it was not too challenging to reproach a man for violating father-son solidarity. The next

---

55. For Plangon's status as a wife, rather than a concubine, see Rudhardt 1962, 49–50; Mossé 1991, 276–77; Patterson 1991b, 281, 283.

two cases demonstrate the rhetorically more difficult task of presenting a conflict with a father from a son's perspective in a way that would not damage the son.

Euctemon's Disputed Estate (Is. 6)

Isaeus 6 involves a dispute over Euctemon's estate. Two possibly illegitimate sons of Euctemon contended with an adopted heir of Euctemon's dead son, whose claim to the estate was legally complex and questionable (Is. 6.3–5; Wyse 1904, 484), and whose adoptive father was dead and was known to have quarreled with his birth father over the inheritance. The murky nature of the competing legal claims made the quality of the son's relationship with his father an important issue, both because it affected the jury's opinion of the disputants, and because it could help the jurors guess what the *kurios*'s preference might have been.

The speaker for Euctemon's grandson, Chaerestratus, tried to show that despite a quarrel with Euctemon over the inheritance, Chaerestratus's father, who was his ticket to the inheritance, had been a true son to Euctemon both legally and morally.

The speech shows two different types of efforts to contend with the problem. One was to take advantage of the speech being delivered by a supporting speaker and a friend of Chaerestratus, that is, an outsider, to allow the speaker to criticize Euctemon. This criticism would not incur the jury's ire or call into question whether Chaerestratus or his father deserved to have been Euctemon's heirs, as would criticism from a family member, of whom more loyalty was expected (Is. 6.1–2, 17; Rubinstein 2000, 29). The other was for the speaker to mitigate Euctemon's culpability for the misdeeds attributed to him.

Hence he presented the elderly Euctemon as the victim of a "mishap" (*sumphoron;* Is. 6.18), manipulated by a conniving woman who took advantage of his enfeeblement as a result of drugs or illness or some other cause to get him recognize the elder of her two sons as his own. This argument made use of a law that allowed one to contest a will, and possibly an adoption, that had been made under the influence of drugs, disease, insanity, old age, or a woman.[56] Rhetorically, it softened the speaker's

---

56. Is. 2.1, 13–14, 19–20, 25, 38; 6.21; 7.1; Dem. 44.68; 46.14; Hyp. 3.17. The author of *Ath. Pol.* 35.2 suggests the legal abuse of these disqualifications. See also Wyse 1904, 248; Harrison 1968, 1: 87 with n. 2; MacDowell 1978, 101; Thompson 1981; Just 1989, 209–10; Rubinstein 1993, 62, 80–81; Rhodes 1993, 443–44; Hunter 1994, 12.

criticism of Euctemon. Ideologically, it appealed to the belief that a legitimate male member was unlikely to disrupt the relationships within the *oikos*.

The speaker explained that Philoctemon had initially objected to the recognition, which he had known to be false, but had changed his mind when Euctemon threatened to marry another woman and legitimize his children with her, and his relations begged him to put an end to the embarrassing conflict. The matter ended in a compromise: Euctemon and his phratry agreed to register Alce's son as his, while he agreed to bequeath the child no more than a small, defined portion of his estate, thereby leaving Philoctemon as his main heir (Is. 6.19–25, 29).

This account reinforced the idea that Philoctemon was Euctemon's main heir without suggesting that Philoctemon's actions were motivated by the wish to retain exclusive possession of his father's property. It transformed the public quarrel between father and son into the irrational act of a sick and manipulated man and promoted the son's moderation, kinship solidarity, and filial piety (Is. 6.23–24).

Apollodorus in Court (Dem. 36, 45, and 46)

Demosthenes 36, 45, and 46 involve a dispute between Apollodorus, the late Pasion's elder son, and Phormio, Pasion's freed slave, who managed Pasion's bank and shield factory. In his will, Pasion, himself a former slave, directed that Phormio marry his widow, Archippe, and serve as a guardian of his younger son, Pasicles.[57] At some point, Phormio distributed the common property, upon which Apollodorus had been drawing heavily. Apollodorus sued Phormio for embezzlement (Dem. 45.3–4; 36.14). Demosthenes 36 was Phormio's defense, which the court upheld. In Demosthenes 45 and 46, Apollodorus charged that the court's former verdict was based on false testimony.[58]

Apollodorus sought to discredit Phormio without discrediting his father.[59] He did so by slandering Phormio and playing upon the jury's fears of status inversion. Without any hard evidence, Apollodorus claimed

57. Dem. 36.30–31. Archippe's civic status is controversial: Trevett 1992, 19 n. 4; Carey 1991; Ogden 1996a, 131–34; Pomeroy 1997, 184–88, with n. 90; Cox 1998, 140 n. 45. What is important to our purpose is that Apollodorus gives his audience no reason to think that she was less than a citizen.

58. Apollodorus's career, expenses, and this legal case: E. E. Cohen 1991, 252–58; Trevett 1992, 9–49 (who questions Apollodorus's contentions); Cox 1998, 90–91; 193–94.

59. See [Dem.] 52.4, 11 for Apollodorus's defense of his father's reputation in an earlier case.

that Phormio had forged Pasion's will and seduced Archippe. Ignoring the fact that Phormio was no longer a slave, he made much of Phormio's origin in bondage. Playing on the Athenian's image of the slave as the opposite of the free adult male, he depicted Phormio as an alien criminal, hostile to honor and lacking in gratitude, and charged him with having cunningly stolen his master's money, house, assets, and wife.[60] A free man and Athenian citizen, Pasion never would have given his wife to a slave (Dem. 45.35; 46.13). To reinforce this point, he suggested that his mother had committed adultery with Phormio, and that Pasicles was Phormio's son.[61]

With his lack of respect for his mother and his aspersion of his brother, Apollodorus risked offending jurors who disapproved of involving the courts in family feuds. To deflect such criticism, he presented himself as an Athenian patriot and a free man who had been victimized by a slave. He was careful as well to exempt his father of responsibility for the scandalous and to play on the fears of the all-male jury that the *kurios* and his household were vulnerable to the machinations of greedy and lustful people.

THE OBLIGATIONS OF KINSHIP

The expectations of amity, solidarity, loyalty, and mutual aid that applied to the father-son relationship also applied to the adult man's relationships with his siblings and kin. To defame the characters of opponents, speakers accused them of mistreating close relatives. Accusations included fratricide (Is. 9.17), incest (Lys. 14.28), selling a sister abroad (Dem. 25.55), and eliminating one's brother-in-law (Is. 8.41), as well as a more general failure to support, protect, and care for relatives (e.g., Dem. 48.53–56). In practice, support for kinship ideology tended to weaken with the person's distance from the nuclear family, but that did not prevent speakers from drawing on the ideology for more remote kin when it suited their purpose.[62]

60. Dem. 45.3, 27, 30, 39, 73. On the image of slaves in Athens, see Vogt 1974, passim; Raaflaub 1983, esp. 533–34; Golden 1985; O. Patterson 1982, 30, 86–90; Cartledge 2003, esp. 141–51; Cox 1998, 190–94. On slaves and deficient manliness, see p. 133 below.

61. Dem. 45.3, 27, 39, 84. Cf. Davies 1971, 429; Hunter 1994, 53, 224 n. 37; Pomeroy 1997, 189–90; Cox 1998, 91. Apollodorus's treatment of his mother in court was quite utilitarian. In a different trial, he used his mother's illness to impress his audience with his self-sacrifice for the city: [Dem.] 50.60–63. He also used his brother's testimony to support an earlier litigation: [Dem.] 49.42–43.

62. Cf. Is. fr. 1 (Forster); Humphreys 1985b, 324–25; 1986; Hunter 1994, 48–55. Humphreys points to a stronger solidarity among birth relatives than among married re-

Several speakers criticized their opponents' failure to care for their wards, usually the orphaned children of close kin. An Isaean speaker impugned the defendant's character and rights to an estate by pointing out that he had evicted his female relatives from his property, even though he was their *kurios* and trustee (Is. 5.10). Lysias made this obligation a central component of his oration against Diogeiton, who had married his daughter to his brother, Diodotus, and following Diodotus's death, took care of his estate. He was accused of mistreating his brother's children, his own grandchildren (Lys. 32). After explaining to his grandsons that he could no longer support them because he had fallen on hard times (Lys. 32.9), the wealthy Diogeiton had heartlessly and shamelessly robbed and dispossessed his own fatherless grandchildren (Lys. 32.11–18).

As we have seen, Athenian law required her nearest male kinsman to marry a single heiress *(epikleros)* when she came of age (Is. fr. 26 [Forster]) or, alternatively, to provide her with an attractive dowry so that a more distant kinsman would do so.[63] The law sought to secure the family property within the kin group, since a woman was not permitted to become the legal proprietor of an *oikos,* and to provide the single heiress with the male protection she was deemed to require.

The practical and sentimental mingled, too, in the orators' expectations. The orations reveal an unabashed acceptance of the idea that men sought and enjoyed the utilitarian advantages of marriage with a well-to-do heiress, which included the inheritance of her *oikos* by his sons by her, the income he could derive from her assets, and the likely prospect that he would be able to incorporate them into his household. An Isaean speaker deemed it senseless, as well against the law (or custom), for a relative not to marry an heiress, because it would improve her children's claim to the property (Is. 3.50).

But there was also criticism of men who mistreated heiresses. An Isaean speaker (Is. 10.19) argued that the reason his father had not claimed an estate that should have gone to his mother was the threat by her relatives to dissolve the marriage by invoking the law permitting a kinsman to dissolve an *epikleros*'s marriage to an unrelated man.[64] The

---

lations: 1985b, 1995, cf. 1986b, 59, 74–75, 91; and esp. Cox 1998, passim. Our discussion suggests that the ideology of kinship solidarity was less discriminatory in its expectations.

63. See n. 13 above.

64. Harrison 1968, 1: 132–38; Schaps 1979, 25–42; Just 1989, 95–98; Hunter 1994, 15–16; Cox 1998, esp. 94–99, but see Patterson 1998, esp. 97–101, 256 n. 70.

speaker sought to win the jury's favor by showing that his mother's relatives had abused their family connection and the law to deprive her of the possessions of the *oikos*.

Conversely, speakers tried to win approval by citing their fulfillment of their obligation to marry an heiress ([Dem.] 53.29). When the heiress was poor, the speaker could pass himself off as a self-sacrificing individual who had done his manly duty in supporting and protecting his kinswoman. For example, Andocides told the jury that when his uncle died, leaving two daughters and heavy debts, he had arranged that he and another cousin would each marry one of them. He told his cousin that that they should act like "good men" *(eiē andrōn agthōn)*—words connoting moral uprightness and noble, manly conduct—and honor their family ties, and that they should not reject the daughters because of their poverty in favor of more lucrative matches. Had their uncle been alive or died rich, they would have asked for the daughters in marriage as their next-of-kin. Now, as persons of *aretē*—moral excellence—they should do the same. Only unscrupulous men would leave poor heiresses in the lurch.[65]

Speakers also manipulated the obligations that men had to help their relatives in the legal sphere. The man prosecuting Agoratus for the murder of Dionysodorus claimed that he was representing the victim, who was his cousin and brother-in-law (Lys. 13.22, 41). Theomnestus said that he was suing Stephanus to avenge the misery that the latter had inflicted, not only on himself, but on his wife (Apollodorus's daughter), his sister (Apollodorus's wife), Apollodorus, and his nieces, fearing that, being so closely related to them, he would be considered extremely cowardly (or unmanly) *(anandrotaton anthrōpōn einai)* if he failed seek justice for their sake.[66] His mention of the social pressure exerted on him to prosecute Stephanus indicates the link the ancient Athenians made between the manly duty of revenge and a man's obligations toward his family.

Another obligation was to give testimony and dispositions on their relatives' behalf (Is. 9.25; [Dem.] 49.37, 41). Yet a third expectation was

---

65. And. 1.117–21. For doubts about Andocides' virtuous conduct, see MacDowell 1962, 12–13, 145–46; Schaps 1979, 30–31.

66. [Dem.] 59.11–12. Cf. Plato *Rep.* 8 549c–550b. Carter 1986, 9; Carey 1992, 84; Christ 1998, 161–62. Rubinstein 2000, 131–48, 156–62, has argued, however, that relatives and friends in public actions played down their relation to prosecutors to highlight the communal nature of the trial. On the manly duty of taking legal revenge: Hunter 1994, 127–28; Christ 1998, 123, 154–59.

that men refrain from suing their relatives. Even more than other persons, relatives were expected to resolve their disputes through mediation or arbitration.[67] Persons involved in litigation with their kin apologized for or deprecated the act, justified their suit as unavoidable or just, and claimed that the fault was with their kin. An Isaean speaker depicted relatives bringing him and his brothers to court to contest a will as shameless and unkinly, and the whole affair as unseemly (Is. 1.5–6). A Lysian speaker described quarrelling with kin as "most shameful" *(aiskhiston)*, observed that jurors disapproved of men who were so unable to endure being outdone by their kin that they took them to court, and protested that he would not be doing this if his kinsmen's injustice had not demanded it (Lys. 32.1). Mantitheus described his suit against his half brother Boeotus as "most painful" and embarked on only under compulsion.[68]

More affirmatively, a Demosthenean speaker took credit for offering to share his inheritance with his brother-in-law rather than undertake a trial and risk mutual recriminations (Dem. 48.8). The speakers protest too much. Kin did sue kin, indeed, almost every property dispute was between kin (e.g., Is. 9).

Of course, the obligations of adult men in their family roles were not always consistent with one another. An oration written by Demosthenes a few years after he came of age (Dem. 27) illustrates the conflicting responsibilities of the *kurios,* son and heir, and kinsman. The oration involved a suit against Demosthenes' elder cousin, Aphobus, who, in accordance with the will of Demosthenes' father, had served, along with another cousin and a family friend, as one of Demosthenes' guardians *(kurioi)* after his father's death. Demosthenes charged Aphobus with squandering and mismanaging the better part of his father's estate.[69]

Demosthenes was acting within his rights and within expectations concerning the *kurios:* to recover what was his, restore the household to the sound state in which his father had left it, and punish those who had wronged him and his father. Yet because he was acting against relatives, he could be faulted for undermining kinship loyalty.

67. Athenian arbitration: Hunter 1994, 55–67; Rhodes 1995, 305–6; Thür 1995, 325–29; Scafuro 1997, esp. 34–38, 117–41, 386–99.
68. Dem. 40.1. See also Is. 5.29; 9.23; fr. 22, 43 (Thalheim); Ant. 1.1; Dem. 27.65; 48.1; [Aristotle] *Rhetoric to Alexander* 36.1442a–b; Wyse 1904, 186–87; Hunter 1994, 55, 58; Christ 1998, 168–73. For criticism of the view that family solidarity gave way to individualism in fourth-century Athens: Rubinstein 1993, 7–10; Scafuro 1997, 281–83.
69. Plut. *Demosthenes* 6; Pomeroy 1997, 162–68; Mirhady 2000, 181–204.

To counter the risk, Demosthenes emphasized that his guardians, not he, had violated kinship obligations. At the beginning of the oration (Dem. 27.4–7), he portrayed his father making his will on his deathbed, when his children were only seven and five years old, and entrusting them to the guardians. He had given Demosthenes' sister in marriage to one of the cousins-guardians, Demophon, and Demosthenes' mother in marriage to another, Aphobus, in the hope that these added bonds of kinship would induce them to look after the children's interests even better. At the close of the oration, Demosthenes concluded that "they thought nothing of kinship, as though they had been left to us not as friends and relatives but as most hated enemies" (Dem. 27.65).

Demosthenes won his suit, yet the problem of violating kinship solidarity resurfaces in Demosthenes 29, in which he worries that his efforts to exact the damages the court had awarded him will lead to accusations that he is ruthless, cruel, and ungrateful.[70]

Kinsmen as Threats

In practice, the ideology that called on men to put themselves at the service of their families and kin gave way to economic considerations and agonistic drive. In fact, kin could, and apparently did, pose a major threat to the *oikos*, especially when its *kurios* was childless.

In Athens, the right to the property of a childless man was given to the *ankhisteia*, a group of kinsmen and affines, down to the sons of cousins on the father's and mother's sides, with a clear preference for the agnatic kin.[71] Yet a relative's right to the property of the *oikos* was ranked lower than the right of an adopted male heir. Subscribing to the view that the kinship group had first claims to the *oikos*, most childless *kurioi* followed the rules of intestate inheritance and choose a near relative as heir.[72] When a *kurios* exercised his right and did not do this, however, his action voided his kin's rights to his property (Harrison 1968, 1: 82–96). Close kin were likely to dispute the adoption, arguing that they had better claim to the property by virtue of their closer and more cor-

---

70. Dem. 29.2; cf. Aes. 1.102–4; Lys. fr. 43 (Thalheim). Demosthenes' concern was justified: Aes. 2.99.

71. Broadbent 1968, 231–35; MacDowell 1978, 98–108; Littman 1979, 5–7, 15–17; Pomeroy 1997, 19–21; Patterson 1998, 88–89.

72. Just 1989, 92–93; Foxhall 1989, 26–32; Hunter 1993, esp. 106; cf. Rubinstein 1993, 24, 79; Cox 1998, 128–29.

dial relationship to the deceased, and that they were following his true intentions.[73]

The adoptees countered that a successful challenge would undermine the *oikos* and make it an empty place.[74] This line of argument reminded the jurors that the *kurios* was responsible—as were they as well—for perpetuating the *oikos*.

Apparently, such appeals to the jurors played on genuine concerns. Indeed, a relative who had his own *oikos*, as did the disputants in Isaeus 2, 7, and 9, was likely to annex one he inherited to it, terminating its independent existence, since it would not make sense to maintain two separate estates. Frequent accusations that claimants to an estate wished to increase their own fortunes suggested that this was a likely scenario (e.g., Is. 1.47; 8.3, 43; 9.26; Dem. 43.67–68, 80; 44.64). In a variation on the theme, an Isaean speaker told of a case where the husbands of sisters who inherited their brother's *oikos* sold all its possessions and left it "shamefully" *(aiskhrōs)* and awfully "abandoned."[75]

The Athenian *kurios* regarded it as one of his primary duties to protect the *oikos* from the dangers of the outside world. This role was integrated into Athens's civic ideology, and speakers often reminded their male audience of the dangers that their wives, children, houses, and ancestral tombs faced from enemies.[76] In reality, Athenian *oikoi* and their occupants were rarely subjected to attacks by foreign powers. The danger came rather from other Athenians, especially kinsmen. It appears that men, in their roles as family members or kinsmen, not only paid tribute to familial and kinship solidarity but also violated, manipulated, or ignored it.

THE *KURIOS* AND HIS FRIENDS

The ancient Greeks looked to both friends and relatives for *philia* (love, friendship), a word that covered a wide range of affections and connotes

73. See, e.g., Is. 2; 4; 5; Dem. 43; 44. Adoption as a way of bypassing the claims of close male kin to one's estate: Rubinstein 1993, 80–86, and 62–86, 92–97; Cox 1998, e.g., 6–9, 148–151. On preference of friends to relatives, see D. Cohen 1991c, 84–85; Cox 1998, 194–202. Challenging adoptions: Hunter 1993.

74. Is. 2.1, 15, 35, 37, 46; 7.43. Cf. Is. 3.61; 7.31–32; 9.7; Isoc. 19.34–35.

75. Is. 7.31; cf. Dem. 43.69. Hunter 1993; 1994, 12, 50–51, seems to have a more charitable view of kin's actions, but see Rubinstein 1993, 45, 51, 57–61, 92–104.

76. Dem. 19.65, 86, 125; 23.55–56; Din. 1.65; cf. Dem. 11.9; 15.10; 18.215; 19.310; Aes. 3.156–57; Lyc. 1.16.

reciprocal obligations and mutual sympathy. Words such as *epitēdeios* and *oikeios* could mean either a close relative or an intimate friend, whether he was a relation or not.[77] Like trusted relatives, the good friends of the *kurios* regularly entered the protected territory of the house and were intimately involved in the life of the *oikos,* which they could join through adoption or marriage.[78] Kinsmen, for their part, might well become friends, especially when they were from the same neighborhood (deme) and roughly of the same age and social background.[79] Moreover, the orations suggest that it was not enough for an heir to be a kinsman of the testator; it was also important for him to be a friend.[80] Friends seem also to have provided the Athenian man with a second tier of support, whether in place of, in conjunction with, or against his kin.[81]

Friends could also be viewed as a threat, however. One Isaean speaker argued that a childhood friend of an uncle of a claimant to an estate had persuaded the former to claim it unjustly (Is. 5.7, 40). A second speaker asserted that friends had helped his nephew in his designs on his property (Is. fr. 1 [Forster]). Moreover, the case of Menecles, discussed above (Is. 2), indicates that friendship with a stranger could augment the pool of potential heirs, undermine the claim of relatives to the inheritance, and disrupt relationships within the family. An Isaean speaker observed that testators (presuming they had no direct male heir) who disliked their kinsmen might prefer to leave their property to friends who were unrelated (Is. 4.18). Even where inheritance was not an issue, friends could compete with kin for the resources of the *oikos.* The Athenians deemed providing assistance to friends as proof of goodness and selflessness. Entertaining friends, drinking, and gambling with them (e.g., Dem. 38.27; cf. Lys. 24.5) were rarely singled out for praise, of course (cf. Lys. 25.4).

An adult male was expected to play the same protective, caring role with his friends as with his family members and kin. In Isaeus 7, the

77. Foxhall 1998a, 59; Konstan 1997, 64, with n. 15, but also 54–56. Greek friendship: Konstan 1997, 1998, and the following notes

78. Friends and the *oikos:* e.g., Is. 2.3–5; 9.4; Lys. 1.18; fr. 120 (Thalheim); Ant. 1.14, 29; [Dem.] 49.40–41; cf. [Dem.] 59.22. D. Cohen 1991c, 84–91; Gallant 1991, 146–57; Hunter 1994, 127–28; Cox 1998, 168–70; 194–202.

79. Dem. 27.4; 53.4; 54.7; Aes. 1.42; cf. Arist. *EN* 8.12 1161b33–35. Age and friendship among kin: Humphreys 1986b, 89–90.

80. Is. 1.4; 7.36; Hunter 1993, 105–6; Rubinstein 1993, 66–67.

81. Friends mediating disputes between kin: Dem. 41.14; Dem. 48.40; Lys. 32.11–12; rendering legal assistance (including against kin): Is. 5.8; 6.54; Lys. 8.18–19; 15.12; frs. 119, 120 (Thalheim); Dem. 29.22; [Dem.] 50.26; 54.33–35; Aes. 1.47; Isoc. 21.1, 8–9, 20; cf. Dem. 43.7; 53.14. See also Lavency 1964, 85; Dover 1974, 175–76; Humphreys 1985c, 316–25; Todd 1990b, 23–31; Hansen 1991, 211; Rubinstein 2000, 128–31, 159–63.

speaker claimed that the late Apollodorus, son of Thrasyllus, had adopted him as his heir and had bequeathed his estate to him rather than to a blood relative. The speaker strained to convince his hearers that Apollodorus and his own grandfather were sufficiently close friends that Apollodorus would have wanted to take this step. As evidence of their friendship, he said that his grandfather had helped Apollodorus recover money embezzled by his guardian, in gratitude for which Apollodorus had helped pay his grandfather's ransom when he was captured in war, served as his surety until the full sum was paid, and given him money when he fell on hard times (Is. 7.7–10; cf. Isoc. 19.10–12, 18–29). The different Isaean speaker makes similar assertions of friendship with the man whose inheritance he claimed: he had set sail with the man on a life-threatening mission and shared the hardships of captivity with him (Is. 6.1–2).

Aristotle divided friendship into a variety of categories and subcategories, including friendships that are useful, pleasurable, and, the highest form, those that are selfless and inculcate virtue in both men.[82] The forensic speechwriters acknowledged these categories, but were content with a simpler division: the speakers and their friends were loyal and selfless, their rivals and their friends were partners in crime.[83] On the assumption that like sought out like (Is. 2.43), speakers boasted of keeping good company and avoiding bad.[84]

Athenians based their opinion of a man, inter alia, on the way he treated, and was treated by, his friends.[85] As evidence of worthiness, speakers boasted of their generosity to his friends and noted that they had friends and resources as proof of their power.[86] Conversely, speak-

---

82. *EN* 8–9. Utilitarian friendship: Dem. 23.134; Lys. 8.18; Millett 1991, 109–26, esp. 111–15. Konstan 1995, 330–33; 1997, 53–92, focuses on its disinterested affection; cf. Foxhall 1998a, 57–67; Mitchell 1997, esp. 8–9. Political friendship: Connor 1971, 35–86; Hutter 1978; Strauss 1986, 20–28; Herman 1987; Mitchell and Rhodes 1996; Konstan 1997, 60–67; Mitchell 1997, 41–46; and, on a theoretical level, Scofield 1998.

83. Good friends: e.g., Ant. 4.4.1; Is. 6.1; Dem. 21.17; cf. Ant. 5.34; Dem. 36.1. Conspiratorial or evil friends: e.g., Lys. 8.8; 12.62–64; Dem. 33.18; Din. 1.33; cf. Lys. 20.12; 24.2.

84. Moving in bad company: Lys. 3.12–18; 4.7; 23.11; Dem. 21.71–74; 25.52; 54.8, 33–35; 59.40; cf. Dem. 61.18. Judging one's character by the company he keeps: Aes. 1.152–53.

85. E.g., Lys. 6.23; 9.13; Is. 2.43; Dem. 54.43.

86. Generosity to friends: Ant. 2.2.12; Lys. 19.56. Friends and power: Dem. 21.111; 53.1; Lys. 8.7. Cf. Dem. 21.20; Arist. *Rhet.* 2.5.14 1382b35–1383a5. Being friendless and poor: Dem. 21.96. Attacking a man as a service for a friend, or attacking an opponent's friend: Lys. 26.15; cf. And. 1.49, 53; Dem. 21.116; Hyp. 3.31; cf. Arist. *Rhet.* 1.12.2–4 1372a11–21.

ers denigrated their adversaries by impugning the character of their
friends (Aes. 1.42) or by accusing a man of mistreating friends when he
was miserly and selfish (Is. 5.35, 43), a cheat (Is 5.40), an informer (Lys.
6.23; Dem. 21.122), an ingrate (Dem. 37.15), or an accessory in friends'
deaths (Lys.12.67; cf. 14.27; Hyp. 5.20–21).

In Demosthenes 53, Apollodorus exploits the ethos of friendship to
avenge himself on Arethusius and his brother Nicostratus, arguing that
two slaves who were asserted to belong to Arethusius's brothers, one of
whom was his erstwhile friend Nicostratus, were actually the property
of Arethusius himself. The purpose of providing this information was to
support Apollodorus's argument that the slaves should be seized to repay
a fine that Arethusius owed the state.

Yet only about a third of the speech deals with the ownership of the
slaves. In the first two-thirds or so, Apollodorus describes his friendship
with Nicostratus and then Nicostratus's subsequent betrayal of him.[87]
He paints himself as Nicostratus's good neighbor and devoted friend,
and Nicostratus as a false friend turned enemy for financial gain. He and
Nicostratus were neighbors of about the same age who had gradually become very close and developed a relationship of mutual help and support: He had never refused Nicostratus's requests for assistance, and had
asked Nicostratus to manage his estate when he was away ([Dem.] 53.4).

When Nicostratus was kidnapped, Apollodorus had come to his
friend's rescue. He describes his conduct in a mixture of emotional and
instrumental terms aimed at proving his deep feeling for Nicostratus and
the lengths to which he had gone to help him. Thus, he relates that he
had grieved for *(sunakhthestheis)* and pitied *(eleēsas)* Nicostratus
([Dem.] 53.7–8), had given money to Nicostratus's brother to get him
back from his kidnappers, had sold precious items from his inheritance
to give Nicostratus a large sum toward his ransom, and had borrowed
in order to lend him money for the rest of the ransom ([Dem.] 53.6–13).
He claims that Nicostratus had wept and appealed to his friendship, and
that he had responded as a "true friend" *(alēthinos philos),* noting that
he had done more for Nicostratus than the latter's own kin.[88]

87. [Dem.] 53.4–16. For the case, see Millett 1991, 53–59; E. E. Cohen 1992, 210–13.
Christ 1998, 177, doubts their friendship, while Johnstone 1999, 81–82, emphasizes Apollodorus's wish to defend his honor and disgrace his opponent. For a similar accusation of
betrayal: Lys. frs. 39.6.iv–v (Gernet-Bizos).
88. [Dem.] 53.12. Altruistic male friends and their sharing of joy and sorrow: Gallant
1991, 155–58; Millett 1991, 109–59; Gill et al. 1998, esp. the contributions of Zanker,
Herman, Konstan, and Gill, as well as van Wees (1998b).

In contrast, he describes Nicostratus's conduct as that of a man who had pretended friendship in order to obtain instrumental benefits, and then, rather than reciprocate, or even show gratitude (cf. Dem. 37.15), had turned against Apollodorus so that he would not have to repay the loan that he, Apollodorus, had taken out on his behalf.[89] He claimed that Nicostratus had conspired with his adversaries to support them in a suit that Apollodorus had brought against them and revealed his arguments to them. He had charged Apollodorus with being a public debtor, obtained a judgment against him, and forced his way into his home, and seized his property. Nicostratus had also joined his brother in vandalizing Apollodorus's garden, ambushed him, and punched him in the face ([Dem.] 53.14–16).

The lengthy depiction of this friendship betrayed in a legal action concerning an entirely unrelated matter attests to the importance that Athenians attributed to a man's conduct as a friend. Evidently, Apollodorus chose to focus on the friendship as his chief strategy in winning over the jury. The strategy had its risks, however. Taking legal action against a friend carried the same opprobrium as taking legal action against a relative (Lys. 12.67; Aes. 1.131). Apollodorus had to convince the jurors that Nicostratus had betrayed him, rather the other way around. In essence, he was asking them to render their verdict less on the ownership of the slaves than on Nicostratus's disloyalty.

THE *KURIOS* AND THE STATE

The social, political, and legal ties between the *oikos* and polis tended to blur the boundaries between the private and the public spheres. Men were expected to use their private wealth for public purposes, to sponsor dramatic productions, and defray the costs of building and maintaining the Athenian navy. The state had a stake in legitimate paternity and intervened to settle family feuds.

These ties were often given the foreground in trials. The jurors, who represented the state, were concerned with the impact of the contenders' conduct and their own decisions on the polis as a whole. Moreover, the

---

89. For lending motivated by noncommercial considerations, see Millett 1991, index, s.v. "*eranos*-loans," and 53–59 on Apollodorus's transactions in this case. Apollodorus's reference to his youth ([Dem.] 53.12), with its connotations of naïveté and strong emotions (Arist. *Rhet.* 2.12.5–8 1389a6–25), served to exacerbate Nicostratus's villainy and betrayal.

jurors' verdicts were apparently affected by their views of the contenders' performance in their personal and civic roles.

Athenians wished to see the man's role in the state and his role in the family as complementing one another, assuming that men would behave as citizens as they did in their families. Speakers argued that a man who humiliated and harmed a member of his family would treat fellow citizens the same way ([And.] 4.15). If he squandered the family fortune, he would squander public funds (Aes. 1. 28–29). If he mistreated his parents, he would mistreat the citizenry (Dem. 25.66; Aes. 1.28; cf. [Aristotle] *Rhetoric to Alexander* 3.1426b4–7). In the review *(dokimasia)* of candidates for public office, this assumption informed the inquiry into how the candidate treated his parents (Din. 2.17; *Ath. Pol.* 55.3).

Speakers linked the man's family and civic roles in currying favor with the jury and criticizing their adversaries. In one and the same breath, Lycurgus asked the jury to convict Leocrates of the public crimes of desertion and treason and the private offense of depriving his forebears of their burial rites (Lyc. 1.147; Lacey 1968, 272 n. 203). Conversely, an Isaean speaker boasted simultaneously of his commendable handling of his wards' estate and his contributions to the polity (Is. 11.38–50). Another Isaean speaker declared that he would show him to be a most villainous person *(ponērotatos)* with regard to the polis, his relatives, and his friends (Is. 5.35).[90]

But the speakers also reveal awareness that duties to family and the polis could conflict, and they were evidently somewhat ambivalent about which duties to prioritize. On the one hand, a Lysian speaker urges jurors to show their anger against the defendant's relatives and supporting speakers, who had asked that he be pardoned but did not try to persuade him to obey the city's orders (Lys. 14.20). On the other hand, a speech written by Dinarchus (1.58–59) approves the acquittal of a man charged with a crime against the state (perhaps desertion or treason: Worthington 1992, 222), because he had gone to help out his stepfather. Aeschines disparages an opponent for not using his power as a member of the Council to help a relative obtain a small subsidy from the state to which he was entitled (Aes. 1.104). A Demosthenean speaker implies that a public figure could be forgiven for proposing an unjust law if his motive had been, inter alia, to help a relative (Dem. 24.67, 195). These orations reflect the belief that, given a conflict, a man's natural inclination will be

90. Cf. Is. 7.30–32; Dem. 19.201; Pearson 1981, 75–76.

to choose his responsibilities to his family above his responsibilities to the state, and, moreover, their understanding and acceptance of that choice.

Other orations, though, grapple with the conflict. In a speech charging Aeschines with dishonesty, disobedience, and disloyalty as a member of the embassy sent to Macedonia in 346, Demosthenes discounted the pleas of Aeschines' brothers on his behalf. Acknowledging the belief that a man should come to his brother's aid in court, even if the brother is guilty, he argued that while it was up to Aeschines' brothers to think of Aeschines, it was the duty of the jurors to convict wrongdoers and uphold the laws of the state (Dem. 19.238–39). This argument handled the potential conflict between a man's obligations according to his role: as kin, the man might choose his obligations to his family; as a juror, he should prioritize his duties to the state.

In his suit against Polycles, Apollodorus deals with the conflict in a single individual ([Dem.] 50). Polycles had been appointed to replace Apollodorus at the end of the latter's obligatory term of service as a trierarch (a citizen who helped to equip and maintain Athenian warships and often captained them). But Polycles failed to take over the ship until more than five months after Apollodorus's term of service officially expired. Apollodorus lodged the suit to punish Polycles and secure reimbursement for the extra expenses he had incurred during those months. Apollodorus expatiated on his dedicated service as a trierarch and his expenditure on the equipment of his ships and the sailors' pay, and contrasted Polycles' reluctance to serve the state either in his person or with his purse.

Of special interest here is a short section toward the end of the speech in which Apollodorus emphasizes his status as family man ([Dem.] 50.59–64). He had never left the ship, he told the jury, even though his mother was sick and dying, his wife ill, his children small, his estate in debt and hounded by creditors, his wells dry, and his vegetable garden not growing. He had longed to see his unhappy family, and had shed tears knowing their straits, but had clung to his duty to serve the state: "Yet, in spite of these things that happened to me, I did not consider my private affairs to be more important than yours [i.e., the state's], and I thought that it was incumbent on me to rise above [*kreittōn einai*] the money that was spent, and the *oikos* that was neglected, and my sick wife and mother, so that no one would accuse me of deserting my post and rendering my ship useless to the polis" ([Dem.] 50.63).

This heartrending account need not be taken at face value. Apollodorus's concern for his dying mother is at odds with his presentation of her in his quarrel with Phormio, discussed above, over his father's estate (Dem. 45.84). His rendition of his motives artfully makes his concern about being charged with desertion if he left his ship an incentive for his dedicated and patriotic service. Moreover, like other public benefactors, Apollodorus did not impoverish himself because of his public service; he went on to perform additional costly public services *(leitourgiai)* later in his career.[91]

Apollodorus dramatizes the conflict between *oikos* and polis, I argue, because the Athenians looked for such conflict when they tested the civic credentials of a man, especially a rich man. Evidence of personal loss was proof of good citizenship and patriotism, and as such, it was supposed to help Apollodorus to gain a favorable verdict in his suit. A Lysian speaker makes a similar argument, contending that his spending on the city without even considering that his children would become much poorer; his record of military service, during which he had risked orphaning his children and making his wife a widow for the good of the state; and, generally, his concern about not being able to perform his assignments eagerly *(prothumōs)* all contradict the charge against him of taking bribes and entitled him to the jury's consideration and a verdict of acquittal (Lys. 21.23–25). Another client of Lysias lays similar claim to the jurors' consideration in arguing that his father's spending on the city had greatly diminished his assets (Lys. 19.61–62; cf. Dem. 47.54). Apparently, jurors approved of citizens spending their money "eagerly" *(prothumōs)* in the public interest, as the Lysian speaker cited above puts it, and not complaining about the state's demands on them. Such complaints might put the jurors as state representatives on the defensive, as beneficiaries of the state's exactions, or even to shame. Indeed, a Demosthenean speaker charges that his adversaries deserve no recompense from the state, because they have not spent their money on it but on themselves. He suggests, apparently without any proof, that they complained, or would complain, that the state took away their property. Their claims were as shameful and as damaging to the good name of the state, a noteworthy contrast to those who "eagerly" *(prothumōs)* performed all their obligations to the city (Dem. 38.25–26).

Yet Apollodorus's and others' rhetoric of conflict between polis and

---

91. See Davies 1981, 83: "[I]t should have been formally impossible for the liturgical and eisphora [property tax] systems by themselves as socio-economic mechanisms to push a man into poverty." I do not contend that Apollodorus's account is utterly false. Cox 1998, 155–66, has assembled cases of the ruinous impact of absence on the household. On Apollodorus's self-sacrifice, see Roisman 1999, 157–58.

oikos should not be read as reflecting a simple prioritization of public duty. Neglecting one's private affairs was not socially approved of (Lys. 25.1). The Athenian male was expected to fulfill both his private and his public obligations. Thus Apollodorus takes care to show that he has been both an exemplary citizen and an exemplary family man, even when the two roles collided.

The orations point to similar problems and pressures in reconciling the role of friend and citizen. Being a good friend and being a good citizen went hand in hand so long as the friend was upright and civic-minded. Speakers depict friends and friendships that fell short of this ideal. They drank, fought, and inflicted bodily harm.[92] Such behavior, the friendships that underpinned it, and the men who engaged in it are generally presented as a threat to public order.

Speakers also charged citizens with ranking personal friendships above the interests of the state. Aeschines, for example, commends Athenian leaders of past generations who brought motions against their friends for proposing illegal laws. He contrasts their civic-minded conduct and concern for Athenian democracy with the behavior of the generals of his own time. In helping their friends as supportive speakers, even though the former have proposed illegal measures, the generals display a lack of gratitude to the state that has honored them, proof of their subversive conduct (Aes. 3.194–196). Other speakers call upon jurors to punish friends of a defendant who support him in court even though they know that he is guilty of acting against the public interest, or because they share in his wrongdoing (Lys. 27.13; 30.31–34; Lyc. 1.135; cf. Dem. 21.127, 212).

As with kin, however, the Athenians half-expected friends to rank mutual solidarity ahead of commitment to the polis and obedience to its laws.[93] One Lysian speaker acknowledges that friends may gain a good reputation for saving one of their own from charges of military desertion, but tells the court that punishing public enemies would be more virtuous (Lys. 14.19; cf. 26.15). Speakers take it for granted that friends, like kin, will lie for one another in court, and may even cite friendship as

92. Good friends and citizens: Lys. 19.56; Isoc. 15.99, and see Konstan 1998, 54–55; cf. Rubinstein 2000, 162. On bad company, see n. 84 above.

93. On friends' solidarity, see Arist. *NE* 8–9, 1159b–1160a7, and, e.g., Meier 1990, e.g., 117–19; Millett 1991, 109–26; Mitchell 1997, 10–16, 22–28; Foxhall 1998a, esp. 53–56; Rubinstein 2000, 161–63. Konstan 1997, 54–67; and Rubinstein 1998, 134–39; 2000, 159–63, argue, however, that the public interest was valued more highly than friendship.

a somewhat mitigating explanation for a man's giving false testimony (Dem. 29.22). This assumption—or practice—seems to have been so ingrained that Lycurgus had to make a point of stating that in helping friends and relatives, a man should stop short of taking a false oath (Lyc. fr. E.3 [Burtt]).

On the other hand, Lysias criticizes Theramenes for prosecuting and causing the execution of his best friends because they had been oligarchs (Lys. 12.67). His criticism suggests that even the democratic jury had little sympathy for men who harmed their friends, including in defense of democracy. Even Aeschines, who criticizes generals for putting personal friendship above the good of democracy, in the same speech faults Demosthenes for serving as prosecutor in the impeachment of a general who had been his father's friend and who had shared with Demosthenes the intimate experiences of friendship in the form of joint military service, dining, sacrificing, and making libations.[94]

It would be unproductive to dismiss these inconsistencies as the orators' talking from both sides of their mouths. The Athenians expected men who had to choose between state and friend to be loyal to both. They sympathized with friends who helped each other even when they sinned against the city, but they also expected them to rise above their comradeship in defense of the public interest. Each choice might be justified—or denounced—in light of its special circumstances, different masculine or civic norms, and the speaker's position in a given dispute.

Andocides 1

Expectations of the Athenian man, as son, kinsman, friend, and citizen, are brought together in Andocides' defense against an incriminating charge *(endeixis)* brought against him in 399 (And. 1). Suspected of the participating in the Hermes and Mysteries affairs of 415, Andocides had been arrested for mutilating the *Hermai,* statues of Hermes that stood in front of Athenian courtyards and in the streets, and for profaning an Athenian Mystery cult, crimes punishable by death and the confiscation of one's property. He saved his life by turning informer. Shortly afterward, he left Athens. He returned after the restored democracy issued a

---

94. Aes. 3.51–52. Similar complaints: Aes. 2.22, with Demosthenes' reply: Dem. 19.188–91. On Aes. 3.51–52, see Rubinstein 1998, 136, and 131–39, for the conflict between personal enmity and friendship with magisterial duty.

general amnesty in 403, regained his citizen's rights, threw himself into public life, and made enemies.

He was charged with participating in the Mysteries of 400 in violation of a decree that forbade anyone who had confessed to having committed impiety, as he had, to enter the temples and the agora. Moreover, during those Mysteries, he had committed the illegal act of laying a suppliant wreath on an altar at the Eleusinium. Andocides' response to these charges was that the decree had been rescinded with the general amnesty of 403, and that the wreath had been laid by his accuser, Callias, a distant relative by marriage, in order to frame him.

More relevant to our concern here is his defense against the charges that in order to save himself in the earlier *Hermai* and Mysteries affairs, he had informed against his father, relatives, and friends, causing the death of the latter. Underlying these accusations was the Athenian assumption that a man who betrayed his family and friends to save his life would also betray the polis to the same ends. In his defense, Andocides relied upon the same assumption of consistency in public and private conduct to present himself as a model son, friend, kinsman, and citizen who had acted not out of cowardice but for the benefit of all concerned.

To do so, he had to reconcile the irrevocable. On the one hand, there was the code of friendship that obliged one to keep silent about the wrongdoings of family members and friends (Dem. 21.117). Even though the jurors represented the state, they did not care for informers and actually expected Andocides to have shielded his fellow men, especially family members, from the power of the state. Indeed, his enemies made much of his informing, presenting it as shameful in the extreme ([Lys.] 6.23; cf. 6.3, 53). And Andocides conceded that that people thought him base and a coward for informing on his father, friends, and relatives to save his own skin (And. 1.19, 54, 56–57).

On the other hand, there was the mutilation of the *Hermai*, a crime so serious that a man who identified the perpetrators should have been considered a good citizen. In addition, the jury in the restored Athenian democracy had cause to be wary of men who were more loyal to their friends than to the state. Such men, in the late fifth century, had formed the political clubs called *hetaireiai*, or comradeships, which had helped overthrow the democratic regime in Athens.[95]

95. The locus classicus is Thuc. 3.82.4–6. *Hetaireiai*: Calhoun, 1913; Sartori 1957; Longo 1971; Connor 1971, esp. 25–29, 35–86; Aurenche 1974; Missiou 1998, 193–96.

Andocides strenuously denied that he had informed, whether against his father, his relatives, or his friends, and blamed these acts on others.[96] Furthermore, to emphasize the value he placed on kinship loyalty, he stressed his astonishment and outrage that the prosecution would charge him with such contemptible behavior (And. 1.19–22, 40–42). To indicate the value he placed on loyalty to friends, he told the jury that he had promised the leaders of the mutilation, which he claimed he had known about but did not participate in, that he would not reveal their identity, and that he had kept his promise (And 1.63–67).

Admitting that he had given information on men suspected of acting against the state, Andocides insisted that he was urged to inform by a close relative, and that his informing had been reluctant, selective, and essential to save, not his own life, but the lives of others. He had informed only on four men, all of whom had already been denounced and whose fate had been sealed (And. 1.51–57). He and his family and associates were in a dark jail, close to being executed, when a cousin with whom he had grown up begged him to save his father, his brother-in-law, and himself, as well as scores of other innocent persons who were wrongly accused. His dilemma, he told the jury, had been to inform on the guilty or to doom his innocent family and associates to imminent and wrongful death: "Am I to look on while my own relatives are about to be executed unjustly and be put to death . . . and three hundred Athenians are about to be executed unjustly?"[97]

Andocides also asserted that he had acted for the good of the polis, freeing it from the fear and panic that had gripped it after the mutilations. Nor was he the coward that he was accused of being. Using military images, he drew a picture of himself as a heroic warrior who had refused both ignoble death and shameful survival, and who had driven terror from the polis and averted injustice (esp. And. 1.56–57).

In sum, Andocides portrays himself as man who meets, and even exceeds, masculine expectations in his conduct as son, kinsman, friend, and citizen. He is truthful, has acted responsibly, and puts his family and the state above his own welfare. With this tactic, he reconciles the conflict

96. And. 1.48–68. MacDowell 1962, 169–71; and Strauss 1993, 192, argue that Andocides did inform on his father, but Edwards 1995, 21–25, credits Andocides with being truthful in denying the charge.

97. And. 1.51; cf. 53, 59, 66, 68–69. On dramatic qualities in this speech, see Ober and Strauss 1990, 256–58; and see also Roisman 1999, which expands on some of the points made here. On the roles of father and son in this trial, see Strauss 1993, 187–99. On oligarchic motifs in the speech, see Missiou 1992, 51–53.

between a man's duties to his family and friends and his civic duty, offering the jury a comforting, if simplistic, picture of consistency. We cannot know whether Andocides' self-portrait was responsible for his acquittal. What is certain is that he was quite adept at manipulating masculine images and ideology when his conduct in his different male roles came under attack.

Judging by the orations, it could not have been easy for the Athenian man to meet the expectations of him as a *kurios,* husband, son, kinsman, friend, and citizen. The insistence on congruence in a man's behavior in his family, with his friends, and toward the polis was an expression of the idea that a man's character remained the same, whatever his role. This idea is behind Andocides' boast that he is an *anēr aristos,* "an excellent man" (And. 1.67), who has brought only good to his family, his friends, and the state. Like other stereotypes, the notion of congruence could be used to simplify the process of assessing a man, and it probably provided a comforting sense of coherence.

It did not encompass all of the reality, however. The orations make it clear that in fulfilling his masculine obligations in one role, the Athenian male could be faulted for neglecting or violating them in another. The orations do not provide a clear hierarchy of roles or guidelines for choosing one set of responsibilities over another. They show us men pouncing on their adversaries and, conversely, defending themselves from the incessant faultfinding that stems from the ambivalence and diversity of the expectations.

This situation meant that the Athenian man had to decide for himself how to act in any given situation, with no guarantee that his conduct would be defensible in court or in public opinion. The uncertainty probably made for a good deal of tension, but it may also have been liberating. For in the contradictions lies the space for choice, and for the self-assertion that is inherent in choosing.

CHAPTER 3

Manly Shame

Honor and shame were essential qualities in Athenian manhood, integral to virtually every aspect of the man's being and life as the Athenians conceived of them. We have seen that young men were accorded less honor than their elders and deemed to have a proclivity for shaming, or dishonoring, others (Lys. 24.16; Dem. 54.21; 55.7). Men who fulfilled their duties to family and polis were considered honorable; those who acted negligently in their roles as *kurioi* or friends were deemed dishonorable (And. 1.57; Is. 3.51; 7.31, 39; Dem. 40.24, 49).

Other masculine activities and roles were also perceived, partly or wholly, in terms of honor and shame. When the Athenian man went to war, he proved his manhood by acting honorably in battle. When in court, his manliness was part of his self-portrait as a man of honor.[1] Indeed, the Athenian conception of honor was largely androcentric. A Xenophantic speaker claims that the pursuit of honor *(philotimia)* separates a man *(anēr)*, that is, a real man, from an animal or a mere human being *(anthrōpos;* Xen. *Hiero* 7.3). Women were also deemed to have or to lack honor, of course, but their honor was mainly passive and anchored in the domestic sphere: their lineage, marital ties, and chastity. The active, and public, pursuit of honor was the province of men.[2]

---

1. E.g., Lyc. 1.49; And. 1.56; cf. Fisher 1998b, 70–71; Allen 2000, 60–62; Gilmore 1990, 20, 31.
2. Cf. Dem. 10.71. For the close links between man (but not woman) and honor in Athens, see Cole 1996, 229. Active and visible male honor: Fisher 1998b, 70; cf. Dover

Honor and shame turn up in many of the orations and in most of our literary sources.[3] Their ubiquity has to do with the egalitarian premise that practically every Athenian man has honor and hence can be dishonored by both his own actions and those of other men. The orations are more informative about shame, perhaps because their agonistic purpose encourages an interest in other people's discomfiture and a proneness to exploit it rhetorically. They deal with shame as *aiskhunē* and *aiskhros* (shameful), terms that often denote dishonor or disgrace, rather than as *aidōs,* which connotes the inhibition stemming from respect for convention.[4] This chapter focuses on the expectation, revealed and manipulated in the orations, that men are guardians against shame in both the public and private realms, and the dilemmas attendant on that expectation.

GUARDING AGAINST SHAME

With some reservations, ancient Athens can be viewed as a shame culture, that is, a culture that emphasized the power of shame in guiding moral behavior. Good name, public persona, and public opinion shaped the outlook and conduct of individuals and the community.[5] Shame was a potent instrument of social control. Although a client of Lysias's ranks the fear of law above the fear of shame as a deterrent to illegal and immoral acts (Lys. 7.15), the rhetor Hyperides, like others, treats fear *(phobos)* and shame *(aiskhunē)* as complementary forces, inducing conformity and obedience to law.[6]

In addition, worthy and unworthy men seem to be distinguished by their susceptibility to shame. In his oration on the Chersonese, Demosthenes declares that while the slave does his duty out of fear of bodily punishment, a free man finds shame *(aiskhunē)* a sufficient motive (Dem. 8.51; cf. 4.10; 10.27; Dover 1974, 228). A Demosthenean speaker classifies men into three groups: the best men do what is right by the prompting of their nature; ordinary men are deterred from wrongdoing

---

1974, 226–27; D. Cohen 1991c, 79–81, 94–96; and in the modern Mediterranean: Peristiany 1966a, 183–84; Herzfeld 1985, 79–84.

3. Dover 1974, 226–42; Fisher 1992; Cairns 1993.

4. Cf. Erffa 1937, passim, esp. 6–9, 59–61, 187–90; Loraux 1986, 185–86, 415–16; cf. Cairns 1993, esp. 48–51.

5. Dodds 1951, with the critique in Cairns 1993, 27–47, esp. 44.

6. Hyp. fr. D 12 (Burtt). See also Dem. 54.23. Cf. Thuc. 2.37.3; Plato *Menexenus* 246d–247c; in Sparta: Plut. *Cleomenes* 9.

by their fear of shame and public opinion; and wicked men are corrected by punishment (Dem. 25.93), implying that they are not moved by shame.

In his funeral oration in honor of the dead in the battle of Chaeroneia (Dem. 60), Demosthenes contrasts shameful *(aiskhros)* fear, which leads soldiers in an undemocratic *dunasteia* to flee danger, with the positive fear of shame *(aiskhunē)*, which leads soldiers in a democratic society, where there is free speech and cowardice can be exposed, to fight to the bitter end, however afraid they may be. Athenian soldiers, he asserts, "fearing these things [being accused of cowardice] . . . [and] the subsequent reproaches, stoutly stood their ground in face of the impending danger posed by their adversaries, and chose a noble death over a shameful life" (Dem. 60.25–26). Shame, then, was a bulwark of masculine courage and military might.[7]

Among the many duties of the Athenian man was the duty to guard against shame both by avoiding shameful actions himself and by condemning the shameful deeds of others. Thus, Aeschines begins his speech against Timarchus with the declaration that his motive in bringing Timarchus to trial is, not only to obtain remedy for the personal injury he has suffered from Timarchus's attempts to bring an unjust legal action against him, but also to defend the laws and the city from the shame brought about Timarchus's immoral behavior. It would be "most shameful" not to speak out against Timarchus's depraved lifestyle as a male prostitute.[8]

Even so, speakers are careful to say that they do not intend to humiliate an adversary but rather to protect the public welfare, in which case such exposure was considered legitimate. By consorting with many men, Aeschines argues, Timarchus disgraced not only his own body but the entire city (Aes. 1.40). Lycurgus asserts that in deserting Athens after its defeat in Chaeronea, Leocrates disgraced the city whose ancestors had died for its good name (Lyc. 1.82). And Demosthenes contends that a law proposed by Leptines would put the city to shame by undermining the obligation to honor a benefactor and the code of reciprocity (Dem.

---

7. Cf. also Dem. 22.31; 60.28–29; Lys. 2.25; Din. 1.79; Arist. *EN* 3.6 1115a12–14; 3.8.1116a17–20; Wyse 1904, 221; Loraux 1986, 134–35, 210–11, 284; Cairns 1993, 375, with n. 94. See Aes. 2.180–82 who presented the sacrifice of his honor as greater than the sacrifice of his life, and Halliwell 1991b, 286.

8. Aes. 1.1–3; cf. Dem. 23.5. Most scholars agree that Aeschines' high-minded exposé of Timarchus's misconduct was designed to neutralize the legal danger he posed to him: E. M. Harris 1995, 96, 201 n. 41; Fisher 2001, 2–6. For the motif of shame in Aes. 1: Fisher 2001, index, s.v. "Shame."

20.10; cf. 20.135, 139–40; Dover 1974, 227). The Athenians viewed themselves as a cohesive moral community, in which the men of the city shared responsibility for standing sentry against dishonorable conduct.

They monitored shameful conduct of women for much the same reason. In his speech against the courtesan Neaera, Apollodorus warns the jury that Neaera will bring shame to the city and calls upon the jurors to punish her so as to preserve its honor and laws and to maintain the honor of the women of their *oikoi*, thereby linking the masculine duty to defend the city and its prestige and a man's duty to defend his family and its honor.[9]

THE RHETORIC OF MILITARY DEFEAT

The obligation to guard against shame was especially salient in the military sphere. The idea that honorable death in battle was preferable to ignoble cowardice was a cornerstone of the Athenian ideology of masculine honor, a commonplace that speakers could take for granted and use to their own ends. A corollary was the sense that defeat in battle was somehow shameful. It may have been one of the many ramifications of the competitive spirit that infused classical Greece.[10]

In Athens, a man (or a state) was judged as good at something (*agathos*) or as possessing *aretē* (excellence) to the extent that he demonstrated superiority over others. The rhetoric in trials and in the assembly was often comparative; denigrating others' performances in order to extol one's own was common practice.[11] Contests (singular, *agōn*) of various sorts were a legitimate and valued means of proving men's worth, increasing their honor and prestige, and, no less important, putting their defeated rivals to shame.

To a large extent, war was seen as a contest in which Athenians proved their superiority and manly worth.[12] In his eulogy, composed perhaps for the soldiers who fell in the Corinthian War, Lysias says that

---

9. [Dem.] 59.107–9, 114. Cf. Dover 1974, 229; and for traditional societies: Gilmore 1990, 43–44, 131.

10. Honorable death and shameful cowardice: e.g., Lys. 2.23; Lyc. 1.102–10; Aes. 2.181; cf. Dem. 4.47. For the many facets of Greek competitions, see Adkins 1960; Gouldner 1965; Connor 1988; Poliakoff 1987; Ober 1989, 250–51; Winkler 1990a, 47; Halperin 1990, 36–37; Wilson 1991, 165; Christ 1998, 34–39, 160–92; Rubinstein 2000, esp. 19–21; 172–84. Competition and testing distinguish men from women, according to the anthropologist David Gilmore (1990, 11–12).

11. E.g., Lys. 14.14–15; Is. 7.38–39; Dem. 51.7; 60.10–11; Hyp. 6.37–38.

12. Loraux 1986, 95–96; Connor 1988; Scanlon 1988; Winkler 1990a, 33; Croally 1994, 120–22.

following the Persian Wars, the Athenians "set Greece free following many toils, most conspicuous struggles *[phanerōtatōn agōnōn]*, and most evident risks, and proved their fatherland to be the best" (Lys. 2.55). Earlier in this speech, he boasts that the Amazons had ruled over many peoples until they met their match in Attica in Athenian men. The victory exposed the Amazon women's aberrant masculinity, obliterated all traces of them, and demonstrated the Athenians' manly valor *(aretē)* (Lys. 2.4–6).

In view of the perception of victory as honorable and defeat as inherently shameful and (explicitly or implicitly) unmanly, dealing with a military defeat both posed a challenge for Athenian orators and provided an opportunity. It posed a challenge mainly for the writers of funeral orations when they tackled the subject of defeat. It gave forensic orators an opportunity to use it against their opponents.

Funeral orations *(epitaphioi)* were delivered at public funerals for Athenian soldiers killed in the democratic city's wars. Inspired by the competitive ethos of displaying worth through ranking, the orations lauded the superior merit and honor of Athens's fallen warriors, called on the living to emulate them, and commended the Athenian community for its unsurpassed excellence in manly courage, justice, and leadership.[13]

But how could the orators extol the soldier-citizens of Athens when Athens lost in the contest of war? The answer is that they crafted their speeches as works of self-praise and self-persuasion. A funeral oration attributed to Lysias (Lys. 2) and Demosthenes' oration for the soldiers killed in the battle of Chaeronea (Dem. 60) showed how the Athenian orator fulfilled the communal wish not to let the results of a lost contest turn into a national disgrace.[14]

In his survey of Athenian military history, the Lysian speaker avoids any suggestion that the Athenians who had died in the battle of Aegospothamoi, in which Sparta defeated Athens in 405, were respon-

---

13. Loraux 1986, esp. 59–61, 95–97, 105–7, 134, 138–41, 184–88; cf. also Strasburger 1954; Ziolkowski 1981, 157–58; Frangeskou 1999, 329–36. My discussion supplements, but differs from, the observations of Loraux 1986 and Thomas 1989, 229–32, on defeat and on the links between manhood and contest in the funeral oration.

14. For the controversy over whether Lysias wrote the speech, see Frangeskou 1999, 317, with nn. 10–11. I follow the scholars who regard Lysias as the speech's author, although it is highly unlikely that he delivered it. I am also in agreement with those who support the authenticity of Demosthenes' authorship of the funeral speech in his corpus (Dem. 60): Loraux 1986, 8–10, 346, nn. 62–63; Frangeskou 1999, esp. 317 n. 10, 329–36. I do not discuss the Platonic parody of the funeral oration in the *Menexenus* because of its distinct comic nature.

sible for the loss. Instead, he blames the defeat on divine intervention and
the ineptitude of commanders (Lys. 2.58), exculpating the rank and file.
Moreover, although he goes into some detail about the deleterious consequences of the defeat, he does so mostly from the perspective of the
Greek world, rather than from that of Athens, thus creating a distance
between defeat and disgrace for the city (Lys. 2.59–60). The Athenian democrats who went into exile following the defeat and the institution of
a pro-Spartan regime in Athens, he points out, were ashamed of the defeat—as only worthy men can be. Their shame and anger, and the wish
to restore democracy, drove them to fight resolutely for the glory of
Athens and its political concord (Lys. 2.62–63). Their noble conduct following the defeat showed in turn that their enemies' victory was not a
proof of their *aretē* (Lys. 2.65).[15]

Demosthenes uses similar tactics in his funeral oration for the soldiers
killed in the battle of Chaeronea in 338, in which Philip of Macedon defeated a coalition led by Athens and Thebes. Significantly, Demosthenes
deals directly with the loss of the battle only at one point in his eulogy
(Dem. 60.19–22). To prove that the Athenians were not responsible for
the defeat, Demosthenes observes that in any battle, one side is bound to
be victorious and the other defeated. Fallen soldiers do not partake of the
defeat. All the soldiers who died at their posts, Macedonians and Athenians alike, are deserving of honor (Dem. 60.19). This view clearly
works in favor of the losing side (Loraux 1986, 140–41). After exoner-
ating the dead soldiers, Demosthenes establishes the superiority of the
living ones by interpreting Philip's decision not to invade Attica after
Chaeronea as proof of his reluctance to engage Athens's valorous warriors again (Dem. 60.20).

Demosthenes accounts for the battle's unhappy outcome by insisting
that Philip won not because of his *andreia*, or manly courage, but because of his experience and *tolma*, a somewhat negative term for daring,
which, under certain circumstances, might connote recklessness or
thoughtlessness rather than true courage.[16] Equally important, Demosthenes displaces responsibility for the defeat onto fortune *(tukhē)* and the
will of the gods, *daimōn*, over which men have no control, or, alternatively, onto the commanders of the Thebans (not the Athenians), who

---

15. For the ways the Athenians dealt with their defeat in the Peloponnesian war, see
Lévy 1976, 40–43, and more recently Wolpert 2002, esp. 120–22, whose observations I
independently share.

16. For the difference between *andreia* and *tolma,* see pp. 190–92 below.

failed to make correct use of troops full of fighting spirit and longing for honor (Dem. 60.21–22).[17]

In the Athenian representation of military defeat, then, results were immaterial. What counted were the warriors' motives, courage in battle, and valorous deaths, which together repelled the shame that was potentially attendant on losing. [18]

Forensic speeches following military defeat share with the funeral orations a determination to preserve masculine honor, but they also exploit the shame of defeat to arouse their hearers' outrage against their adversaries. Thus, blaming the general Lysicles for the death of 1,000 citizens at Chaeronea, the capture of 2,000 more, and for the subsequent enslavement of Greece by the Macedonians, Lycurgus calls him a reminder of the fatherland's shame and disgrace (Lyc. fr. 10.1 [Burtt]). In indicting Leocrates for leaving Athens in the aftermath of the defeat, he describes the panic and social disorder in Athens, calling it a time of "danger and shame [aiskhunē]" (Lyc. 1.43), when free women presented a "sight unworthy [anaxiōs . . . orōmenas]" of themselves and the polis as they crouched in doorways, in full public view, inquiring about their men (Lyc. 1.40). At the same time, though, wary of offending the jurors' sensibilities, Lycurgus borrows motifs and style from the funeral orations and presents the defeated Athenians as scoring a victory on the field (Lyc. 1.47–49).

Aeschines, whose conciliatory attitude toward Macedonia contrasts sharply with Lycurgus' anti-Macedonian stand, shows similar caution in describing Athenian losses and uses a similar tactic to assail his lifelong political rival Demosthenes in opposing a motion to crown Demosthenes for his services to the city. Once the protector of other Greeks, he says, Athens now finds itself competing (agōnezetai) not for leadership but for the soil of the fatherland. Like Lycurgus, Aeschines links the actions of his adversary to the city's sorry state. He blames Demosthenes, who had consistently urged the Athenians to confront Philip, for the destruction of the armies and navies of several Greek city-states, including Athens, and for orphaning their children (Aes. 3.134, 136, 155–57). He accuses

---

17. See also Dem. 18.193–194, 200, 207, 290, 303; cf. Thuc. 2.87.2. Loraux 1986, 141, argues that *tukhē* gives all the worth to the dead, but nothing to the survivors of defeat. No such distinction is made in Dem. 60.19–22.

18. For more devaluations of enemies' victory, see Dem. 18.146, 245–246; cf. Plato *Menexenus* 243d, with Thomas 1989, 230; Loraux 1986, 140; Usher 1993, 254.

him, moreover, of fleeing the battle and leaving his shield behind.[19] Honoring him with a crown would be tantamount to making a trophy for their own defeat (Aes. 3.156)—an ironic claim because trophies were made by the victor from the shields of the vanquished, in this case, Athens. But Aeschines, too, is careful not to impugn the valor of the Athenians, inserting in his narrative of defeat a laudatory remark about the *andres agathoi* who died in the war and contrasting them with the cowardly Demosthenes (Aes. 3.152).

In his response, Demosthenes uses the same values to turn the tables on Aeschines. He faults Aeschines for stressing the results of the battle and, using arguments reminiscent of the funeral orations, emphasizes the noble purpose of the contest and the contestants' motivation (Dem. 18.199–200). Athens would have gone to war, he contends, even if the consequences had been known in advance, because the Athenians have their manly and agonistic reputation to maintain. Throughout history, he says, Athens has distinguished itself "by taking risks and competing *[agōnizomenē]* for primacy *[prōteion]*, honor *[timē]*, and fame *[doxa]*" (Dem. 18.203). Athenians must not trade their heritage and destiny for servile security under the dominion of a tyrannical power. The defeat of Athens is a temporary setback; what counts is the eternal participation in the contest and the participant's noble aims (Dem. 18.199–205).

In the funeral and the forensic orations, speakers strive to preserve the masculine image of Athens in the face of military defeat. The genre permits them to proclaim that the Athenians collectively can never lose and never be dishonored—and to place the blame for defeat on individual citizens, bad generals, or supernatural forces. This rhetoric contrasts sharply with the orators' treatment of Athenian victories. No speaker attributes Athens's victories to divine power or the enemy's inept leadership. On the contrary: the victories prove the Athenians' superior *andreia*, valor, justice, and noble motives.[20]

SHAME AND VIOLENCE

Like other Mediterranean peoples, the ancient Athenians believed that every man received a measure of honor at birth from his family, lineage,

---

19. Aes. 3.148, 159, 175–76, 245, 253; cf. Din. 1.12, 81; Hyp. 5.17; Wankel 1976, 866, 1078–79.
20. Lys. 2.4–53; Dem. 60.6–11; cf. Hyp. 6.35; Plato *Menexenus* 240a–246a.

and national affiliation.[21] This honor, however, had to be zealously guarded against internal and external threats. A man might shame himself by showing lack of restraint (see, e.g., Dem. 61.20) or disrespect for convention (see, e.g., Is. 1.5). He might be shamed by other men. Reprehensible acts, moreover, could shame the victim as well as the perpetrator. Evidently, Athenian men were particularly vulnerable to deliberate attempts on the part of other men to shame them.

Physical violence unconnected to war and sport could also tarnish manliness in ancient Athens. If the aggressor had more power and status than his victim; if his attack violated conventions (e.g., if he attacked a guest); or if the aggressee was unfairly victimized (e.g., attacked without provocation), the act was thought shameful. More often, however, physical violence was perceived as an affront that shamed the recipient. It constituted a crossing of boundaries that violated a man's body.[22] The human body, especially that of a free adult male, was protected by lines of defense, among them his honor and ability to deter attack, as well as by laws and social norms, including Athenians' respect for the free man's personal autonomy. An attack exposed the weakness of these defenses. It reduced a free man to the status of a slave, against whom physical force could legitimately be used. In his speech against Meidias, Demosthenes observes that a man who struck another with a lash was treating him like a slave.[23]

The speaker in Isocrates 20, who is prosecuting one Lochites for assault, points out that crimes against the body are more serious than crimes against property (Isoc. 20.1–2). The severity of the injury, he contends, in response to the argument that he had not been badly injured, is less relevant than the hubris of the attack and the affront *(aikia)* and dishonor *(atimia)* sustained (Isoc. 20.5–6).

The orations often connect physical violence to the wish to hurt and humiliate the victim.[24] Low-level violence also seems to have been rather common.[25] The orations describe brawls perpetrated by young men and

---

21. Di Bella 1992, esp. 152–57.

22. Many studies of Greek sexuality discuss the connection among honor, shame, and the body: Foucault 1978, 1985; Dover 1973 [1988], 1989; Halperin 1990; Winkler 1990a.

23. Dem. 21.180, and see Dem. 22.55; 24.167; cf. Hyp. fr. 36.3 (Burtt); Garlan 1988, 197–200. Torturing slaves: Thür 1977; Gagarin 1996. Slaves, however, could not be hit, violated, or killed at will: Allen 2000a, 109–11; and corporal punishment of citizens was not avoided at all cost: Allen 1997.

24. E.g., Ant. 2.1.6–8; Lys. 1.44; 3.6–8; Dem. 21.38, 71–74; 47.38–39; 54.4–18; Aes. 1.58–59; cf. Isoc. 20.2–3.

25. Cf. Lys. 3.42–43; Dem. 54.14; 47.19; Aes. 1.135; Winkler 1990a, 49.

old; fights involving individuals and also cohorts of friends, who came
to one another's aid; and feuds in which violence begat violent and nonviolent conflicts, sometimes for years on end.[26]

The Athenians had laws against deliberate wounding, assault, rape,
slander, and hubris—an umbrella term that included slander, causing serious injury, and other offenses.[27] But it remained for the speakers to persuade the jury to convict or acquit and to impose a penalty. In doing so,
they addressed and manipulated the jury's concerns about shame and in-
advertently pointed to the ambivalence with which Athenian men viewed
the use of violence to inflict shame.

In two speeches, both speakers make the shame of violent attacks
stick to the aggressors, while seeking to galvanize the jurors' sympathy
for the shame inflicted on their victims. One speech was written for Ariston against Conon and his sons (Dem. 54; see pp. 17–20 above). The
other was delivered on behalf of Teisis against Archippus, who allegedly
tied his guest Teisis to a pole, whipped him on two occasions, and locked
him in a room overnight (Lys. fr. 75 [Thalheim]). The speakers pin the
shame on the aggressors chiefly by treating the assaults as hubristic acts,
which made the violence more reprehensible, deserving of harsh punishment, and shameless and unmanly, in the sense that hubris constituted a
violation of the expectation that men would exhibit self-control and
compete equitably (Dem. 54.1, 4–5, 8–15, 20, 23, 28, 43; Lys. fr. 75
[Thalheim]). In another case, a speaker admits having used his fists in a
nasty feud with an Athenian named Simon over a boy lover, but tries to
reach the jury by contrasting his sensitivity to shame with the shameless
insolence of his opponent (Lys. 3.4, 6–7, 9, 13, 17).

These and other speeches pay tribute to the official disapproval of recourse to violence in a feud. Nonetheless, they also hint at a culture in
which a moderate level of violence—and the shame that went with it—
was tolerated.[28] So does Ariston when he tells the jury that Conon will
dismiss the assault on him by claiming that "things of this sort are natural for young men" (Dem. 54.14; cf. Isoc. 20.5). The speaker for Teisis
suggests that some citizens and foreigners who saw how Teisis had been
treated were exasperated with the state for not immediately and publicly

26. Humphreys 1986b, 59, 67; D. Cohen 1991c, 85–86; 1995, 131–34, 186. Friends'
moderating feuds: Isoc. 18.9–10; Dem. 41.14; 42.11. Ongoing feud: Lys. 3.19; 4; Dem. 21;
54; D. Cohen 1995a, 131–35.

27. MacDowell 1978, 109–32; Fisher 1992; 2000; Todd 1993, 268–79; D. Cohen
1995a, 87–142.

28. See Fisher 1998b, 75–77, 86–87; Herman 1994, 101–5.

punishing criminals—and with jurors who sometimes declined to punish senseless bullying (Lys. fr. 75 [Thalheim]; cf. Dem. 21.36–37). Lastly,
Simon's adversary explains to the jurors that, although Simon has broken his skull, he does not think it appropriate to charge him with a crime.
Severe punishment (exile), such as was imposed for premeditated murder, he adds, should not be meted out for unintentional injury resulting
from drunken rivalry, playfulness, slander, or a fight over a *hetaira* (Lys.
3.40–43). Each of the above speakers had his own self-serving reasons
to raise these points, but together they pointed up the Athenian ambivalence toward the acceptability of violence.

Ambivalence also complicated the response of men to shame. That a
man of honor should retaliate after he had been shamed was generally
accepted. The question was whether he should strike his opponent or
take him to court.

Officially, peaceable resolutions were encouraged. A good deal of approval of attempts to avoid violent feuds is found in the orations, and
outsiders were expected to intervene and stop altercations, if need be by
force. The law against assault, for example, punished the man who hit
his opponent first.[29]

At the same time, some Athenians took the obligation to retaliate with
physical force very seriously. Alluding to the assumption that men were
inclined to respond with physical aggression to the shame of being in-
sulted, Ariston tells the jury that there are laws even against speaking
evil, so that the words will not escalate into a chain of violent reactions,
leading to bodily harm or murder (Dem. 54.18–19).[30] Antiphon's speech
written for a fictional homicide case also suggests that for some, recourse
to physical violence to avert shame was the preferred response. The prosecutor surmises that the murder was the culmination of a lengthy legal
feud; he suggests that the defendant was willing to take the chance of
being caught and punished, because he thought it more honorable or
right *(kallion)* to take revenge and suffer for it than to refrain from retaliation in a cowardly *(anandrōs,* unmanly) way and be ruined by an opponent's legal action.[31] Athenian homicide law did not recognize shame

29. Commending avoidance of violence, and outsiders' intervention in a feud: e.g., Lys.
3.10, 13, 16; [Dem.] 53.17; cf. Theophrastus *Characters* 15.6; Hunter 1994, 138–39;
Christ 1998, 192. Punishing first strike: chapter 1, n. 23.
30. Halliwell 1991b, 284; D. Cohen 1995a, 135; cf. Pitt-Rivers 1966, 55.
31. Ant. 2.1.8. Retributive killing and its prevalence in legal thought: Carawan 1998,
200–201, 286.

or the wish to avoid it as justification for killing. But the prosecutor's hypothesis suggests that Athenian men could appreciate the possibility that masculine shame was sometimes stronger than the fear of breaking the law and, in this case, of incurring pollution as well.[32]

The alternative to the use of violence to restore lost honor was legal action. Although extolled in the speeches—by speakers who took this route—the legal option was not so simple. The toleration of moderate violence and the ambivalence with which Athenian society regarded retaliatory violence were obstacles. This ambivalence enabled a pleader to present an adversary's violence as a crime against the laws, honor, masculine and civic restraint, and the social and political order, and a defendant to portray legal action as an illegitimate substitute response to a violent act.

The proper response to insult and dishonor occupies a central place in Demosthenes' celebrated speech against Meidias (Dem. 21).[33] The incident that occasioned the speech occurred during the festival of the Dionysia in 348, when Demosthenes was serving as a *khorēgos* (producer and financier) of the men's dithyrambic chorus for his tribe.[34] On the day of the performance, Demosthenes' enemy Meidias entered the crowded theater and struck Demosthenes in the face.

As Demosthenes tells it, the punch was the culmination of fourteen years of harassment, physical bullying, verbal abuse, and use of the courts by Meidias to shame Demosthenes and deprive him of his wealth and his rights. Although the formal charge was malfeasance—wrongdoing at the festival—Demosthenes asked the court to take into consideration a litany of offenses that Meidias had purportedly committed against him before, during, and after the festival, including breaking into his home when he was a young man and hurling abuse at his mother in front of his young sister (Dem. 21.78–80); underhanded acts to prevent him from winning a choral competition; false charges of desertion, murder, and of being responsible for Athenian military difficulties in Euboia (Dem. 21.103–4, 110), and efforts to disqualify him from membership in the Council (Dem. 21.111).

---

32. Cf. Antiphon *(Sophistes)* fr. 44 A (DK); Carawan 1998, 198–99. According to Arist. *EN* 4.5 1126a7–8 not responding to insults was servile.

33. Dem. 21: E. M. Harris 1989; MacDowell 1990; Wilson 1991; D. Cohen 1991a; Fisher 1992, esp. 44–51; Ober 1994b; D. Cohen 1995a, esp. 88–101. The following is a revised version of Roisman 2003.

34. I follow here MacDowell 1990, 1–28, for the circumstances of the trial and the nature of the charges, and see also Fisher 1992, 38, with n. 13.

This litany came in support of his claim that Meidias's punch was a hubristic act, that is, an insolent and premeditated assault with the intention of dishonoring its victim.[35] Demosthenes tried to make the punch a matter of public interest and to obtain a conviction and more severe penalty than the punch alone would have warranted. But his interpretation of the incident also appealed to the Athenian male's high sensitivity to honor. Masculine honor in ancient Athens was largely proactive and often exhibitionist. Demosthenes crafted much of his speech to justify his legal action and physical inaction in response to this public humiliation.

His justification hinged on the claim, made implicitly and woven into the legal arguments, that seeking legal redress was no less manly than violent retaliation. In refusing to retaliate in kind, Demosthenes maintained, he had been *sōphronōs*, meaning that he had acted responsibly, moderately, and with self-restraint (Dem. 21.74). Moreover, the court was the proper guardian of the law and of the safety of all the people of Athens (Dem. 21.76). Gabriel Herman has argued that these assertions appealed to the dominant code of behavior in Athens, which held personal honor in low regard and emphasized civil conduct and nonretaliatory response. This code, he claims, had replaced the more traditional notion that men should defend their honor by taking personal action.[36]

It seems to me, however, that Demosthenes' need to explain his preference for legal redress, and to present it as the only legitimate response to Meidias's action, implies that his recourse to the court was not universally accepted. The ideology of self-restraint and the rule of law and the ideology of physical, and preferably immediate, defense of one's honor, seem to have coexisted for Athenian men.[37]

The two ideologies were associated with different ideals of manhood. Men who were self-controlled and restrained, nonviolent, and public-spirited went to court. Those who were courageous, high-spirited, and unwilling to brook slights to their honor retaliated physically. Behavior

35. E.g., Dem. 21.6–7, 25–26, 77–109. Law of hubris: Gagarin 1979; MacDowell 1990, 18–23; D. Cohen 1991c, 176–180; Fisher 1992, 36–85; D. Cohen 1995a, 94–95; cf. Dover 1974, 226–27; Rowe 1993, esp. 399.
36. Herman 1993, 1994, 1995, esp. 48–51; cf. 1996.
37. Cf. D. Cohen 1995a, 126. Herman 1993, 408; 1994, 109, acknowledges such coexistence but then goes on to describe the two modes of behavior almost as incompatible ideal types. See the criticism of W. V. Harris 1997; Schofield 1998, 39; Fisher 1998b, 72, 80–86; 2000, 88; cf. Rhodes 1998, 156 n. 47; Christ 1998, 161–66. Fisher, whose interpretation is close to the one offered here, thinks that Athenians were encouraged to seek revenge through the courts, but that grievous hubris legitimized a swift physical response; and see similarly Harris 1997 and Allen 2000a, 126–28. There was no agreed-upon measure of the gravity of an offense or insult, however.

that was regarded as prudence and self-discipline in the first view was seen as timidity and unmanly shamelessness in the second. The dichotomy is noted by Plato, who points out misconceptions that led the democratic man to identify *sōphrosunē* (moderation, resisting pleasures) with *anandria* (cowardice or unmanliness) and *anaideia* (shamelessness).[38]

The challenge that Demosthenes faced was to convince his audience that a man who sought to defend his honor through legal action was not timid or unmanly, and that he himself was no less of a man because he did not use his fists. He addressed these issues by claiming that the demos had expressed indignation and anger at Meidias, and many citizens had pressured him to bring this rash *(thrasus)*, disgusting *(bdeluros)*, and no longer restrainable *(oude kathektos)* person to justice (Dem. 21.2, cf. 21.23). These remarks pertained to the Athenians who shared Demosthenes' preference for the legal defense of honor over the physical and were aimed at isolating Meidias and putting him in an adversarial position to the people. They can also be viewed, however, as Demosthenes' effort to impress upon his listeners that his choice of legal action enjoyed popular approval, which would never be given to a litigant whose conduct and manhood were in question.

He then presented himself as a brave defender of democratic Athens who was fulfilling his civic responsibilities. Meidias was an arrogant, insolent bully who assaulted anyone who stood in his way (21.1, 17, 115, 135, 185, 203–4), flaunted the laws (Dem. 21.7), and disgraced the name of Athens (Dem. 21.32). He also used his great wealth and power to ruin his poorer and less powerful adversaries rather than to benefit the public (Dem. 21.98, 109, 122, 138).

The democratic ideology of Athens allotted honor to both strong and weak, poor and rich, aristocrats and nonaristocrats. Demosthenes accordingly claimed that in pressing charges, he sought revenge in the form of public service (Dem. 21.28, 30, 40, 127, 207), and also because some of Meidias's victims did not respond to his bullying out of fear of his power and wealth (Dem. 21.20).[39] With such assertions, he highlighted his manly fulfillment of his civic duties, and his manly courage—which contrasted with the fear that deterred Medias's victims from taking legal action. According to this line of reasoning, legal action was the manly thing to do.

38. Plato *Rep.* 8 560d–e. Cf. Thuc. 3.82.4. Although Plato is not an unbiased source for democratic attitudes, his observation pointed to a lack of agreement on basic values and attitudes. *Sōphrosunē* and *andreia:* pp. 176–78 below.
39. Wilson 1991, 169–70; Fisher 1998b, 81.

Demosthenes also emphasized his virility by drawing attention to his
military record of service in the infantry and as a trierarch (21.133, 154).
To describe his legal actions, he marshaled military metaphors, comparing his response to Meidias's accusations against him to repelling a military onslaught (*diōtheō:* 21.124) and declaring that he would have been
a "deserter from the ranks of justice *[leloipenai . . . tēn tou dikaiou
taxin)]*" had he not brought Meidias to trial (21.120; cf. 21.3).

In addition, Demosthenes made a manly impression by expressing
sympathy for physical responses to insult. In explaining his decision
to prosecute Meidias, Demosthenes touted the virtues of restraint and,
furthermore, asked that his case serve an example *(paradeigma)* that
would teach his fellow Athenians to fight against hubristic men not
with impulsive violence but with legal action (Dem. 21.76; cf. Isoc.
20.8). He gave the example of two men who had killed in response to
being struck. The first, a wrestler, killed another athlete (a pancrati-
ast) because he thought that he was treating him insolently in a private get-together. Euaeon, the second, killed a man in revenge for a
single blow (Dem. 21.71–72). These examples brought home the disastrous consequences of responding to violence in kind and supported Demosthenes' declared preference for restraint. Yet, at the
same time, Demosthenes expressed sympathy for the murderers: "It
wasn't the blow that made him [Euaeon] angry, but the dishonour
[atimia]; nor is being hit such a serious matter to free man (though it
is serious), but being hit insolently *[to eph' hubrei]*. . . . That's what
rouses people, that's what makes them forget themselves, if they are
not accustomed to being insulted" (Dem. 21.72; MacDowell's translation, 1990, 131–33). Rather than condemn the killers, Demosthenes
said that he fully sympathized with Euaeon and anyone else who took
the law into their own hands when they were dishonored *(atima-
zomenos)*.[40] This sympathetic gloss seemed to have been directed at
Athenians with nagging doubts about Demosthenes' manhood and the
validity of his mode of retaliation.

Demosthenes depicted Meidias as, in contrast to himself, the incar-
nation of aberrant masculinity, who trampled men weaker than himself
underfoot and failed to contribute to the public good. Meidias, he
added, had shirked his military duty and then rode to the military cam-

---

40. Dem. 21.74. Cf., however, Allen 2000a, 125.

paign on the island of Euboia in a silver *astrabē* (mule chair), such as was used by women and invalids, taking wine and goblets along (Dem. 21.133).[41] The obvious implication was that Meidias had been soft and unprepared for the rigors of battle. Demosthenes treated Meidias's subsequent naval service in the same way. In 357, the Athenians had solicited emergency donations of triremes—warships—in order to free the island of Euboia from a Theban invasion. Meidias donated a ship and later served on it, probably as its captain. Demosthenes contended, however, that Meidias had donated the ship out of cowardice *(deilia)* and unmanliness *(anandria)*, in a ploy to avoid more dangerous service in the cavalry. He had sent a surrogate to command the ship as long as it looked as if he could stay safely on land and had boarded it only when the risk that he would have to fight in the cavalry recurred (Dem. 21.160–66; cf. 21.174). This interpretation of Meidias's conduct, based on the ascription of motives that could not have been known, sought to deprive Meidias of his claim to honor, manliness, courage, and use of his wealth and person in service of the state. It was possible because the rules governing reputation allowed men to invalidate substantive proofs of honor and masculinity on the basis of the individual's alleged motives.

Ironically, the speech may never have been delivered. Aeschines, followed by Plutarch, argues that Demosthenes "sold" his case to Meidias for monetary compensation. Since Aeschines was Demosthenes' enemy, his account is not above suspicion.[42] Whether or not he went through with his suit, however, the arguments he makes suggest that Athenian men sought to avoid shame and retaliate for insults but disagreed about how to do so.

THE RHETORICAL MANIPULATIONS OF SHAME

The orators' manipulated inconsistencies or contradictions in the expectation that men stand up against shame to benefit their clients.

The use of shame to promote conformity and moral conduct was supposed to complement the wish of Athenian men to protect their honor.

---

41. For the chair: Schol. Dem. 21.133 (469a Dilts); Lys. 24.11; MacDowell 1990, 351; Wilson 1991, 184. For Meidias as a stereotypical rich man: Ober 1989, 209–10; 1994, 94; D. Cohen 1995a, 98–99.

42. Aes. 3.52; Plut. *Dem.* 12.2–6; *Moralia* 844d. On the controversy: Dover 1968, 172–74; E. M. Harris 1989, esp. 132–36; Fisher 1992, 38; Ober 1994b, 91–92; Rubinstein 2000, 209. MacDowell 1990, 23–28, is undecided.

Yet some orations convey sympathy for men who averted shame not by refraining from misconduct but by wrongdoing or by concealing their misconduct.

According to Aeschines, high officials who mismanaged public revenues often engineered public commendations for their services before they presented their accounts at the end of their tenure *(euthunai)*. Later, when the officials faced criminal charges, the jurors were ashamed to convict those they had earlier proclaimed to be just and virtuous. A law was subsequently passed forbidding crowning an official prior to audit, although Aeschines adds that the law was frequently circumvented (Aes. 3.9–11). Aeschines volunteered this information so that he could say that his foe's passing his *euthunai* did not mean that the man was innocent. What is relevant to our concern is that he explained, and to some extent excused, the willful miscarriage of justice perpetrated by the jurors because of a wish to save face and avoid shame.

In Demosthenes 22, the speaker sought to overcome the jurors' apparent reluctance to inflict shame on men of their ranks. He charged that Androtion had proposed an illegal resolution to grant the Athenian Council the customary honor of a crown at the end of its term, even though it had been negligent in carrying out its duties. In an attempt to avoid punishment, Androtion asked the jury not to disgrace the five hundred men of the Council by depriving them of their reward. The public interest, Androtion's prosecutor countered, must be ranked above the shame of individuals and groups. Moreover, only Androtion and people of his ilk and not the other councilors would be shamed (Dem. 22.35–37). The prosecutor's arguments stressed the corrective and didactic value of shame but also tried to allay Athenians' wariness of fully exploiting the weapon of shame.

The same prosecutor also charged that Androtion had revealed facts about the private lives of the people from whom he collected taxes: this one had been a slave, that one's father or mother had worked as a prostitute, another had fathered a child by a prostitute, and yet others had committed this or that crime. Here his arguments were that Androtion had been elected to collect taxes, not to shame people with their private circumstances, and that even if his allegations were true, he should not have made them public (Dem. 22.61–62; cf. Dem. 25.89). Although the arguments are obviously tendentious, they show that the disclosure of people's misconduct or misfortunes could be considered an illegitimate violation of privacy and a transgression against the honor to which all Athenian citizens were deemed to be entitled.[43]

Athenian males faced many situations in which any course of action they took could be called shameful. A clever speaker could use the dilemma inherent in such situations to his advantage by ranking the shames that threatened him in accordance with his personal interests. When Mantitheus attempted to prevent his half-brother Boeotus from changing his name to Mantitheus, he weighed the shame inherent in airing a family feud in public against the shame that the change of name threatened to cause him. The change would mean that his half-brother would share or usurp Mantitheus's status as the recognized head of their father's *oikos* and his role in preserving the name and memory of his ancestors.[44] If he failed to take preventative action and relinquished something that rightfully belonged to him without a fight, Mantitheus risked losing his honor and manhood. He would not have fought his kinsman (literally, "someone under the same yoke"—*zugomakhein*), Mantitheus maintained, if it were not that the change of name would have brought him great *atimia* (dishonor) and a reputation for unmanly cowardice (*anandria;* Dem. 39.6; cf. Is.1.5). In offering this justification, Mantitheus manipulated the rival claims to shame in the hope that the jury would approve of his choice.

A similar ranking of shame in accordance with the speaker's legal needs is found in two speeches by Lysias. In his speech against Theomnestus, a Lysian speaker justifies a somewhat problematic suit for slander by stating that although suing for slander is viewed as a servile and overly litigious act, he deems it shameful not to punish a man who has defamed his own and his father's good name (Lys. 10.2–3). Yet in the oration against Simon, a different Lysian speaker claims that he has re-frained from bringing legal action against Simon, who had struck and in-sulted him, so as to avert the disgrace (e.g., ridicule) he would incur when the source of their quarrel, their amorous rivalry over a boy, was made public in court (Lys. 3.3, 9). Unlike the former speaker, who took legal

43. For speakers who professed reluctance to describe adulterous affairs, wishing not to incur the resentment of their victims, see Aes. 1.107; [And.] 4.10; and more generally, Lys. 3.3; Arist. *Rhet.* 1.12.35 1373a33–35; D. Cohen 1991c, 129; 1995, 155; Scafuro 1997, 212–16; cf. Du Boulay 1974, 82–83.

44. Fathers gave names to their sons in an attempt to preserve the fame *(kleos)* and memory of themselves and their ancestors: Svenbro 1993, 64–79; cf. Todd 1993, 281; Ogden 1996a, 96–98, 192–94.

action at the risk of ill repute, this litigant justified his legal inaction by ranking the shame of damage to his name higher than the shame of not punishing insults and blows.

Speakers also manipulated the conflict between honor and pragmatism. Of course, Athenians' hope was that the honorable choice and the pragmatic choice would be one and the same. But if the two conflicted, honor should prevail.[45] In his speech against Leptines, Demosthenes thus described the character of the Athenian polis—that is, the character of Athenian men—as "truthful and worthy, and, in matters of money, not seeking what is most profitable, but doing what is honorable *[kalon]*" (Dem. 20.13; cf. Dem. 58.29; Lys. 19.15). For this reason, men often discounted or denied the motivating power of self-interest. A wealthy depositor in a bank who sued to get his money back, for example, argued that he was much less concerned about losing his money than about appearing greedy and unjust, and, consequently, being slandered all his life (Isoc. 17.1).

A more radical approach, used by Demosthenes in a speech he wrote for the former slave Phormio, was to elevate the practical. Phormio's former master, Pasion, had willed him his widow in marriage. Apollodorus, Pasion's son, questioned both the validity and the legality of the arrangement.

Demosthenes handled the matter by extolling the practical value of such unions, adding that marriages between free women and bankers who, like Phormio, were former slaves who had become wealthy in their trade and had been rewarded with Athenian citizenship, were not at all uncommon (Dem. 36.28–29). Clearly, Demosthenes was trying to minimize the shame inherent in marrying a social inferior.[46] He then went on to reconcile the potential contradiction between the masculine concern for *doxa* (reputation) and the expectation that a man act rationally and pragmatically in looking after the interests of his family. Pasion did not disgrace himself or his sons *(oud'. . . hubrizon)* in marrying his widow to Phormio, Demosthenes declared, but rather guaranteed the perpetuation of his business, as a good kurios should, by bringing a highly knowledgeable and trustworthy manager into the family. In acting pragmatically *(ta sumphorenta)*, Pasion acted properly *(kalos)*. Apollodorus,

45. Honor combined with advantage: Lys. 19.61; Dem. 14.28; 20.12–14; *Pr.* 50.2. Self-interest and honor or justice in philosophy: Nill 1985; in the orators: Adkins 1960, ch. 10. Pragmatism in forensic speeches: Lavency 1964, 174–82.

46. For the important role the slaves and wives played in banking, see E. E. Cohen 1992, 70; 2000, 44, and for Dem. 36.28–29, 30: 2000, 141, n. 56.

in contrast, was a vain elitist who cared neither for the welfare of his oikos nor for the benefit that preserving his family's wealth would bring to the city (Dem. 36.30–31, 44, 57; cf. 22).

Yet Demosthenes added a reservation to his reconciliation of expediency with honor. For men like themselves, citizens by birth, Demosthenes acknowledged to the jury, "it is not proper to choose a great amount of money over birth," thereby restricting the choice of an expedient marriage over a prestigious one to former slaves, like Phormio and presumably Pasion, who had acquired their citizenship as a reward for their wealth and merit and, in his view, were obliged to make sure that they retained that wealth (Dem. 36.30). Demosthenes' remarks suggests that the Athenians' standards of honor and propriety were not uniform across social classes but subject to ranking in accordance to one's social position.

The ideology of shame, then, was inconsistent and limited. The speeches indicate, moreover, that the injunction—sometimes explicit, always implicit—that Athenian men guard against shame was an unattainable ideal subject to manipulation. They show the temptation to avert shame by hiding misconduct, and the social opprobrium one risked in exposing the shame of others, even though the threat of such exposure was a valued tool of social control. They show how speakers could exploit the multiplicity of acts that might be called shameful to their own benefit, and use contradictions between shame and practicality to justify deviations from the straight and narrow.

CHAPTER 4

Manhood and Social Standing

Any student of the relationship between manhood and social standing in Athens must ascertain the term that best describes a man's social position. Although Solon's reforms of 594 officially divided the Athenian citizenry into classes defined by property, ancient sources used many other terms to designate social position. Privileged Athenians were often referred to as *khrēstoi* (worthy ones), *aristoi* (best), *plousoi* (rich), *euporoi* (well-propertied), *gnōrimoi* (notables), *eugeneis* (well-born), *kaloi k'agathoi* (beautiful and good). The less fortunate were known as *penētes* (poor or beggars), *aporoi* (propertyless), *ptōkhoi* (destitute), *hoi polloi* (the many), *to plēthos* (the majority), *dēmos* (commoners), and, derogatorily, *ho okhlos* (the mob). The terms were overlapping and vague, referring simultaneously to a man's wealth, status, birth, occupation, and moral standards.[1]

I mainly use the terms "elite" and "masses" respectively for the men who stood on the upper rungs of the social and political ladder and those below them—although when other collective nouns, such as "upper classes," "lower classes," "rich," and "poor," suit the content, I have availed myself of them as well.[2] I identify members of the elite in Athens in terms of Aristotle's

---

1. For these terms see, e.g., Davies 1981, 10–14; Sinclair 1988, 120–123, and the notes below. There was not complete agreement on their application: cf. Aristotle's (*Pol.* 4.3–4 1291b7–30) and Demosthenes' (8.66; 10.68; 60.27) use of the same attributes to identify both notables and demos.

2. Elite and masses: Ober 1989, esp. 11–17, 192–96; cf. Davidson 1997, 227–38. For emphasis on class distinctions, see Davies 1984, 13–14; de Ste. Croix 1983. For the ter-

characteristics of the rich and the notable, namely, their wealth, lineage, and education (although not moral standards; Arist. *Pol.* 4.3–4 1291b7–30), and by their political activity, lifestyle, and social prestige. No single attribute was sufficient to gain a man entry into the elite and no single lack excluded him (see, e.g. Dem. 3.29; 22.47; 58.63). The masses, who were often identified with the demos, or common people, were often poor, but also included more prosperous families who lacked social and political prominence.

This chapter examines the ways in which perceptions of masculinity were colored by social and economic status, and how the elite and the masses perceived each other's manhood.

SUPERIOR MANHOOD AND ELITE STATUS: THE EROTIC ORATION (DEM. 61)

Among Demosthenes' speeches is an erotic work entitled *Erōtikos* (Dem. 61), which was aimed at an elite, or elitist, readership. It is an essay addressed by a man to a prospective young male lover named Epicrates. Although Demosthenes' authorship of this essay has been questioned since antiquity, its inclusion in the oratorical corpus, its affinity to several fourth-century works of a similar nature, and its intended elite audience make it a valuable document.[3]

The most extensively documented form of Greek homosexuality is pederasty, the relationship between an *erōmenos,* a beloved, a youth between the age of puberty and the time when his face or body began to be covered with hair, and an *erastēs,* the lover, a man often in his twenties through early to middle thirties. The lover served as the social and intellectual mentor of the *erōmenos;* according to Plato, this was the relationship's sole purpose.[4] Even if it was not practiced only

minology of the poor, see Markle 1985, 267–71. The distinctions between strata within the classes of Strauss 1986, 42–43, 61–63, 100–101, and Sealey 1993, 22–26, do not apply to the subject under discussion.

3. The first-century reader Dionysus of Halicarnassus denied Demosthenes' authorship of speech 61 (*Demosthenes* 44). Among his modern-day followers are Blass 1898, 3.1: 406–8, and Carlier 1990, 312. Clavaud 1974, 85, dates the work to 340–323, and D. Brown 1977, 86–87, to 345–335; cf. Buffiere 1980, 405. For the affinity of the work especially to Plato's *Symposion* and *Phaedrus* (esp. 227b–234c), and to Xenophon's *Memorabilia,* see Blass ibid. and Clavaud 1974, 70–83; cf. Fisher 1998, 95. For its elitist nature, see below and D. Brown 1977, 85, 89–93 (whose view of the *erōtikos* as a political pamphlet I do not share).

4. The seminal work on Greek homosexuality is Dover 1989. See also Foucault 1985; Reinsberg 1989; Halperin 1990; Winkler 1990a, 45–70. For criticism of Dover's thesis, see, e.g., D. Cohen 1991b; Cohen and Saller 1994; Davidson 1997, 167–82.

among the elite, pederasty was readily identifiable as an elitist practice.[5]

The anonymous author of the work describes it as an epideictic piece,
whose function is to praise its subject and show off the skills of its com-
poser. His assertion that he composed the essay with future readers in
mind and his denigration of plebeian contestants for Epicrates' favors
(Dem. 61.2, 23–24, 32, 35, 39, 48–52), suggest that the target audience
was more exclusive than that of most of the speeches in the oratorical
corpus, which address the popular Assembly and courts.

Young Epicrates is described as the epitome of the Athenian ideal of
manhood. His enamored suitor credits him with manly courage (Dem.
61.8, 22, 26, 28, 30), discretion and self-restraint (Dem. 61.7–8, 17, 30,
cf. 61.32), diligence (Dem. 61.24, 26, 37), and intelligence (Dem.
61.37–39); with the pursuit of honor and avoidance of shame (Dem.
61.5, 19–20, 35, 55), and the ardent and competitive striving for excellence beyond that of all others (passim). These ideals were much the
same as those for mature men, although Athenian youths were deemed
less capable of fulfilling them than their elders.

In eulogizing the youth, the author of the erotic essay highlights Epicrates' embodiment of the Athenian elite's ideals of masculinity. He includes him among the *kaloi k'agathoi* (beautiful and good; Dem. 61.1,
54) and *beltistoi* (the best; Dem. 61.23). In lauding the young man's
courage, he focuses on Epicrates' decision to train for the *apobatēs* race,
a chariot race that included mounting and dismounting from the chariot and running.[6] This race is open only to citizens, not to slaves and
aliens, he notes, and only the best men *(beltistoi)* participate in it. He
praises it as the most solemn and beautiful *(semnotatos* and *kallistos)* of
all contests (61.24), as far more noble than running and boxing (cf. Isoc.
16.33), as augmenting the participant's courage and manliness (Dem.
61.22–28), and links it to an ancient aristocratic tradition. Every reader
or hearer of this oration knew that while boxing and running were relatively egalitarian sports, the *apobatēs* was a rich man's sport, because it

---

5. Fisher 2001, 58–60, 276–85, argues for the adoption of pederastic practices and
ethos by democracy, but the evidence he uses (esp. Aes. 1.131–40) shows also their clear
aristocratic affinities. See also Carter 1986, 63–64; Ober 1989, 250; Shapiro 1992, 71–72;
Hubbard 1998, esp. 59; Cartledge 2002, 91–105. Greek homosexuality could extend beyond pederasty to relationships that crossed class and age hierarchies. See Hubbard 2003;
Golden and Toohey 2003.

6. The Athenian *apobatēs* and its elitist character: Gardiner 1910, 237–39; Clavaud
1974, 127 n. 4, 135–137; D. Brown 1977, 91; Kyle 1987, 188–89; Crowther 1991; Golden
1997, 329–30, 333; 1998, 3. For military prowess, elitist attitudes, and homosexuality:
Ogden 1996b, esp. 116, 139. Cf. Clavaud 1974, 135–37, 197 n. 4.

required leisure and the money to pay for the chariot and training the horses. The implication is that the social elite viewed themselves as manlier than men of lower social status.[7]

The author, however, avoids a direct equation between masculine merit and membership in the social elite. He suggests that the elite held themselves up to higher standards than others, but his specific reference is to innately superior men. While men of obscure and lowly nature *(aphanē kai tapeinēn tēn phusin)* might act dishonorably without rebuke, any lack of regard for matters of honor brought disgrace on those who were admired and publicly conspicuous (Dem. 61.35). He advises Epicrates to distinguish between social esteem acquired through luck, wealth, or physical prowess, and that attained through education, hard work, and self-improvement, because these acts reveal the person's character and inner merit (Dem. 61.37–39). He cites the example of Solon, who rose from humble origins by dint of his own formidable intellect and achievements (Dem. 61.49–50). Character, he suggests, is more important than birth.

And yet, in steering Epicrates away from the social recognition acquired by luck, wealth, or physical prowess, he dismisses the prestige that can be won by commoners *(phauloi)*, implying that true distinction earned through manly virtue *(andragathia:* Dem. 61.37–39) is the province of the socially superior. His emphasis on education in mathematics, rhetoric, and philosophy, as opposed to practical training, as a means to honor and advancement (Dem. 61.43–44, 48, 54–55) does not really imply opening the door to all deserving young men; for in fourth-century Athens, few people outside the elite could afford such education (Ober 1989, 115–16; 156–91). Near the end of the composition, the author makes his elitist perspective quite clear, declaring that the city needs the traditional *kaloi k'agathoi*—socially prominent men of high intellectual and moral standards—to save it from the misfortunes brought upon it by leaders chosen from the commoners *(tois tukhousi)* (Dem. 61.54–55).

Different Strokes for Different Folks

The association between superior manhood and superior social class seems to have been made by the demos as well. Arguing against an ad-

---

7. For the link between resources, horsemanship, lineage, and exclusivity, see Isoc. 7.44–45; Clavaud 1974, 127 n. 4; Golden 1990, 71–72; 1998, 5–6. Golden 1998, 3, 157–75, argues that the *apobatēs* was unique even within equestrian events.

versary whose ancestry went back to the venerated slayers of the Athenian tyrant Hipparchus, an Isaean speaker reminded the jury that the tyrannicides had been honored not for their lineage but for their *aretē*, reputation *(doxa)*, and manly virtue *(andragathia)*—attributes that his rival lacked (Is. 5.46–47).[8] But his need to emphasize that excellence and manliness were not a function of status but character points to Athenians' inclination to overlook it and associate masculine and moral virtues with men of distinguished origin.

The association of superior manhood with superior social status is also implicit in the double standard of behavior for the elite and the masses. This double standard appears in a passage in Demosthenes' speech against Androtion referring to Solon's law forbidding male prostitutes to propose laws and speak in public. This law, the speaker claims, is not aimed at the many, who tended not to speak in public. It is, however, aimed at the politically active—that is, at members of the political elite—and is intended to protect Athenian democracy from the machinations of corrupt politicians (Dem. 22.30–32). The implication is that male prostitution by commoners who are not active in public affairs can be tolerated, either because it is less shameful for them than for their social superiors or because commoners behavior does not have the ability to harm the state. The passage implies that the nonelite, whom the orator was addressing, expected the elite to meet higher standards of sexual probity than the demos.[9]

THE UNMANLY ELITE

The elitist claim to superior manhood was not universally accepted in ancient Athens. Orations often refer to members of the elite whose conduct and lifestyle violate masculine conventions. Perhaps ironically, these allusions are made not by commoners but by members of the elite themselves, to whom most of the speakers in the orations can be considered to belong. The fact that these references are found in speeches written by different speechwriters is an indication of the pervasiveness of these views.

Oratorical references to the elite as unmanly focus on several interrelated themes: sexual excesses, self-indulgent lifestyles, the use of wealth in the pursuit of false honor, and hubris.

8. Cf. Lys. 18.11; Arist. *Rhet.* 2.15 1390b19–31; Wyse 1904, 482.
9. See Fisher 2001, 52–53. Halperin 1990, 98–99 has used Dem. 22.30–32 to tie the effeminization of the lower class to their poverty, but no such link is evident in the text.

Elite Excesses and Unmanly Conduct

Several orations attack the egocentric, self-indulgent excesses of the elite, depicting sexual indulgence, rowdiness, and profligate spending. Thus, a speaker alleges that while living in the northern city of Abydus, the elder Alcibiades had behaved lawlessly and shown lack of moral discipline *(akolasia)*, adopting the locals' indecent sexual practices (Ant. fr. 67 [Blass]). Another speaker charged that this Alcibiades and a friend had first shared a local woman and then, later, her grown-up daughter by one of them, each averring that the other man was her father (Lys. fr. 4 [Thalheim]). The speaker of a fictional speech attributed to Andocides makes the slightly less scandalous charges that Alcibiades brought *hetairai* into his marital home, fathered a son with a captive Melian woman, and was most shamefully greedy *(aiskhrokerdestatos)* in his extravagant expenditures for his personal comfort and pleasure ([And.] 4.14, 22, 32]. In a character assassination of Alcibiades' son, Lysias includes the young man's all-night reveling, keeping an *hetaira,* male prostitution, and incest (Lys. 14.25, 28, 41). Speakers in the Demosthenean corpus accuse Androtion of prostitution (Dem. 22.31–32); Phrynion of drinking heavily, behaving rowdily, and having sex in public with an *hetaira* ([Dem.] 59.33); and Apollodorus of living *aselgōs* (wantonly), going about with three slaves in tow, and wasting his patrimony on fine clothing, *hetairai,* and other insatiable appetites (Dem. 36.45). Aeschines depicts Timarchus as an incontinent person who could resist no pleasure and who hired himself out as a male prostitute to support his vices after he had wasted his patrimony (Aes. 1, passim, esp. 42, 95–96). The wealth and social position of the accused were of the essence in most of these allegations.

Excess and self-indulgence were viewed as unmanly in ancient Athens.[10] Men who were driven by their appetites and wants and who spent lavishly to support them violated the masculine ideal of self-restraint; they more closely resembled the Athenian stereotype of women as consumers than that of men as producers.[11]

Thus Aeschines contrasts Timarchus's conduct with that of the *metrios* or *sōphrōn* man (Aes. 1.51, 122), claims that Timarchus played the part of the woman in his sex for sale, and observes that this unre-

10. Foucault 1985, 63–77; Winkler 1990, 49–50; Carson 1990, 142; Davidson 1997, 174.
11. On the spendthrift: Hunter 1994, 12, 103, 110; Davidson 1997, passim. On man as producer and women as consumer: e.g., Xen. *Oec.* 3.15 and Pomeroy 1994, 271; cf. Vernant 1989.

strained behavior might be a natural impulse in women but was unnatural in men (Aes. 1.111, 185). To highlight their targets' self-indulgence and slur their masculinity, several orations speak of their wearing a *khlanis*, a fine-quality woolen cloak.[12] Aeschines, for example, told jurors that they would find it hard to tell whether the soft and refined clothes that Demosthenes wore belonged to a man or a woman (Aes. 1.131).

Extravagance and self-indulgence also undermined the elite's fulfillment of their obligations to their families (Dem. 36.45; [And.] 4.14; Aes. 1.95–96). Some speakers linked unmanly behavior to disloyalty, political subversion, and antidemocratic proclivities. Aeschines emphasizes that Timarchus's inability to control his appetites made him prone to crime, serving a tyrant, and attempts to overthrow the demos.[13] The Demosthenean speaker who accused the prominent politician Androtion of male prostitution explained that people of his sort posed a danger to democracy, because to avoid being shamed by their reprehensible behavior, they would try to overthrow Athens's democratic regime, in which people were free to criticize wrongdoers, whatever their status, and to establish an oligarchy, where criticism of public figures was forbidden. Alternatively, he claimed, they would try to corrupt the demos to make them more like themselves (Dem. 22.31–32).

Many Athenians were receptive to linking the elite's lack of restraint to antidemocratic proclivities, because the latter also implied deficient manhood. This implication is evident in Demosthenes' and Aeschines' contrasting of free and courageous democrats to cowardly oligarchs, and in Aeschines' contrasting of democratic self-restraint and moderation to oligarchic license (Dem. 60.25–26; Aes. 3.168–70). Athenians thought a man who would subvert democracy was one who would subvert morality, deprive Athenians of their manly freedom, and legitimize unmanly conduct.

Wealth versus Honor: Meidias and Phaenippus

Although the Athenians certainly did not disapprove of wealth, Athenian civic ideology ranked it below honor, and sometimes counterposed

---

12. Dem. 21.133; 36.45. See MacDowell 1990, 352; cf. Hunter 1994, 103; and more generally: Dover 1974, 111–12. For the Athenian dress code, see Halperin 1990, 186 n. 82; Geddes 1987; cf. Bassi 1998, 98–119.

13. Aes. 1.190–91; Davidson 1997, 282, 292–93, 301; Fisher 2001, 350.

the two.[14] Claiming that Androtion confused symbols of honor (crowns) with symbols of wealth (cups and plates), a speaker depicted valuing wealth as vulgar, maintained that wealth was worthy only if it was spent for the honor of the city, and warned that rich men who pursued wealth for its own sake might sully their honor (Dem. 22.75–76). Similarly, two funeral orations directly counterpose wealth and pleasure, which Athenians associated with the elite (as well as with the Persians), to honor and *aretē*. In his funeral oration for the dead of Chaeroneia, Demosthenes asserts that good men *(andres agathoi)* scorn the acquisition of wealth and the pursuit of pleasure in favor of *aretē* and honor (Dem. 60.2). A Lysian speaker lauds the Athenians who fought in the Persian wars for having chosen freedom and *aretē* over servile infamy and wealth as subjects of their Persian foes.[15]

Men of wealth were expected to spend generously to finance state-sponsored dramatic and choral performances, to pay war taxes, and to equip and command warships. Some of the obligations were anchored in law, but voluntary contributions were also expected.[16] In the speech against Meidias, Demosthenes contrasts Meidias's failure to properly perform the public services incumbent on a man of his wealth and social position with his extravagant spending on himself. After discounting Meidias's public services as trivial, self-seeking, and falling short in comparison to his own public contributions, Demosthenes asserts that Meidias has built a large mansion that overshadows the houses of his neighbors; drives his wife about in a carriage pulled by expensive imported horses; and walks around the marketplace with his servants, talking loudly of drinking horns and cups. The mass of Athenians do not benefit from the wealth that Meidias has accumulated, Demosthenes concludes, and he calls upon the jury not to judge a man's love of honor *(philotimia)* by whether he has a big house, many maidservants, and fine garments, but rather by whether the community shares in his good name and love of honor.[17] This normative assertion presents the self-pampering

14. Dover 1974, 111–12; Ober 1989, 205–14, 225–26. Cf. Hunter 1994, 109–11, as well as Dem. 36.30; Hyp. fr. D 17 (Burtt).

15. Lys. 2.33; cf. Dem. 36.52; Lyc. 1.108; Fr. 15.2 (Conomis). See also men whose wealth was attributed to disreputable sources: Dem. 19.114; 45.81; Aes. 2.161; 3.240; cf. Ant. 5.58; Hyp. 4.32. For complaints against using wealth to arouse the jurors' hostility and spare their pity, see Is. 6.59; 11.38; Dem. 27.53; 29.49; Isoc. 15.5, 31; Ober 1989, 225.

16. On the institution of *leitourgia* in the Classical period: Lewis 1960; Davies 1971; 1984, esp. 9–37, 88–132; Millett 1998, 242–53.

17. Dem. 21.154–59. For the concept of *philotimia*, see Dover 1974, 229–34; Whitehead 1983; MacDowell 1990, 378–79; Veligianni-Terzi 1977, 211–12, 223, 268–69,

and conspicuous consumption of a wealthy man as unpatriotic and a travesty of true manliness and honor.

The speech against Phaenippus, concerning a dispute over who should carry out certain civic obligations, the plaintiff or Phaenippus, also brings together the themes of the elite's misuse of their wealth, their deficient public service, and their defective honor. The plaintiff, who claims to have fallen on hard times, depicts Phaenippus as a prosperous young farmer who shirks public duties in favor of ostentatious display and a soft, effeminate life. The only evidence of Phaenippus's pursuit of honor, the speaker says sardonically, is that he is a *hippotrophos agathos esti kai philotimos*, "a good breeder of horses who is a lover of honor" (Dem. 42.24). Horse breeding was a prestigious activity associated with the landed rich, and the words *agathos* (good) and *philotimos* (lover of honor) were both associated with the elite. The speaker then goes on to discredit Phaenippus as so full of self-indulgence *(truphē)* that he has sold his war horse and bought a chariot so as not to have to walk (Dem. 42.20–24).

Yet these two speeches also imply that Athenians were ambivalent about how a man should gain prestige. The conduct attributed to Meidias and Phaenippus strongly suggests that the display of wealth did confer prestige on a man. So does the distinction made by Androtion's prosecutor between crowns, on the one hand, and plates and cups, on the other, as symbols of honor.[18]

Hubris

Last but not least, the elite were susceptible to accusations that they violated expectations of masculine conduct through hubristic behavior. The Athenian conception of hubris covered a wide range of behavior, including unrestrained sexual activity (Aes. 1.108); self-pampering and self-indulgent spending (Dem. 36.42); and offenses against the state, including

---

283–84, 292–93; cf. Davies 1971, xvii–xviii.; Hakkarainen 1997, 14–19, 21. For ranking one's reputation and interests over those of the state: [And.] 4.29; Dem. 21.10, 71–73; 19.237–38; 22.31–32; Ober 1989, 311.

18. Dem. 22.75–76; cf. Dem. 61.38; Thuc. 6.12.2; Theophrastus *Characters* 21, 23; Arist. *Rhet.* 2.12.4–8 1389a6–25; Pitt-Rivers 1966, 60. See Davidson 1997, esp. 183–210. Competitive quest for prestige played a role too; cf. [Dem.] 59.33. Against the view that discounts conspicuous consumption in Athens (Davidson 1997, 227–46; cf. Ober 1989, 205–21), see Aristotle's observation ibid.; Dem. 13.29–30; 23.208, and the archaeological evidence cited by Morris 1994, 69–71, 74; 1999, 64–70; Bergemann 1997, 123–25.

antidemocratic proclivities (Isoc. 20.10; cf. Dem. 21. 202–4), greed and violations of the law (Dem. 45.67), and misuse of public office (Dem. 22.54).

Some orations treat hubris as an attribute of the elite. A Lysian client asserts that hubris is more likely to be shown by men of wealth, who can buy themselves out of trouble, than by those whose poverty obliges them to behave with moderation (Lys. 24.15–18).[19] In the speech against Conon, Ariston describes his attackers as quarrelsome, violent, and verbally abusive; shows them humiliating his slaves, himself, and his comrades; says that they were infatuated with *hetairai* and that they gave themselves crude, offensive names; and presents them as contemptuous of public sensibility and of things sacred.[20] He refers to them as sons of the *kaloi k'agathoi* (Dem. 54.14), thereby linking their hubristic contempt for others and lack of self-restraint with their social status as members of the Athenian elite.

In his oration against Meidias, Demosthenes depicts the defendant as an arrogant bully, and repeatedly associates Medias's hubristic behavior with his superior means. Meidias intimidates his victims with his audacity *(thrasos)*, overbearing *(huperphania)*, aggressiveness *(aselgeia)*, violence *(bia)*, meddlesomeness *(philopragmosunē)*, and resources *(aphormē)* (Dem. 21.137–38). He uses the power that his wealth and status give him to harm members of the demos and to persecute fellow citizens through the courts (Dem. 21.95–96, 98; cf. 21.112). And Meidias gloats over his superabundant wealth and has used it to try to drive him, Demosthenes, into exile and to cover him with shame (Dem. 21.109). Demosthenes urges the jury to confiscate Meidias's wealth so as to rid him of his hubris or at least render it ineffective (Dem. 21.138).

In his summation of his speech, Demosthenes asserts that Meidias thinks himself superior to everyone else, views those less privileged than he as subhuman paupers (Dem. 21.198), and calls the demos unproductive freeloaders who live like parasites on the wealth of the rich and do not contribute to or serve the state as much as they can (Dem. 21.203; cf. 21.22–31).

In the Athenian view, a man had the right to claim superiority when

---

19. Some scholars have found strong literary and comic elements in Lys. 24, but this does not mean that this or other observations lacked validity or persuasive power. For the speech see Usher and Edwards 1985, 263–69; Harding 1994, 202–6; Usher 1999, 106–10; but also Carey 1990.

20. Dem. 54.20, 39. Carey and Reid 1985, 87, 100–101, read Dem. 54.14, 39 as mocking poor people.

he excelled others in his character and conduct, and he was entitled to shame others only when their conduct warranted it. Social and economic advantages did not make a man manlier, since they did not make him morally superior. Hence the elite's use of their resources to seek pleasure and to shame others, their view of themselves as superior to fellow Athenians, and their failures to meet their civic responsibilities meant that they fell short of civic and manly ideals.

It is perhaps ironic, but not surprising, that the manhood of the elite was faulted in connection with the lifestyle, prominence, and wealth that made them members of the elite in the first place. To counter these hostile perceptions, wealthy speakers pled poverty, presented themselves as weak and victimized, and claimed that they lacked legal experience. They portrayed themselves as quietistic *(apragmōn)*, that is, unmeddlesome, men, who lived moderately and modestly.[21] On the positive side, speakers stressed the reputable and manly way in which they had acquired their wealth (i.e., through toil), made contributions to the community, and assisted their friends. Examples abound. Andocides, who came from an ancient Athenian family, included in his defense speech against the charge that he profaned the Mysteries the dual boast that that, after his family had lost their money, he had started a new life of honest toil, and that he learned the meaning of self-control (And. 1.144–45). The prosecutor of Phaenippus bragged that he had earned his wealth through hard bodily toil in the silver mines he leased (Dem. 42.20). The defendant in one of Antiphon's rhetorical pieces boasts of paying war taxes, performing public services, and aiding friends financially, as well as of having acquired his wealth by hard work and not by vexatious litigation (Ant. 2.2.12). A Lysian speaker charged with having taken bribes describes himself as sparing in his private expenditures but taking (socially approved) pleasure *(hedomai)* in making public contributions and performing his duties (Lys. 21.15–16).

MANHOOD AND THE MASSES

Along with a mixed view on the impact of elite status on manhood, the orations present a range of opinions about the impact of association

---

21. Claiming poverty and a weaker position: e.g., Lys. 24.9, 18; Dem. 45.73; cf. Dem. 44.4, 28. Ober 1989, 222–24, aptly describes the fictitious character of the wealthy man pleading poverty as "a poor little rich man," but I cannot share Ober's view that the demos participated in the pretense willingly. Lack of experience: p. 140 below; quietist and the moderate: pp. 179–81 below.

with the masses on manhood. The indigence of the poor, who probably constituted a significant proportion of the masses, was seen as compelling them to act with moderation *(sōphronein)* (Lys. 24.15–18), while the demos as a whole are regularly credited by the orators with moral superiority, civic-mindedness, and sensitivity to the manly values of honor, glory, and justice.[22] This flattering picture undoubtedly reflects the orators' efforts to curry favor with the members of the demos who sat on the juries they addressed. But it also reflects the official ideology of democratic Athens, where all citizens were deemed to have honor, where poverty was expected to evoke compassion, and where humiliating the poor was considered unseemly and a sign of elite haughtiness.[23]

On the other hand, the orations also suggest that the Athenians sometimes associated low economic and social status with deficient manhood. Just as the privileges of the elite were seen as inclining them to self-indulgence and hubris, the deprivations of the poor were seen as inclining them to crime, encouraging unmanly ways of earning a living, and impeding displays of courage and honor.[24] By and large, the orations treat poverty as a liability in the attainment of manhood.

Poverty as an Impediment to the Display of Courage and the Defense of Honor

Athenian manhood tended to be performative. Men were expected to display their manhood through action and speech. The actions included public aggression—such as Conon's victory dance over Ariston's prone body (Dem. 54.9) and Meidias's slapping Demosthenes in the face in a theater full of people (Dem. 21.1)—which could be perceived either as crude, hubristic displays of masculinity or as one-upmanship. They also included acts of courage (Lys. 16.12–17); civic and military service (e.g.,

22. E.g., Hyp. 4.33–36; cf. Aristophanes *Plutus* 563–564; Isoc. 7.4; pp. 134–35 below. Harding 1994, 205–7, however, has argued that the claim that the poor were self-controlled under compulsion was made tongue-in-cheek.

23. Pitying and improper mocking or reproaching of poor men: Is. 5.11, 35; Dem. 18.256; 45.67, 85; 57.36, 42, 45, 52; Din. 1.36. Mocking or feeling contempt for the demos: [And.] 4.16; Dem. 21.198, 203; Aes. 1.173–76; Hyp. 2.2; cf. Din. 1.104. For the poor see n. 2 above and Rosivach 1991; cf. Dover 1974, 109–10.

24. Poverty inducing wrongdoing: Lys. 7.14; Dem. 29.22; 45.44. Yet treating wrongdoing out of poverty with sympathy and indulgence: Lys. 31.11; Dem. 21.182; 23.148; 24.123; 51.11; Aes. 1.88.

Aes. 2.167–69; 3.42–43); and participation in sports or political or legal contests, as well as boasting about doing so.

Many ways of displaying manhood were beyond the means of the poor. Although the orations rarely comment on these matters, they do suggest that the poor were handicapped in displaying their manhood in the legal arena, and deemed lesser men on that account.[25] In ancient Athens, manly courage and self-sacrifice could be affirmed by taking, or claiming to take, legal risks. Among the risks were exposure to damaging countercharges and sometimes partial disenfranchisement and a heavy fine if one failed to secure a minimum proportion of the jurors' votes (Harrison 1971, 175). These were risks only the well-to-do could afford to take.

Although the Athenians believed that unnecessary legal risks should be avoided (see, e.g., Isoc. 18.9–10; Is. 3.46–47), speakers boast of taking such risks and fault their adversaries for failing to do so. In his public suit against Timocrates, for example, the prosecutor Diodorus boasts that he risks losing a large sum of money in defense of the citizenry (Dem. 24.3). Speakers also link the amount of risk a man is taking to the validity of his claims. They cite their opponents' use of legal procedures that carry little or no risk as evidence that the latter's charges are groundless and cite their own readiness to take legal risks as evidence of their innocence or of the justice of their suits.[26]

The orations thus reveal an association between the masculine values of courage, fair contest, and risk-taking, on the one hand, and the economic and socially based ability to conduct high-risk litigation, on the other. In a speech he wrote for Diodorus against Androtion, Demosthenes interprets Athenian legal procedures as allowing different methods of bringing malefactors to justice, depending on the litigant's disposition and financial status. Taking the prosecution of theft as his example, but indicating that the principle can be applied to other crimes as

---

25. For a trial as a contest, see Osborne 1985b, 40–58, esp. 42–44; Todd 1993, 160–63; D. Cohen 1995a; Christ 1998, 34–39. Rubinstein 2000, esp. 18–21, 90–91, 172–98, extends the competition in private and especially in public legal actions to team contests, which could include nonelite members, and argues for a lesser risk in going to court. Yet even she concedes (190, 192) the higher likelihood of men of the elite engaging in agonistic law suits.

26. Avoiding legal risks: And. 1.6; Is. 4.22; 11.31; 12.8; Lys. 19.3; Hyp. 1.8, 12. Taking legal risks: Lys. 14.17; 7.36–38. See Christ 1998, 35–36, 76, 140, 148. Whitehead 2000, 124–25, citing Scafuro, observes a typical plea by defendants for sympathy through claims of being disadvantaged here; but see Is. 3.46–47; 11.31; 12.8, spoken by, or in reference to, prosecutors.

well, he states that a man who is strong and self-confident *(errōssai kai sautōi pisteueis)* can arrest a thief personally *(apagōgē)*, at the risk of incurring a large fine if the arrestee is found innocent; a man who is somewhat weak *(asthenesteros)* can report the criminal to the archons, who will handle the matter *(ephēgēsis)*; a man who is afraid to do even this *(phobei kai touto)* can bring a public action *(graphē)*; and a man who distrusts himself (*katamemphei seauton;* literally, finds fault with himself) and is too poor to pay the fine can sue the wrongdoer for theft in a private action *(dikē)* before a public arbitrator without risking any loss himself (Dem. 22.25–27; cf. Isoc. 20.2).

The speaker's overt aim was to extol a system that ensured that persons of all dispositions and financial capabilities could obtain justice. Yet even though the issue at hand was the risk of a fine, in three of the four procedures, the speaker refers not to the litigant's financial means but to his disposition (cf. Dem. 54.1). Specifically, he names the masculine qualities of strength and self-confidence that the litigant possesses as the determining factor in the choice. The legal procedure that the person has selected is thus an indicator of his manly character. Those unable to pay a large fine tended to be seen as lacking the manly nerve to take the risk, and they may also have had to make do with less justice. For the greater the risk the prosecutor took, the more severe, apparently, the punishment that the defendant might suffer.[27]

The moral disadvantage of a poor man in such a system is evident in Apollodorus's public charge *(apographē)* against Arethusius, a state debtor whose property Apollodorus claimed for the state. To reinforce his claim that he is not acting out of excessive litigiousness or seeking to profit, Apollodorus points out that he risks forfeiting both his money and civil rights should the jury decide against him; boasts that he rejected the less risky option of having someone else file the suit and suffer the damages should he lose; and, if the jury finds against Arethusius, renounces the reward due to those who successfully denounce men found to be state debtors.[28] Through these dramatic gestures, Apollodorus presents himself as a manly citizen who values honor and revenge above money and who meets danger face-to-face on behalf of the state.[29] Only the rich could afford to make such costly public gestures to demonstrate their virility and the purity of their motives.

27. Cf. Osborne 1985b, 43, whose interpretation of this passage has been disputed by Rubinstein 2000, 221–25.

28. [Dem.] 53.1–2. On shielding oneself by using another prosecutor, see Hansen 1991, 192–94; Rubinstein 2000, 198–212.

29. Cf. Dem. 58.45; Christ 1998, 148–49; Johnstone 1999, 81; Rubinstein 2000, 203.

To be sure, the orators did not criticize the poor for avoiding risky legal procedures, as they did the rich. Such criticism would probably have been considered unseemly and antagonized the jury. In addition, it is likely that the poor were not expected to take the same risks as the rich. Nonetheless, the poor, in contrast to strong, confident men of wealth, were seen as weak, fearful, and unable to defend their interests, their honor, or the public good in court.

Negative Perceptions of the Indigent and Lowborn (Dem. 18–19)

Members of the masses could also come under fire for the types of work they did. While idleness was deemed reprehensible in men of all classes, and working was valued in principle, not all work was deemed equally suitable for a man.[30] The Athenians looked down on indoor work, which was typically done by women and slaves; work for hire, which limited the freedom of the worker and subjected him to the wishes of his paymaster; and work serving or catering to the needs of others, which was scorned for similar reasons. The scorned occupations also included banausic occupations, that is, menial crafts.[31] These were despised as done by children, women, slaves, and aliens, who were excluded from the category of adult manhood and barred from Athenian citizenship. Examples abound. Aeschines disparaged Demosthenes as a knife-maker's son (Aes. 2.93). The fifth-century politician Cleophon was denigrated as a lyre-maker (And. 1.146; Aes. 2.76), and his contemporary Hyperbulus as a lamp-maker (And. fr. III.2 [Maidment]), implying that men who engaged in such occupations fell short of Athenian expectations of the elite.

The masses' expectations of their political leaders inform two orations in which Demosthenes rails against his longtime rival Aeschines. To undermine Aeschines' elite status and leadership claims, Demosthenes associates him and his family with poverty and low birth, as well as with demeaning, unmanly, and morally corrupting occupations.

Demosthenes came from a family privileged by wealth and connec-

---

30. Garlan 1980; de Ste. Croix 1983, 179–92; Balme 1984; Thompson 1987, 28–29; Rosivach 1991, 192–93; Loraux 1995, esp. 44–50; Wood 1996, 129–31; Golden 1998, 146–57; D. Cohen 1998, 58–61; Morawetz 2000, 15–48; cf. Wood 1988, 137–45.
31. On the image of banausic work and its association with noncitizens: Isager and Hansen 1975, 50–52; Whitehead 1977, 109–21; Raaflaub 1981, 305–13; Usher 1993, 262; Cartledge 2002, 148–50; Morawetz 2000, 15–19. For similar attitudes among traditional Andalusians: Gilmore 1990, 48–49, 223–24. Personal freedom: e.g., Wallace 1994a.

tions, while Aeschines was born into one that, in Edward Harris's description, "was not poor, but without the advantages of birth and wealth that would have enabled Aeschines and his brothers to gain easy acceptance into the circle of respectable society" (Harris 1995, 28). Aeschines entered the elite when he became a prominent and powerful politician, although his early acting career and marriage into an important Athenian family might have earned him an elite status even before he had become active in politics.[32] In his attack, however, Demosthenes cites the ignominy of Aeschines's family background and his youth, and the degrading work in which he and his family had purportedly engaged.[33]

In the first speech (Dem. 19), delivered in 343, accusing Aeschines of misconduct as an envoy to Philip of Macedonia, Demosthenes claims that as a boy Aeschines had assisted his mother in conducting raucous initiation rituals into religious cults, that as a man he was employed as a lowly secretary to public officials, and that as an adult he had eked out a meager living as a bit-part actor (Dem. 19.199–200). He described one of Aeschines' brothers as a painter of alabaster boxes and drums, and his other brothers as junior clerks and underlings of officeholders, noting that these are respectable occupations but not suitable for commanding officers in the Athenian army. Aeschines' father, he disparages as an elementary schoolteacher (Dem. 19.237, 249, 281).

Thirteen years later, in a speech defending a proposal, which Aeschines had opposed in court, to honor him for his services to the state (Dem. 18), Demosthenes disputed Aeschines' moral right to oppose the honor and mocked his and his family's claims to *aretē,* intelligence, and education, as well as their ability to differentiate between virtue and vice (Dem. 18.127–28)—qualities and attainments that, in Athenian thinking, distinguished men from women and, in the view of the elite, the elite from the masses. Elaborating on his earlier descriptions, Demosthenes claimed that Aeschines' mother had practiced "daytime marriage" (apparently a euphemism for prostitution) until she was rescued by a ship's piper, a slave; and that his father had been the slave of an elementary schoolteacher and had suffered the ignominious punishment of being placed in the stocks. He distorted the father's name, Atrometos (literally, untrembling), to Tromes *(trembler)* (Dem. 18.129–30). These depictions

32. Demosthenes' family: e.g., Pomeroy 1997, 162–82; Badian 2000, 12–18. Aeschines' background and early career: E. M. Harris 1995, 17–33; Fisher 2001, 8–14.
   33. Since the information about the family background and career of Aeschines and his family comes chiefly from Demosthenes' biased speeches, I shall not dwell here on the accuracy of his descriptions. For the following, see also Rowe 1966.

brought together imputations of slavish origin, cowardice, and the sexually indecent behavior of related females—all considered transgressions against normative manhood. Based on the Athenian belief that children inherited their parents' characters, Demosthenes could rely on his hearers to conclude that Aeschines' ancestry consigned him to be a cowardly and morally suspect failure.[34]

To the alleged defects of Aeschines' birth and nature, Demosthenes added the defects of nurture. Aeschines, he said, had helped his father at the elementary school where he taught, grinding the ink, wiping the dust off the seats, and sweeping the waiting room (Dem. 18.258). He added that Aeschines' mother had raised him to be a "fine image of a man" *(ton kalon andrianta),* and to excel as a third-part actor, and, when he became a man, had him assist her in her initiations, doing menial tasks during the day and at night mixing the libations and washing and dressing the initiates (Dem. 18.129, 259–60; Ferrari 2002, 125–26). In short, both as a boy and as a young man, Aeschines had depended on others and attended to their needs, performing tasks that were incompatible with manly autonomy and elite status.

Demosthenes sneers at the menial work in which Aeschines engaged as an adult too, calling him a "pernicious" or "abominable" secretary, and sarcastically refers to his clerical work as a "most noble occupation" (Dem. 18.127, 209, 261; cf. 19.70, 95, 314). He also describes him playing bit parts in the service of two other actors (Dem. 18.209, 261–62; cf. 19.246–47, 337). At the same time, he insinuates that Aeschines is an idler and a parasite, comparing him to a *spermologos*—a rook that consumed grain in the fields—and calling him an "agora frequenter" (Dem. 18.127), a man who spends his time milling around in the marketplace, possibly in search of gossip or reasons to litigate.[35]

Demosthenes sought to associate Aeschines' lowly occupations with moral corruption and ineptitude. His description of work in initiation ceremonies in the company of drunks and cult members implies moral corruption (Dem. 19.199).[36] He asserts that as a secretary, Aeschines had behaved badly for a pittance *(ponēron onta)*—implying that he had been

---

34. Cf. Usher 1993, 216; E. M. Harris 1995, 25; Cox 1998, 79–80.

35. Wankel 1976, 2: 676–705, esp. 677–78; Dyck 1985; Harding 1987, 30–31; Ober 1989, 214, 288; Usher 1993, 214–15. Images of the idler: Hesiod *Works and Days* 302–5; Plato *Rep.* 8 565a; Dem. 3.35; 9.57; cf. Dem. 2.23; 8.3; 61.37; Isoc. 7.44; Loraux 1993, 78. Law against idleness: Dem. 57.32; Lys. Fr. 10 (Thalheim); Balme 1984, 142–43; Harrison 1968, 1: 79–80; Wallace 1989, 62–64; Bruyn 1995, 79–81, 111–64; cf. Gilmore 1990, 88–89, but see Todd 1993, 245.

36. Paulsen 1999, 211; MacDowell 2000, 289.

bribed for small sums (Dem. 19.200; MacDowell 2000, 289)—and that he had been dismissed for the very illicit acts with which he charged others (Dem. 18.261).

Demosthenes pours scorn on both the occupations and the poverty that drove the family into such work. He repeatedly refers to Aeschines' early poverty, saying that he had been reared in dire straits and had risen from rags to riches (Dem. 18.131, 258). These references were double-edged. They imply sympathy and understanding for the poor and excuse some of their lapses from the moral ideals of the Athenian elite (Dem. 18.256, 263). Yet by consistently linking poverty with undesirable behavior, he treats it as a condition that predisposes a man to moral and intellectual inferiority, especially when linked to lowly birth.

Demosthenes' portrait was designed to persuade the jury to view Aeschines' claims to elite status as ungrounded. The attack was on Aeschines and not on the masses in general. Nonetheless, it drew on the common perception that poverty, low birth, and low-prestige occupations impaired a man's manhood, as well as his ability to attain moral and intellectual excellence. It also drew on the resentment of social climbing by the masses, who wished to see their leaders as authentic members of the social and moral elite.[37]

A Man's Work: Defenses of Men in Deprecated Occupations (Dem. 57 and 37)

Two speeches in Demosthenes' oratorical corpus that defended people in scorned occupations actually reflect the scorn in which those occupations and the people who earned their living by them were held. One speech was written for the litigant Euxitheus, who had appealed a revocation of his membership in his deme, and so of his citizenship, probably because of doubts about his free birth. Euxitheus aggressively defends his father's status as a free Athenian citizen, before and after he had been captured in a war and sold into slavery (Dem. 57.18), and his mother against aspersions that she has been engaged in selling ribbons in the agora and in wet-nursing—occupations typical of aliens and slaves. He argues that the family has fallen on hard times, calls upon the jurors not to regard poor people and those who work and live honestly with contempt *(atimazete),* and contends that people should feel sympathy for the many free men

37. Sinclair 1988, 121–2, 185, 205, 227; Ober 1989, 112–19, 192–292.

who have been forced by need to take up servile work (Dem. 57.30–31, 35–36, 42, 45; cf. Is. 5.39).

Euxitheus spoke in the indignant tone of a proud but poor Athenian. The stated attitude of this speech is virtually the opposite of that advanced by Demosthenes in his speeches against Aeschines. Yet when a speaker called upon the jury to pity or show understanding of persons forced to work in lowly occupations, he also asked them to make a special effort—to go against the grain in reconciling poverty with honor and independence. He asked them to overcome their poor opinion of people categorized as insignificant, forget their prejudice against servile occupations, and consider the value of hard work or the power of difficult circumstances.

The other speech is the speech Demosthenes wrote for the moneylender Nicobulus against one Pantaenetus in a complex case regarding credit and loans, which reveals both the prejudices against moneylenders and the rhetorical means employed to counter them (Dem. 37).[38] Apprehensive of the effect that the image of moneylenders would have on the jury, Demosthenes tried to forestall Pantaenetus's attack on his client's character. He began by charging that, like a *sukophantēs* (a litigious abuser of the legal system), Pantaenetus relied not on the merits of his case but on extrajudicial factors such as the Athenians' dislike of moneylenders and on the demeanor of Nicobulus, who walked fast, talked loud, and carried a stick—behavior that indicated lack of education, restraint, and gravity, as well as arrogance and the propensity to humiliate others.[39]

Then he moved to dissociate Nicobulus from the stereotype of the moneylender. He had Nicobulus admit that people justifiably hated some moneylenders because they turned lending money into a trade *(tekhnē)*, lacked compassion, and were concerned only with becoming even wealthier, but argued that he himself was different. He shared the popular dislike of moneylenders and was a borrower, not just a creditor; he risked his own person going overseas; and when he made a loan, it was

38. Dem. 37: Finley 1973, 32–35; Isager and Hansen 1975, 191–96; Carey and Reid 1985, esp. 105–17; Millet 1991, 193–196. In Aristophanes *Frogs* 1012–17, Aeschylus disparagingly contrasts men of the agora with model hoplites, and see Bourriot 1972, esp. 34–36; Mossé 1983; D. Cohen 1998, 57–61. Moneychangers and bankers, however, seemed to attract respectable citizens: Millett 1998a, 225; cf. E. E. Cohen 1992, 24.

39. Athenian sycophancy: Osborne 1990, with Harvey's 1990, response. The fullest account of the topic is Christ 1998, with the modifications of Rubinstein 2000, 198–212. The terms "sycophant" and "sycophancy" used here have nothing to do with its common English usage.

to do favors *(kharisasthai)* or to protect himself from losses. As for his gait, he could not help what nature had made him.[40]

Both the attack on Nicobulus's character and the defense drew their inspiration from the Athenian views of the social interaction incumbent upon men. Moneylending commercialized a relationship that Athenians expected to be based on social reciprocity, friendship, trust, alliance, and affection. Moneylenders stuck out as specialists who replaced cooperative interaction and values with the pursuit of selfish gain.[41] In Athenian thinking, they violated the expectation that men who had money would share their wealth with the city and the norm of helping friends and kin, exemplified in the practice of giving loans free of interest and without asking for security.[42]

Demosthenes' strategy was to show how Nicobulus's business conduct was dominated not by the attributes of his trade but by his sociable and manly character. His moneylending practices followed the societal expectations of *kharis* (reciprocal assistance). He sought to protect his earnings, but he never lent money for self-enrichment. Demosthenes transformed Nicobulus's business ventures into a manly feat of courage and risk-taking (cf. Dem. 33.4).

His defense of Nicobulus rested on the distinction between a man's character and his trade—on the argument that character was a truer measure of men. But this strategy suggested the difficulties that the Athenians had in keeping that difference in mind.

All in all, the orations show strong associations between manhood and social position. The manhood of elite's members could be called into question when they misused their resources; the manhood of the masses might be viewed as flawed because they lacked resources or, if they were wealthy, because of the way in which they acquired them.

Yet the links in the orations between manhood and social class do not mean that manhood was a class-determined concept. Members of the

40. Dem. 37.52–56. For ethical interpretations of gait (and dress), see Arist. *EN* 4.3. 1125a13–17; Süss 1910, 253–54; Dover 1974, 115; Bremmer 1991; Hall 1995, 53; Fisher 1992, 48–51, 479; Bergemann 1997, 76–79; Goldhill 1998, 110; cf. Gleason 1995, 60–62; Too 1995, 91. Other hostile interpretations of a man's appearance and gait: Lys. 16.18; Dem. 45.68–69, 77; 54.34; cf. Is. 5.11; Aes. 1.25–26, 131; Theophrastus *Characters* 24.8, 26.4. Greek physiognomy and its rhetoric: Gleason 1995; Hesk 2000, 219–27.

41. Lenders as friends: Shipton 1997, 411–12. The anthropologist Ernst Gellner observes from his reading of premodern Arab history that the unspecialized person constitutes the moral norm. It is he "who can lose himself in a solidarity unit, and gladly accepts collective responsibility" (Gellner 1988, 148).

42. Sharing wealth: Dover 1974, 163. Interest-free loans: Millett 1991, 100, 127–217; E. E. Cohen 1992, 190–91, 207–15.

elite may have claimed that they were manlier than the masses, and some of the masses may have shared their view. But the masses as a whole seem to have regarded much of the elite's conduct and lifestyle as unmanly. They were concerned about the elite's misuse of their social and economic resources and suspected their self-interest and loyalty to Athenian ideals. The masses also seem to have been of mixed mind about their own ability to attain the desirable level of manliness. Along with the elite orators who voiced the sentiments, they apparently felt that their lack of resources forced the poor among them into crime and deprived them of the capacity to display courage and honor. They seem also to have shared the elite's suspicion of low birth and poverty and the elite's scorn for certain ways of earning a living. Yet, at the same time, they could and did point to the supremacy of character over social class and occupation in the evaluation of a man. In other words, elitist and more egalitarian assumptions about one's ability to approach masculine ideals seem to have coexisted. We need not try to reconcile them when the Athenians did not.

CHAPTER 5

Men in the Military

In Athens, all able-bodied men between the ages of eighteen and fifty-nine could be called to military service.[1] The exclusion of women, children, physically frail, older men, and sometimes slaves created an exclusive group of males who valued physical and mental power in general and in the military arena in particular. In the words of the sociologist David Morgan, such exclusivity and division of labor define not only who *does* what but who *is* what.[2]

In the military, Athenian men were able to meet the masculine expectations of courage, strength, fraternity, order, self-control, discipline, self-sacrifice, loyalty, and service to the state, and to defend Athens's cherished ideals of justice and democracy.[3] By serving in the military, a man brought honor to himself and his family and helped to defend the polis and to maintain or augment its wealth, power, and prestige. Dis-

1. *Ath Pol.* 53.4, 7; Hansen 1991, 100. In the period under discussion, men called for service included resident aliens and slaves, but the orators focused on Athenian citizens. Ascertaining how many citizens actually did military service in fourth-century Athens is problematic: see Pritchett 1974, 2: 104–10; Burckhardt 1995, esp. 111–33; 1996, 86–153.

2. Morgan 1994, 166 (Morgan's italics), and see 167–68; Burkert 1983, 47–48; cf. Versnel 1987, 69; Sourvinou-Inwood 1995, 113. Military masculinity in New Comedy: Pierce 1998, 136–39.

3. Sharing dangers with others: Lys. 10.27; Is. 6.1; cf. Lys. 31.7; Lyc. 1.43. Courage and self-sacrifice: Lys. 16.13, 15–16; and good citizenship: Isoc. 18.61; and loyalty to the communities and its ideals: Lys. 2.11–14; 16.3; 26.21–22. On the prominence of these expectations in regard to land and naval warfare, see respectively Hanson 1996, and Strauss 1996, 315–25; Cartledge 1998b, 63–64.

playing courage in war was the traditional way for a man to acquire
aretē.[4]

I shall examine the ethos that sustained these masculine perceptions,
as well as the tension that existed between the realities of war and its ideology. For despite the changing realities of war in the fourth century,
Athenian public discourse held tenaciously to earlier Archaic and Classical values of military service. These values and perceptions had an impact on Athenian rhetoric in court and at the assemblies. Yet adherence
to these values and Athenian attitudes toward military service and its
avoidance were not uniform, but influenced by a man's social and economic status.

THE WARRIOR IDEOLOGY

In Athens, military service came in different forms, which were usually,
but not always, determined by income. Wealthy Athenians served as hoplites (heavily armed infantrymen) in the army, horsemen in the Athenian
cavalry, or trierarchs in the navy. Those less affluent, but with enough
income to purchase a panoply, tended to serve in the infantry, either as
hoplites or as lighter-armed peltasts, while the poor, often identified with
the *thētes,* usually rowed the ships or fought as light-armed troops in the
infantry.[5] The association, however, between income and military function could change according to the circumstances of the campaign or
mission.[6]

Even though many Athenians fought at sea or as lightly armed troops,
the hoplitic ethos of military performance remained dominant. This
ethos promoted the masculine values of courage, stamina, strength,
order, self-control, self-sacrifice, and comradeship in arms. It valorized
facing danger, standing one's ground, and cooperating with fellow soldiers, and relished victory (preferably quick) in a well-regulated, open,
face-to-face confrontation, preferably between nonprofessional soldiers.

---

4. Service and honor: e.g., Lys. 18.7; Dem. 40.25; 60.32; Hyp. 6.27. Helping the polis:
e.g., And. 1.147; Lys. 2.23; Dem. 60.3, 17; 61.30; Lyc. 1.108; Hyp. 6.19; Dover 1974,
165–66, 168; Loraux 1995, esp. 64–68, 75–87, 152–58. These and other sources cited later
in this chapter call for modification of the view that war lost its prestige in the fourth century: Hunt 1998, 194–202, esp. 196.
   5. *Thētes* was originally the term for members of the fourth and lowest income group
in the state.
   6. A. Jones 1960, 30–31; Sinclair 1988, 57; Hansen 1991), esp. pp. 6–7, 45–46,
108–19, 115–16; 1995, 338–49; Burckhardt 1996, 140, 148; Cox 1998, 155–161; Christ
2001, 405. For the following discussion, cf. Pritchett 1974, 147–89.

The model hoplite was the model Athenian man. This view inhered in the contrast that Aeschines draws between his enemy Demosthenes, whom he calls a *kinaidos*, an unmanly creature, and the manly hoplite, who is physically fit and mentally self-possessed *(sōphrōn)* (Aes. 2.151). The hoplitic ideology held sway well into the fifth and fourth centuries, even after protracted, relatively unheroic sieges had replaced pitched battles and citizen hoplites increasingly fought alongside lighter-armed men and alien mercenaries.[7]

The hoplitic ideology and its values were embodied in the institution of the *ephēbeia*.[8] In their service in this institution, eighteen- and nineteen-year-old Athenians performed garrison and patrol duties and were trained to fight with the hoplitic spear and large shield, as well as with the bow, javelin, and catapult, weapons normally wielded by the light-armed troops. The oath they took promised cooperation, disciplined obedience, solidarity, patriotism, honor and fear of disgrace, respect for tradition, and striving for excellence. Both the *ephēbeioi* and the men who wished to mold them into manhood continued to see the essentially archaic hoplitic norms as relevant to the creation of a desirable citizen and man.[9]

The hoplitic ethos was also very much alive in the forensic and deliberative oratory of fourth-century Athens. Lycurgus put elements of the ephebic oath to forensic use in his speech of 330 prosecuting the Athenian Leocrates for treason. Leocrates, he claimed, had disgracefully violated his ephebic oath: he had shamed his sacred arms, deserted his post or the man standing next to him, and failed to defend his fatherland and its gods (Lyc. 1.76–78).

Demosthenes drew on the hoplite ethos in a speech delivered in 355

---

7. Burckhardt 1996, 154–257; Hanson 2000), esp. 219–22. Hoplitic ideology and practices: Ridley 1979; Loraux 1986, 161–63; Vidal-Naquet 1986a, 85–105; 1986b; Connor 1988; Hanson 1989; Lissarrague 1990b, esp. 13–34; Hanson 1995, 219–318; Ober 1996, 35–71; Cartledge 1998b, 61–65. Ober 1991, 188–92; Wheeler 1991, 137–38; and Mossé 1995a, 104–6, have argued for changes in war ethics in the fourth century, and cf. Spence 1993, 171–79; Hesk 2000, 24–29, 115–18. Hoplites and manhood: cf. Winkler 1990b, 28–33; John Henderson 1994, 87–89, 96–97. See Krentz 2002 for postdating the hoplitic ideology to a time after the Persian Wars (490–479) and its projection backward to the Archaic Age; cf. van Wees 2000, 156; Krentz 2000. Undoubtedly, the orators and their audience viewed the values discussed here as ancient.

8. See pp. 12–13 above. I share the objections of Rawlings 2000, 238–41, to Pierre Vidal-Naquet's (1986a) structuralist characterization of the ephebes as antihoplites. See Siewert 1977, 102–4.

9. Cf. Strabo 10.4.16. For recollection of these values at ceremonial occasions, see Humphreys 1985b, 206–11; Loraux 1986, 26–27, 355–56; Goldhill 1990, 107–14; Raaflaub 1996, 157; Tsitsiridis 1998, 397–99.

against Leptines, whom he prosecuted for proposing a law abolishing certain exemptions from *leitourgiai,* or public services. He contrasts the service of the general Conon in rebuilding the walls of Athens with Themistocles' accomplishment of the same task. Asking the audience's indulgence for slighting the latter's work, he maintains that Conon's contribution should nevertheless be viewed as greater and nobler, because Themistocles had tricked the Spartans, while Conon rebuilt the walls after defeating the Spartans in battle. Openness was better than stealth; it was more honorable to attain one's ends through "victory"—implying open and morally unambiguous confrontation—than through trickery.[10] Apparently, Achillean straightforwardness was still more highly regarded than Odyssean craftiness.

In the speech commonly known as the *Third Philippic,* delivered to the Assembly in 341, Demosthenes expresses a more complex attitude.[11] At that time, the Athenians' interests in the Thracian Chersonese in northeastern Greece were being threatened by Philip of Macedonia. Demosthenes uses the occasion to reiterate his call to check Philip's expansion, while rebutting speakers who claim that Athens can win against Philip, because he is weaker than the Spartans of former years were.

Demosthenes condescendingly points out that times have changed, especially in warfare. In the old days, the Spartans had come in the summer, spent four to five months invading and devastating Attica with an army of hoplites and other citizens, and then gone back home. They had conducted themselves in an Archaic or, more correctly, civic-minded manner *(arkhaiōs eikhon, mallon de politikōs),* never resorting to bribery but following the rules of war and fighting openly. Now, however, most (peoples) are undone by traitors and none by pitched battle *(parataxeōs)* or war. Philip marches wherever he wishes and is followed, not by a phalanx of hoplites, but by an army of lightly armed troops, cavalry, archers, and mercenaries. He attacks a people divided against themselves, lays siege, and pays no heed to whether or not it is the fighting season. Demosthenes advises the Athenians not to look back naïvely to previous wars against the Spartans and rush into a full confrontation,

10. Dem. 20.72–74. On Dem. 20, see Sealey 1993, 126–27; Badian 2000, 27–28. For Demosthenes' comparison, see Hesk 2000, 45–49, 104–6. Since the hoplitic ethos embraced more than one kind of warfare, it could include Conon's defeating the Spartans at sea. Nouhaud 1982, 219, has noted Demosthenes' silence about Conon's use of the Persian fleet to defeat the Spartans. On the gap between ideology and practice concerning military deception, see Krentz 2000.

11. Dem. 9: Schaefer 1885–87, 2: 442–67; Sealey 1993, 180–82; 233–35. See also Polybius 13.3–6; Krentz 2000, 177–78; Hanson 2000, 204, 225, n. 7.

but rather to defend themselves by moving into the Macedonians' territory, harassing them, but avoiding close combat, because they are better trained (Dem. 9.47–52).

Demosthenes' opposition of the two modes of warfare is impressive both rhetorically and in its sobriety. According to him, the days of the regulated, agonistic, and open battle between hoplite forces are long gone. Victory is now achieved more by suborning traitors among the enemy than by the manly courage of hoplites standing their ground against other hoplites.

Yet Demosthenes is not really ready to renounce the hoplitic ethos. The Spartan way of warfare may have been a noble anachronism in 342, but not so the values that supported it.[12] As Demosthenes sees it, a citizen warrior is more patriotic than a paid mercenary, open confrontation is more honorable than winning through trickery or protracted siege, and a hoplite is worthier than a light-armed trooper (Dem. 9.48–50). Demosthenes the pragmatist recommends not engaging Philip in a frontal *agōn*. But the rhetor, the patriot, and the man-hoplite in him cannot allow the Macedonians to score an honorable victory. In a way, his advice to harass Philip's land followed the dignified Spartan precedent of invading and devastating enemy territory.

All three speeches show that hoplitic values and ideology remained highly relevant to the assessment of men and of government policy in the second half of the fourth century. Several factors may account for resilience of the hoplitic ethos. These include traditionalist tendencies in popular ideology, the popular identification of the hoplitic with the noble, and the possibility that generations of Athenian farmers, who typically fought as hoplites, helped preserve the legacy of hoplitic values (Hanson 1995, 260–61). There was also an element of escapism in seeking to disengage from a messy and inglorious reality and falling back on an ethos offering clear rules of conduct and unambiguous choices.[13] Whatever the reasons for their persistence, hoplitic values were part and parcel of the hegemonic masculine ideology of Athens.

Yet in spite (or because) of the important role that martial ideology played in Athens, its basic values were not clearly defined. Even the meaning of military courage and cowardice were open to divergent interpretations.

---

12. Demosthenes' description of the Spartans here cannot be easily reconciled with the argument (for which see Bradford 1994, esp. 78; Hesk 2000 31–32) that they were consistently and stereotypically portrayed as duplicitous. See also Aes.1.180–81.

13. On Greek traditionalism and nostalgia, see Humphreys 1986a; 1997, 216–18; cf. Bassi 1997, 214–15.

MILITARY COURAGE AND ITS RHETORIC

In ancient Athens, as elsewhere, courage was seen as a quintessentially masculine quality.[14] Women were not regarded as bereft of courage, but men's courage was viewed as much greater. Manly courage in women could be perceived as aberrant. In the account of the Amazons in the Lysian funeral oration, the speaker describes these women warriors as having been "viewed as men for their courage *[eupsukhia],* rather than as women for their nature." When they met their match in "brave" Athenian men, however, the crushing Athenian victory exposed their folly *(anoia)* and showed that their "spirit" was that of women (Lys. 2.4–6).[15]

Courage took on other prototypically masculine qualities, namely, reason and self-control. This association is implicit in Demosthenes' funeral oration for the Athenian soldiers who died in the battle of Chaeroneia. All *aretē*, Demosthenes declares, begins with intelligence *(sunesis)* and ends with courage *(andreia;* Dem. 60.17; cf. Gorgias 82 B6 [D-K]).

Indeed, manly courage was conceptualized not so much as an inherent personality trait but as an ethos—a set of ideals and code of behavior—that was developed through education and socialization.[16] Hyperides stresses this in his funeral oration for the dead of the Lamian War, where he observes that raising and educating Athenian children in self-control *(sōphrosunē)* makes them into brave men *(andres agathoi)* who show valor *(aretē)* in battle (Hyp. 6.8). The cultivated courage denoted by the Greek terms *andreia* and *eupsukhia* was sometimes contrasted by the Athenians with *tolma* or *thrasos. Tolma* referred to an innate quality with positive and negative meanings—audacity and daring, on the one hand, rashness, on the other—which was often associated with thoughtlessness, lack of shame or decorum, disregard for rules, undue

---

14. Dem. 60.29; cf. Lyc. 1.100–101; Arist. *Politics* 3.2 1277b20–23; cf. 1.5 1260a22–24. This chapter focuses primarily on courage in its military context. For additional discussions of the concept, as well as of cowardice, see pp. 142–45 and 188–92 below; Romilly 1980; Smoes 1995, 99–280; Hobbs 2000, on courage in Plato. This and the following section are a revised version of Roisman 2003.

15. Feminine courage: See n. 14 as well as Loraux 1995, 80–81, 242–43; Hobbs 2000, 68–75.

16. Aristotle *EN* 3.8 1116a17–29; cf. Xen. *Symposion* 2.11–12; *Cyropaedia* 12.7; Thuc. 1.84.3; Reden and Goldhill 1999, 267–71 (based on Plato's *Laches*); and the following notes. Thuc. 4.126.4–6 gives a fine example of military courage, and see Romilly 1956.

aggressiveness, and impulsive, irresponsible conduct. The term *thrasos,* which in the speeches normally denotes unwarranted or harmful over-confidence, is also used to describe a rash disposition.[17] Of the two types of courage, the Athenians generally preferred the cultivated, thoughtful *andreia* to the natural, emotional *tolma* and *thrasos.* This valuation is ev-ident in Hyperides' assertion that "audacious men *[oi . . . thraseis]* do all things without thinking *[aneu logismou],* but men of good courage *[oi . . . tharraleoi]* meet the dangers they face undauntedly after reason-ing *[meta logismou]*" (Hyp. fr. A 4 [Burtt]).[18]

The funeral orations celebrate Athens as a manly nation, whose sol-diers' courage, public consciousness, and sense of justice legitimize its claim to the leadership of Greece. They praise Athens as a democratic polis of *andres agathoi* whose ancestors surpassed their fellow Greeks in valor, self-sacrifice, and hoplitic values.[19]

Yet defining a courageous warrior remained problematic. Like other manly virtues in ancient Athens, courage had to be confirmed and vali-dated by others. And it was frequently a subjective matter. This subjec-tivity, in addition to agonistic attitudes toward other people's courage, afforded speakers rhetorical opportunities to apply their own standards to particular cases and individuals. The funeral orations show a consen-sus about the masculine bravery of soldiers who had died fighting for their country, but no such consensus emerged regarding the living.

The flexible ascription of courage to individuals and groups can be seen in the different ratings of service in the infantry and cavalry. At times, speakers imply that the infantry is a more dangerous service than the cavalry and thus demands greater manly courage.[20] Other passages,

---

17. Positive *tolma:* e.g. Lys. 2.40, 50, 68; 16.17; Dem. 1.24; 3.30; Aes. 2.182; cf. Lys. 6.49; 34.11; Dem. *Lett.* 1.13; Lyc. 1.131, 143; Is. 9.35. Harmful daring: aggressiveness: Lys. 24.24; cf. Lys. 3.45. Brazenness (often coupled with shamelessness), e.g., Is. 3.51; Lys. 10.6; 26.3; 31.1; Dem. 19.72; 22.31; 24.182; 38.5; 40.53; Isoc. 17.14; cf. Dem. 18.220; 25.9. Lacking in decorum: Dem. 5.4; Aes. 3.241. Disregard of rules and laws: e.g., [And.] 4.27; Lys. 6.9; 15.3; Dem. 42.1; 57.59; Din. 3.3; Isoc. 18.3. Associated with lying and cheating: e.g., Lys. 7.17; 12.2; 16.8; 19.51; 30.24; 32.15; Dem. 25.28; 28.9; 36.17; 40.28, 58. Thoughtlessness: Plato *Laches* 193a–d. For audacity's association with intimidating and powerful people, see [And.] 4.17; Dem. 21.20, 66, 98, 191, 201; 22.25.

18. See also Arist. *EN* 3.7 1115b24–1117a27; Hunter 1973, e.g., 49–50, 68–69; Carter 1986, 11; Loraux 1995, 241–44; Hobbs 2000, 79–80, 116–22.

19. Lys. 2.7–9, 11–14, 23–24, 55; Dem. 60.10–11; Hyp. 6.17–19; cf. Lyc. 1.70, 83, 105; Andoc. 1.107; Isoc. 7.74; Missiou 1992, 51–52; and, generally, Ziolkowski 1981; Lo-raux 1986, 96–97 (but see her comments at 106, 387 n. 132).

20. Esp. Lys. 16.13, and see 14.7, 9; cf. Bugh 1988, 135, 150–53; Spence 1993, 168–172. For ranking hoplites in relation to rowers and lightly armed troops, see Bourriot 1972, 25–41; Humphreys 1993, xvi–xvii. See in addition Raaflaub 1994, 138–42; 1996,

however, suggest that the cavalry was viewed as being just as risky as the infantry and that the men who fought in it were regarded as equally brave.[21]

Often the comparison was to the credit of the person in question, with speakers buttressing their claims that they had faced danger with derogatory remarks about fellow Athenians who tended to their own affairs and security. In claiming that he had volunteered for a particularly risky mission, stood in the front line of fighters, and been among the last to leave the battlefield, Lysias's young client Mantitheus compared himself to men who had sought less risky service, stood in the rear, and left the battlefield early, including a certain Athenian who had accused everyone else of cowardice (Lys. 16.15–18). In this way, Mantitheus, who was suspected of oligarchic tendencies, sought to establish his democratic credentials by advancing monopolistic claims to courage and patriotism at the expense of other Athenians.

Similar claims are found in other orations. Demosthenes contrasts Meidias's efforts to evade dangerous military duty with his own participation in an expedition (Dem. 21.133). Apollodorus compares Polycles' dereliction of duty with his decision to risk his life and spend his capital ([Dem.] 50.59). A Lysian speaker burnishes claims about his own and his father's courage and military service with repeated references to a slanderous allegation that the man he is prosecuting threw away his arms and fled the battlefield.[22] Lastly, a client of Isocrates claims that, unlike other trierarchs who had become demoralized and tried to avoid service following the Athenian defeat at Aegospotamoi in 405, he and his brother had spent their own money on a crew and inflicted damage on the enemy. And when the Spartan admiral Lysander threatened to execute anyone who brought grain to Athens, and no one dared violate his edict, he and his brother had intercepted a shipment and distributed the grain in the city, a good deed for which they were publicly honored.[23]

In all the speeches discussed in this section, courage and contribution to the city's war efforts are juxtaposed with poor performance or cow-

---

155–56; Cartledge 1998b, 62–64; cf. Hanson 1996, 306; 2000, 220, 229, nn. 32–33; Burckhardt 1996, 195; Bergemann 1997, 79–80; but see also n. 69 below.

21. Is. 6.5; Dem. 21.102–14; Lys. 20.24–25. The speaker who calls Alcibiades the Younger a coward for choosing cavalry service over infantry service observes in the same speech that fighting in the cavalry also entails risk (Lys. 14.7, 14).

22. Lys. 10.21–25, 27–30. See also Lys. 10.1, 9, 12; Edwards and Usher 1985, 229–58; Hillgruber 1988.

23. Isoc. 18.60–61. For the *topos* of the ideal citizen soldier and its use by a number of authors, see Burckhardt 1996, 179, 194, 216, 254–55.

ardice. In a society where men competed for honor and feuded publicly, there was an incentive to dispute what courage meant and how risk should be faced. Suffice it to note that Isocrates' client and the other trierarch, Meidias, are respectively depicted as brave and as cowardly for putting out to sea in the service of their polis.

THE RHETORIC OF WAR AND PEACE

The ambiguities surrounding the questions of what courage was and when it was displayed also informed the rhetoric of war and peace. The Athenians readily admitted that peace was better than war.[24] Nonetheless, war was more prestigious than peace. Occasionally, Athenians celebrated peace on stage, in religious festivals, and in the visual arts. But Athens was full of monuments, paintings, sculptures, and inscriptions commemorating military events and victorious generals and their armies, and religious, dramatic, and sporting events reminded the Athenians of their martial virtues.[25] The funeral orations proclaim that the highest honors are to be attained in war. A speech attributed to Demosthenes, for example, recalls the glories of the martial past when Athens had ruled the other Greeks, exacted large sums of money from them, and erected trophies commemorating its victories on land and sea, and laments that in peace, contemporary Athens has squandered its wealth and lost allies won at war.[26]

The prestige of war seemed to have given speakers who advocated taking a belligerent option a rhetorical advantage, since it was easy to identify peace or the reluctance to go to war with cowardice *(anandria)* (Lys. 34.11; Aes. 2.137; cf. Dem. 15.28; 19.218–219; Thuc. 6.13.1). A speaker in one of Demosthenes' preambles seeks to curb popular enthu-

---

24. Dem. 5.24–25; 8.52, 56–57; 19.88; Aes. 2.176–177; cf. Dem. 10.55, 58; 19.92–93, 336; And. 3.1, 12; Herodotus 1.87.4; 8.3.1; Thuc. 2.61.1; 4.59.2, 62.2; Xen. *Poroi* 5.5–13; Isoc. 8.19–20, but cf. Isoc. 8.5–8, 36. [Aristotle] *Rhetoric to Alexander* 2 1425a10–1425b16 lists arguments for and against going to war.

25. Raaflaub 2001. According to Bergemann 1997, 43–44; cf. 63–65; 79–83, the most popular renditions of masculine activity in fourth-century Athenian grave reliefs were of men engaged in war. On peace *(eirēnē)* in Athenian public art after the Peloponnesian War, see Stewart 1997, 152.

26. Honors in war: Lys. 2.76, 79–81; Hyp. 6.40; Dem. 6.33, 36. Glorifying war and lamenting peace: Dem. 13.26–27; cf. Dem. 2.24–27. See also Dem. 19.269; Lyc. 1.49. A pro-Spartan interlocutor in Isocrates' *Panathenaicus* (12.242) presents the admittedly extreme position that lovers of peace are neither acquisitive nor effective guardians of what they have, while lovers of war are able both to take what they desire and to keep it. Those who acted in the latter way are deemed the most accomplished among men: *ha poiousin oi teleioi dokountes einai tōn andrōn.*

siasm for a military action by asking his audience not to consider people courageous just because they advocate marching out with an army, nor to deem those who oppose them cowards (Dem. *Pr.* 50.1). In several speeches, Demosthenes tries to find a way around the association between war, courage, and masculinity to urge restraint; in others, he applies the rhetoric of masculinity to advocate military expeditions.

Demosthenes encountered the challenge of opposing a campaign early in his political career. In 354, following a report that the Persian king planned to attack Greece, the Athenians deliberated whether or not to fight him. As Demosthenes relates, several orators apparently advocated an immediate military response in alliance with other Greeks (Dem. 14.8). In his speech *On the Symmories* (companies) (Dem. 14), however, Demosthenes advised against taking hasty action.[27]

Those who supported a military campaign had in their favor both the Athenians' longing for their fifth-century empire, which had been founded on victories over the Persians, and the prestige war held for Athenian men.[28] In his speech, Demosthenes sets out to counter this double allure by assuming the pose of a mature adult who favors cautious, measured steps. Although approving preparations for a defensive war, if one is necessary, he calls the advocates of war rash and impetuous *(tois de thrasunomenois)*. Their courage is more evident in their words than in their deeds. It is not difficult to acquire a reputation for *andreia* (manly courage), he says, or to appear clever in speech when there is danger. But what is both difficult and proper is to show manly courage when facing danger and to give more thoughtful advice than another would (Dem. 14.8).

In posing this contrast, Demosthenes crafts a subjective and self-serving definition of courage, which simultaneously restricts courage to the battlefield and extends it to the giving of the most sensible advice. Although he nowhere disavows the valor of war, he divests his rivals' call for war of its masculine appeal and emphasizes the masculine values of rationality and restraint.[29]

After his plea for prudence and restraint was accepted (so he says:

27. For *On the Symmories:* Carlier 1990, 78–99; Sealey 1993, 128–29; Lane Fox 1997, 177–81; Badian 2000, 28–30.

28. Dreams of empire: Badian 1995.

29. Cf. Dem. 14.28; *Pr.* 45.2–4; Aes. 2.177. Praising caution and deliberate pace: Carter 1986, 46; Crane 1998, 205. For a similar challenge in opposing a military operation and the use of a similar rhetorical strategy to meet it, see Thuc. 1.80–85. For Thucydides' influence on Demosthenes: Yunis 1996, 240–41, 269–77.

Dem. 15.6), Demosthenes did an about-face. In a series of speeches, especially in the first and third *Philippics* (Dem. 4; 9), the three *Olynthiacs* (Dem. 1–3), and *On the Chersonese* (Dem. 8), delivered between 352/351 and 341/340, he urges the Athenians to march against Philip.[30] Nonetheless, on at least one occasion during this period, he characterizes those who advocate war against Philip as doing so *thraseōs* (boldly, rashly) (5.24) and ignoring the disastrous consequences Athens is likely to suffer. But during these years, his calls for war are far more frequent than his pleas for peace.[31]

In calling for military action, Demosthenes had to contend with the difference between Athenian ideology and practice. Despite the prestige of war as an arena for the display of masculine courage, there was considerable hesitation about taking up arms, even when Philip's expansionism threatened Athenian interests. The city's military record in the fourth century was checkered, raising questions about the wisdom of fighting campaigns in which victory was uncertain. Some Athenians regarded certain campaigns as superfluous, or thought they served private interests, and citizens of all social strata seem to have been reluctant to serve in them. Moreover, campaigns were inadequately funded, because Athens's resources were channeled into civilian projects instead.[32]

Demosthenes offered practical solutions to these difficulties, including launching shorter campaigns (Dem. 1.27), rotating service to reduce the hardship to individuals (Dem. 2.31), shifting money earmarked for civic uses to military purposes, and paying the troops in full (Dem. 3.10–11, 33–34).

But he no longer considered such practical solutions sufficient. To convince his audience of the necessity of taking military action, he appealed to their masculine ethos. In the first *Olynthiac*, he asks whether listeners are not ashamed to lack the courage *(ou tolmēsete)* to do to Philip what Philip would do to the Athenians if he could (Dem. 1.24). In the first and third *Philippics*, he calls permitting Philip's expansion to go unchecked an act of "cowardice" *(anandria* in Dem. 4.42; *kakia* in Dem.

---

30. My discussion focuses on speeches whose authorship and actual delivery are fairly secure. Speeches whose authorship is uncertain or that do not focus on military expeditions (Dem. 5, 6, 10, 13–15) are referred to in the notes.

31. Badian 2000, 29–33, thinks that moderation did not help Demosthenes' political career.

32. Questioning campaigns: Lys. 25.30; Aes. 2.79, 173–77; 3.82; cf. Dem. 8.52; 10.59–60. Funding expeditions: see below. For the Athenians' preference for channeling revenue into the Theoric Fund, which paid for the festivals, see Dem. 1.19–20; 3.18–19; Badian 1995, 100–6; Leppin 1995, 558–66; E. M. Harris 1996.

9.67) that shames the entire nation, and declares that if the Athenians allow Philip to keep what he has taken without doing anything about it, "we are soft" *(malakizometha).*[33]

Seeking to stir up the agonistic drive in his listeners, he contrasts their conduct with that of the tremendously energetic and enterprising Philip and accuses them of passivity, regarded as a feminine trait.[34] In the second *Olynthiac,* he observes that while Philip participates in the toils of the campaign, we "sit here doing nothing" but procrastinate, pass resolutions, and ask questions (Dem. 2.22–25, 27). In his oration on the clash with Philip over the Chersonese, he rebukes the Athenians for their refusal to serve or pay war taxes, while Philip actively pursued his conquests.[35]

He also confronts the Athenians with their failure to take advantage of the opportunities that come their way. To Athenians, acting decisively at the right time was a sign of alertness, intelligence, and courage.[36] Thus in the first *Philippic* and the first *Olynthiac,* Demosthenes notes the Athenians' failure to seize the opportunities at hand because of their indecisiveness and dithering and warns that "we waste the time for action in preparation, and the opportunities for action will not wait on our inertia and pretence of ignorance." He also faults them for failure to face their difficulties resolutely; and worries that negligence and indolence will cost them dearly.[37] In the third *Olynthiac* and other speeches, Demosthenes tries to shame the Athenians into fighting, appealing to their high regard for leadership: their failure to do their duty is what has prevented them from stopping Philip, he says, and going to war will show them to be true leaders, worthy of their ancestors.[38]

When Demosthenes opposes war, he equates courage with rashness. But when he urges military action, he characterizes inaction as shameful and cowardly. He is able to accomplish this rhetorical feat because of the elasticity of the Athenian concept of masculine courage.

---

33. Dem. 9.35. The term *malakizometha* is from the unamended manuscript. Cf. Dem. 11.22; 15.23, 28.

34. Feminine passivity: Halperin 1990, 133; Loraux 1986, 147.

35. Dem. 8.21, 23, 36, 53. See also Dem. 6.1–4; 9.9–10; 10.3; cf. 14.15.

36. Courage and opportunities: Aes. 3.163; pp. 144–45 below. The Greek concept of *kairos* is most fully discussed by Trédé 1992. Opportunity and political leadership: Plato *Statesman,* with Lane 1998, 137–46, 182–94; Trédé 1992, 189–244, 291–94.

37. Dem. 4.37; 1.7–8, 14–15. See also Dem. 4.12; Trédé 1992, 232–35. For perversion of reality and satire in Dem. 4: Rowe 1968, esp. 368, 373; Harding 1994, 211–12; cf. Sampaix 1937, esp. 312–15. This, however, does not affect the point about missed opportunities.

38. Dem. 3.3, 23–24; 8.49; 9.19; 73–74. See also Dem. 6.8–11; 10.24–25, 46, 73; 13.33–35; cf. 11.22; 13.25.

THE MILITARY MEASURE

Military service was not just a testing ground for masculine courage in Athens. It was also a civic obligation anchored in law and a civic virtue expected of Athenian men.

Male citizens between the ages of eighteen and fifty-nine were subject to call-up as infantry or cavalry soldiers, initially from lists of conscripts *(katalogoi)*, then, from some time in the first half of the fourth century, by designated age groups.[39] Wealthy men, whether citizens or resident aliens, could be drafted to serve as trierarchs in the Athenian fleet, in which capacity they were usually required to equip and maintain the ships and crew as their *leitourgia*. Men who failed to perform their military duties adequately could be charged with a variety of offenses, including draft dodging, deserting their posts, throwing away their shields, and cowardice. Technically, each violation seems to have had its designated legal procedure, but they all came under the heading of public legal action *(graphē)* and carried the same severe penalty: *atimia*—loss of citizen's rights, including participation in public affairs, the right to plead a case in court in person, and the right to appear in certain public places, all on pain of summary arrest and execution.[40] The double title of a comedy by Aristophanes' contemporary Eupolis, *Astrateutoi* (Draft Dodgers) and *Androgunoi* (Womanish Men), suggests that their manhood was also subjected to mockery.[41]

In addition, the Athenian state incorporated the requirement of military service into several judicial and administrative procedures called *dokimasiai*. These procedures were applied to establish a man's qualifications for citizenship, whether by birth or naturalization, and for public office. Every candidate for state office, however minor, could be subjected to them. Although many reviews were probably pro forma, they could still provide an opportunity for the candidate's opponent to question his loyalty to the polis and disparage his battlefield experience, and for the candidate to proclaim his patriotism and military credentials.[42]

---

39. Hamel 1998, 24–28; Christ 2001.

40. *Atimia* was also hereditary. See MacDowell 1962, 110–11; Harrison 1971, 2: 32–33; Pritchett 1974, 2: 233–35, 238; Schwertfeger 1982, 264–65; Todd 1993, 106, 183.

41. Eupolis frs. 35–47 (K-A); Dover 1989, 144–45; Hubbard 1991, 82–83. Aristophanes, too, made jokes about throwing away one's shield and draft dodging: *Acharnians* 600–601; *Birds* 290; *Clouds* 353; *Frogs* 1014–15; *Women at the Thesmophoria* 827–29; *Wasps* 19, 592.

42. See esp. Lys. 16; 31. *Dokimasia:* Din. 2.17; Aes. 3.14–15; *Ath. Pol.* 45.2–3, 55.2–3; Bugh 1988, 53–54 (on cavalry); Rhodes 1993, 614–19; Hansen 1991, 218–20, 267; Robertson 2000; its political use and abuse: Roberts 1982, 20–21; Adelaye 1983.

It was possible, then, to introduce a man's military record in court as evidence of his moral and manly character, his contributions to the public weal, and his qualifications for political and military leadership.

Claimants and Defendants

Most of the claimants and defendants featured in the orations came from the social and financial elite. The military service expected of them included fighting and financial contributions in the form of war taxes and *leitourgiai* for military projects. Claimants and defendants often cited their or their ancestors' and relatives' performance of these duties as proof of good character and good citizenship, along with other marks of public virtue.[43]

Failure to serve marked a man as disreputable and was presented as grounds for conviction. Thus the speaker who accused Andocides of profaning the Mysteries asked the court: "On what consideration should you acquit Andocides? As a courageous soldier? But he has never left the city on any campaign" ([Lys.] 6.46). Nichomachus's prosecutor posed a similar question: "Why should anyone acquit him? Is it because he has participated in many land and naval battles facing the enemy as a courageous man *[anēr agathos]*?"[44]

Politicians

Military service was regarded as an important qualification for public office and political leadership.[45] Mantitheus tells his hearers in the *dokimasia* examining his credentials to serve on the Council that he dwells on the fervor with which he carried out his military duty in case any of them "is angry with persons who claim the right to manage the city's affairs but run away from its dangers" (Lys. 16.17).

In his oration arguing against awarding Demosthenes a crown for service to the city, Aeschines seeks to undermine Demosthenes' political contribution by repeatedly, and perhaps falsely, asserting that he had fled the battle of Chaeroneia.[46] In *On the False Embassy*, Demosthenes iden-

---

43. E.g., Is. 4.27–29; 5.41–46; 7.37–41; Lys. 21.3, 6–11, 24–25; 18.21, 24–25; 19.56–57; 25.4, 12–13; fr. 45 (Medda).

44. Lys. 30.26. See also Dem. 54.44; Lys. 10.27–28; 21.20; 26.21–24.

45. For the division in fourth-century Athens between military and political leadership, see Dem. 18.245–47; Isoc. 8.54–55; Davies 1984, 124–27; Hansen 1989a, 25–33; cf. 34–72; Ober 1989, 119–21; Hansen 1991, 268–71.

46. Aes. 3.148, 152, 159, 175–76, 181, 187, 244, 253; cf. Din. 1.12, 71, 79, 81. See also Plut. *Dem.* 20.2; [Plut.] *Moralia* 845F; Aulus Gellius 17.21.31. Carlier 1990, 221;

tifies Aeschines as a pretender to military merit, noting that he denigrated the military service of the demos "as if he himself were a stupendous warrior" (Dem. 19.112–13). These imputations did not necessarily accord with the facts. In response, Aeschines recounts the military expeditions in which he has participated and the distinctions that he has won (Aes. 2.167–169)—a reply that further shows the importance of military service for a public career.[47]

Apparently, the Athenians identified courage and morality as martial qualities and, at least to some extent, viewed soldiers as superior to politicians. This is evident in a story told by Aeschines in his effort to deny Timarchus the right to speak in public, that is, to engage in politics. At a meeting of the Spartan Council of Elders, Aeschines says, a man who was an excellent speaker but lived shamefully had almost persuaded the Spartans to vote his way. But just as the Council was about to vote, one of the elders warned against following the advice of an immoral man, and called forward another man, less talented in speech, but a splendid warrior, distinguished by justice and self-control *(dikaiosunē* and *enkrateia),* to reiterate more or less what the first had said, the point being that the Spartans should not heed a criminal and a coward.[48]

The story links morality to soldiering in several ways. It is set in Sparta, renowned for both its asceticism and its military might; it depicts the Spartan elders as respected, feared, and elected to office because they live moderately and morally *(sōphrōn);* and it contrasts a pretender to political influence with a preferred political actor in whom military prowess is combined with justice and self-control. Allegorically, the pretender refers to Timarchus and Demosthenes; Aeschines plays the role of the respected elder; and Sparta is the state whose wisdom Athens should emulate.[49]

The story identifies the political message with the messenger rather than with its content.[50] By describing the preferred speaker as less tal-

Worthington 1992, 147–48; and Mossé 1994, 115, regard the charge against Demosthenes as slanderous.

47. Cf. Dem. 19.282. For Demosthenes' assertion and Aeschines' response: Burkhardt 1996, 237–39; Paulsen 1999, 406–9.

48. Aes. 1.180–81. Plutarch liked Aeschines' story: *Moralia* 41b, 801b–c; cf. 233a; Aulus Gellius 18.3; Philo 195b, and see also Bers 1997, 162; Fisher 2001, 327–31.

49. That Aeschines brought no evidence of Timarchus shirking military service or acting in a cowardly fashion suggests that no such evidence existed: Burckhardt 1996, 238, n. 302; Fisher 2001, 250.

50. The idea that the character of the speaker affected the value of his message is stated more directly in Aes. 1.31 and Isoc. 15.278.

ented in speech than the "corrupt Spartan," Aeschines' story opposes the "speech" through which so much of politics is conducted to the more obvious and more masculine "action" of the military man.

Generals and High Military Commanders

Fourth-century Athenian generals were more professional than their predecessors, more instrumental in affecting the city's military fortunes, and accordingly received greater official honors.[51] The Athenians know how to honor brave men, Lycurgus says: other cities put up statues of their athletes, but Athens erects statues of victorious generals and the slayers of the tyrants (Lyc. 1.51).

The primary criterion for a great commander was obviously victory on the field (see esp. Dem. *Pr.* 50.3; cf. Lys. 18.3; Isoc. 15.116). Commanders meeting this criterion were commended in the orations for their personal courage (Din. 1.76), leadership (Hyp. 6.11, 15, 24), self-sacrifice (Dem. 20.82; Hyp. 6.10), probity (Dem. 20.82; Hyp. 6.9–10), for defending the city's inhabitants (Dem. 20.68–69, 72; Hyp. 6.35–36), for preserving or restoring its liberties, and for augmenting its honor and wealth (Dem. 20.74–80; Hyp. 6.11). In eulogizing the general Leosthenes, who fell in the Lamian War against Macedonia, Hyperides adds prudence *(phronēsis)* (6.38), mastery of controllable events (6.13–14; cf. Dem. 4.39), and foresight and strategic ability (6.15). He also praises Leosthenes for his ability to persuade the allies of Athens to accept his control (6.14) and to inspire bravery, endurance, loyalty, and sacrifice among his troops (6.3, 23–24, 29, 35–40). The general Chabrias is commended for protecting his troops from harm (Dem. 20.82).

Exaggerated though the praise may have been, the victorious commander emerges as the epitome of Athenian masculinity: outperforming others in the most competitive of endeavors, showing personal courage in the face of death, conferring benefits on the community; and, furthermore, possessing many virtues that win him admiration not only on the battlefield but also in the personal and community roles in which Athenian men were expected to excel.[52]

High military commanders appear to have been held in greater esteem

---

51. Professionalism of military leadership: Lengauer 1979. Honoring generals: Sinclair 1988, 177–79; Hakkarainen 1997, 20, 24–28.

52. For the ideal Hellenistic general, including his masculine characteristics, see Beston 2000.

than other men, including, and perhaps especially, politicians. Aeschines brands Demosthenes a dangerous usurper of power who, although a mere orator and politician, has the audacity to claim that he has benefited the city more than the generals who have fought for it, and who has threatened to sue any generals who oppose his proposals to go to war with Philip. He is, in fact, little more than a man of words, who boasts of nonexistent accomplishments, as opposed to accomplished generals who lack verbal ability to describe their achievements. Another speaker belittles Demosthenes' services as an envoy as a mere fraction of the services that the general Timotheus, a man of deeds rather than of words, and his father, the general Conon, had rendered Athens.[53]

Reservations about the Military Measure

Yet even while Athenians associated military service and military men with personal and civic virtues, they also had reservations about the military yardstick.

One concern was that a man's military record could be misused to deflect the course of justice. In a case against Eratosthenes, whom he charged with responsibility for his brother's death during the rule of the infamous Thirty (404–403), Lysias warned the jury that Eratosthenes might resort to what he described as a "customary" expedient among Athenians of building a case not on its merits but on service as soldiers, commanders of warships, and conquerors of cities. Lysias challenged Eratosthenes to prove that he had inflicted as many injuries on the enemies of Athens as on its citizens (Lys. 12.38–40, and see also Dem. 21.172).

Moreover, most of the praises of generals in the orations are of generals fallen in battle or long dead, who had become exemplary figures, free of human flaws and limitations (Dem. 18.314–319). The orations are more critical of living generals and commanders. In his first *Philippic,* Demosthenes observes acidly that "every general has been tried for his life in the people's courts two or three times, but none has dared to fight the enemy to the death" (Dem. 4.47). In two speeches written by Dinarchus, speakers accuse commanders of bribe-taking (Din. 1.74) and treachery (Din. 3.12–13). Demosthenean speakers refer to generals violating the terms of their command and committing financial impropri-

---

53. Contrasting Demosthenes with generals: Aes. 3.145–46, 181, 229; Din. 1.16–17. Of course, politicians (including envoys) and generals were sometimes grouped positively: Lys. 26.20; Dem. 18.204–5; 21.145; 24.135; Aes. 2.184; Isoc. 12.143.

eties ([Dem.] 49.9) and charge them with deception, unreliability ([Dem.] 50.15, 23), defrauding the state (Dem. 24.173), and failing to give good council (Dem. 18.170). Isocrates reproaches the Athenians for electing persons of poor judgment and low intelligence as generals (Isoc. 8.54–55), and for choosing men of robust physique rather than sagacity and good citizenship (Isoc. 15.106–27). Not surprisingly, then, during the period discussed in this study, a fair number of generals were convicted and severely punished for failing to give a satisfactory account of their performances and of the money they had spent on their campaigns.[54] It is significant that the orations often criticize generals as a class, which suggests that, alongside the tribute paid to them, there were doubts about their probity, loyalty, public spirit, judgment, and even military competence, as well as resentment of their arrogance and influence. Demosthenes' observation that generals make easy scapegoats for the failings of their troops seems to have been on target.[55]

Perhaps more fundamentally, the orations also provide indications of an agonistic apprehension about the impact on the rank and file of the city's armies of the civic honor and esteem accorded victorious generals. The exclusive attribution of victory and the honor that derived from it to the victorious general clashed both with reality and with Athens's democratic ideology. On the field, the general fought alongside the rank and file, and his contribution to the actual fighting was much the same as that of every other soldier.[56] Ideologically, singling out the commander conflicted with the conviction that victory was the product of a collective masculine effort, embodied in the phalanx or the trireme.[57]

The apprehension is evident in Hyperides' funeral oration for the fallen in the Lamian War. Although he takes the unusual course of emphasizing the individual accomplishments of the general Leosthenes, Hyperides feels obliged to add that his praises commend not only Leosthenes' leadership but also the courage of all the troops (Hyp. 6.15). In his argument against awarding Demosthenes a crown, Aeschines reminds his hearers that when the forefathers of the Athenians had built war memorials, they had refrained from inscribing the names of the vic-

---

54. Pritchett 1974, 2: 4–33; Roberts 1982, esp. 178; Hansen 1975, esp. 74–120; Knox 1985, esp. 135–38, 142; Sinclair 1988, 163–76; Hamel 1998, esp. 135, 145–57.
55. Dem. 3.17. Blaming military defeats on generals: Lys. 2.58; Dem. 60.21–22; cf. Dem. 18.245; 19.147; 58.55; Pr. 30.1; pp. 68–70 above. When it served a speaker's purpose, however, the blame could be shifted to a rival politician: Dem. 19.334–35.
56. Pritchett 1974, 2: 276–90; Wheeler 1991; Beston 2000, 321–22.
57. Thomas 1989, 214–15.

torious generals on them, lest they seem to be honoring the generals more than the ordinary warriors (Aes. 3.183–86).

Andocides manipulates these apprehensions, saying that military commanders benefit their country by exposing their soldiers to danger and fatigue and by spending public money. When they err, the demos pays the price. Moreover, although the demos rewards military leaders with honors and crowns, the far worthier man *(polu pleistou axios anēr)*—namely, the lower-level soldier—is the one who puts his own life on the line.[58]

There seems to have been, as well, some resentful apprehension of generals as men who abuse their powers and look down on those who elected them. A Lysian speaker, who had been fined by his generals for allegedly slandering them, protests that the generals had unjustly called him up for service repeatedly, slandered him personally, and unlawfully fined him. He adds that their behavior shows that they held justice, law and "the many," in contempt. He also complains about their overall disdainful, impious and violent ways (Lys .9.6–7, 11, 13–18).

The Athenians' ambivalence about this, like their ambivalence about other matters, enabled orators to assume contradictory positions in accordance with their interests. A speaker who called up a general as a supporting speaker relied on the public's respect for generals' authority and prestige. But he could also stir up resentment of their perceived arrogance, abuse of a privileged position, and lack of commitment to the public good.[59]

In *Against Leptines,* Demosthenes endorses the lavish rewards the people have bestowed on the generals Conon and Chabrias so that he can denounce a proposal that the Assembly abolish the exemptions from certain *leitourgiai* that had been accorded to men who had made extraordinary contributions to the city, as well as to their descendants (Dem. 20.68–87). But, in a speech written for Aristocrates' prosecutor, Demosthenes argues that the mercenary leader Charidemus does not deserve honors and reminds the jury (much as Aeschines had) that their Athenian ancestors had shown that gratitude to victorious generals

58. And. 2.17–18. Missiou 1992, 42, rightly observes in And. 2.17–18 an oligarchic claim for *aretē* that is based on facing risk and financial sacrifice; cf. Thuc. 8.65.3; *Ath. Pol.* 29.5. But it surely struck a chord in the hearts of democrats as well; cf. Lys. 28.4. Andocides' complaint comes with a lineage: Homer *Iliad* 2.225–42; cf. Euripides *Andromache* 693–98.

59. Aes. 2.149; Lys. 14.21–22; Aes. 1.32; cf. Lys. 15.4, 8; Aes. 3.196; Isoc. 15.131; Rubinstein 2000, 166–67; Fisher 2001, 274–76.

should be expressed, not by erecting bronze statues or dispensing excessive rewards, but "in a manner that was worthy both to the recipients and themselves," namely, by electing them to command the brave and noble men of Athens (Dem. 23.196–98; cf. 13.21–22).

THE DOUBLE STANDARD

The centrality of military service in the evaluation of manhood stands in contrast to rebukes of Athenians for shirking their duty to fight and pay war taxes, hiring mercenaries to fight in their stead, and responding slowly, and ineffectively to the military threats they faced. While these charges were probably exaggerated, they were not groundless.[60] Athenians had many reasons for their reluctance to go to war. Nonetheless, although the laws against dereliction of duty applied to all violators without distinction by social class, the orations suggest that there was considerably more sympathy for men of lower social status and means who opted out of serving than for men of higher social status and means who did the same.

Affluent men who met the legal requirements for service might be faulted for failing to meet the social expectations of them. Although Athenian law permitted trierarchs to contract out their military service, a Demosthenean speaker reminds his audience that following an Athenian naval defeat, trierarchs who had contracted their duty to others had been charged with treason and desertion (Dem. 51.8). Demosthenes condemns Meidias for having contracted out of his ship to avoid danger and compares him unfavorably with other trierarchs who had served in person.[61] Two orations also reported charges of desertion against upperclass men whose valued public activities exempted them from military duty. Meidias had hired a sycophant to charge him with deserting his expedition to Euboia, where he was to serve as a hoplite, Demosthenes says, even though his role as a khorēgos (producer) of a chorus at the Dionysia Festival exempted him from military service (Dem. 21.103).

---

60. Shirking obligations: Dem. 1.6, 24; 2.25–27; 8.21, 23; cf. Dem. 4.7; 14.15. Hiring mercenaries: Dem. 3.35; 4.24; Isoc. 8.44–45; cf. Dem. 4.9–10. Ineffective responses: e.g., Dem. 2.12–13; 3.4–5; 4.26–27, 36–37. Assessing the Athenian military policy and conduct: Burckhardt 1995, 126–33, esp. 128 n. 126, 129 n. 129; 1996, 181–223, esp. 220; cf. Pritchett 1974, 2: 104–12; Hanson 1995, 483 n. 13. On the navy, see Amit 1965, 31–34; Cawkwell 1984.

61. Dem. 21.155, 163–66. Substitute trierarchs: Amit 1965, 111–12; Jordan 1975, 73, 79–80, 134–37; Cawkwell 1984, 340–41; MacDowell 1990, 372–73; Gabrielsen 1994, 96–101, 220. Expectation of personal service: Gabrielsen 1994, 37, 97, 237 n. 46.

Mantitheus's brother, also a hoplite, was charged with desertion even though he was entitled to an exemption as a chorister (Dem. 39.16–17). Apollodorus accuses Stephanus of having obtained an unwarranted conviction for desertion against a tax collector whose duty exempted him from service.[62] Although convictions were not always obtained, the charges of desertion and criticisms of contracting out suggest that public expectations of the elite were higher than the legal requirements.

The orations convey the sense that when the masses shouldered a military burden, members of the elite should as well. This sense is evident in two cases in the Lysian corpus: in one, the speaker claims that the wealthy and politically active Andocides had never fought for Athens, while many men had sacrificed their lives or money for the city ([Lys.] 6.46); in the other, the speaker asserts that Alcibiades the Younger—a member of the elite by virtue of his birth and lifestyle (Lys. 14.23–28)—had avoided danger while other soldiers had shown up at their assigned positions despite their sickness or poverty.[63]

Athenians appear to have expected less of the poor. In a speech charging Polycles with failing to relieve him of his duties as a trierarch at the stipulated time, Apollodorus lists the great financial and personal damage this dereliction of duty had caused him.[64] But Apollodorus applies different standards to the rowers who manned his ship. Unlike the trierarchs, who were men of means and social status, the rowers were drawn mostly (although not entirely) from among poor citizens (the *thētes*) or aliens or slaves. They were not usually conscripted but hired for service.[65]

62. [Dem.] 59.27. For a reconstruction of the case in Dem. 39.16–17: MacDowell 1989a, 71–2; cf. Carey and Reid 1985, 179–81. For Dem. 21.103 (and 21.15): MacDowell 1990, 9, 238; Pritchett 1974, 2: 233, n. 11. On [Dem.] 59.27, see Kapparis 1999, 222–25. One or two Athenian chorus directors are reported to have been convicted for not performing military service, but the circumstances of the cases and their economic status are unknown: Dem. 21.58–60; MacDowell 1990, 279–81.

63. Lys. 14.14–15; cf. Ant. 87 B 57 (D-K). The extant oratorical sources report considerably more on public enforcement of the laws against desertion against prominent hoplites, sea captains, and the well-to-do than against seamen. See Lys. 10.1; 14 and 15; Dem. 21.103, 110, 163–65; 39.17; 51.8; 59.26–27; cf. Dem. 18.107; 50.63; Aes. 2.148; Xen. *Hell.* 6.2.13, and, possibly, Lyc. 1.77, 147. Charges of evading service in nonoratorical sources: Storey 1989; Christ 2001, 409. The difference may be partly explained by the elite's exploitation of the legal system in their rivalry for power and prestige, although such exploitation must have been enhanced by the demanding expectations of military service of the upper class.

64. [Dem.] 50. For the speech, see Jordan 1975, 212–15; Cawkwell 1984, 334–40; Trevett 1992, 12–13, 36–41.

65. Manning the ships: *Ath. Pol.* 24; [Xen.] *Ath. Pol.* 1.2; Jordan 1975, 102–3, 202, 208, 210–30; Morrison 1984. Rosivach (1985 [1992], esp. 41, 53–57) and Gabrielsen (1994, 106–8) believe that service was voluntary, but M. H. Hansen (1985, 22–23; cf. 1991, 37, 45–46) argues that conscripted *thētes* were used on a regular basis. Slaves as row-

In 362, however, when Apollodorus was called to serve as a trierarch and to take a ship on a mission in the northern Aegean, members of the demes (townships) were conscripted for naval and hoplitic duty. The conscription was apparently necessary because Athens faced some serious crises.[66] It is against this background that Apollodorus reports successive instances of rowers' failing to report or deserting his ship ([Dem.] 50.6–16, 22–23).

The sources do not specify the extent of desertion or how typical this behavior was.[67] Nonetheless, although it is clear that the dedication and patriotism of these rowers could not be relied on in the city's hour of need, Apollodorus's report shows considerable understanding of them. He presents the failure of the conscripted sailors to report for duty (except for what he describes as a few incompetents), and the subsequent desertion of the sailors hired to replace them, in a factual manner, with little, if any, moral aspersion ([Dem.] 50.7, 11). His focus is, instead, on the idea that they could not be expected to serve without pay. A ship "comes apart," Apollodorus told the jurors, when its sailors were not paid; sailors are prone to desert when they have no way of providing for their households while they are at sea.[68] He gave the sailors who stayed with his ship when it temporarily returned to Athens extra money to leave with their *oikoi,* because he understood their need and the strain they were under ([Dem.] 50.12–13). He explains the sailors' third desertion by stressing that they had not been paid for two months and could see no prospect of being paid in the near future. Although there is a note of criticism of the more skilled rowers who had left him for a better pay ([Dem.] 50.14–16; cf. 50.65), Apollodorus points an accusatory finger at the state and the generals for not meeting their obligations to them. In describing another incident of desertion, he suggests that because the sailors had been paid barely enough to sustain themselves and were hungry, they had come to the end of their tether and did not want to continue to endure the fatigue, exposure to the elements, and danger of protracted military service at sea ([Dem.] 50.22–23).

---

ers: Rosivach 1985 [1992], 51–53; Burckhardt 1995, 120–26; 1996, 96–98, 105 n. 140; Hunt 1998, esp. 40–41; 87–101 (disputing Welwei 1974).

66. Cawkwell 1984, 335–37; Burckhardt 1995, 124–25.

67. For desertion in the last stage of the Peloponnesian war, see Gabrielsen 1994, 122–25, and add Plut. *Lysander* 4.4–5.

68. Many of the hired rowers were probably Athenian citizens. Grain at the time was scarce and expensive, which made Apollodorus's offer of cash for rowing attractive. Cawkwell 1984, 338, denies that the rowers were citizens, but cf. Hornblower 1991, 1: 198–99.

Apollodorus shows no analogous sympathy for Polycles' dereliction of his trierarchic duties ([Dem.] 50.24). Citing Polycles' statement that he would not take the ship before his co-trierarchs showed up ([Dem.] 50.37), he deems it a poor excuse, and urges the jury to uphold the law and punish Polycles so as to preserve the honor of the law and to deter other trierarchs from failing to serve ([Dem.] 50.57, 65–66).

It is possible that Apollodorus's presentation of the sailors' conduct and motives aimed to deflect charges that they had deserted him because of his deficient trierarchy and poor treatment of them. Moreover, his display of understanding for the motives of the deserters probably did not hurt his case, since it was not unlikely that many jurors had experienced similar predicaments. Nonetheless, the fact that he excuses the rowers' conduct and could make Polycles' tardiness and poor execution of his military duty appear worse than the rowers' draft dodging and abandoning of their ship shows a double standard in relation to dereliction of military duty and links the expectations of military service to social class and economic status.

Apollodorus takes care to show Polycles' dereliction of duty, but he also emphasizes his own fulfillment of military duties incumbent on him. He recounts the financial sacrifices he made during his service, and stresses that he served his entire term, and even more, in person—that is, that he had met both the legal requirements and the social expectations of military service. He had not behaved like one of those disorderly *(akosmoi)* rogues *(ponēroi)* but was sincere in his pursuit of honor *(philotimia)*, useful *(khrēstos)* to the city, and well-disciplined *(eutaktos)*. In contrasting his behavior to theirs, Apollodorus lays claim to the patriotism, prestige, and masculinity associated with military service among the elite.[69]

Judging from Apollodorus's explanation of the rowers' motives, Athenians recognized that the rich could afford to serve and thus had no compelling reason not to fulfill their masculine duty. This view seems to have been behind the complaint made by another trierarch, possibly Demosthenes (Blass 1893, 242–49), about the injustice of punishing poor sailors who deserted, but not trierarchs who did not personally sail with their ships (Dem. 51.11).

---

69. [Dem.] 50.63–64; cf. Isoc. 18.58–61. It has been claimed that Athenian rowers suffered from a low military prestige: see n. 20 above. I do not think, however, that it affected attitudes toward their desertion or draft dodging, and in any case, the oratorical corpus provides no evidence for the inferior ranking of rowing in comparison to hoplite or cavalry service. See Plato *Laws* 707a–b; Hunt 1998, 123–26; Strauss 1996, 320–21; 2000, 276.

Like other matters related to Athenian manhood, the uses of military service seem to have been affected by class rivalry. Along with the link between military excellence and upper-class status, there was a perception of the affluent elite as soft and unruly—and thus unmanly—warriors. In Plato's *Republic,* Socrates tells of lean, sunburned poor soldiers mocking the fat, pale, out-of-shape rich soldiers who fight alongside them.[70] Xenophon describes elite warriors (cavalrymen and hoplites) as insubordinate, and characterizes naval forces, manned mostly by the lower class, as disciplined and orderly.[71] Demosthenes contrasts wealthy Meidias, who had gone to war in a silver *astrabē* (mule chair), taking along his wine and goblets, with the tough and disciplined infantry, who appeared in good formation and properly armed (Dem. 21.133). The stereotype is also evident in two other orations, where signs of effeminacy observed in members in the lower classes are blamed on their elite leaders (Dem. 8.32; [Dem.] 50.35).

The elite may well have had to contend in court with both higher expectations and suspicions of deficiencies. But an understanding of the financial constraints that impeded the military performance of the masses was not necessarily joined with esteem. At least some members of the affluent elite viewed the masses as failing to shoulder an equal share of the military burden. In the *Second Olynthiac,* for example, Demosthenes ironically divides the Athenian Assembly into three classes: politicians who behave like tyrants; the *leitourgikos* class who pay for and serve in the military; and the rest—that is, the masses—whose only business is to vote against the second class.[72]

However, Demosthenes sometimes has wealthy and powerful adversaries, whom he depicts as deficient in their own military service, express contempt for the military service of the demos. In *On the False Embassy,* Demosthenes reports that Aeschines descended from the speakers' podium after the demos had shouted him down during deliberations over a peace treaty with Philip. There were many who heckled, Aeschines declared, but few who fought when the need arose, "as if he [Aeschines] himself were a stupendous warrior" (Dem. 19.112–13). In his speech

---

70. Plato *Rep.* 8.556c–d. Cf. Eur. *Phoenician Women* 597. Plato is speaking of oligarchy here, but the *topoi* of the fearful, effeminate rich and the courageous poor are applicable to Athenian democracy as well: see Grossmann 1950, 106–11; Eherenberg 1951, 243; cf. Humphreys 1993, xvii–xix; Spence 1993, 198–202. The need for physical conditioning in battle: Plato *Laws* 832e–833a; *Protagoras* 326b–c; Xen. *Mem.* 3.12.2; cf. Ridley 1979, 528–47.

71. Xen. *Mem.* 3.5.18–19. Cf. Thuc. 2.89.9; Xen. *Oec.* 8.4–7; but see Isoc. 12.116.

72. Dem. 2.30; cf. Dem. 19.113; Aristoph. *Assembly Women* 197–98.

against Meidias, Demosthenes reports that Meidias blamed Athens's military setbacks on the reluctance of the demos to serve, refused to contribute to the city's war efforts because the money would be doled out to the demos, and refused to serve as a trierarch because the demos refused to embark on the ships (Dem. 21.202–4). Demosthenes' purpose in both cases was to sway the jury against his rivals. Yet his presentations also point to the existence of elitist complaints about the people's poor military spirit.

Thus, the military yardstick for judging character and contribution to the civic good was complicated by class considerations and rivalries. The uneven application of this measure to the rich and poor made it possible for the wealthy to boast of military records as a sign of civic virtue and masculinity, while looking down on the demos as less manly. The demos applied the military yardstick more stringently to their social superiors, but did not accept the implication that their lesser service made them less masculine and less worthy of honor and social esteem.

In sum, despite the changing realties of war in the fourth century, Athenian public discourse held on tenaciously to archaic (or archaizing) values and perceptions of military service. The hoplitic ethos, which highlighted honor, cooperation, disciplined obedience, solidarity, patriotism, and striving for excellence, as well as the attainment of victory in a well-regulated, open, and face-to-face confrontation between nonprofessional soldiers, underpinned the image of the ideal military figure, whether simple soldier or general, but also that of the desirable citizen and man.

The elasticity of the concept of courage, a quintessential masculine value, made it possible for orators to argue both for and against military action. And the belief that key masculine values—courage, strength, endurance, fraternity, order, self-control, discipline, self-sacrifice, loyalty, service to the state—were particularly well manifested in military service made it a standard by which Athenians could judge one another in court, politics, and public office.

Nonetheless, the importance of military service as a measure of manhood and a man's fitness for public office did not mean that military men were unequivocally idealized, or that all men who failed to serve were unequivocally condemned. Generals as a group came in for severe criticism, and the military yardstick was applied unevenly to the rich and poor.

CHAPTER 6

The Struggle over Power

Next to sexuality, the most common theme in studies of masculinity, modern and ancient alike, is the drive for power. A few examples will serve to illustrate this point: The sociologist Steven Goldberg argues that patriarchy is a universal pattern because it is anchored in men's preoccupation with power, rooted in their unique neuro-endocrinological makeup. The psychoanalysts Gerald Stechler and Samuel Kaplan attribute contemporary men's aggressive power struggles to the male need to assert the self, arguing that men relate to the world under the assumption that passivity will undermine their identity. As for "the Greek world of war and adventure," Nicole Loraux asserts, "power is in essence and by definition virility." Michel Foucault explains Greek sexuality as a product of the struggle for power in the community to which the sexual partners belonged.[1]

This chapter focuses on the struggle over political power between the demos and the orators, against the backdrop of Athenian perceptions and expectations about masculinity. *Demos* is a multifaceted term that can denote either the common people or, as used in this chapter, the Athenian citizenry, or people, as a whole in their capacity as decision-

---

1. Goldberg 1993, esp. 77–102. Stechler and Kaplan 1980; cf. Stechler 1987; Loraux 1995, 119; Foucault 1978, 1985; and see Halperin 1990. Cf. Loraux 1993, 87–88, for Athenian politics and civic imagery as exclusively masculine; and Van Northwick 1998 for manhood in Sophoclean Oedipus. The following is an expanded and revised version of Roisman 2004.

makers in the governing and judicial institutions of Athens.[2] In democratic Athens, the power of the people was considered supreme, yet litigants and political leaders sought to harness that power to attain goals and outcomes desirable to themselves, the community, and the state. Promises that adherence to their advice would result in collective benefits failed to relieve the tensions between speakers and their audience, who were aware of, and sensitive to, their own primacy and control. This chapter examines the asymmetrical relationship between speakers and their audiences and the key ways in which this relationship affected the manner and contents of their addresses.

THE MANLY DEMOS: THE INSTITUTIONAL AND IDEOLOGICAL BASES OF THE POWER AND MANLINESS OF THE DEMOS

Athenian democracy invested the demos, that is, the entire citizen body, with manliness, both by conferring supreme political power on them and by attributing masculine qualities, especially courage and freedom, to them.

Athenian democracy granted all adult male citizens the same civic and political rights, regardless of social class: state benefits, representation in the judicial system, equal treatment under the law, and the right to participate, vote, and hold office in the political, administrative, and judicial bodies of the polis. The Assembly *(ekklēsia)* passed laws, elected officials, served as a court on special occasions, and discussed proposals brought to it by the Council or individuals. The Council *(boulē)* was an administrative body that supervised officials and state functions and prepared the agenda for the Assembly. The jury courts dealt with most judicial matters in the city. The Assembly, whose average attendance may have been 6,000 men, was open to all citizens who wished to be present. The Council consisted of 500 members chosen by lot from candidates from all the districts of Athens. The jury courts, which varied in size and number, consisted of citizens-volunteers who were selected by lot to form panels of *dikastai,* or jurors. Men who attended the Assembly received modest payment for their services. The officeholders, who also received payment, were either selected by lot from all Athenian citizens or elected by popular vote. Although schematic and simplified, this description of the working of Athens's government and judicial system shows that in this democratic city, the demos reigned supreme.

2. Esp. Hansen 1991, 303.

Because political and judicial decisions were made by majority vote, the masses controlled these institutions rather than any individual or subgroup, including the politically active orator-politicians. These self-selected individuals, variously and often interchangeably termed *rhētores* (orators), *hoi legontai* (speakers), *sumbouloi* (advisers), *politeuomenoi* (politicians), and *dēmagōgoi* (leaders of the people, demagogues), stood out from the citizen body as a whole.[3] Drawn mostly from the political and social elite of Athens, they were conspicuous in popular deliberations, and because of the intense rivalries among them, they frequently resorted to the courts. They were not elected but depended upon the citizenry for support in the various governing and judicial bodies.

Speakers stress the political and judicial power of the demos. In his speech against Meidias, Demosthenes told the jurors, "The laws are strong thanks to you, and you thanks to the laws" (Dem. 21.223–24). Apollodorus, in his speech against Neaera, felt the need to caution the people that the law set limits on their power: "Even though the demos of the Athenians is the supreme *kurios [kuriōtatos]* of everything in the polis, and can do whatever it wishes . . . it has laid down laws *[nomoi]* for itself according to which it must act in making someone a citizen when it so wishes" ([Dem.] 59.88). Thus, despite the difference in their views of the relationship between the law and the power of the demos, both speakers viewed the demos as holding supreme power, able to do pretty much as it wished.[4]

Speakers seem eager to acknowledge the demos's power to decide on critical issues (Ant. 2.2.13; Din. 1.106–7), reward and punish (Dem. 19.177), or consider proposals and supervise state organs (And. 2.19). Even though certain Athenians had on occasion risen to great power in the Assembly, Demosthenes asserts in *On the False Embassy*, "in the law courts, no one to this day has ever become more powerful than you, or the laws, or the [juror's] oath" (Dem. 19.297). In *Against Leptines*, he observes that, in contrast to Sparta and other oligarchies, "among us the people are the *kurios* of the state, and [we have] curses and laws and other safeguards to prevent anyone else from becoming the *kurios*" (Dem. 20.107). Although obviously designed to impress the jurors, these

---

3. For the terms and their ranges of meanings: Dover 1974, 25–26; Mossé 1984; Hansen 1989, 1–24, 93–127; Ober 1989, 105–8, 110–18; Hansen 1991, 143–45; Mossé 1994, 124–53; Yunis 1996, 7–12, 272–73.
4. For the structure of power in Athens, see, conveniently, Kapparis 1999, 360–62; Marowetz 2000, 142–50. Practical curtailments on the demos' power: Hansen 1991, 300–304; Mossé 1994, esp. 173–78.

remarks reflect the prevailing view of the demos as the supreme power in the polis.

Because power and privilege were closely associated with masculinity in Athenian thinking, the demos's political power invested it, a priori, with masculinity. The association is evident in Demosthenes' contemptuous description of the people as "most manly" *(andreiotatos)* for resigning their control, power, and honor to politicians, who, he claims, abuse, humble, and subordinate them (Dem. 3.30–32, and below).

The democratic ideology of Athens also bolstered masculinity. In his funeral oration for the dead in the battle of Chaeroneia, for example, Demosthenes assumes an association between the frank speech *(parrhesia)* of Athenian democracy and the masculine values of honor, patriotism, and military valor.[5] Similar links are to be found in Alcibiades the Younger's claim that his democratic ancestors had taught the citizens courage, which enabled them to defeat the barbarians at Marathon single-handedly (Isoc. 16.27).

Of the masculine qualities identified with Athenian democracy, freedom had special meaning.[6] Free status, attained at birth, but also through manumission, was a sine qua non of Athenian citizenship; only free citizens could speak, vote, and hold public office. The orations consistently associate freedom with qualities and behavior that are becoming to a man, and slavery, whether literal or figurative, with unmasculine behavior (e.g., Dem. 45.27; Dem. 24.124; Aes. 2.173). Aeschines, Demosthenes sneers, "cowered like a slave" (Dem. 19.210). He also associates freedom with the ability to feel manly shame, contrasting this with the slave's fear of corporal punishment (Dem. 8.51). Aeschines calls Timarchus a "slave to the most shameful lusts" and lauds chaste Athenians who live like "free and honorable men."[7]

The orations consistently identify democracy with freedom and present individual Athenians or the entire demos, especially the exalted demos of times past, as having fought and died in the name of liberty (Dem. 15.17; 18.208; 59.96; Hyp. 6.10, 16, 24, 40). Demosthenes

---

5. Dem. 60.25–26. The oligarchs naturally had their own political definition of manhood: see, e.g., Theophrastus *Characters* 26.2. Freedom of speech: Raaflaub 1980; Halliwell 1991a; Monoson 1994b, 174–85; Sluiter and Rosen 2004.

6. Greek freedom: Raaflaub 1983; 1985, esp. 233–46. Freedom and masculinity: Just 1985; Cartledge 1998b, 56; cf. Svenbro 1988, 188; Cartledge 2002, 118–51; Marowetz 2000, 33–41. Aristotle *Pol.* 1317b10–16, however, is critical of democratic freedom.

7. Aes.1.42, 156. Servility and dishonorable or unrestrained conduct: Lys. 10.2; Dem. 22.53–54; cf. Dem. 18.296. Slaves as deficient in reason and intellect: DuBois 1991, 6; Rosivach 1999, 142–57. See also Hunt 1998, 50–53, 126–32.

rouses his hearers against Philip by telling them that the Macedonian is resolved to destroy them because he knows that, given their tradition of liberty and fighting to preserve it, they will stand up to him and never consent to be slaves (Dem. 8.42, 60). The speaker of a funeral oration attributed to Lysias reminds his audience that the restorers of Athenian democracy in 404/3 had been "persuaded by [their] nature" to imitate "the ancient valor *[aretē]* of their ancestors" and had fought for freedom (Lys. 2.61–62). Athenian men were expected to choose death over slavery (Dem. 18.205; cf. Lys. 2.62). The possession of liberty confirmed the manhood of the demos, and men who fought for freedom were portrayed as having demonstrated the prototypically masculine virtues of courage, honor, service to their country, and *arēte*.[8]

The orations also suggest that the demos perceived themselves as morally superior to most of the orator-politicians who addressed them, and to the members of the elite whose cases they judged. In an oration he wrote for the prosecutor of Timocrates, Demosthenes contrasts the high-mindedness *(megalophrosunē)* of the jurors and their uncompromising upholding of justice with the self-serving conduct of politicians, who make laws to cover up their own transgressions (Dem. 24.123–24). In an oration written for an *eisangelia* (impeachment) on behalf of an elderly citizen charged with bribe-taking by the politically active Polyeuctus, Hyperides describes the democratic jury (as opposed to the prosecutor and his ilk) as objective judges and protectors of the public interest (Hyp. 4.32–36). The Athenian Diodorus presents the demos as more dedicated to honor, military glory, and tradition than the politician Androtion (Dem. 22.75–76). More ambiguously, speakers often claim that the jurors have been misled by exploiters of their natural goodness and magnanimity *(philanthropia),* or what Kenneth Dover calls their "manly simplicity" *(euētheia).*[9]

The moral superiority of the demos justified their judicial and political power. Their civic and manly tasks, including guarding the community from shame and disorder, were thought to have enormous consequences for the future of Athens. In his speech against Timarchus,

8. Esp. Lys. 2.18, 33, 41–42, 44, 55; Hyp. 6.19. Also relevant are Lys. 18.24; Dem. 9.70; 10.4, 50; 18.99; 23.124; Lyc. 1.147.

9. Dover 1974, 23, 201–2. The people's *euētheia*: Dem. 19.103; 24.52; 25.12; *Pr.* 24.2; Din. 1.104; their *philanthropia*: Dem. 20.165; 23.156; 25.81. Confidence in the demos's sense of justice allegedly justified Antiphon's client's willingness to put himself in the hands of the jury: Ant. 5.8; cf. 2.4.1; 6.51; Is. 9.35; Dem. 57.56. See Dem. 21.2 for the people's sense of justice in the assembly.

Aeschines calls the jurors the guardians of the laws laid down by Solon for ensuring *sōphrosunē*—normative morality and moderation—among men of all ages (Aes. 1.6–7). Jurors, the Demosthenean speaker of the first speech against Aristogeiton asserts, ensure that "good men will have an advantage over wicked ones." They protect Athens's fine and noble qualities—moderation *(sōphrosunē)*, respect *(aiskhunē)* for parents and elders, and good order *(eutaxia)*—against everything shameful *(aiskhros)*, shameless *(anaiskhuntos)*, rash *(thrasus)*, and impudent *(anaidēs)*. The speaker emphasizes their weighty responsibility and manly duty by depicting virtue in feminine terms as under siege by more robust evil qualities: "For wickedness *[ponēria]* is bolder and greedy, while good and noble conduct *[kalokagathia]* is quiet *[hesukhion]*, hesitant *[oknēron]*, slow *[bradu]*, and terribly easy to take advantage of" (Dem. 25.24). Only men of high moral standards could carry out such a mission.

For both institutional and ideological reasons, then, speakers who wished to persuade a popular audience to do their bidding had a difficult task. They faced men who were and thought themselves powerful, were proud of their freedom, viewed themselves as manlier than the orators, had morality on their side, and had considerable discretion in deciding for or against them. The speakers' efforts to deal with this asymmetrical relationship created a power struggle, which is apparent both in the ways the speakers address their audiences and in the latter's conduct.

THE POWER STRUGGLE

In Athenian democracy, the main mode of communication in the courts, the Council, and the Assembly was speech. Any citizen who had not run afoul of the law could address the Assembly and bring his case before a judicial body.

The orator, as the focus of attention in these forums and a master of words, also had the advantages that came with social position and wealth. And yet the speakers, like other sources, paint a picture of tumultuous interchanges.[10] Speakers had to make themselves heard above the audience's clamorous din *(thorubos);* to contend with mockery,

---

10. Calhoun 1913, 121–123; Cronin 1936, esp. 35–43; Bers 1985; Hansen 1987, 69–72; Sinclair 1988, 205–7; Hall 1995, 43–44; Lanni 1997; Tacon 2001.

heckling, protests, and other interruptions;[11] to respond to hostile or challenging questions;[12] and to try to persuade audiences who refused to listen to them or even aggressively silenced them.[13] At times, the din could also be caused by cheering, applause, or other expressions of encouragement and support.[14] Either way, though, the participation of the audience was an expression of their power and determination to exercise it, which undermined the speaker's structural advantage and reminded him that his right to speak depended on his hearers' forbearance and goodwill.

Encounters with unbridled mass audiences could, then, be an intimidating experience and required the orator to display courage and to have ability to control the crowd if he were to succeed as a public speaker. Describing how *hoi polloi* made the ground and the rocks tremble and echo with uproar in the Assembly, law courts, and other public gatherings, Plato compares the demos to a huge, powerful beast that public speakers have to tame (Plato *Rep.* 492b–c, 493a–d).[15] The author of the manual *Rhetoric to Alexander* has a defendant quiet the clamorous jurors by requesting them not to scare him, a man who in any case faces fearful legal danger (18 1433a10–13). Partly in reproach, partly in acknowledgement of the prevailing norm, Isocrates justifies his avoidance of public activity on the grounds that he lacks the boldness and loud voice to contend with the power of the crowd (Isoc. 5.81; 12.9–10; *Letters* 8.7).[16]

Plato feared that the audience would intimidate young and inexperienced speakers, who would succumb to the views of the demos, rather than leading them on the path of wisdom and righteousness.[17] The ora-

---

11. Heckling and protests: Lys. 12.73; Dem. 19.113, 122; *Pr.* 4.1; 21.1; Aes. 1.78; 2.51, 84; Lyc. 1.52; Demades frs. 16, 20 (de Falco); cf. Aristophanes *Acharnians* 37–39, 59–64; *Assembly Women* 143–44; Xen. *Hellenica* 1.7.12–13; Plato *Laws* 876b; [Arist.] *Rhetoric to Alexander* 18 1432b11–1433a29. Mockery and jeering: Dem. 19.46; Aes. 1.80; cf. 1.82–84; Plato *Euthyphro* 3b–c; *Protagoras* 319c; Plut. *Dem.* 6.3. More references in: Cronin 1936, 38; Bers 1985, 6–9, 12; Lanni 1997, 184 n. 8, 187, and Tacon 2001, 182–92.

12. Dem. 8.38, 70; 10.11; cf. Thuc. 4.28.1–3

13. Dem. 18.143; 19.15, 45; 45.6; Aes. 2.4, 153 (with Cronin 1936, 40–41); cf. Isoc. 8.3; 15.22; Xen. *Hellenica* 1.4.20; 6.5.49; Plut. *Dem.* 25.6.

14. E.g., Dem. 5.2; 10.44; 21.14.

15. Cf. Plato *Laws* 876b; Yunis 1996, 147–49.

16. Too 1995, 75–98. Speakers' complaints about the unfair advantage enjoyed by opponents blessed with loud or beautiful voices: Dem. 19.206, 339; 57.11; cf. Is. 6.59; Millett 1998a, 217–18; Easterling 1999, 154–60.

17. See also Xen. *Mem.* 3.7.1, 5; cf. Plut. *Moralia* 41c; [Arist.] *Rhetoric to Alexander* 18 1433a15–16.

tions do not, however, depict cowed, acquiescent orators. Rather, they suggest a power struggle vigorously engaged in by male contenders.

In *On the Embassy*, Demosthenes describes speech as a unique power *(dunamis)*, which differs from other powers in that, while those can generally be effective on their own, speech depends on those who listen to it. Speech, Demosthenes relates, can be "broken through" *(diakoptō)* when the audience "resists" *(anthistēmi)* it (Dem. 19.340). This language, with its quasi-military associations (e.g., power, break through, resist), is that of conflict between two strong forces (cf. Dem. 18.277).

Images of power struggle are also found in Aeschines' appeals to his audience to enforce the "rule of relevancy" and stick to the issue, an injunction anchored in the oath taken by litigants in both private suits and in homicide cases.[18] In practice, relevance was subjectively defined and included more or less related grievances and offenses, the characters of the parties in the dispute, and a large variety of issues.[19] Nonetheless, Athenian pleaders often urged the jury not to let their opponents deceive or confound them by digressing from the issue of the dispute. In his speech against Timarchus, Aeschines advises the jurors to "do as at the horse races: drive him [Demosthenes] in the track of the case" (Aes. 1.176). In his oration against Ctesiphon, he urges his hearers to "be like the boxers in athletic contests you see competing with each other for position; in the same way, you, too, must spend the whole day fighting with him [Demosthenes] about the disposition of his argument, and you must not let him step outside the limits of the issue of illegality; you must sit there on guard, lying in wait for him as you listen, and drive him back to the argument about illegality, and watch out for his attempt to divert the case" (Aes. 3.206; trans. Carey 2000, 235). Both images refer to the world of sport, in which contenders vied for position using their strength, cunning, and wits, and define the relationship between the demos and the speaker as a fierce masculine competition.[20]

18. Private oaths: *Ath. Pol.* 67.1; Cronin 1936, passim, esp. 30–46, but see Rhodes's reservations in 1993, 719; Harrison 1971, 2: 163. The oath taken in other courts had a similar clause: Biscardi 1970, 219–22; Scafuro 1997, 50–51, and Harris 1994, 133, 149 nn. 5–7. Homicide cases: Ant. 5.11; 6.9; Arist. *Rhet.* 1.1.5 1354a21–24; cf. 1.1.10 1354b31–1355a3; Lys. 3.46; Lyc. 1.12. Warning for the jurors to watch for irrelevant arguments: e.g., Lys. 9.1–3; Dem. 40.61; Hyp. 4.4, 10; cf. Is. 10.21–22; Dem. 18.123; 58.23–26. Relevance in the assembly: Dem. *Pr.* 56.2.

19. Dem. 18.9, 34; 57.33, 66; Hyp. fr. 2, 4.4, 31 (Burtt); cf. Dem. 19.192, 213; 56.31; 57.63.

20. Wrestling and judicial contests: Garner 1987, 61–62. Aeschines' fondness for athletic metaphors: Ober 1989, 283, and Golden 1998, 158–59; Fisher 2001, 324, but see Lane Fox 1994, 138–39.

Recognizing the power of their audience, speakers try to transform their hearers from spectators and judges into active participants in their struggle against their opponents. They urge them to challenge the statements of a rival, question him, jeer at him, express anger at him, silence him, or simply refuse to listen to him.[21] This does not, of course, stop them from complaining when a rival does the same, or when audiences disrupt them (e.g., Hyp. 1.11; cf. Dem. 2.29; 8.32). Nor does it keep them from jeering, heckling, protesting, and interrupting themselves (e.g., Dem. 19.23; 59.43).

More directly, speakers ask to speak without clamor or interruption. To some extent, appeals vary in tone with the speaker's status, subject, and forum. In the orations addressed to the Assembly, for example, Demosthenes, acting in the capacity of a political adviser, assumes an authoritative tone, reminding his hearers that it behooves them to listen to him, because he is speaking on matters of public concern (Dem. 5.3, 14–15; 13.3, 14; *Pr.* 21.4; 26.1; 44.2; 56.3). Probably to avoid antagonizing the jurors, the tone is humbler, however, in a Demosthenean speaker's address to the court on behalf of a litigant in danger of losing his citizenship and possibly his freedom.[22]

On the whole, it appears that speakers took their noisy audiences in their stride. Skilled speakers made good use of the time allotted to them, ignored interruptions, responded to challenges on the spot, and tried, sometimes successfully, to intimidate or stare down clamorous audiences.[23] They knew that for all the boasts of Athens's free speech, to exercise it, they would have to claim it for themselves, aggressively if need be—against a citizen body who considered interrupting to be their right and privilege, and against rival politicians, who instigated the crowd or adopted its tactics.[24]

21. Calls to question and challenge a rival: Is. 3.79; Dem. 20.131; Aes. 3.207–8; Isoc. 20.22; to jeer at him: Dem. 18.52 (with scholia ad loc.); cf. 18.23; to express anger at him; Aes. 1.174; cf. Dem. 19.302; Lyc. 1.16; to refuse to listen to a rival or to silence him: Dem. 19.75; 21.40; 23.219; 24.65; Aes. 3.201; cf. Lys. 13.83; Dem. 19.82; 21.28. Lanni 1997, 187–89, regards appeals to bystanders as a way to educate the jury and check their potential abuse of power. I agree that they were intended to exert pressure on the court.

22. Dem. 57.1, 50. The handbook [Aristotle] *Rhetoric to Alexander* 18 1432b34–1433a 29 draws a finer distinction in advising litigants to rebuke unruly jurors in the name of fairness and justice at the beginning of a speech, or if the hecklers are few in number. If the clamor is universal, however, the litigant should reproach himself so as not to arouse the jurors' ire.

23. These methods, however, seem to have been viewed as preemptory and arrogant: Lys. 12.74; Dem. 21.194; 25.95; Aes. 1.34.

24. Based largely on Aeschines 1.33 and 3.4, scholars assume that around 346/5 a new measure was introduced to curb heckling—by rhetors, not the popular audience—in the assembly: Fisher 2001, 163–64, with bibliography.

In claiming the right to speak, speakers showed their mettle and took the first step in contending with the asymmetrical power balance that they faced. They still faced the challenges of establishing their leadership and persuading the powerful demos to follow their counsel, and they often contended with these challenges by manipulating masculine values and perceptions.

HANDLING SUSPICIONS OF THE
POLITICAL LEADER AS A MAN OF WORDS

The Athenians acknowledged the paramount role that speech played in their democracy. Some eighty-five years after Thucydides' Pericles argues that "discussion" *(logos)* is an essential precursor of wise action (Thuc. 2.40.2), Demosthenes tells the Assembly that the democratic *politeia* (government) is based on words (Dem. 19.184; cf. Isoc. 4.48–49).

At the same time, Athenians were wary of speech. The orators repeatedly contrast words unfavorably with deeds. Phrases such as "words without action seem vain and empty" (Dem. 2.12) and "deeds surpass words" (Dem. 10.3) are liberally sprinkled throughout the orations, as is praise of those who have benefited the polis "in word and deed" and criticism of those whose words and deeds are discrepant.[25] These sentiments reflect the conviction that words are ineffective without deeds, that deeds are the surer index of character and manhood, and that words can cover up unworthy and unmanly conduct. Demosthenes, for example, defines the Athenians' failure to back up their professed support for the Rhodian democrats against the island's oligarchy as unmanliness or cowardice *(anandria)* (Dem. 15.28; cf. 14.8). Aeschines sets Demosthenes' "beautiful words" against his "trivial deeds" and "evil life" and links the discrepancy to Demosthenes' alleged cowardice and licentiousness (Aes. 3.174–75; cf. 3.168).

The Athenians were sensitive to the dangers inherent in speech, especially eloquent speech in the service of political or judicial persuasion. They, like other Greeks, viewed persuasion as essential in leading the

25. Praise: e.g., Aes. 3.49; Dem. 21.190. Criticism: e.g., Is. 2.31; Dem. 6.1–3. Contrasting words and deeds: Lys. 19.61; Is. 2.31; Dem. 4.30; 6.1–3, 29; 8.73, 77; 13.32–33; 14.41; 18.122; *Pr.* 45.3; cf. Lys. fr. 1 (Thalheim); Dem. 9.15; *Pr.* 50.1. Harmony between words and deeds: Dem. 9.1, 21.190; *Pr.* 9.2; Aes. 3.49; Hyp. fr. D 11 (Burtt); Din. 1.17; cf. Dem. 18.179; Aes. 3.191; Plato *Laches* 188c–e. Praises for people who benefited the polis in words and deeds are formulaic in Athenian honorary decrees: Veligianni-Terzi 1997, 213–226, 231–232.

people toward right action, but also as a dangerous power that could lead them astray.[26] Persuasion (Peithō) was personified as an assistant to Aphrodite and presented as a seductress who, like desire, could occupy a man's mind and subjugate him to her will.[27] This notion is reflected in Aeschines' claim that Demosthenes compares Aeschines' rhetorical powers to the irresistible and destructive power of the Sirens' song (Aes. 3.228). Able speakers were thus cast in a sinister light, their skills presented as threatening the reason, discretion, and even independence of the Athenian male. Speakers accuse smooth-talking rivals of mendacity and associate them with magicians and wizards (singular, *goēs*).[28]

Hyperides viewed orators (and generals), with their double-edged power of persuasion, as "men who are able to harm the city" (Hyp. 4.27), in contrast to private citizens. According to Aeschines, Demosthenes is a sophist, a teacher of rhetoric, who uses his rhetorical skills to hoodwink, shame, and mock the jury, win renown and profit at their expense, and distort the laws.[29] Depicted as stronger than other members of the demos, a skilled speaker was seen as undermining the democratic principle of fair trial *(agōn)*, which stipulated that, as in any contest, the contestants' advantages were to be evenly distributed.[30]

To dispel these concerns, speaker-politicians insist that their words are consistent with their deeds, while the words and deeds of their rival are inconsistent (e.g., Dem. 18.57, 122; Aes. 3.248). Their rivals are fabricating, but they are telling the truth (Aes. 2.147; Dem. 6.31; 18.141). In the law courts, litigants depict themselves as young or inexperienced, unskilled, and hence truthful speakers—even where their orations have been written by expert speechwriters—and ask for the jury's special forbearance and protection.[31] And they maintain that their rivals abuse their

26. Gorgias *Helen* 9–14; Kennedy 1963, 3–14, 26–51, 125–57; Dover 1968, 25–28; Romilly 1975; Buxton 1982, esp. 10–24, 48–66, 105–14; T. Cole 1991, 148; Zeitlin 1996, 136–43; Detienne 1996, 77–80; Hesk 2000, 170–71, 196–98, 206–41.

27. Humphreys 1993, xxvi–xvii; Brockreide 1972; Kely 1973; Rothwell 1990, 26–43.

28. Dem. 18.276; 19.104; 29.32; Aes 2.124, 153; 3.137, 207; Din. 1.66, 92, 95; Burke 1972, 257; Worthington 1992, 261; Hesk 2000, 213. Able speakers deceiving the jurors: e.g., Dem. 22.4; 32.31; 48.36.

29. Aes. 1.125, 173–75; 3.16, 202. Cf. Dem. 19.246, 250; 35.40–41; Lyc. 1.138.

30. Is. 8.5; 10.1; Lys. 19.1–3; Dem. 18.3–4; Hyp. 1.19–20; 4.27–30; 5.25–26. Cf. Isoc. 15.258; Astydamas [II] in *Tragicorum Greacorum Fragmenta* 1.60 T2a, with Page 1981, 33–34. See also Romilly 1975; Ober 1989, 170–77; Hansen 1991, 144; Whitehead 2000, 147; cf. Christ 1998, 193–224.

31. Ant. 5.1–7, 79; Lys. 12.3; 17.1; fr. 20 (Thalheim); Is. fr. 8 (Forster); Dem. 27.2; 34.1; 36.1; 38.6; 41.2; 44.3–4; 58.41; Hyp. 1.10, 20; Ober 1989, 174–77.

rhetorical powers for personal ends, whereas they themselves use their powers of persuasion for the good of the polis.[32]

HANDLING SUSPICIONS OF THE POLITICAL LEADER STEMMING FROM HIS ACTIVITIES IN THE PUBLIC REALM

To ensure that state offices and institutions would be filled by upright, useful citizens, Athenian law established minimum requirements for public office and permitted individuals to subject candidates to the procedure of *dokimasia* (review) to determine that the requirements were met. The legal requirements were being male, born of Athenian parents, and a proven member of one's phratry and family, as well as treating one's parents well, paying one's taxes, and serving in the army (see esp. *Ath. Pol.* 55.3)—conduct showing that the candidate had fulfilled the masculine roles of son, citizen, and soldier. It is possible that the *dokimasia* was also required of public speakers. According to Aeschines, Athenian law barred men from speaking in public if they had maltreated their parents, dodged the draft or showed cowardice in battle, worked as prostitutes, or squandered their patrimony (Aes. 1.28–30). These prohibitions seem to have been aimed at ensuring that only men of sound, manly character and conduct could hold political power.[33]

The informal expectations of political leaders resembled the legal requirements. In his speech against awarding Demosthenes a golden crown, Aeschines lists five qualities that distinguish a friend of the people *(dēmotikos)* from an oligarch: (1) being freeborn on both parents' sides, (2) having a family that has served the democracy, or at least has no animosity toward it, (3) being temperate and moderate *(sōphron, metrios)* in daily life, (4) having good judgment and speaking ability, and (5) possessing a courageous spirit *(andreion einai tēn psukhēn)* (Aes. 3.168–70). Although Aeschines' aim in naming these qualities was less to establish objective criteria for a political leader than to rule out Demosthenes, Athenians generally expected these characteristics in their political leaders. [34]

32. Dem. 18.236, 277, 280–284; Aes. 2.118; 3.220; cf. Dem. 18.66–69; 180; *Pr.* 7.2
33. *Dokimasia:* p. 117 above. For the debate about reviewing rhetors: Harrison 1971, 2: 204–5; Ober 1989, 119; Worthington 1992, 235–36, 304–5; Lane Fox 1994, esp. 150–51; Fisher 2001, esp. 157–59.
34. Demosthenes' response: Dem. 18.122. Judging by the orators, the expectation of politicians to act as the demos's "lovers," for which see Wohl 2002, esp. 49–58, must have lost its appeal in the fourth century.

Yet along with their high expectations, the Athenians apparently had grave apprehensions about their leaders' potential to do harm. Thus, in explaining the need for those merits, Aeschines emphasizes not their intrinsic worth but rather their value in protecting Athenian democracy against politicians who would harm it. Free birth is necessary because men who are not free might resent the laws that secure the state's democracy.[35] The absence of any legacy of family animosity ensures that a leader does not have old scores to settle. Moderation and self-control reduce the likelihood that he will take bribes to support an extravagant lifestyle. A courageous spirit will prevent him from abandoning the demos in times of danger (Aes. 3.168–70). Aeschines does not explain the need for good judgment with reference to some harm, but his statement that good judgment is more important than speaking ability probably alludes to the Athenians' wariness of the harm that could be done by a persuasive speaker.

The perceived need to guard against politicians' propensity to harm the demos is also apparent in a Demosthenean speaker's advocacy of strict laws and harsh penalties governing individuals' obligations to the state, in contrast to more lenient laws and milder penalties governing their obligations in private life. According to the speaker, such severity is required "so that politicians will not do you [the demos] so much damage" (Dem. 24.192–93).

To convince their hearers that they will not use their power to harm the demos, politicians often differentiate themselves from their rivals on the basis of qualities associated with normative manhood, including civic courage and personal probity.

Civic Courage

Military service was a major requirement for political leadership, both legally and in terms of popular opinion (see esp. Lys. 16.17). According to Aeschines, men who were too cowardly to defend the state had no right to advise it either (Aes. 1.29). But courage on the battlefield was not enough. Political leaders were also expected to show courage in their civic activities. Aeschines, as noted, deemed a "courageous spirit" (Aes.

---

35. Presumably the laws Aeschines has in mind are the laws barring slaves from citizenship, although this is not entirely clear. Elsewhere, Demosthenes suggests that a man of servile background feels resentment toward the people because he cannot hide the shame of his birth (Dem. 24.124).

3.170) essential to ensure that that political leaders would not flee in time of trouble. The same conviction lies behind Demosthenes' comparison of oligarchically inclined politicians to soldiers who leave their posts in violation of their general's orders (Dem. 15.32–33).[36] The claim that he himself had done just this is used by several speakers to cast aspersions on Demosthenes' fitness for public office. A speaker prosecuting Demosthenes on a charge of taking bribes accuses him of having used his position as envoy to escape Athens after the battle of Chaeroneia, amid rumors that Philip was going to invade its territory (Din. 1.80–81). Aeschines and Hyperides allege that Demosthenes has chosen the Piraeus, the city's port, as his home so he can easily get away, leaving the demos leaderless (Aes. 3.209; Hyp. 5.16).

Both Aeschines and Demosthenes depict their rivals as lacking the courage politicians require if they are to perform their civic duties properly, while conversely presenting themselves as possessing it. Aeschines consistently portrays Demosthenes as a coward both in battle and in his political life (e.g., Aes. 2.139; 3.81, 155, 161). In *On the Embassy*, which deals with the Athenian embassies that were sent to Philip to discuss a peaceful resolution of the dispute with Macedonia, he claims that Demosthenes' timidity has jeopardized Athens's interests abroad, while implying that he, Aeschines, has the civic courage required for political leadership.[37] Aeschines asserts that during the first Athenian embassy to Philip in 347, Demosthenes had showed his "cowardice" *(deilia)* (Aes. 2.22) and proved that he had no claim to being the city's benefactor (Aes. 2.24). Each of the ten Athenian envoys to Macedonia was to deliver a speech to Philip and his attendants, with Demosthenes, the youngest of the ambassadors, speaking last. With a view to demonstrating Demosthenes' failure of nerve and his own skillful performance of his ambassadorial duties, Aeschines first describes his own address in lengthy, loving detail, depicting himself as having reasonably, but tactfully, pointed out that Philip owed a debt of gratitude to the Athenians and had a moral and legal obligation to restore the city of Amphipolis to them. In contrast, Demosthenes, who had earlier boasted of his rhetorical ability, lost his bearings after a miserable preamble and was unable to continue, despite Philip's gentle prodding (Aes. 2.21, 34–35). The king did not even

---

36. For the image of desertion in Demosthenes' speeches, see Ronnet 1971, 161–62.

37. Aes. 2.20–39. For discussions of the following episode (reported differently in Plut. *Dem.* 16.1), see Schaefer 1885–7, 2: 202–4; Carlier 1990, 150–52; Sealey 1993, 151, 304 n. 70; E. M. Harris 1995, 57–60, 194 n. 42; Bers 1997, 167–73; Paulsen 1999, 322–23, 450–51. Cf. Badian and Heskel 1987.

refer to him in his reply (Aes. 2.38). Although one may wonder whether any actual harm was caused by the incident, the message of the story is that Demosthenes' failure was cowardly, disgraced the city, and rendered his ambassadorship useless, proving his unfitness for positions of public responsibility—while Aeschines' intrepid presentation of Athens's position proved his own fitness for the task.

During the second embassy, in 346, Aeschines said, the Assembly had given a broad mandate to the envoys "to negotiate any other advantage" they could with Philip, a reference, probably, to persuading Philip to move against Thebes, then Athens's rival. The wording was intentionally vague so that should Philip refuse, the Assembly could avoid embarrassment and deflect the Thebans' anger onto the envoys (Aes. 2.101–5).

As Aeschines was explaining this broad understanding of the instructions to his fellow envoys, he says, Demosthenes rudely interrupted with the demand that they refrain from meddling and adhere to a narrow interpretation of their mission. Demosthenes admitted to being "soft" (malakos, a descriptor with feminine characteristics), fearful of distant dangers, and deliberately choosing not to see the opportunity at hand. He declared that he would not be called to account (e.g., risk standing trial) for Philip's wars, for saying things that he had not been instructed to say, or for doing things that he had not been instructed to do. Aeschines depicts a fearful politician who placed his personal welfare above that of the demos and prevented the envoys from persuading Philip to move against Thebes (Aes. 2.106–7).[38]

Demosthenes, on the other hand, depicts himself, in On the Chersonese, as the sole politician with the courage to advise the Assembly that Athens should reject Philip's request that it cease its support of hostilities against him in Thrace. Although Philip's supporters in Athens malign him as a cowardly politician who will "not risk" (oude kinduneuein) making an unpopular proposal, and who is "lacking in daring" (atolmos) and "soft" (malakos), in reality he is more courageous (andreioteros) than his rash and impulsive (itamōs) political adversaries.[39] Speaking in the third person, he offers proof of his claim to courage, contrasting politicians who, concerned with their own interests and indifferent to the well-being

38. For the episode and Aeschines' reliability here: Paulsen 1999, 362–66. Trédé 1992 has observed a contrast between Aeschines' more active approach to seizing opportunities and Demosthenes' view that opportunities should be seized only at moments of great destiny or danger to the city. Both approaches required courage and determination.

39. For a similar approach in On the Symmories: Dem. 14.8. Cf. Dem. 3.32; 4.51; 18.219–20.

of the state, are unwilling to take political risks and pander to popular opinion with those who are willing to hazard their personal welfare for the greater good. The former he characterizes as "rash" *(thrasus)*. The latter he extols in a sweeping generalization that equates political courage with true manliness: "But whoever in your best interests frequently opposes your wishes and never speaks to gain popularity, but always for what is best . . . this man is courageous" (Dem. 8.68–69). Finally, in somewhat clichéd fashion, he depicts himself as a lone sentinel protecting the demos from the machinations of other rhetors by risking the people's wrath to offer them his beneficial counsel. In contrast to most other politicians, who act out of greed and ambition, he consistently offers "advice that diminishes me in your eyes, but that, if you follow it, will contribute to your greatness" (Dem. 8.70–71).[40]

Aeschines and Demosthenes focus on different aspects of the politician's civic courage. Aeschines stresses the need for courage in dealing with foreign leaders, Demosthenes on the need for courage in dealing with the demos.[41] Aeschines argues that the courageous politician seizes opportunities and accurately assesses the enemy's intentions. Demosthenes stresses the courage the politician needs to stand up to the demos and tell them, not what they want to hear, but what they need to hear. For all their differences, however, both speeches portray a politician's lack of courage as harmful to the state. And both draw on the Athenians' expectation that political leaders show manly courage in justifying their own political service or proposals and denigrating those of their rivals.[42]

Personal Probity

The Athenians wished to see their public figures as *metrioi,* that is, as men of moderate, conforming disposition who, despite their elite status, resembled ordinary citizens *(idiotai).*[43] As the young Epichares puts it in his speech against Theocrines, the city's elders have told him that Athens

40. Poking fun at the commonplace of the politician as lone sentinel: Aes. 2.8; Dem. 25.64. Uses of the cliché: e.g., Dem. 5.5; 21.189–90; 24.157; cf. Dem. 15.6; Lyc. fr. A1 (Burtt); Dover 1974, 29–30; Ochs 1996; Heath 1997, 233 (in comedy).

41. Of course, neither limited displays of courage to either foreign or domestic affairs: e.g., Aes. 2.181.

42. See also Dem. 3.21–22; 9.2–3; 18.263; 19.208; 21.172; Aes. 1.105; 3.160, 163; cf. And. 2.4; Monoson 1994b, 182–83; Balot "Free Speech, Courage, and Democratic Deliberation," in Sluiter and Rosen 2004.

43. Moderation and being a *metrios:* pp. 176–84 below. For the term *idiotēs/ai,* see Mossé 1984; Ober 1989, 108–12; Rubinstein 1998.

"fared best when moderate and self-restrained men administered it" (Dem. 58.62; cf. Din. 2.8). Such men embody the ideal of personal probity, a broad concept referring to a man's behavior toward his family and household and his friends, as well as to his sexual activity. As an aspect of manliness, personal probity was an important qualification for public activity or office.

The Athenians tended to view personal behavior as a reliable indicator of public behavior.[44] Their logic was anchored in two related convictions: behavior was an indicator of character, and character was a stable element that manifested itself consistently in every area of a person's life.

In his speech on the embassy to Philip, Demosthenes draws on the perceived link between private and public behavior in telling a salacious story about Aeschines' misconduct at a banquet in Macedonia. When a young Olynthian woman, whom the host had brought to serve as a female companion, was reluctant to sing and dance, Aeschines and another guest became enraged. They called for a slave to bring a whip; when the girl began to cry, the slave tore off her dress and lashed her on the back. Demosthenes dwells on the girl's free birth, modesty, and vulnerability and the drunken abuse and out-of-control behavior of Aeschines and his cohorts (Dem. 19.196–98; cf. 19.309). To Athenians, inebriation, rage, and violence against a free and modest girl was hubristic, bullying, tyrannical behavior that overstepped the bounds of the self-control expected of the Athenian male. To ensure that the utterly reprehensible nature of such behavior did not elude his audience, Demosthenes prefaces his account with the statement that it will show that Aeschines and his friends had been the most ineffective and depraved of all the envoys to Philip, whether official or private, and with the contrasting story of an actor who rescued young Olynthian girls whom Philip's forces had captured (Dem. 19.192–195).

Demosthenes also ties Aeschines' misconduct at the symposium to his role as envoy: the story of his abusive behavior circulated to Arcadia, Thessaly, and beyond (Dem. 19.198). Aeschines' lack of personal probity thus made him unfit to represent the polis abroad or guide the Athenians at home.[45]

---

44. Aes. 1.28–30; 3.77–78; cf. Din. 1.71; Dover 1974, 302–3; Strauss 1993, 43–53. Personal attributes, public persona, and leadership: [Aristotle] *Rhetoric to Alexander* 38 1445b32–33; cf. Bourdieu 1991, 107–59.

45. Aeschines denies the story altogether and claims that the audience drove Demosthenes off the podium when he tried to tell it: Aes. 2.4, 153–58.

Aeschines makes much the same argument against his opponent Timarchus, whose immodesty, drunkenness, and lewdness, he claims, cause good people to feel ashamed that they have permitted him to serve as an adviser to the city (Aes. 1.26). He pays particular attention to Timarchus's alleged prostitution as grounds for depriving him of the right to speak in public. Although a legal occupation in Athens, male prostitution was viewed with disfavor. Men who engaged in it were forbidden to address the public, make proposals, and hold certain offices. Aeschines and Demosthenes agreed that a man who sold his body was likely to sell out the interests of the polis as well.[46] Aeschines, however, also stresses the effeminate nature of Timarchus's behavior, calling him "a man with a male body who has committed womanish acts." No discerning man would "employ as an adviser someone who abused nature and himself" (Aes. 1.185). Men who violate the "natural" distinction between the genders, he implies, are not fit to act as political advisers.[47] Indeed, elsewhere in the speech, he links Timarchus's female role in homosexuality to crimes against the polis. A man who charged Timarchus and his lover Hegesandrus with embezzling public funds joked that Hegesandrus had previously been the wife of another politician, but was now a man to Timarchus (Aes. 1.110–11).[48]

Public Behavior

A variety of gender-related actions in the public realm also distinguished the beneficial from the harmful political leader. These included arrogant and hubristic treatment of the demos, shameless behavior or behavior that shamed the city, acting out of greed, lack of consistency and steadfastness, slavish or servile conduct, and bribe-taking.[49]

---

46. Aes. 1.28–29; Dem. 22.30–32. Additional aspersions on politicians as male prostitutes: And. 1.100; Aes. 2.23, 88; "Introduction" n. 35. See Dover 1989, 23–31, Foucault 1985, 219; Winkler 1990a, 58–59; Halperin 1990, 94–99; D. Cohen 1991c, 230–31; 1995, 143–62; Wallace 1993, 1994a; but also Patterson 1998, 130–32, and Fisher 2001, 36–53.

47. Dover 1989, 6; Fisher 2001, 340.

48. James Davidson's (1997, 270–74) downplaying of the sexuality in the insult makes it lose much of its meaning; and see Fisher 2001, 248–49. For charges of sexual misconduct against the politicians Alcibiades the Elder and his son, see p. 89 above.

49. Hubristic and arrogant conduct: Dem. 21.131, 200–204; 25.41; Aes. 1.175; cf. Dem. 19.242. Political shamelessness: Dem. 7.17; 18.139; 19.16; Aes. 2.57–59; 3.105; Din. 1.48. Bringing shame to the city: Dem. 24.205; Aes. 1.120; Hyp. 2.9; cf. Dem. 20.28; Behaviors making the individual unfit to lead it: Din. 1.93; Dem. 22.47. Placing personal interests above those of the public: And. 2.2–3; Lys. 28.13; enriching oneself at the city's expense: e.g., Lys. 12.93; 27.9–10; Dem. 3.29; *Pr.* 53.3; cf. Din. 1.89, 114; Dem. 5.12. Greed leading to betrayal: Dem. 18.294–95; 19.28; Hyp. 5.35; making illegal proposals:

All these were obviously harmful in their own right. Of note here is that they could also be used as yardsticks of political behavior, because they were viewed as unmanly. Arrogance and hubris were viewed as distortions of masculinity. The capacity for feeling shame was deemed essential to manhood, while the preservation of personal and national honor was considered a duty of all good men. The inability to control one's greed was an instance of unmanly lack of self-control, while politicians who changed their political stands were suspected of lacking manly perseverance and endurance.[50] The link that was drawn between the harmfulness of the behavior and its unmanliness was strongest, however, with respect to servile conduct or attributes and bribe-taking.

Accusations of slavishness and servility were flung at rivals for supporting Philip's position in the conflict with Macedonia (Dem. 19.258–60), showing antidemocratic proclivities (Hyp. 2.10), and tailoring their speeches and proposals to the wishes of the demos (Dem. 13.19). They rested on the centrality of freedom to the self-identity of the Athenian male and the concomitant perception of subservience as low, depraved, and unmanly. Even though in law and practice the offspring of freed slaves could hold most political offices, the idea was so incongruous that Demosthenes could discredit Aeschines by alleging that he had slaves for ancestors. Such ancestry, he contended, cast in doubt Aeschines' integrity and his loyalty to the demos (Dem. 18.129, 131; 19.209–10).

Analysis of words frequently associated with bribery suggests the largely passive and unmasculine nature of the bribe-taker.[51] The bribe-taker took and received *(lambanō, dekhomai)* rather than gave, was paid a fee *(misthos)*, hired himself out *(misthoō)*, sold (himself, the public interest, the city, etc.; e.g., *apodidomai)*, and was corrupted *(diaphtheiromai)*. Orators accused him of selling his honor and freedom of speech (Dem. 19.142; Din. 2.1; cf. Dem. 19.118); of being greedy (Dem. 23.201;

Dem. 24.65; and selling the city's honors: Dem. 23.201. Servility and bribe-taking, pp. 148–49 below.

50. Arrogance, hubris, and shame: pp. 73–79 above. Greed: pp. 173–76 below. Inconsistency: pp. 199–203 below.

51. Bribery in Athens: Wankel 1982; MacDowell 1983; Strauss 1985; Harvey 1985; Herman 1987, 73–81; Sinclair 1988, 180–86; Ober 1989, 204–5, 246–47, 278–79, 331–33; Bauman 1990, 82–94; Reden 1995, index, s.v. "bribery"; Kulesza 1995; Mitchell 1997, esp. 181–86; Taylor 2001a; cf. 2001b. The characterization of the vocabulary of bribery as neutral in Taylor 2001a, 52, is based on two words alone: *dora* (gifts, bribes), and *dorodokia* (gift giving, bribery).

Harvey 1985, 102–3) and willing to jeopardize the city to satisfy his greed—instead of protecting it as a man should (Hyp. 5.25). They faulted politicians who took bribes with unmanly and uncivic excess and hedonism. Demosthenes charged that Philocrates spent the money he had received from Philip on sex and food (Dem. 19.229), while Aeschines asserted that Timarchus had spent bribe money on his mistress (Aes. 1.115). Orators characterize the bribe-taker's position as inferior and subordinate to that of the bribe-giver. Demosthenes calls Philocrates, Aeschines, and others Philip's "hirelings" (singular, *misthōtos*) (Dem. 9.54, 18.21, 52; 19.110); Aeschines claims that Demosthenes followed orders from his paymasters (Aes. 3.218). Bribe-taking was held responsible when politicians changed their stance on public issues and violated the expectation that men stand their ground (e.g., Dem. 19.9–16; Aes. 2.79).

THE DEMOS'S POWER AND APPEALS TO PITY

The speeches addressed to the Athenian courts contain repeated appeals for pity.[52] Speakers "begged of" *(exaiteō, deō)* and "supplicated" *(hiketeuō* or *antiboleō)* the jurors to "take pity" (mostly *eleeō*) on them, "save" *(sōzō)* them, or "come to [their] aid" *(boētheō).*[53] Apparently, speakers often accompanied their appeals for pity with tears and wailing, designed to arouse sympathy for the sufferer and anger at his adversary or the alleged perpetrator of the offense.[54] In some cases, they brought their small children or elderly parents and other relatives to court, or described the suffering the latter would endure as a result of an unfavorable verdict.[55]

52. Athenian pity: Dover 1974, 195–201, 269–70; Pucci 1980, 169–74; and more generally: Romilly 1979, esp. 25–196; Arnauld 1990, 106–8. Appeals to pity in courts: Johnstone 1999, 109–25; Allen 2000a, esp. 148–51, 194–95; Konstan 2001, 27–48.
53. For example, *eleeō:* Lys. 18.1; 19.53; *exaiteō:* Lys. 20.35; Dem. 21.99; *deō:* Dem. 54.2; *sōzō:* Dem.57.3; *hiketeuō* and *antiboleō:* Is. 2.44; *boētheō:* Dem. 27.68; 58.69.
54. Shedding tears in court: e.g., Ant. fr. D 1 (Maidment); Lys. 27.12; Dem. 21.99; 37.48; 39.35; 45.88; 53.29; [And.] 4.39; Lyc. 1.150; Isoc. 18.35–39; Johnstone 1999, 172. For tears, display of emotion in public, and masculinity: Loraux 1986, 45; 1995, 157 (based on Plato *Pheidon* 117c–e), and 1998, esp. 10–12, 20–24; Carson 1990, 138; Arnauld 1990, 53–55, 64, 83–84, 102–8; Stears 1999. Cf. Dem. *Letters* 2.25, and Dover 1974, 167; van Wees 1998a, 16–19.
55. Producing or invoking family members in court (with a preference for children and mothers): e.g., Lys. 7.41; 20.34–36; Dem. 21.99, 186, 188; 25.84; 40.56–57; 57.70; 58.3; Aes. 2.148, 152, 179; Hyp. 4.41; cf. Isoc. 15.321; Xen. *Hell.* 1.7.8; Plato *Apology* 34c; Aristophanes *Wasps* 568–74; Carey 1989, 140. Pitiable gestures and dress: Arist. *Rhet.* 2.8.14–15.1386a29–1386b7. On the performative aspects of requests for pity: Johnstone 1999, 114–20; Rubinstein 2000, 154–56.

These appeals reflected the uneven power relationship in the Athenian courts, where the jurors decided for or against the speaker and, in the event of the latter outcome, had considerable latitude in setting the penalty. A speaker on behalf of the freed slave and banker Phormio explicitly links the jury's demonstrations of power and of pity in his request that they "not show him [Phormio] pity when he has little to gain by it, but now when you have the power [literally, are *kurioi*] to save him" (Dem. 36.59). Charged with homicide, Euxitheus reminds the court "that I deserve pity from you more than punishment . . . and that your power *[humeteron dunamenon]* to save me justly should always be mightier than my enemies' ambition to destroy me unjustly" (Ant. 5.73).

In power relationships, pity, or mercy, is typically shown by the stronger and more powerful.[56] In appealing for the jurors' pity, the speaker acknowledges the jurors' preferred position and simulates supplication to move his more powerful hearers to grant his wish.[57] The tone of the more fulsome appeals may be illustrated by a passage from Demosthenes' case against his cousin and guardian Aphobius, whom he accuses of appropriating his inheritance from his father:

> Come then to our aid, aid us, for justice, for your own sake, for ours, for my father who has passed away. Save us, pity us, since these, although relatives of ours, did not pity us. We have fled to you for protection. I supplicate you, I entreat you in the name of your children, of your wives, and of the good things that you have, so that you may enjoy them. Do not disregard me and do not cause my mother to be dispossessed of her remaining hopes in life or to suffer undeservedly. (Dem. 28.20)

In begging so humbly and effusively, Demosthenes represents himself as a helpless dependent of the powerful jurors, whom he seeks to turn into his champions. Such appeals were supported by the Athenian conviction that pity was a moral virtue intimately linked to the manliness of the demos.[58] Thus a Demosthenean speaker asserts that the laws of Athens and her *politeia* show pity *(eleos),* forgiveness *(sungnomē,* also

56. Johnstone 1999, 109–25; Konstan 2001, 50. It is true that the emotive power of the appeal to pity could make the relationship between the pitier and the pitied more balanced, but at the same time, it acknowledged the preferred position and greater power of the former.

57. Johnstone 1999, 115–17, 123. I do not share Johnstone's view, based on Plato's *Apology* 34c–35b, that supplication feminized the suppliant: Socrates was hardly a typical Athenian, and Plato limited this observation to the elite.

58. Stafford 1998, 51, notes that, unlike most other personifications (e.g., justice, peace) in Greek, pity *(eleos)* is in the masculine gender.

translated as sympathy; cf. Konstan 2001, 39–40), and other qualities "that belong to free men" (Dem. 22.57). In the funeral oration attributed to Lysias, the speaker claims that pity and love of justice for the weak had led the warriors of Athens to risk their lives to aid families, friends, and others who needed them (Lys. 2.14, 39, 67). Pity is thus presented as promoting manly acts and affirming an array of manly attributes, including freedom, heroic valor, self-sacrifice, protectiveness, and friendship.

The speakers suggest that pity is an inherent quality of Athenian jurors and other representatives of the demos. Each juror brings to court "pity, forgiveness, and humaneness" that stem "from your nature," says Aristogeiton's prosecutor (Dem. 25.81). A Lysian speaker commends the members of the Council hearing his case for their "renown for showing pity even for persons who had suffered no hardship" (Lys. 24.7; cf. Isoc. 15.20).

The view of pity as a virtue of the demos and the view of the jury as naturally and, on the whole, properly moved by pity came together to create two conundrums: being merciful to a guilty party would undermine the jurors' mission of meting out justice, and in any trial, pity could be shown to only one of the contending parties. To address these concerns, speakers bring pity and justice together in a single construct and make the jurors the guardians of both, but while defendants equated the request to spare them with justice, prosecutors often warned the court not to let pity subvert the course of justice or the laws.[59]

Thus, defendants frequently contend that they deserve pity because they are innocent or because their cause is just (e.g., Ant. 2.2.13; 3.2.2; 5.73; Lys. 4.20; Isoc. 16.48; cf. Lys. 3.48). They appeal to the jurors as protectors and caretakers who ensure justice for the weak—the poor, orphans, minors, and, more generally, innocent persons who have suffered calamities or face suffering undeservedly.[60] The triple themes of pity, protectiveness, and justice for the weak come together in Aeschines' appeal against charges of misconduct as an envoy to Philip and other po-

59. Pity and justice: Allen 2000a, 168–96; Konstan 2001, 27–4, 37–42 (chiefly in Lysias). For the view of the defendant as the weaker party in a trial: Johnstone 1999, 94, 97, 111–12; Rubinstein 2000, 220.

60. Pitying the poor, weak, and defenseless: in addition to chapter 4 n. 23 above, see e.g., Dem. 38.20; cf. And. 1.148–49; Dem. 19.309–10. Pity for victims of unwarranted suffering and injustice: e.g., Dem. 1.6; 2.6–9; Lys. 6.56; 31.10–11; 32.19; Dem. 28.18; Isoc. 14.52; Arist. *Rhet.* esp. 2.5.12 1382b24–26, 2.8.1–2, 13–15 1385b11–19, 1386a24–b7; cf. *Poetics* 6.2 1449b, 13.5 1453a; [Arist.] *Rhetoric to Alexander* 34 1439b26–36, 36.1445a2–12; Konstan 2001, esp. 43–48; 128–36.

litical crimes. Highlighting the vulnerability of his father, brothers, and children, Aeschines implores the jury to avert the disasters that will befall them if he is convicted (Aes. 2.179). The jurors' protective role is stressed even more forcefully in Andocides' defense against the charge that he had violated the rules prohibiting supplication during the Mysteries. Appealing for his life, Andocides tells the jury that he has no family to help him: "[Y]ou must be my father, and brothers and my children. It is to you I come for a shelter and you I entreat and supplicate" (And. 1.149). The comparison of the jurors to his family resonated, because Athenian men as warriors and *kurioi* were expected to protect, care for, and provide justice to the weak, and especially to the women, children, and other dependents in the household.

It was also necessary, of course, for speakers to persuade the jury to reject their opponents' pleas for pity—a necessity that, by its nature, fell to prosecutors rather than claimants. The main argument they made was that the person in question was guilty and did not deserve pity, and that its dispensation would distort the course of justice and harm the innocent. In Dinarchus's orations against Philocles and against Demosthenes, both accused of bribe-taking, the prosecutors point to the damage to the laws, justice, and the state, here depicted as the innocent party, should the jury pity the defendants.[61] Other speakers warn jurors not to misplace their innate compassion (Dem. 25.81) and maintain that wrongdoers avoid punishment and pervert the course of justice by taking advantage of jurors' humanity *(philanthrōpia),* mildness *(praotēs),* forgiveness *(sungnomē),* simplicity *(euētheia),* easygoing ways *(rathumia),* or accommodating natures *(eukherēs).*[62]

In some cases, speakers equate displaying undeserved pity with feminine weakness. Lycurgus contends that the defendant Leocrates will try to exploit the "wet," pliant side of the jurors' nature *(tēn hugrotata autōn tou ēthous:* Lyc. 1.33). The implication is that the jurors should affirm their masculinity by justly convicting the defendant. In a speech accusing Timocrates of passing an illegal law, Demosthenes has Diodorus charge that Timocrates has taken unfair advantage of the ju-

61. Din. 1.109; 3.19–20. See also Lys. 11.9; 14.40; 15.9; 28.11; Dem. 21.225; cf. Dem. 19.228; Romilly 1979, 113–26. Claims that the men sitting in judgment are the ones who deserve pity: e.g., Lys. 27.12; 28.14: Dem. 19.283; Lyc. 1.141.

62. Humanity: Dem. 23.156; 24.51. Mildness: [Lys.] 6.46; Dem. 24.51; 58.55; *Pr.* 6.1; Hyp. 5.25 (with humanity). Forgiveness: Din. 1.55, 57; Simplicity: n. 9 above. Easygoing ways: Dem. 22.78. Accommodating nature: Dem. *Pr.* 42. For additional examples of pity misplaced, see, e.g., Lys. 22.21; Dem. 19.310; cf. Lys. 6.3; Dem. 21.148; Lyc. 1.143–44, 148. See also Loraux 1995, 47, 267 n. 20; Whitehead 2000, 437–38.

rors' kindheartedness and indulgence (Dem. 24.51), commend the latter for their "pity for the weak," and admonish them that the accused does not, however, deserve this pity (Dem. 24.170–71). A little later in the speech, he equates indulgence toward criminals with effeminate softness *(malakisthentas)* and injustice (Dem. 24.175; cf. 21.184). Assertions like these simultaneously compliment the Athenians on their kindness and question the soundness of their judgment, because they yield unduly to the unmanly side of their nature.

The orators thus present themselves as the most qualified to determine when pity is warranted and when, conversely, it resembles feminine indulgence, undermining justice and harming the state. Whichever side the speakers come down on, however, both their appeals for pity and their arguments against it acknowledge the jurors' superior power in the hierarchy of Athenian democracy.

THE DEMOS'S POWER AND APPEALS TO *KHARIS*

In addition to appeals for pity, the orations also contain repeated appeals for *kharis,* which is best translated as grace, favor, gratitude, kindness, or thanks, but which usually refers to the reciprocity due for favors or services rendered, even when these were expected or mandated. Pleaders in Athenian courts often treat *kharis* obligations as equitable compensation and ask for favorable verdicts in return for services rendered to the state (especially in the form of *leitourgiai* and courageous military service) by themselves or their ancestors. The essential argument is that the dispensation of *kharis* is the right and just thing for the jurors to do.[63]

Like pity, *kharis* was an important Athenian value, applied to private relations and public affairs. Failure to reciprocate a favor or service could mark a man as *akharistos,* that is, as ungrateful, untrustworthy, or antisocial. Demosthenes alludes to this perception when he declares, albeit with obvious self-servingness, that while a donor should properly

63. See, e.g., Is. 7.41; Lys. 25.12–13; fr. I.6.ii (Gernet-Bizos); Dem. 58.66–67; Isoc. 18.16–18, 58, 66–67; cf. And. 1.141–3; 4.42; Aes. 2.169–171. On *kharis,* see Davies 1984, 92–96; Ober 1989, 226–33, 245–47; Millett 1991, 123–126; 1998b; Gallant 1991, 141–69; Missiou 1992, 32–40, 116–24; Seaford 1994; Konstan 1997, 81–82; Johnstone 1999, 100–108; Rubinstein 2000, esp. 213–20. For the rules governing exchange and reciprocity see, generally, Sahlins 1972, 185–275; Bourdieu 1977, esp. 10–15; Reden 1995; cf. Hands 1968, 26–48. Johnstone 1999, 102–4 and Rubinstein 2000, 215, have rightly noted that requests to reward a service were made more often by defendants, and requests to deny *kharis* by prosecutors.

forget the favors he has done, "one who receives benefits should re-member his obligation for all time" if he is to "act like an honest *[khrestos]* person."[64]

The ethos of *kharis* was applied to the relationship between politi-cians and the state. The young Epichares depicts his adversary and fel-low politicians as ungrateful to the state and the demos, to whom, he claims, they owe their prosperity.[65] Demosthenes argues that Aeschines owes his present wealth and position to the demos and is "ungrateful and villainous by nature" for failing to show them the "gratitude" they de-serve (Dem. 18.131). These and similar arguments (e.g., Hyp. 5.29–30; Aes. 3.196) are, of course, partisan pleadings. Nonetheless, they showed how readily the relationship between the demos and public figures could be depicted in terms of *kharis* obligations.

The orations also assume that the state should show *kharis* to indi-viduals who have aided it. In advocating the repeal of Leptines' law that deprived the families and offspring of persons who had benefited the state of special tax exemptions, Demosthenes observes that those who do not reciprocate favors do wrong *(kakia)* (Dem. 20.6). The law would bring "disgrace" *(aiskhros)* to the city; its citizens would be viewed as "envious, untrustworthy, and ungrateful" (Dem. 20.10). The state's *kharis* obligations are also implicit in litigants' candid declarations that by performing political and military duties with ardor and zeal, they have intentionally placed the state under an obligation to do them jus-tice (Lys. 16.15–17; 20.31, 33; cf. fr. 45a [Medda]).

And yet the demand for *kharis* entailed difficulties for the speakers. How might they persuade the jury to withhold *kharis* from opponents without feeling they were violating social and moral norms? One ap-proach was to denigrate opponents' behavior in the *kharis* relationship by belittling their motives or the quality of their service.[66] The other ap-proach, which often accompanied the denigrating tactic, was to present

64. Dem. 18.268–69. Failures to return favors: e.g., Is. 9.23; Dem. 25.56–58; 49.1; Aes. 2.150. Aristotle discusses *kharis* in the *Rhetoric* 2.7 1385a16–b10 from the giver's point of view and as an act of altruistic kindness.

65. Dem. 58.63. Ober 1989, 245–46 argues that the people regarded the elite as in their power and in debt out of *kharis* because they allowed the politicians to enrich them-selves through public service; cf. Herman 1987, esp. 75–97. It is also possible that elite members' references to this functional arrangement aimed to maintain the demos' toler-ance of their power and the opportunities of profiting from it.

66. Is. 5.36; Lys. 26.4; 30.16; Dem. 21.152–59; 23.184; 36.41–42; cf. Dem. 18.3; Arist. *Rhet.* 2.7.5 1385a34–1385b5.

the jurors' *kharis* obligation as incompatible with—and less important than—their obligation to mete out justice.[67]

Despite the normative quality of *kharis*, expectation of it—unlike expectation of pity—entailed an insidious threat to the power of the jurors vis-à-vis the speakers. It placed the jury in the pleader's debt, circumscribed the jurors' prized freedom of action and decision, and reversed the power relationship between the jurors, or demos, and the individual pleader.

Athenians prized givers over receivers in *kharis* relationships. The speaker of the Lysian funeral oration maintains that the Athenians who had fought at Marathon against the Persians had refused help from allies because "rather than owe gratitude for their salvation to others, they preferred that the rest of the Greeks be indebted to them."[68] Demosthenes claims that the distribution of public funds by politicians rather than the people turns the latter into beneficiaries of the politicians' favors, deprives them of their power, transforms them into "underlings and inferiors," and undermines their manliness by leading them to "owe gratitude for what is your own" (Dem. 3.30–31).

Speakers who appealed for *kharis* thus had to mitigate the threat to their hearers' freedom and superiority and to assuage anxiety about their rank and power. They did this through what may be called a rhetoric of *kharis,* in which the request—or demand—for *kharis* as due by justice appears in conjunction with a range of other arguments and pleas, each of which was designed to reduce the tension inherent in the *kharis* relationship.

One example of this rhetoric can be found in a Lysian speaker's defense against the charge of a crime against the state, where a guilty verdict could have resulted in his impoverishment and loss of citizenship (Lys. 21). The speaker appeals to the ethos of *kharis,* arguing that the jury's failure to reciprocate his wartime services to the state makes an unfavorable verdict doubly unjust: unjust because he is innocent, and unjust because *kharis* requires that he be rewarded, not punished. He thus

67. [Lys.] 6.8; Dem. 19.238; Din. 3.21; Lyc. 1.139–140; cf. Lys. 15.9–10; Isoc. 18.34. Other reasons to withhold *kharis:* Lys. 12.80; 14.31; 30.27; Dem. 19.91–95. Comparing one's service with an opponent's lack thereof: e.g., Is. 4.27–29; 7.35. Millett 1998b, 249–50; Johnstone 1999, 104–6; Rubinstein 2000, 214–15.

68. Lys. 2.23; cf. Thuc. 2.40.4–5. *Kharis* and superiority: Reden 1995, 79–85. Missiou 1992, esp. 28–32, 109–39, distinguishes between traditionally aristocratic *kharis* with expectations of return and an uncalculating democratic *kharis.* But, as these pages show, nonoligarchic speakers freely ask the democratic demos to reciprocate favors done.

claims to be owed a debt of gratitude, tries to shame the jury into re-
quiting it, and highlights the material advantage that the demos stands
to gain from reciprocating past services with a favorable verdict, all while
proclaiming that he is not asking for any recompense and taking care to
assure the jurors that he is not challenging their superiority and his dependence on them (Lys. 21.11–13). Finally, he makes a plea for pity for
himself and his children (21.25).

Such ploys appear in many other orations, all designed to maintain
the balance between speaker and jury, individual and demos. By pre-
tending not to demand a reward, the speaker assumes the pose appropriate to the weaker party in a transaction (e.g., Dem. 45.78, 85; cf.
46.13; 59.89). By stressing the utilitarian aspects of the jurors' *kharis* obligations, he turns *kharis* from a requirement that implies compulsion
and inferior status into a voluntary act—and transforms the jury from
claimant's debtor into the city's benefactor.[69] Finally, yoking the plea for
kharis to a plea for pity enveloped it in a deferential wrap that placed the
speakers in the politically correct hierarchical relationship to their free
and powerful hearers.[70]

With their appeals for pity and *kharis,* speakers strive to direct the
people's power to punish and reward without appearing to threaten it.
They present themselves, however, as the appropriate persons to determine when and how to apply these values.

THE MANHOOD OF THE AUDIENCE AND THE SPEAKER

A more assertive approach challenged the superiority of the demos, questioning its manhood, and affirming the speaker's own manliness and
leadership capacities. This approach was made possible by the license
given by Athenian democracy to all of its citizens to employ free and
frank speech *(parrhesia)* for the benefit of the state.

Speakers chiefly question the demos's manhood in speeches addressed
to the Assembly. In *On the Chersonese,* for example, Demosthenes insinuates that rival politicians emasculate the demos by making the
people appear frightening and tough in the Assembly but lazy and contemptible in war. Using demagoguery and currying favor *(kharizo-*

69. The utilitarian argument came in the form of promises by individuals to benefit the
state: And. 2.2; Is. 6.61; 7.41–42, or claims that rewarding benefactors would serve as an
example to others: Lys. 18.23; 20.31; [Dem.] 50.64; cf. Dem. 20.7.
70. E.g., And. 2.6–9; Lys. 3.47–48; 7.30–31; 18.1–10, 27; 20. 33–36; Is. 7.37–38;
Davies 1984, 96–98; Ober 1989, 228–30; Millett 1998b, 244.

menoi), they induce the people to listen to popular debates from the perspective of their (the demos's) *truphē*—a word variously translated as complacency, softness, or luxury—and with an ear to what flatters them and gives them pleasure *(hedonē)* (Dem. 8.32–34; cf. 9.4; 18.138; Aes. 3.127).

Elsewhere, Demosthenes points to the demos's complicity in its disempowerment and emasculation. In the *Third Olynthiac*, he claims that in the days when Athens ruled the Aegean, the politicians did not flatter the demos; they lived modestly like the rest of the population and dedicated themselves to the public weal. The people, for their part, were the master *(despotēs)* of the politicians through their control of all state benefits, honors, and offices. But in the inglorious present, the politicians dispense state funds and public honor, while the people, stripped of power, are tame, subservient, and act like an underlings *(en hupēretou kai prosthēkēs merei gegnēsthe);* in a most unmanly fashion (literally, and sarcastically, in a most manly fashion: *to pantōn andreiotaton)*, they thank the politicians for what is in fact their own (Dem. 3.21–32).[71]

Speakers also criticize the people's functioning in two specific areas associated with Athenian manhood: action and intellect, while indicating their own superiority with various degrees of explicitness.

As we saw in chapter 5, in his efforts to rally the Athenians to check Philip's aggression, Demosthenes faults his hearers for lacking the manly qualities of courage, leadership, responsibility, and the readiness to take action and to seize opportunities. To these reproaches may be added his criticisms of their laziness, shortsightedness, and unreasonableness; their bestowing their honors on unworthy political actors; and their talking rather than doing.[72]

At the same time, Demosthenes conveys the idea, although not in so many words, that he is a better man than his hearers. He does so by drawing attention to his own proactive, self-sacrificing, courageous, and civic behavior in fairly close proximity to faulting the demos for the opposite conduct. In the *First Olynthiac,* he reproaches the people for shortsightedness, idleness, and seeking pleasure, and he then declares

71. Cf. Dem. 13.26–31; 23.206–10; Isoc. 8.129–30; Ober 1989, 319–20. Cf. Xen. *Oec.* 7.10 with Pomeroy 1994, 272, for the vocabulary of taming women.

72. Invoking actions combined with criticism: e.g., Dem. 1.6–11; 3.9, 20, 33; 4.7–10; 8.76–77. Inaction, feebleness, and cowardice: Dem. 3.31; 4.8, 10, 42; cf. 19.224; shortsightedness, delaying and missing opportunities: Dem. 1.8–10, 15; 4.37; 10.29, 54; refusing to do their duty and evading responsibility: Dem. 3.3; 4.7; 8.22; lack of reason and yielding to pleasure or anger: Dem. 1.15; 4.38; 6.27, 34; honoring unworthy politicians: Dem. 8.66; cf. 23.197–98; talking instead of doing: e.g., Dem. 3.4–5, 15; 4.36–37; 8.22.

that even though he is aware that Athenians are prone to punish rhetors who speak their minds, he subordinates his own well-being to the welfare the people (Dem. 1.15–16). In the *Third Olynthiac,* after berating the demos for having lost the "courage to act and fight," he likewise implies his readiness to suffer the consequences of speaking plainly (Dem. 3.30–32). A similar declaration in the *First Philippic* (4.51) follows a string of rebukes to the demos for being indecisive, careless, indolent, apathetic; for having shirked their duties in the past and failing to take action against Philip in the present; for talking but not doing, missing opportunities, lacking initiative, mismanaging their war preparations; and, last but not least, for cowardice.[73]

The importance of intellect to the Athenian man's perception of himself is suggested by the many occasions on which speakers shower praise on their hearers for their intelligence and rationality.[74] Nonetheless, speakers openly reproach their audience in the Assembly, Council, and law courts for a variety of intellectual lapses. Among his litany of failings, Demosthenes condemns the demos for lacking good sense (Dem. 2.26), deluding themselves (Dem. 10.49), and being easily duped by deceptive speakers (Dem. 19.83–84; 20.3; 24.161; cf. *Pr.* 25.1). In his *Third Philippic,* he attributes such behavior to his audience's "folly and madness" (Dem. 9.54–55). He and other speakers rehearse errors of judgment in the courts and Assembly: in allowing guilty persons to go free (Dem. 18.132–34; 21.37; 23.206), in letting their carelessness, gullibility, or emotions—whether of compassion, resentment, jealousy, good nature, or any other—undermine their decision-making (Aes. 3.192; Dem. 19.103, 228; 22.78; 25.12; 51.15; *Pr.* 24.2; 46.3; Lys. 26.1–2; cf. Lyc. 1.33), for their lack of good sense in relying on unprincipled men as character witnesses (Dem. 23.146–47) or officeholders (Lys. 30.28); for their failure to discern the corruption and self-interest of their leaders (Lys. 27.10–11); and for their inability to tell honest politicians from their opposites (Dem. 19.226–28; cf. 18.149).

Some speakers heighten their criticism by preceding it with praise of the demos's intelligence (Dem. 6.27; 23.145–47; Aes. 1.178–79). The demos, they imply, are misusing good minds—they are capable of acting differently. This and other criticisms also imply that the speakers them-

73. Dem. 4.2–3, 7–8, 12, 33, 40–42. See also Dem. *Pr.* 38.3. Cf. Ober 1989, 318–32; Russell 1990, 206–7; Roisman 1999.

74. E.g., Dem. 6.18; 9.15; 10.13; 19.161; 23.109; Is. 11.19; Ober 1989, 157, 163–65. Cf. Dem. *Pr.* 44.1; 45.2; Thuc. 1.84.3; Yunis 1996, 40–43, 78.

selves possess the clarity of vision, strength of character, and discretionary powers that their hearers lack. Speakers emphasize their superior acuity, for example, by expressing astonishment at their hearers' failure to see "the obvious." A Lysian speaker marvels that his hearers are ready to listen to and tolerate the wrongs inflicted by their allegedly oligarchic opponents (Lys. 34.2). Demosthenes is astonished that his hearers fail to grasp the danger that Philip poses to Athens and the need for active measures to stop his expansion (Dem. 2.24–6; 4.43; 6.6); that oligarchies in other Greek states threaten their own democracy (Dem. 15.19); and that Aeschines is so evidently evil (Dem. 18.159).

The primary function of the rebukes is instructional and corrective, but by their nature, they also challenge the demos's sense of superiority and convey the message that they need the speaker to prod and guide them, to show them the error of their ways, and to point out the right course of action.

In his speech in 346 in favor of preserving the peace with Philip despite its shortcomings, Demosthenes sets out to establish his credentials to advise the demos by reminding them of his superior foresight and knowledge in previous situations. He was the only politician, he claims, to warn them against the disastrous decision to send aid to Plutarchus of Euboia (Dem. 5.3–5). It was he who exposed the actor Neoptelemus as Philip's agent, although doing so provoked the people's resentment against him (Dem. 5.7). He had warned them not to believe claims made by Athenian ambassadors that Philip would benefit Athens and not harm their ally Phocis. In all these instances, events had proved him to have been correct. Demosthenes tactfully attributes his clear vision not to superior intelligence but to good fortune and his lack of interest in personal gain (Dem. 5.10–12). Yet his discourse about his perspicuity and record of courageous speech gains much of its strength from its juxtaposition of these with images of misguided people who follow their own untutored impulses or the bad advice of rival politicians and learn only when it is too late that their orator is wiser than they are.[75]

In his speech *On the Crown*, Demosthenes depicts himself as the city's savior at a time when the people were confused and he had the unique knowledge and presence of mind to come to their rescue.[76] Drawing a vivid picture of the fear and disarray of the polis following Philip's cap-

---

75. See also Dem. 6.29–34; 19.19–28, 41–46. For more implied claims to be sound of mind: Dem. 2.22; 9.20; 15.11; [And.] 4.13.
76. Dem. 18.168–79. See Yunis 1996, 268–77.

ture of the Phocian city of Elateia in 339, which left Boeotia and Attica exposed to a Macedonian invasion (Dem. 18.168–69), Demosthenes contends that even though the fatherland was crying out for salvation, not a single general, orator, wealthy man, or ordinary citizen had responded to the herald's call for suggestions. They lacked the firsthand knowledge of the sequence of events and deep understanding of Philip's character and policies that only he, Demosthenes, possessed. His expertise had made it possible for him to stand by his post and provide counsel—and comfort—for the people in their hour of need (Dem. 18.173). He reminds his hearers that he had calmed the Athenians' fears by sharing with them his understanding of the situation, and that the advice he had given had resulted in an alliance between Athens and Thebes and the removal of the threat posed by Philip's capture of Elatea (Dem. 18.188).

On the Crown was delivered in 330, eight years after the defeat of Athens and Thebes in Chaeroneia, so Demosthenes' foresight could have been called into question, as indeed, Aeschines had done in his speech against Ctesiphon. In his speech on the crown, Demosthenes defends his advice, even though it had not worked out in the long run. At the core of his defense is his presentation of himself as the ideal rhetor, as he defines him shortly after his recapitulation of his speech to the Assembly: seeing the likely course of developments from the outset, foretelling and issuing warnings, overcoming impediments in the government, and creating a positive atmosphere and motivation to act (Dem. 18.246; cf. 4.39; 25.33). He had done these things under the most difficult circumstances and when no one else in Athens had risen to the occasion. The demos had acknowledged his leadership at the time by universally approving his speech, and he had followed through on his proposal by persuading the Thebans to ally themselves with Athens and doing everything else that was necessary from start to finish (Dem. 18.174–79).

Demosthenes presents himself as an adviser who has the civic courage and soundness of mind to lead the demos, and the demos as needing his leadership. He possesses superior knowledge, understanding, and judgment. He is the true defender and protector of the demos. In short, Demosthenes strives to make the demos dependent on him alone as their adviser *(sumboulos)* or guide. One may wonder about the congruity between Demosthenes' efforts to make the people dependent on him and his earlier criticism that they had lost their manly attributes through their dependence on the politicians who controlled public revenues (Dem. 3.31).

The orators' criticisms of the people's judgment and manly spirit, and their attendant claims of their own superiority in these respects, reversed the accepted hierarchy between demos and speaker and probably carried some risk of offending. It is not accidental that such criticisms were not voiced by litigants whose personal possessions, rights, or life were at stake, and who sought, instead, to sway their hearers with appeals to pity and *kharis*.[77] The more vigorous reproaches cited in this section were voiced in the Assembly by Demosthenes, who had not much to lose, probably only his popularity, and that only temporarily. Where public policy was at stake, reproaches were regarded as part and parcel of speakers' role as advisers, and as an acceptable means of educating the people to become better citizens and prodding them to make correct policy decisions. They were made against the background of the license given by Athenian democracy to all of its citizens to employ free and frank speech *(parrhesia)* for the benefit of the state.[78]

Nonetheless, for all his criticisms, Demosthenes never challenges his hearers' manhood completely. On the contrary, his message is that if they mend their unmanly ways, they will regain their power. A clear example is the *First Philippic,* where Demosthenes mixes harsh reproaches of the demos's unmanly submissiveness, laziness, apathy, and procrastination with assurances that every citizen can "become his own master" if he heeds Demosthenes' call to "put aside his hesitation," perform his military duties, and stop dithering (Dem. 4.7–8, 10, 36–38). Implicit in the exhortations that precede or follow the rebukes is a call to the demos to reassume their masculine responsibilities and regain their lost manhood by heeding his advice (Dem. 1.6–10, 14–15, 20; 2.13; 3.15–16, 34–35; 8.46).

The interactive character of Athenian oratory and the rhetors' recriminations shows that the demos and the orators who sought to lead them were actively engaged in a power struggle in democratic Athens. The values and perceptions of manhood were part and parcel of this struggle. In the courts and the Assembly, orators faced audiences who perceived themselves as more manly, powerful, and virtuous than they, and who often flexed their muscles in unruly behavior. The orators in

---

77. Indeed, cautious litigants attributed their censure of their audience to other men: Lys. fr. 75 (Thalheim); Isoc. 18.10, 36; Dover 1974, 23.

78. E.g., Dem. 3.3. For the constructive role of *parrhesia* and the legitimacy of reproaches, see, Dover 1974, 23–24; Monoson 1994b, 175–78, 182–84; and Wallace and Balot in Sluiter and Rosen 2004; but see also Roisman 2004.

turn manipulated the values and rhetoric of manhood in efforts to influence or lead the demos.

To handle concerns that speakers could undermine the people's power and harm the polis, orators present themselves as conforming to masculine expectations and their rivals as deviating from them. Litigants pay respect to the demos's perception of their superiority in the Athenian hierarchy in their appeals to the jurors' pity and *kharis*.

Other orators warn that rival politicians seek to deprive the demos of their political power and masculinity; they also raise questions about the demos's masculinity. Together, the rebukes and the self-presentations aim to make the demos dependent on the speaker, encourage them to accept his guidance, and legitimize his sway over them.

All in all, the orations point up the very close connection between political power and manhood in fourth-century Athens. And they show that speakers who wished to control the powerful and manly demos had to demonstrate that they were manlier, not only than their rivals, but than the demos themselves.

CHAPTER 7

Men, Desires,
and Self-Control

In chapter 6, I discussed the struggles over power between the demos and
its leaders and the role that the rhetoric of masculinity played in them.
The subject here revolves around a different sort of power struggle, this
one between a man and his own desires or appetites.

As they fashioned a positive or negative manly image, speakers appealed to an ethic of restraint. In so doing, they chastised young men,
delinquent *kurioi*, and members of the elite for lacking in restraint or
committing hubristic and out-of-control assaults. Indeed, orators express
and manipulate the perceived threat posed by pleasures in general, and
bodily appetites for sex and wine and the inordinate desire for more (i.e.,
greed) in particular, to the city's social, political, and moral order.[1] Yet
the Athenians' attitudes toward men controlled by these desires, and especially by sex and wine, were not one-dimensional. They ranged from
fear and resentment to sympathy and understanding, and so created an
ambivalence that speakers could manipulate. Orators also took advantage of the ill-defined nature of the virtues of self-control, moderation,
and quietism in order to assert or dispute an individual's worth as a man,
citizen, and moral person.

1. The desires discussed here are mentioned in the orations with greater frequency than
others and are especially relevant to our subject. Examining other desires or emotions is a
task of immense proportions. See, e.g., Allen 2000a on anger and its discourse.

GIVING IN TO PLEASURES

The Athenians regarded pleasures as forces that could lead men into violating key masculine social and political ideals, including independence and honor.[2] In a speech accusing Timarchus of male prostitution, Aeschines describes the defendant as a slave to the most shameful pleasures *(douleōn tais aiskhistais hedonais)*—namely, gluttony, lavish eating, flute girls (who might be called upon to provide sexual services as well as music), *hetairai,* and gambling—and "to all those other things none of which should control the noble and free man" (Aes. 1.42).[3] Incontinence and impulsive bodily pleasures *(hai propeteis tou sōmatos hedonai),* he adds, drive people to crime, the killing of fellow citizens, antidemocratic conspiracies, and disregard of shame or of punishment for misdeeds (Aes. 1.191). Aeschines' ability to tie appetites and incontinence to such wide-ranging destructiveness tells us about how inclusive the Athenians' concern about men who succumbed to them was. Demosthenes confirms the linkage of appetites to matters of national security by comparing Aeschines to several Greek politicians who had betrayed their countries to Philip and Alexander. These men had thrown out the freedom and independence by which Greeks had formerly gauged their welfare; instead, they shamelessly measured their happiness by their stomachs (i.e., pleasures) (Dem. 18.294–96).[4]

In his funeral oration for the fallen at Chaeroneia, Demosthenes presents the search for pleasure as undignified and petty. The Athenian war dead, *andres agathoi* and models of patriotic manhood, motivated solely by eagerness for *aretē* and praise, look down on the living Athenians, who are preoccupied with wealth and the enjoyment of pleasures *(kata ton bion hedonōn apolauseis hupereōramenas:* Dem. 60.2; cf. Aes. 1.160). Along similar lines, a Lysian speaker argues that the most laborious *leitourgia* (public service) is to lead an orderly and self-restrained *(sōphrōn)* life and not allow oneself to be overcome by pleasure or greed (Lys. 21.19; cf. Is. fr. 35 [Forster]). Yielding to pleasures, then, was a mark of deficient manhood and citizenship; it contributed to servility,

2. For *akrasia,* lack of control over appetites, as well as *akolasia,* self-indulgence, see Aristotle *EN* 7.3.9–12 1147a24–1147b8; North 1966, index, s.v. *akolasia;* Foucault 1985, 63–77. Gosling and Taylor 1982, which focuses on the philosophical works, and Davidson 1997, chs. 5–9, expand the investigation to other sources.
3. Enslaving pleasures: Just 1989, 170–71; Thornton 1977, 44–46.
4. But cf. Aes. 2.152.

disgraceful and self-indulgent conduct, and criminality, and diminished the noble ambition for valor, honor, and civic excellence.

The practitioners of the rhetoric of masculinity utilized this attitude in several ways. In the Assembly, Demosthenes condemned succumbing to pleasures and urged the Athenians to fight Philip. The search for pleasure made them lazy and passive, instead of active; it left them prone to follow bad leaders and miss valuable opportunities to improve the polis's situation (see pp. 156–58 above).

Denunciations of giving in to pleasure are even more prevalent in the court speeches. Wishing to create a paradigm of the criminal or violator of decent norms, some speakers attribute the pursuit of many pleasures and a multiplicity of related offenses to their adversaries. In a short fragment from a speech of Lycurgus's in an unknown context, which has survived in a Latin version, the speaker ascribes lust, plunder, greed, deviant sexuality, and cowardice to different parts of the defendant's body (Lyc. fr. 14.4 [Burtt]). In the space of a few sentences, a speaker accuses Alcibiades the Younger of dereliction of his military duty and charges him with sexual promiscuity, immoderate drinking, betrayal of his father, gambling, wastefulness, attempts to kill his friends, and crimes against citizens, aliens, and his own family (Lys. 14.25–28). Typically, accusations of this sort were directed against members of the elite who had the means and the leisure to pursue a life of pleasures.

But the most glaring example of criticism of yielding to pleasures is surely Aeschines' speech against Timarchus, whom he accused of male prostitution and extravagance, which disqualified an Athenian from speaking in public (Aes. 1.29–30). Aeschines expanded his accusations into a comprehensive character assassination and drew a picture of a man driven by pleasures to violate almost any rule of masculine and civic conduct. From a young age, he claimed, Timarchus had provided sexual services to many a man for fees and other rewards because he could not control his own appetite for sex and spending. His lifestyle revolved around drinking, extravagance, sexual license, gambling, and violent confrontations (Aes. 1.39–43, 51–62, 70, 75–76, 95–96). Timarchus was not just a disgrace and menace to himself. He offended communal sensitivities and decorum when, as a speaker in the Assembly, he threw off his cloak and, like an athlete, exposed his half-naked body, which was marked with signs of drinking and wantonness (Aes. 1.26). In this way, Timarchus violated the boundaries between controlled environments that permitted male nudity, such as the gymnasium, and those that required decency.[5] After he had consumed his own resources and those of his *oikos,* he profited from public activity because he was a slave to his pleasures (Aes. 1.105–6, 154).[6] While in office, he put himself up for hire by taking bribes, extorted the allies of Athens to finance his shamelessness, and hubristically treated them as disgracefully as he treated his own body (Aes. 1.107–8, 113–16; cf. 1.188). In sum, Timarchus's conduct was dishonorable, harmful, and surely unmanly.

Even though the detailed delineation of Timarchus's incontinence is exceptional in the speeches, it shares with other discourses the aim of destroying a rival by revealing his inability to resist his desires. And yet the Athenians were also willing to indulge some transgressions.

AMBIVALENCE ABOUT YIELDING TO EROS

Athenian men actively pursued love and sex and perceived them as pleasurable and culturally approved experiences. Yet they counseled self-restraint in pursuit of sexual gratification or love as well. A client of Lysias's, who was involved in a violent dispute over a male lover, put this expectation into words: everyone has desires, "but the best *[beltistos]* and most restrained *[sōphronestatos]* man is the one who can bear his misfortune in the most orderly way *[kosmiōtata]*" (Lys. 3.4). Sexual desire and nonconjugal love affairs constituted threats to one's manhood, to the performance of the roles of a *kurios,* kinsman, and citizen, and to the entire polis.

Passion was deemed a threat to reason because the wish to satisfy it baffled one's mind and could lead one to hurt oneself or those associated with one.[7] An Isaean speaker argued that young men's inability to control their desire had caused them to lose their minds and commit the grave error of marrying *hetairai* (Is. 3.17). Even more disconcerting was infatuation that victimized family and kin. As we have seen, some *kurioi* who were in love with a mistress or an *hetaira* failed to transfer the household and its possession to legitimate kin or wasted its resources on

---

5. Cf. Humphreys 1993, xvi; Osborne 1997, 506; Stewart 1997, 27. Davidson 1997, 262–63 argues that Aeschines here silences Timarchus, who is allowed to speak only through his body, while Fisher 2001, 154, sees here a reference to Timarchus's unesthetically aging body. For self-restraint and body language: Dem. 19.251; 45.68; 61.13.

6. Just 1989, 229–30, 346–51; Davidson 1997, 255–59; Sissa 1999, 153–60; Fisher 2001, esp. 174–75, 229–31, 346–51.

7. Cf. Xen. *Oec.* 12.13–14 (especially in relation to homosexuality); Pomeroy 1994, 318; Dover 1973 [1988], 271–72; 1974, 175–80, 205–16; Just 1989, 166–77.

these women (see pp. 138–41 above). Adulterers, who were equally prisoners of lust or love, dishonored and destroyed families too. Such men threatened the state because of the likelihood of their fathering illegitimate children who might claim rights in the household and the city.[8] Another public concern revolved around the danger to the morality of children, who did not know how to defend themselves from such men. Aeschines surveyed various regulations concerning Athenian schools, and other environments where adults and children met, in light of one interpretative principle: they were intended to prevent men from corrupting and seducing boys.[9] Finally, erotic desire for a female or male, especially when mixed with wine, competition, and youth, caused violent or licentious behavior.[10]

Athenians' critical views of men under the influence of love or desire should be put in perspective, however. Relationships with mistresses and *hetairai,* for example, were not automatically condemned. Some speakers refer to men with mistresses, including adversaries, without any moral judgment (Is. 3.39; Dem. 23.55; 59.21–22, 24, 122; Lyc. 1.17, 55). Even criticism of adulterers ranged in level of intensity from high to moderate resentment (p. 35 above). Finally, there is the telling advice given in a fourth-century rhetorical manual, attributed to the sophist Anaximenes, to a speaker who is forced to admit a charge: he should seek "to compare your own deeds as much as possible to the habits of the majority of mankind by saying that most people, or even everyone, do this kind of thing in a way that happens to be done by you. If it is impossible to demonstrate this, one must take refuge in misfortunes or errors and try to gain forgiveness by claiming what is common to human beings: passions that drive out our reason, which are *erōs,* anger, drunkenness, pursuit of honor, and their like" ([Aristotle] *Rhetoric to Alexander* 7 1429a10–19).

How should we account for attitudes that ran from the understandable, even excusable, through the neutral, to the strongly critical? It appears that concerns about yielding to erotic desire and other pleasures

---

8. Dem. 48.35–36; Lys. 1.2, 4, 26, 33; Aes. 2.177; pp. 34–36 above.

9. Aes. 1.9–12. See D. Cohen 1991c, 176–80, but also Golden 1990, 57–62, esp. 58; Fisher 1992, 41–42; 2001, 36–37, 129–35; Cole 1984. Ford 1999, 242–43, shows Aeschines' partisan interpretation of these laws, but my interest is in his appeal to common concerns.

10. Lys. 4.8; Aes. 1.58–59, 135; cf. Davidson 1997, esp. 213–15; and pp. 170–73 below.

were balanced by an acknowledgment that succumbing to them was common, and hence deserving of sympathy.[11] Orators found these ambivalent attitudes both challenging and useful. Generally, speakers claimed sympathy for themselves, or for those whose actions they wished to excuse, but denied it to their adversaries. When arguing against men whose misconduct was related to desire, they stressed the destructiveness of being consumed or overwhelmed by desire to counter the view that succumbing to pleasures mitigated misdeeds. Conversely, when charged with such misconduct, they portrayed themselves, or their relatives, as having put up a good fight against their desires (cf. Aristotle *EN* 7.7 1150b7–12), or at any rate as sympathetic victims. Examples of first rhetorical tactic include Aeschines' charges against Timarchus described above, speakers' railings against adulterers and those who associated with *hetairai* (pp. 134–41 above), and a Lysian speaker's counteraccusations against a man who had charged him with premeditated wounding. In arguing that his accuser's behavior had been beyond the pale, he described him as being sick with love *(duserōs)* for a female slave whom the two had shared, in "a way that is contrary to other people's."[12] Enflamed by this woman, he had gotten violently drunk and feigned an injury, as a result of which the speaker might now lose his fatherland and life (Lys. 4.8–9, 18–19).

The Rhetoric of Exculpatory Passion: Hyperides' Against Athenogenes (Hyp. 3)

A prime example of the appeal to the jurors' empathy for men defeated by eros is surely *Against Athenogenes,* a speech written by Hyperides for a client who had fallen in love with a young male slave (Hyp. 3).[13] The speaker claimed that he had approached the slave's owner, Athenogenes, with an offer to buy the boy's freedom, but Athenogenes played the reluctant seller. In stepped Antigone, a former courtesan, madam, and Athenogenes' *hetaira,* and offered her services as mediator. In fact, she was privy to a plot against the speaker. A meeting was arranged, during which

---

11. See, e.g., Arist. *EN* 7 1149b4–6, and Halperin 1990, 68; Jeffrey Henderson 1990, 5; cf. Dover 1973 [1988], 270–71, and 1974, 205–16. Loraux 1995, 9–10, even has argued for the male's wish to appropriate the intensity of pleasure reserved to females. Thornton 1997, esp. 11–67 privileges the Greeks' fear of the dark sides of sexual desire, while Calame 1999, 91–109, stresses its unifying power.

12. Sexual passion as a disease: Thornton 1997, 33–35.

13. For the case, see Whitehead 2000, 265–351. An appeal to the extenuating force of love and desire can also be detected in Dem. 40.51 and Is. 6.18.

Athenogenes advised the lover to buy the boy, his father, and his brother, as well as a perfumery shop that the slaves helped to run. To ensure that no one would "corrupt" the boy, he should buy them all outright. The transaction involved paying the slaves' business debts, which Athenogenes claimed were small, but which actually amounted to the hefty sum of about five talents. Athenogenes even arranged that at the time of the signing of the contract, no one would be able to advise the buyer that he was falling into a trap (Hyp. 3.1–8, 23–24).

To get his client out of this bad deal, Hyperides counterposes popular morality, and the jury's sense of fairness and empathy for victims of love, against the written agreement his client had signed.[14] He casts the speaker as a naïve man who had come from the country and was not experienced in the tricks of the market (Hyp. 3.26).[15] Consumed with love and passion, he was too befuddled to make a sound business decision, which was why he had put his faith in Antigone: "that is how, I reckon, *erōs* makes a person lose his wits, taking a woman as a partner" (Hyp. 3.2). Hyperides' client had listened to the reading of the sale agreement, but he had been in a rush to conclude it (Hyp. 3.8). Appealing to both sympathy and justice, the speaker calls for the law to arbitrate between them, because it was made neither by people in love (like him) nor by conspirators (like his adversary) (3.21). He also offers a dubious analogy between a will, which could be legally invalidated as a result of the influence of a woman on the testator, and himself, who had been persuaded, even compelled, to sign the agreement by Athenogenes' *hetaira* (Hyp. 3.18). In conformity with the stereotype of courtesans, who are condemned in the speeches for ruining men financially, he depicts Antigone as a sneaky, ill-famed woman with a reputation for cleaning out the assets of a wealthy *oikos* (Hyp. 3.3).[16] Her partner, Athenogenes, was allegedly a noncitizen, who hung about in the agora and made his living from lowly trades such as speechwriting; moreover, he was a cheat, a traitor to his city, and had abused the hospitality of the Greek city of Troizen (Hyp. 3.19, 29–32, 35). Hyperides' client argued that he deserved the jurors' sympathy because, having succumbed to desire, he

14. Appeal to fairness: Hyp. 3.13, 22; Colin 1946, 192; Scafuro 1997, 61–62. See Dem. 37.39–43 for a similar attempt to invalidate an agreement based on the unfavorable circumstances under which it was made, and Aes. 2.166 for the case of a naïve beloved taken advantage of by his lover, Demosthenes.

15. Scafuro 1997, 63–64; Whitehead 2000, esp. 270–71.

16. *Hetairai* as the cause of economic losses: p. 39 above; Davidson 1997, 194–205; Kapparis 1999, 7.

had been fleeced by Athenogenes and his mistress.[17] The court could come to the rescue. The jurors no doubt experienced similarly strong desires. They would, it might be hoped, protect one of their own from a plot hatched by inferiors and non-Athenians.

Hyperides was clearly trying to mitigate the culpability of an infatuated wastrel. The argument he supplied to his client may be compared with an Isaean speaker's charge that his rival to an estate had squandered his inheritance on the pursuit of boys (Is. 10.25), or with a Demosthenean speaker's harsh criticism of his adversary's lavish spending on a woman whom he described as a *hetaira*, which had impoverished his own sister and her children (Dem. 48.53–56). At the same time, Hyperides' speech illustrates why it was necessary for adversaries of men like the speaker, whose yielding to love and desire could earn them more sympathy than reproach, to offset this effect by expanding on the dangers and evils of submission to both.

AMBIVALENCE ABOUT YIELDING TO WINE

The speakers' frequent references to the combination of love or sex with wine indicate that the Athenians viewed the two appetites similarly.[18] By and large, the ethics of drinking wine—like that of sexual activity—reflected masculine concerns and tended to privilege male consumers.

In the taverns of Athens, free men, women of low repute or origin, and slaves could share wine in mixed company.[19] At home, however, only free adult males were approved as drinking companions. Men considered drinking by female members of the family as improper or subversive when it was not associated with religious and festive occasions or medical treatment. They reasoned that since women could not control their appetites and were incapable of coping with the power of wine to loosen inhibitions, they would disgrace themselves and the males associated with them.[20] This view can be gleaned from Apollodorus's de-

17. Cf. [Aristotle] *Rhetoric to Alexander* 7 1429a15–16; Colin 1946, 188–90, 193–96.
18. Sex and wine: Lys. 1.12; 4.7; Dem. 21.138; 47.19; 54.14; Aes. 1.70. Drinking in Athens: in addition to n. 24 below, see also McKinlay 1951; Lissarrague 1990b; Davidson 1997, esp. 36–69, 147–59; cf. Younger 1966, 109–11. Davidson 1997 also discusses addiction to expensive food, which is not as telling on manhood as wine drinking.
19. Davidson 1977, 53–61, characterizes taverns as plebian institutions as opposed to the more elitist *sumposia* (banquets). The oratorical sources concentrate on drinking in the upper class.
20. Just 1989, 186–87; Davidson 1997, 53–60. The disapproval of female citizens' drinking is much in the background of jokes about their fondness of wine: Aristophanes *Lysistrata* 113–14, 195–205; *Thesmophoriazousae* 630–33; Oeri 1948, 13–15. Cf. Aelian *Varia Historia* 2.38.

scription of the drunken Neaera having sex with multiple partners while her male companion, Phrynion, was asleep ([Dem.] 59.33). Hence, women of the house were barred from convivial occasions where wine and food were served—be they dinners, drinking parties *(potoi)*, *sumposia* (banquets), or *kōmoi* (post-party revelries, which often included serenading a loved one, altercations, and other mischief). Conventions restricted the consumption of alcohol at home to male participants in these social gatherings and to unrelated female companions and attendants who catered to their needs, either *hetairai* or flute girls.[21] When minors are mentioned in a drinking environment, it is usually at a *sumposion* or a *kōmos*, with the suggestion that they, like the female participants, provide sexual services to the older participants.[22] Thus the masculine attempt to monopolize legitimate wine drinking and its pleasure in the household defined the free male group through exclusion.

Within the group of males, drinking wine was socially condoned, and Athenian men who drank water instead of wine were considered unsociable and sour.[23] There were, however, rules and rituals pertaining to wine consumption, which generally called upon men to drink in moderation or in controlled environments, such as *sumposia*, or even *kōmoi*.[24] Moderation in drinking was commendable because it showed a man's self-restraint and did not impair his cognitive powers (esp. Isoc. 1.32; Arist. *EN* 7.3 1147a–b). It also often prevented unruly behavior, shame to the drinker or to those he humiliated, and altercations that might result in bodily harm, including violent death (Lys. 1.45; Dem. 32.27; 54.25). The disapproval of immoderate drinking is best illustrated by the adult Athenians' views of the young as addicted to pleasures, among which wine drinking played a prominent role. In his literary speech *Antidosis*, Isocrates describes the best of the young of his day as spending their time in drinking parties, get-togethers, indolence, and play, while the worse displayed their excessive *akolasia* (lack of discipline or self-indulgence) by drinking in public places and looking for cheap thrills in gambling houses and schools for flute girls. (Isoc. 15.286–87; cf. Isoc.

21. Identifying women as *hetairai* by their drinking and dining in male company: Is. 3.14; [Dem.] 59.24, 33, 48; cf. Keuls 1985, 175, 177; Kapparis 1999, 219–20.

22. Lys. 14.25; Dem. 19.199; cf. Golden 1990, 10.

23. Dem. 6.30; 19.46; Lucian 58.15; Dover 1968, 150–51; Davidson 1997, 155–56; MacDowell 2000, 226, comments on the limited disapproval of such men.

24. Frontisi-Ducroux and Lissarague 1990, 227, 230; Murray 1990b. For Greek opinions on moderate and excessive drinking, see, e.g., Theognis 479–83; Eubulus in Athenaeus *Deipnosophistae* 2.36b–c = fr. 94 (K-A); O'Brien 1992, 102–3, 234–39; Schmitt-Pantel 1992, 85–86; Murray and Tecusan 1995, esp. ch. 6; Davidson 1997, 194–205.

7.47–49; Hyp. 5 fr. a). These images of the youth were used, as we have seen, by both the prosecution and the defense in the case of young Ariston against his assailants, Conon and his son, with both sides describing their adversaries as drunken brutes (Dem. 54.3–5, 7–8, 14; and see also pp. 117–21 above).

Disapproval of drunkenness was not, however, limited to the young. Demosthenes cites drunkenness, together with lack of control and unseemly dancing, to illustrate the undignified and shameful behavior of Philip II in his court (Dem. 2.18–19). Intoxication underlined the abusive treatment of men and women, as in the case of drunken Simon, who, along with some friends, burst into the house of his rival for a youth, shamed the rival's female relatives, and attacked him and tried to kidnap the youth (Lys. 3.6, 12–18). Timarchus's drunkenness preceded his and friends' invasion of Pittalacus's house, which led to physical abuse and the destruction of his property (Aes. 1.58–59). Inebriation was behind Aeschines' maltreatment of a free Olynthian woman at a banquet he attended while on a mission to Macedonia as an Athenian envoy (Dem. 19.196–98).

But as with sexual desire, attitudes toward intoxication were hardly uniform, not even regarding the young. A Demosthenean speaker argues that the old tolerated (or are supposed to tolerate) the young's lack of moderation in expenditure, drinking, and play (Dem. 25.88). This ambivalence often surfaces in cases involving violent conduct by young men and adults, in which intoxication could serve to prove either an intention to harm and insult or its absence (and in that case make the attack less serious and humiliating). In Antiphon's fictional trial of a young defendant charged with killing an older man, for example, both the killer and his victim are accused of having started the fight when drunk (Ant. 4.2.1, 3.2; cf. Ant. 4.4.2). Moreover, the prosecutor calls for the defendant to be found guilty, not of the relatively excusable offense of manslaughter, but of murder, because he killed his victim out of drunken hubris and loss of restraint (Ant. 4.1.6).[25] Demosthenes, however, thought drunken attacks more excusable than sober, premeditated hubristic acts (Dem. 21.38, 73–74, 180).

According to Aeschines, when Timarchus and his friends sought (unsuccessfully) to reconcile with Pittalacus and ameliorate his disgrace fol-

25. Disapproval of drunken assault: Ant. 4.4.6; Arist. *EN* 3.5 1113b 25–1114a; *Pol.* 2.9.9 1274b17–23. Wine and hubris: MacDowell 1990, 18–23; Fisher 1992, esp. 16–17, 99–102, 206–7.

lowing their mistreatment of him, they pleaded with him not to prosecute them, alleging that what they had done had merely been drunken,
playful mischief *(pragma paroinia)* (Aes. 1.61; cf. Ar. *Wasps* 1256–61).
Simon's adversary similarly attempted to belittle the significance of the
injury he had inflicted on his opponent, as well as to disprove his intention to kill him, when he argued that it would be terrible, or strange
(deinos), to severely punish wounds resulting from drunken rivalry *(ek
methēs kai philonikias)*, or from play, or from slander, or from fighting
over a *hetaira*. He added that everyone regretted such conduct once they
had regained their senses (Lys. 3.43). A different Lysian speaker, in a
speech concerning an attempted homicide, tried to have it both ways. He
pleaded reduced culpability, arguing that his entry into the house of his
rival over a woman, and his wounding of him there, had been un-
premeditated and the result of his intoxicated state and his search for
boys and flute girls at the time of the incident. At the same time, however, he claimed that he had been forced to defend himself against a
lovesick opponent who had a proclivity for belligerence and getting
drunk (Lys. 4.6–8).

   Drunkenness was thus pleaded both in a bid to excuse violent conduct
and as evidence of an opponent's violent nature and lack of restraint. At
the core of these attitudes was the unresolved conflict between the social
and masculine injunction to control oneself when drinking and the admission that wine was often stronger than self-control or cultural inhibitions. This made the plea of drunkenness useful for rhetorical purposes, because it could both support arguments regarding a person's
responsibility for a misdeed and brand his misbehavior as only mildly re-
proachable and, hence, insufficient to convict him or to undermine his
reputation for being of otherwise reasonable and restrained character.[26]

THE EVILS OF GREED

Like sex or wine, greed (mostly *pleonexia*, in its negative sense; *kerdos*:
gain, profit, in their negative sense; *philokhrēmatia*: love of money; and
aiskhrokerdeia: shameful gain) was viewed as an appetite, linked to loss
of reason and control, and contrasted with wisdom, self-restraint
(sōphrosunē), and justice (Lyc. fr. 14.4 [Burtt]; Dem. 26.25; Plato *Laws*

---

26. Excusing and indulging drunkenness: Arist, *Rhet.* 2.25.1402b8–13; cf. Philippides
F 27 (K-A); Lys. 1.12; Hyp. 2.3; Carey and Reid 1985, 78; Scafuro 1997, 246–59; Davidson 1997, 151.

831c–e). Unlike sex or wine, however, greediness had no redeeming features.[27] It manifested itself in harmful forms such as immoderate acquis-
itiveness, stinginess, or, conversely, excessive spending and covetousness.
Greed was held responsible for the depletion of households, the betrayal
of kin and acquaintances, and other violations of the norms regulating
masculine roles within the family and the kinship group. Speeches concerning disputed property and inheritance illustrate these ill effects. An
Isaean speaker claims that his mother has been robbed of her right to an
estate by her uncle and her brother, both of whom he describes as money-
grubbers *(philokhrēmatountes)* (Is. 10.17). A different Isaean litigant
charges that shameful and excessive interest in money makes his uncle
covet his and others' properties (Is. fr. 1 [Forster]). Demosthenes describes
the embezzlement of his inheritance by relatives and guardians as "great
and manifest shamelessness" *(megalē kai periphanēs anaiskhuntia)* and
"excessive and terrible greediness" *(huperbolē deinēs aiskhrokerdeias)*
(Dem. 27.38). The culprits are "most insatiable for money" *(aplēstotatois
khrēmatōn)* and "desirous of money" *(khrēmatōn epethumoun)* (Dem.
27.60–61; cf. Dem. 27.46; 29.4, 48).[28] The attribution of greed to legal
adversaries thus showed them to be abusers of the power, privileges, and
responsibilities that the Athenian society and law entrusted to male
kin.

The desire to have more was perceived as unbounded. It controlled
conduct in private and public life.[29] An opponent lambastes Alcibiades
the Elder for having raised the tributes paid by Athens's allies, which had
made them hostile to the city, and then making personal use of public
funds. Alcibiades had also displayed greed *(pleonexia)* and arrogance in
his private life when he extorted huge sums of money from Callias, his
brother-in-law, for marrying his sister and siring a child with her. He
plotted to kill Callias for his wealth, hubristically and tyrannically
robbed, hit, imprisoned, and took money from fellow citizens, and
showed himself to be a money-grubber *(philokhrēmatos)* by his spending ([And.] 4.11–13, 15, 27, 32). The speaker does not attribute Alcibi-

27. Balot 2001's thoughtful investigation of greed in Athens has distinguished between
its meanings as a wish to have more goods and the wish to have more than one's fair share,
which was especially offensive to democratic ideology.

28. See also Is. 1.7–8; 9.23–26; Lys. 32.11–18; cf. Is. 2.29; Theophrastus *Characters*
9, 30. Undue and servile love of money: Dover 1974, 111, 170–75.

29. This notion of greed is used to reverse effect by Apollodorus, who claims that his
father, Pasion, could not have sided with one party in a dispute for the sake of personal
profit, because his *leitourgiai* and benefactions to the polis show no indication of any
shameful wish for gain on his part ([Dem.] 52.26).

ades' destructiveness to greed alone, but his depiction of him elaborates on how a greedy and powerful man could endanger both *oikos* and polis.[30]

Demosthenes' depictions of greedy men are less venomous but no less censorious. He portrays both Timocrates (in a speech written for the Athenian Diodorus) and Stephanus, son of Menecles (in a different speech written for Apollodorus) as men whose relationships with family, friends, or the state had been corrupted by their greed. In *Against Timocrates*, Diodorus charges that bribes and shameful gain had moved Timocrates to propose a law to change the procedure of arrest for debt, which would allegedly benefit special interests and political allies but would harm the state (Dem. 24.65, 196). He adds that insatiable greed *(aplēstia)* had prompted Timocrates to aid the politician Androtion in wronging the people and in embezzling public money (Dem. 24.174). Finally, Diodorus stokes the jurors' outrage at a man whose love of money had perverted his filial and fraternal obligations. Timocrates, he says, is such a miser and so pitiless that he had refused to help his own father get out of a public debt, and had given his sister in marriage to a non-Athenian for financial gain. A person who had done such things to his family would surely put his public services and decrees up for sale (Dem. 24.200–203).

The portrait of Stephanus, whom Apollodorus charged with giving false testimony on behalf of his adversary, Phormio, highlights the moral turpitude of a man driven by greed. The speaker depicts Stephanus as a parasite who sucks rich men dry. After ditching the banker Aristolochus when the latter had become impoverished, he had attached himself to Phormio. Bound by no sense of friendship or gratitude, Stephanus had refused to help Aristolochus's son to pay his father's debts. He treated citizens with disrespect, and showed no concern for kin or even for his own good name. Thinking only of how to get even more, he, a rich man, shamefully hid his wealth to cheat the state out of its *leitourgiai*. Stating the obvious, Apollodorus observes that wealth does not justify wrongdoing, and asserts that Stephanus's conduct is due to his *aiskhrokerdeia*, *pleonexia*, hubris, and the wish to defeat the laws. He concludes this character assassination by accusing Stephanus of being merciless to those who owe him money, including his kin (Dem. 45.63–70).

In these cases, yielding to the shameful and selfish desire for gain

---

30. Gazzano 1999, 64–65; Gribble 1999: 132–34; Balot 2001, 195–196; cf. Wohl 2002. 139.

clashed with the conduct expected of a man in his roles as a *kurios,* family man or kinsman, friend, and citizen. Greed dethroned trust, loyalty, the pursuit of good name, and conformity to customs and laws.

At times, however, speakers focus on the effects of greed on the polis arguing that it eviscerates the patriotic and manly duty to sacrifice interests, assets, and even one's life for Athens (Dem. 47.3; 51.10–11; 58.29; Lyc. 1.57; cf. Dem. 14.32; 49.65–67). Politicians made a popular target for charges of greed; they put private interests ahead of those of the public, it was suggested, thereby betraying public trust and endangering the country.[31] Aeschines and Demosthenes trade accusations that bribe-taking and the quest for profit dominate their respective political careers.[32]

Greed, then, disrupted the quality of life at home and in the city and subverted the values and the security that sustained both institutions. This perception was used by orators (and often by prosecutors who probably wished to provide the defendants with a common, but base, motive for their alleged misconduct) to depict their adversaries as undeserving of a favorable opinion in view of their mean character and failure to overcome their greed.[33]

THE RHETORIC OF SELF-CONTROL

The Athenians hoped that men governed by greed and other desires would be punished by the courts or public opinion. But no less important was internalizing self-control. The concepts of *sōphrosunē* (self-control or restraint) and its cognates, as well as being *metrios* (in its sense of being moderate), conveyed the ability to master appetites and emotions.[34] Children, youths, and women, as well as men, were expected to practice *sōphrosunē.* According to the orators, each of these groups had its special challenges. Children must learn discipline and sexual mod-

31. Esp. Hyp. 5.34–35; Harvey 1985, 102–3; Balot 2001, 225–30.
32. Aes. 3.218; Dem. 19.28; cf. 8.71; 18.295–96; 19.223. For additional violations of communal values attributed to greed: Dem. 37.53; Lys. 12.19; Is. 9.26; Isoc. 21.6.
33. I have limited my discussion to cases where the sources explicitly name greed as motive or attribute. Constraints of space prevent me from discussing cases where greed is all but stated: e.g., Is. 4; 5; Aes. 1.102–6, 170–72; Dem. 32.
34. North 1966; cf. Cairns 1993, 314–21. See Dover 1974, 59, and Fisher 1992, 8–9, 13–18, for the limitations and merits of Aristotle's definition of *sōphrosunē* in *Rhet.* 1.9.9 1366b13–15 and *EN* 3.10 1118a2–1118b8. *Metrios:* Morris 1996, 22; cf. North 1966, 138.

esty.[35] Young men were expected to be shy, respectful, and modest.[36] For women, *sōphrosunē* prescribed sexual chastity, reserved conduct, and conformity to familial roles.[37] These forms reflected the values of adult males, who were, in turn, subjected to higher standards because they were thought more capable of controlling themselves than any other group.[38]

Sōphrosunē was associated with other manly virtues. In the "Erotic Oration" included in Demosthenes' corpus of works, Epicrates, a young, but mature, male youth, is said to possess beauty of body, *sōphrosunē* of soul, and manliness *(andreia)* in both (Dem. 61.8, 13). Aeschines contrasts the *kinaidos,* a womanish, incontinent man of pathic predilection, with a hoplite with a well-built body and a *sōphrōn* mind (Aes. 2.151).[39] A Demosthenean speaker similarly contrasts democrats, who live under the rule of laws and are self-restrained *(sōphrones)* and good *(khrēstoi),* with those who live under oligarchy, who are cowards *(anandroi)* and slaves (Dem. 24.75). In addition to being associated with a manly body, temperance, and freedom, self-control was often linked to martial masculinity. Demosthenes praises Athenians who displayed *sōphrosunē,* manly courage *(andreia),* and justice when they camped next to Theban domiciles on the eve of Chaeroneia (Dem. 18.215–16). Both Hyperides and Aeschines link self-control to courage and military valor. Because the Athenians had brought up their children in full *sōphrosunē,* Hyperides says, the latter displayed superior *aretē* in battle (Hyp. 6.8). Aeschines contrasts a Spartan who fought splendidly in war and led a life of justice and self-control *(enkrateia)* with another Spartan who was a

---

35. Aes. 1.6–7, 139, 158, 187, 189; 2.180; cf. Isoc. 9.22.

36. Dem. 25.24, 88; 61.17, 20–21; Aes. 2.180; cf. Is. 1.1; Dem. 19.285; 54.1; Plato *Charmides,* esp. 158c; Cairns 1993, 314–15; Fisher 2001, 60–67.

37. Lys. 1.10; Aes. 1.182; [Dem.] 59.86, 114. On female propriety, esp. in tragedy, see North 1966, 69–71; Cairns 1993, 306; cf. Carson 1990, 142.

38. According to Aeschines (1.11), forty was the most *sōphrōn* of ages. See also Aes. 1.18, 48; Hyp. 5.21; *Ath. Pol.* 56.3, with Rhodes 1993, 625–26; Aristotle *Rhet.* 2.14 1390b4–16. Although Socrates' pupils apportioned *sōphrosunē* equally between men and women (Plato *Meno* 74b; Xen. *Oec.* 7.15, 26), Aristotle seems to have been closer to the popular view ranking masculine self-control, which he grants to the ruler (male) rather than to the ruled (female), as higher; *Pol.* 1.3 1260a14–24; 3.2 1277b17–25; North 1966, 25, 129; Foucault 1985, 85–86; cf. 63–77; Whitehead 1993, 71; Pomeroy 1994, 275. *Sōphrosunē* and honesty in Greek epitaphs: Dover 1974, 67–68; Whitehead 1993, 71–72.

39. See Davidson 1997, esp. 167–82, and Fox 1998, 7–13, for criticism of Winkler 1990a, 45–47, 56–56, who has made the *kinaidos* a major cultural marker in Greek male ideology. It is probably not an accident that Aeschines is exceptional among the extant orators in finding a use for this term (Aes. 1.131, 181; 2.88, 99, 151; 3.167).

coward and villain.[40] Self-control and moderation were associated with other masculine and civic attributes, such as rational sensibility, good reputation, sensitivity to shame, respect for elders and civic order, modest lifestyle, obedience to law, justice, and public service. Conversely, lack of control *(akrasia)* and absence of *sōphrosunē* were associated with masculine deficiencies, including the loss of reason, indecent or shameful behavior, brutal and hubristic conduct, and self-indulgence.[41]

Thus, it paid to convey the impression of being in possession of self-control and moderation, especially in the jury courts (Dem. 21.185). In spite of his desire for the love of a youth, the Lysian speaker of *Against Simon* had contended with it most properly (Lys. 3.4). He had tried hard to avoid getting into fights with Simon (Lys. 3.13, 32) and had refused to sue him, so that his opponent would not be punished too severely (Lys. 3.40). Affecting similar attitudes, Ariston chose a legal action against Conon for assault on a scale befitting his youth (Dem. 54.1). He kept his distance rather than sue Conon's sons for the wrongs they had done him during military service (Dem. 54.6) and proclaimed himself to be a moderate person *(metrios)* who was never seen drunk or violent (Dem. 54.15–16). Both speakers show how the Athenians' approval of moderate and self-restrained conduct could be exploited in cases involving battery to exaggerate an adversary's brutality and support the speakers' claims that they had not been the initiators of their respective fights.

Moderation helped create a wholesome man whose good citizenship or public services were complemented by a modest personal lifestyle.[42] According to the rules of *kharis,* such men deserved favorable consideration from the jury, because their moderate personal lifestyle made them harmless, useful citizens, and hence beneficial to the state. An Isaean

---

40. Aes. 1.180–81, and see also p.119 above. Courage and *sōphrosunē*: North 1966, 144–46; cf. Thuc. 1.84.3, with Hornblower 1991, 1: 129; Wheeler 1991, 138; Smoes 1995, 78–97. The concepts of *andreia* and *sōphrosunē* could collide, however: Dem. 61.30; Isoc. 12.197–98; Plato *Rep.* 4 429a–431d, with Hobbs 2000, 137–74; *Symposion* 196c–d; *Meno* 74a–b; Arist. *Pol.* 1 1260a20–23, 3 1277b20–4; North 1966, e.g., 97, 108, 144, 170–73, 190, 195; Dover 1974, 66–67.

41. Moderation and rationality: And. 1.145; Dover 1974, 121–22; and good name: Lys. 19.16; Isoc. 18.32; and sensitivity to shame: Aes. 3.11–12; and respect for others: Dem. 25.24, 88; Aes. 1.22; and modest lifestyle and ideal political virtues: Dem. 3.25; 58.62; and obedience to law: Dem. 24.75; 26.25; and justice: Dem. 26.25; Isoc. 16.28; and public service: Lys. 21.19; Dem. 38.26. Moderation was also used to denote honesty (Lys. 19.54; 29.24) and decent character (Hyp. 4.12). Lack of *sōphrosunē*, however, was linked to irrational conduct: Is. 3.17; Dem. 26.25; to shameful conduct: Dem. 2.8,18; 25.24; to hubris: Lys. 26.5; Dem. 21.128; and to self-indulgence: Aes. 1.95.

42. See, in addition to the following cases: Is. fr. 35 (Forster); Lys. 16.3 (although also 16.19); 21.18–19; 26.3; Dem. 38.26; Hyp. fr. B 23.

speaker claimed that Apollodorus, son of Eupolis, his adopted father, was a wealthy man and a moderate citizen *(metrios politēs)*, who did not covet or forcibly try to appropriate other people's property, but kept to himself and lived modestly, so that he could give money to the state whenever the need arose. The speaker consequently asked the jury to reward Apollodorus's exemplary personal restraint and public work by honoring his wish to adopt him, a useful citizen in his own right, as his son (Is. 7.39–41). In his defense against charges of illegally attending the Mysteries of 400, Andocides cited his self-control and claimed a debt of gratitude from the city for his ancestors' brave and dedicated public services. He maintained that he was a good citizen, and that, having learned from his mistakes, he knew how to be self-controlled and sensible *(to sōphronein kai orthōs bouleuesthai)*, adding for good measure that his many powerful friends could be useful to the city (And. 1.141–45; cf. And. 2.5–6). In his prosecution of Stephanus for false testimony, Apollodorus supported his claim to a favorable decision by denying charges of immoderate conduct, boasting of personal moderation and public generosity, and depicting his rival, Phormio, as lacking in moderation. He refuted the accusation that his demeanor was offensive or hubristic by arguing that he was moderate *(metrios)* in his expenses and much better ordered *(eutaktoteros)* in his life than his adversary or other people. He had shown great munificence to the polis and the people, a generosity apparently made possible by his modest lifestyle (Dem. 45.77–78). Apollodorus portrayed Phormio as a corrupter of men and women, hubristic in conduct and a profligate (Dem. 45.78–80). All three speakers assumed that the jurors were morally obliged to reward men whose self-control benefited the state, and, moreover, that it was in their interest to do so. Young Ariston alluded to this perception when he warned the jury that if they believed men like his brutal, licentious, and hubristic assailants, useful people (like himself) would not benefit from living as *metrioi* (Dem. 54.14–15). A failure to reward moderation would encourage moderate men to join the ranks of those who threatened the city's social order.[43]

Equally useful in court was the closely related image of being a quiet or unmeddlesome man (often, *apragmōn*).[44] Such a man minded his own

<hr />

43. For the power of moderation in private life and a record of public service to atone for transgressions against the state, see Lys. 12.38; 21.3, 6; cf. Lys. 14.41–43; Dem. 25.76; *Lett.* 3.24–26.

44. Ehrenberg 1947; Dover 1974, 187–90; Harding 1981; Lateiner 1982; Carter 1986; Demont 1990; Christ 1998, 66, 165.

business and tried to keep out of public life and avoid confrontation, including the agonistic activity of litigation. These qualities helped litigants
to deflect allegations of litigiousness and portray the charges against
them as unfair and malicious. The quiet man's image suited several masculine perceptions as well. His lack of experience in court, as opposed to
his rival's skills, appealed to the agonistic, democratic, and masculine
ethos of a fair and equal contest and invited the jurors' sympathy. Seeking a compromise before going to trial showed that he was a reasonable
and nonconfrontational person who curbed the drive for destructive
feuding and vengeance. Such a man was the prosecutor of Spudias. In a
case concerning the property of their mutual father-in-law, the speaker
argued that he had been compelled to go to court, that he had made every
effort to avoid litigation, but that his mild and considerate approach to
Spudias had been met with disdain. He also depicted his opponent as a
man who frequently used the courts and portrayed himself as fearful that
his lack of experience would hamper the presentation of his case (Dem.
41.1–2; cf. 41.24).[45] Mastering his fears, however, he had taken Spudias
to court. Indeed, as Matthew Christ (1998, 166) has noted, the quiet person displayed courage when he risked contending with a formidable opponent and was unwilling to suffer wrong passively. A prime example is
a speaker in Antiphon's fictional homicide case who casts himself in the
role of the reluctant, but determined, antagonist. He laments that he has
been forced into court and has had to go against his peaceful nature and
display audacity *(tolma;* Ant. 3.2.1; cf. Aes. 1.1–2).

The frequent use of the unmeddlesome, moderate, or restrained
image led rivals to contest it. This was often done by prosecutors who
were concerned that the defendants' moderation would gain them sympathy with the court. Their primary technique was to unmask an opponent's "true" nature. In the review *(dokimasia)* of Euandrus's background prior to his acceding to the office of archon, a Lysian speaker
predicted that the defendant would ignore the charges against him and
dwell instead on the money his family had spent on the city, his performance of *leitourgiai,* and his victories (in competitions) on behalf of
the demos; he would also describe himself as orderly *(kosmios),* not
rash, given to minding his own business, and moderate *(sōphron).*
Clearly concerned that such a record and lifestyle would outweigh any

45. See also Is. 1.1; Lys. 7.1; fr. 32, 78.4 (Thalheim); Dem. 24.6; 42.12; 54.24; Hyp.
4.21; cf. Lys. 12.4; Dem. 21.83, 141; 37.43; 40.32; Hyp. 3.23, Isoc. 4.157, 227.

of the crimes he attributed to Euandrus, the speaker portrayed the *leitourgiai* performed by Euandrus's father as a ploy to gain public trust, which he later betrayed by helping to overthrow democracy, and Euandrus's quiet moderation as inauthentic and practiced under compulsion (Lys. 26.3–5). Similarly, in a speech written for the prosecutor of Aristogeiton for bribe-taking, Dinarchus suggests that that the defendant will try to portray himself as a man who is *metrios* in character, comes from a good family, has performed noble deeds in private and public, and hence deserves acquittal. In fact, however. the defendant has treated his father shamefully, has a criminal record, has spent time in jail, has lodged false accusations against a priestess and her family, is a state debtor, and is guilty of other misdeeds as well (Din. 2.8–14). Apollodorus was equally anxious to deprive adversaries of any claim they might have to moderation. Since the Athenians appear to have associated restraint and sobriety with a lack of levity, Apollodorus argued that Stephanus's walking along the city walls looking angry was not a sign of sobriety *(sōphrosunē)* but masked misanthropy and a bitter disposition (Dem. 45.66–68). Phormio also behaved modestly *(sōphrōn)* by day, but at night committed acts (presumably adultery) that were punishable by death (Dem. 45.79–80). All these speakers portray other men's restraint and moderation as a guise designed to mislead the jury or persuade the people to reward their allegedly masculine and social conformity. At the same time, their suggestions that a man could easily feign being *metrios* or self-controlled made self-control and moderation disputable attributes and uncertain measures of a man's worth.

What further complicated the use of self-control and moderation in evaluating a man was the fact that these notions were heavy with ambivalent meanings and subjected to partisan judgments. There was disagreement, for example, about the merit of being moderate under compulsion rather than out of volition. Thus, the accuser of Euandrus charged that he deserved no credit for his moderate and peaceful lifestyle because he had no opportunity to be licentious and was prevented from wrongdoing by other people. One should look to Euandrus's oligarchic past, when he could have chosen between these two ways of life but revealed his true nature when he opted for illegal political activity (Lys. 26.5). In contrast, another Lysian speaker claimed that poor, weak men like himself deserved sympathy when they were forced by necessity to be self-restrained (Lys. 24.15–17; cf. Ant. 4.3.2). Alluding to the same attitude, Demosthenes said of Meidias that anyone else who had been voted against for impiety would have adopted a low profile and behaved like a moderate man *(metrios)*, at least till his trial was over, but not Meidias (Dem. 21.199). Apparently, moderation under compulsion could be regarded as either for or against a person, depending on its partisan presentation.

Moreover, speakers took advantage of uncertainty about what qualified as a quiet, restrained lifestyle. Quietism was normally approved in a man, although when it was manifested in lack of involvement in public affairs, it could be subjected to radically different interpretations. In his prosecution of Ctesiphon for proposing to honor Demosthenes with a crown, Aeschines attempted to deflect in advance Demosthenes' contentions that he had spent his time chasing young men in the gymnasia, and not in public service; that he had not prosecuted Ctesiphon in public interest; and that he was silent at moments that called for him to speak up and take part in the city's public affairs. In response, Aeschines complained that the quietness *(hesukhia)* of his life had been slandered. He explained that he chose to keep silent due to his moderate lifestyle *(he tou biou metriotēs)* and had been content with having little rather than being desirous for more. He spoke in public out of free will, when necessary, and in accordance with the democratic principle of allowing people to speak when they so chose, rather than because of the compulsive need to spend that made Demosthenes the obedient mouthpiece of his paymasters (Aes. 3.216–20). Aeschines' quietism, then, did not mean that he was passive, self-indulgent, fearful, opportunistic, or lacking in civic spirit, all faults in a man and a citizen. Instead, he equated moderation and quietness with curbing greed and cherished independence and freedom, the latter a chief marker of Athenian manhood, while imputing to Demosthenes the masculine faults of lack of control over his impulse to spend and of putting himself out for hire.[46]

Yet although Aeschines portrays his quietism as socially approved, Demosthenes depicts it in his defense of Ctesiphon as "injurious" *(adikos)* and "festering" *(hupoulos)*, emphatically distinguishes it from the just, beneficial, and simple quietism practiced by the majority of the citizens, and points out that Aeschines' infrequent public appearances had coincided with the city's times of troubles (Dem. 18.307–8). Demosthenes' distinction between positive and negative quietism tells us little, however, because instead of clarifying what makes the one bad and the

----

46. *Sōphrosunē* and freedom: Pohlenz 1966, 30–34, 67–71, 82, 92–93, 99–100.

other good, he simply labels them as such.[47] That two orators could offer radically different characterizations of the same conduct is explained by the Athenians' uncertainty about how to judge quiet and moderate behavior and by an inclination to assess a man not just by his actions but by motives that could be subjectively assigned to him.

Uncertainty about self-control, love, and desire and its self-interested manipulation is found in Aeschines' speech against Timarchus. Aeschines informs the jury that the defense will claim that Timarchus's respectable loving relationship has been wrongly stigmatized as prostitution. The orator speaking for Timarchus will put Timarchus and his male lovers in the heroic company of other loving couples, such as the democratic martyrs and tyrant slayers Harmodius and Aristogeiton or the Homeric Achilleus and Patrocles. He will praise beauty combined with self-control (sōphrosunē) and point out that Aeschines himself has been involved in similar, but more unseemly, affairs (Aes. 1.132–35). "But I," responded Aeschines, "do not object to legitimate love (erōs dikaios), nor do I say that the outstanding in beauty are prostitutes" (Aes. 1.136). In an attempt to distinguish Timarchus's love affairs from others, including his own, he argues that "I differentiate between loving the beautiful and the sōphrōn [self-restrained], which is an emotion experienced by a soul that is humane [philanthrōpos] and sympathetic [eugnōmōn]; but licentiousness [to aselgainein] for monetary payment is the act of the hubristic and vulgar [literally, uneducated] man. I think that it is noble [kalos; honorable] to be the object of eros without being corrupted, but disgraceful to prostitute oneself, being won over by pay."[48]

Few Athenians were likely to dispute Aeschines' assertion that self-control, moderation, and a virtuous disposition were the cardinal criteria of legitimate love between male partners, or the distinctions he drew between sex for pay and honest love, and between beauty and its corrupters. Yet a closer look at Aeschines' distinctions and characterization of loving relationships shows them to be vague and a bit misleading. He contrasts the rather abstract notion of humane, sympathetic, and noble love with the more concrete love for pay. And, while most Athenians

47. Yunis 2001, 280, identifies the people's quietness in Dem. 18.308 as a reference to the fact that they seldom spoke in the Assembly. Such passivity can hardly be called "just" or "useful."

48. Aes. 1.137. Dover's 1989, 47, translation slightly modified. For interpretations of this passage, see Dover 1989, 42–49; D. Cohen 1991c, 198–199; Davidson 1997, 254–57; Sissa 1999; Ford 1999, 251–54; Fisher 2001, 58–61, 274–82; Ferrari 2002, 138–47.

would have probably have concurred with his (and the defense's) premise that lovers should behave in a restrained way, they would not necessarily have agreed on a definition of restrained love. What Aeschines defined as male prostitution, driven by lust, Timarchus's advocates portrayed as honorable love affairs (Aes. 1.132–34). Moreover, the speaker on behalf Timarchus described Aeschines' courting of youths in the gymnasia as a threat to pederastic love, because Aeschines brought it into disrepute. He behaved like a pest, was a lover of many boys, participated in altercations over them, and composed indecent erotic poems; he was, in short, driven by desire. Aeschines replied that his poems were proper, and expressed universal truths about the difference between noble and ignoble love, which placed his loving practices clearly in the former category (Aes. 1.135–37).

The criteria for distinguishing restrained from unrestrained love and their respective practitioners were, then, far from clear. Acknowledging the difficulties of differentiating between the two kinds of love, Aeschines provided a definition for each and then tried to apply his definitions to a law that forbade slaves to attend the gymnasia by interpreting it in light of a distinction between self-controlled pederasty involving youths and free men, as opposed to lust-governed relationships with slaves (Aes. 1.138–39). Later in the speech, he volunteered to further assist his audience by distinguishing those who possess good looks and have the most restrained *(sōphronestatoi)* lovers from those who use their good looks to disgrace and prostitute themselves, and to name certain individuals in each category (Aes. 1.155–59; cf. 1.140). Aeschines may have sensed that the jurors found it difficult to apply such broad categories to real-life situations and to judge conduct on a continuum between the poles of overtly passionate, disgraceful and patently restrained, socially approved love.[49]

To sum up, self-control enabled men to resist the undesirable and incapacitating influences of desire and, hence, to behave morally. In private and in public, self-restrained men were modest in their needs, and performed the masculine roles of a *kurios*, kinsman, friend, and citizen well. Lack of restraint detracted from one's manliness and was regarded as a source of danger to other men, their values, and their institutions. Yet the

---

49. Dem. 61.1, 3–5, 20–21, also seeks to distinguish between legitimate and illegitimate love, but similarly provides no clear criteria for either. N. R. E. Fisher (2001, esp. 53–67) frames Aeschines' explanations in the context of what he sees as Athenians' attempts to strengthen their political and moral principles faced with the Macedonian threat.

significance accorded to self-control in judging manhood and character encouraged rhetorical manipulation, which was possible because the Athenians were ambivalent about the criteria to use in judging self-restrained conduct. Thus when a Lysian speaker said that the best and most restrained man could manage his desire in the most orderly way (Lys. 3.4), his aphorism provided them with little help in defining restraint and identifying its practitioners.

CHAPTER 8

What Men Fear

As we have seen, orators often bear witness to fear in the experience of manhood in the family, the military, and politics. Following Aristotle, I shall define fear here as the anticipation of something bad in the future (Arist. *EN* 3.6. 1115a9; *Rhet.* 2.5.2 1382a20–1383a13; cf. Plato *Laches* 198b–c). Scholars distinguish between fear and anxiety, which is a general uncertainty about the future. Fear is more concrete and focused, and hence easier to manage, augment, reduce, or even eliminate.[1] The malleability of fear and anxieties invited speakers to take advantage of both. In so doing, they often appealed to the masculine anxiety about the fragility of order and tried to distinguish men who supported order from those who threatened it.

BENEFICIAL AND LEGITIMATE FEARS

Athenians used a man's reactions to fear to assess his character, masculinity, and conduct. They recognized fear as natural to human beings and hence not always reprehensible (Aes. 3.175). In fact, fears for one's reputation, or of the laws, were commendable and deemed beneficial to the state, because they deterred people from wrongdoing.[2] Fear also re-

---

1. Delumeau 1978, esp. 9; Bouwsma 1980, esp. 215–16, 218–19, 222; Naphy and Roberts 1997b, esp. 1–3.
2. Lys. 14.14–15; Dem. 21.196; 60.25–26; Lyc. 1.129–130; pp. 165–66 above; cf. Lys. 20.21. Fear of the gods was commendable as well: see, e.g., [Dem.] 49.67; 59.77. Fear as conducive to women's morality and domestic duties: [Dem.] 59.68; Xen. *Oec.* 7.25.

sulted in prudential action or fostered healthy distrust. Aeschines asserts that democracy was toppled when the people trusted, instead of fearing, politicians who flattered them. Lysias called upon the Greeks at the Olympic Games of (probably) 384 to fear for their future, a probable reference to threats from Persia and Dionysius, the tyrant of Syracuse.[3] Rather than challenge masculinity, then, certain fears had a utilitarian function, useful for the proactive men who served as protectors of the state and its regime.

The Athenians did not expect a man to take a courageous stand against every danger he encountered. In an uneven contest or power relationship, they acknowledged that fear justified the weaker party's reluctance to take a risk and suffer the consequences.[4]

This attitude appears frequently in the speeches. Thus two defendants justified their record under the oligarchy by pleading fear of that oppressive regime. A Lysian speaker on behalf of Polystratus, who was active in an oligarchic government of Athens in 411/10, argued that the reason Polystartus had not opposed the oligarchs was because they executed or expelled people who opposed them, putting fear and dread in the hearts of potential dissidents.[5] The defendant Eratosthenes, who was charged by Lysias with involvement in the death of his brother, Polemarchus, during the tyrannical regime of the Thirty in 404/3, availed himself of a similar defense. Eratosthenes admitted that he had arrested Lysias's brother, but insisted that he had obeyed the orders of the Thirty out of fear (Lys. 12.25). Eratosthenes' confession of a legitimate fear of the strong worried Lysias, who expressed the concern that this explanation might persuade some jurors to acquit him (Lys. 12.50), apparently because it turned Eratosthenes into an unwilling instrument, indeed a victim, of the oligarchic government.

The image of the rightly fearful, weak man helped clients involved in a fight, in which the question of who had started it established the party responsibility for the damage done. A speaker in Antiphon's fictional trial for homicide of a young man who has killed an older person argues

3. Commendable fear of politicians: Aes. 3.234; cf. Dem. *Pr.* 42.2. Fear concerning the future: Lys. 33.6, 8; Diodorus of Sicily 14.109. See also Dem. 19.223–24 and Hyp. 3.13, where fear moves the speakers to deal with danger.

4. Speakers depicted fearful individual Athenians (Lys. 23.15; Isoc. 21.2; Dem. 22.25–27; 39.3), or even the entire nation (Aes. 3.80; Lyc. 1.37, 43) as taking steps to avoid meeting danger. Aristotle's discussion of fear in the *Rhetoric* is dominated by fear of the strong and is devoid of evaluative judgment as well: *Rhet.* 2.5.1–15 1382a20–1383a25.

5. Lys. 20.8. On Lys. 20 and its authorship, see Usher 1999, 115–16; Rubinstein 2000, 152–54. See Lys. 20.18 for a different use of the fear of confronting the strong in this case.

that it was unlikely that the old man had started the fight, because old
men are self-restrained, can handle their wine, and are weak, hence
afraid of youths (Ant. 4.3.2). A Lysian client and Simon's rival for a boy
claimed that he had altered his route to avoid an altercation with Simon
and his companions. He added that people who are fearful run away,
while those who pursue others intend to cause harm (Lys. 3.35–36). Fear
of a stronger party, he implied, was natural, justified restraint or retreat
and reinforced the claim that the adversary was the aggressor. Demosthenes and Aeschines also deemed victims of hubris and brutality who
declined to sue their wealthy, powerful aggressors to be legitimately fearful (Dem. 21.19–20; Aes. 1.64; cf. Dem. 19.80). These speakers had a
special agenda, of course, but they used fear to justify a man's refusal to
face risk, including in cases where he could be seen as a coward or was
expected to retaliate because he had been wronged or humiliated.[6]

OVERCOMING FEAR:
COWARDICE, COURAGE, AND RASHNESS

As opposed to fears that were seen as conducive to masculinity or as deserving of sympathy, others were routinely and severely condemned.
They came under the category of cowardice *(anandria, malakia, deilia,* or
kakia), and were ascribed to men who put their own safety and interests
ahead of the common weal or their own honor. Cowardice, then, involved fears that moved an individual to fail in his duty as a soldier, politician, or citizen (e.g., Lys. 31.7; Dem. 8.68; Lyc. 1.5) or caused capable individuals, or even the state, to shrink from responding to attacks on them.

As the primary meaning of *anandria* and *malakia* (softness) connoted,
cowardice meant lack of manhood. Thus, these and similar words were
often applied to women, slaves, and barbarians.[7] Aeschines' speech
Against Ctesiphon is especially illustrative in this regard. In reference to
the proposal to crown Demosthenes for his public services, he comments
sarcastically on the herald's official salute that accompanied the crowning act: " 'That this man,' if man *[anēr]* he is, 'the Athenian people crown
for [his] *arēte*,' the most evil *[kakistos]*, 'for [his] good manly virtue *[an-
dragathia]*,' the coward *[anandros]* and deserter."[8] Rejecting his rival's

6. See also Dem. 18.245; Hyp. 3.13; cf. Dem. 54.17.
    7. Cowardice and women: Arist. *Pol.* 3.2.10.1277b 22–23; cf. Dover 1974, 100; and
slaves: Dem. 24.75; cf. Hunt 1998, 48, 129, 162; and barbarians: Isoc., e.g., 4.152; 5.137.
    8. Aes. 3.155. For lack of substantial distinction between *arēte* and *andragathia,* see
Adkins 1960, 235; Whitehead 1993, 57–62; cf. Dover 1974, 164–65.

assertions that he had incited the Greeks to revolt against Alexander, Aeschines argued that Demosthenes would never go near a place of danger. He would go where there was money, but he would not act like a man *(praxin de andros ou praxeis)* (Aes. 3.167).

Given the damage cowardice did to one's reputation, good men strained to dissociate themselves from it. Speakers exploited their need to do so.[9] About 403, a Lysian speaker opposed a proposal, backed by Sparta, to limit citizenship in Athens and urged the Athenians to reject it even if it meant going to war. Given Athens's history of fighting for justice and freedom, he proclaimed, it would be shameful *(aiskhros)* and amount to cowardice *(kakia)* if they were not prepared to fight for their freedom now (Lys. 34.11). Similarly, Demosthenes rebuked Athenians as cowards for failing to respond to the danger posed by Philip and to support their ideals with actions. Aeschines used the threat to national honor, not to stir the Athenians into manly action, but to prevent the crowning of the coward Demosthenes.[10]

As Aeschines shows, the damage done to one's honor and reputation by suspicion of cowardice could be manipulated for personal ends. This is confirmed in several speeches in which a desire to avoid the charge of cowardice is used by litigants to justify and dignify their appearances in court. Andocides, who was suspected of having saved his skin by informing on others in the Mysteries affair, says that he wishes to absolve himself of wrong *(kakia)* and cowardice *(anandria)* (And. 1.56). Two other litigants seem more manipulative of this concern, which they use to justify bringing their opponents to trial. Young Theomnestus, in Apollodorus's speech against Neaera, claims that he is suing Stephanus because men call his having failed to retaliate for the wrongs Stephanus has done to him and his relatives very cowardly *(anandrotatos)* ([Dem.] 59.12). Mantitheus defends his legal action against his half-brother for the use of his own name by stating that giving up on his name would be a great dishonor and cowardice (Dem. 39.6; see pp. 142–44 above). Both present their litigation as retaliatory and defensive, and hence free of malicious motives.[11] In addition, they and Andocides used the court to pub-

9. Since cowardice could be attributed to one's nature (Lys. 10.28; Aes. 3.81, 163, 175), it was not easy to erase this shame. Cowardice associated with other moral defects: Dem. 21.172; Aes. 1.105; 2.22.

10. Shaming as cowards: Lys. 34.11; Dem. 1.24; 4.42; 9.35, 67–68; 11.21–22; 13.34; 15.23; cf. 19.218–19; Aes. 3.231, 247. For the Athenians' fearless ancestors, see Lys. 2.15, 23, 63; Dem. 18.98; cf. Lys. 2.29; Thuc. 2.42.4; Hesk 2000, 11–13.

11. See also Lys. 22.1–3; Allen 2000b, 17–18.

licly advertise their compliance with the manly injunction to avoid the disgrace of cowardice.

Manly Athenians, then, feared cowardice, yielded to salutary fears, but suppressed harmful ones. Yet this formula was susceptible to rhetorical manipulation, because defining a man as courageous or a coward and identifying the nature of his fears was done on partisan grounds. For example, while adversaries described Andocides' informing on his relatives and friends as "utterly shameful" ([Lys.] 6.23) and as a cowardly act (And. 1.56), Andocides retorted that his action showed valor *(aretē)* (ibid.). Demosthenes deemed Meidias's donation of a trireme and embarking on it for a campaign cowardice, because his motive was to avoid more dangerous service elsewhere (Dem. 21.160–66). And Demosthenes and Aeschines traded charges that they had prosecuted each other or other Athenians out of cowardice (Dem. 19.221; 18.279; cf. 18.16).

The thin line between cowardice and caution invited rhetorical manipulation as well. Demosthenes labels failure to take military action as cowardice at one time and prudence at another (pp. 114–16 above). In his speech *On the Embassy,* he reports that Aeschines and the politician Philocrates had disparaged his political conduct as lacking in daring *(atolmos)* and cowardly *(deilos);* yet he defines it as prudentially cautious *(eulabēs)* (Dem. 19.206; cf. And. 3.33).

Courageous conduct was no less contestable. A masculine notion, courage stressed the manly qualities of self-sacrifice and self-restraint, endurance, reasoned thinking, and, of course, the ability to prevail over one's fears.[12] Yet claims of courage were not easily admitted, because attitudes toward men facing fear were based less on an impersonal scale of manly values than on the individuals who articulated them.

One example is the subjectively drawn distinction between manly bravery *(andreia)* and rashness *(thrasos* and *tolma* in its negative sense). In a letter attributed to Demosthenes, the writer claims that an opponent "behaves boldly *[thrasunetai]* like a man *[anēr],* but takes the passive part *[paskhei]* like a woman" (Dem. *Lett.* 4.11). The author of the "Erotic Oration" says that people who display their *andreia* might be considered overbold *(thrasuterōn)* (Dem. 61.14; cf. Eurip. *Bacchae* 962). And a Demosthenean speaker calls an adversary charged with breaking his agreement with him "brave *[andreios],* or rather shameless *[anaiskhuntos],*" a qual-

---

12. Public speakers, for example, confessed their fears of addressing the people, then stated that they would speak out anyway for the sake of the polis: Dem. 10.35–36; 23.4–5; *Pr.* 23.2; cf. [And.] 4.1; Loraux 1995, 75–87.

ity normally associated with brazenness (Dem 56.41; cf. Hyp. 4.9; fr. B 17.2 [Burtt]). All these texts point to an ambiguous relationship between rashness and masculinity, which allowed people to identify the two with each other but also to contrast them.

Given this vagueness, some speakers call their conduct courageous rather than rash, while others portray their opponents as rash rather than courageous. In several speeches, Demosthenes distinguishes his own manly courage from his fellow politicians' rashness (Dem. 5.4; 8.68–70; 14.8–9). He and other speakers also deny opponents' courage by labeling them as brazen in view of their opportunistic exploitation of the weaknesses of others. Simon's adversary claimed that Simon had been afraid to bring him to court for four years, but became more brazen *(tolmeros)* once he heard that the speaker had lost some private cases (Lys. 3.20). Similarly, Alcibiades the Younger charged that, as long as his father was alive, his enemies were afraid to display the audacious *(thrasus)* libelous speech they used once he was dead (Isoc. 16.22). As long as the state was prosperous, Demosthenes charged, Aeschines trembled like a hare out of fear of punishment for his wrongdoings; but once the people were suffering (and presumably unable, or too preoccupied, to prosecute him), he became bold *(thrasus)* and showed himself in public (Dem. 18.263). These speakers confirm Aristotle's observation that rash men are braggarts who pretend to be courageous when the occasion warrants it, but in fact are cowards because they cannot endure fear.[13] Yet, the characterization of the above persons as cowards in disguise is questionable at best, because it was their adversaries who linked their daring actions to opportune timing.

Demosthenes, for instance, treats similar actions as displays of courage at one time and as unwarranted audacity at another. In his speech *On the False Embassy*, he denies prosecuting Aeschines for misconduct as an envoy out of cowardice, adding that he derives neither safety nor pleasure in acquiring enemies (Dem. 19.221–24). Yet when Androtion had made similar claim to civic courage because as a public servant he had made enemies and was in danger, Demosthenes, in a speech written for his prosecutors, called him shameless *(anaidēs)* and audacious, using the expression *etolma legein* (literally, "dared to say") (Dem. 22.59). Androtion may have been an impudent and empty brag-

---

13. Arist. *EN* 3.7 1115b29–34; 1116a7–9; 3.8 1116b32–1117a1; cf.Dem. 22.66; Antiphon fr. 56 (D-K), Plato *Laches* 184b–c, 197c–d; *Protagoras* 350a–c; and for boldness based on words alone rather than deeds: Dem. *Pr.* 32.2, 45.2.

gart, but the evidence suggests that such charges were freely bandied about. Indeed, one speaker refers to the practice of treating courage as unseemly boldness when he accused politicians of trying to silence rival speakers who stand for justice by calling them brazen *(thrasus)* (Dem. 51.19; cf. Aes. 2.106).

The terms "courageous," "rash," and "coward, Aristotle observes, are relative: a courageous man seems rash in comparison to a coward and cowardly in comparison to the rash (Arist. *EN* 2.8 1108b19–20). The orators carry this observation a step further. Taking advantage of the subjective line between courage and cowardice, and of the importance of intentions and context in judging an act, they claim masculine courage for themselves and ascribe recklessness or unmanly cowardice to others.

The rhetoric describing men's reactions to fear was supplemented by speakers' appeals to men's fears, and, in particular, to the anxiety about the stability of the social and political order. This anxiety lurked behind many of the fears already noted, including fears for the *oikos*'s welfare, of youthful challenges of adult men, of men driven by desire or hubris, of powerful politicians and skillful speakers, and even of Philip and the Athenians who helped him.

ORDER, FEAR OF DISORDER, AND THEIR RHETORIC

Order, *kosmos* or *taxis* and their derivative notions, originally meant the functional arrangement of troops for or in battle. It evolved to connote, in addition, the more general concept of a regulated existence for both state and individual.[14] On the state and the communal level, order—or even better, good order *(eukosmia)*—meant good laws, regulations, and government, and a sound moral regime. For individuals, order meant conformity to written and unwritten laws, dutiful citizenship, and disciplined, decent personal behavior.[15] Order protected society from descending into anarchy and uncivilized forms of existence. The quest for

14. Greek order: Cartledge, Millett, and Reden 1998, and Piepenbrink 2001, esp. 93–170, which, for the most part, do not address the issues discussed here. On good order in nonoratorical sources: Jaeger 1945, 1: 150–84; Grossmann 1950, esp. 70–89; Kerschensteiner 1960, esp. 10–24; Gold 1977, 3–5; cf. Hobbs 2000, 156–57.

15. Dem. 25.9–11; Aes. 1.22–27, 33–34; cf. Dem. *Pr.* 4; Aes. 3.3–4; 2.108; *Ath. Pol.* 44.3.

order, then, was an attempt to decrease the danger of threatening or unpredictable elements in the human environment.[16]

To a large extent, the concept of order, both in the senses of an organizing principle and of orderly conduct, was male-oriented. The military associations, if not origins, of the concept, and the expectation that adult males would guard it, made attaining and preserving order a masculine concern. Men learned about order in the army, with role assignments, hierarchy, discipline, and cooperation among male warriors; order contributed to victory and honor.[17] Demosthenes, for example, commends the Athenian and Theban armies for their orderly discipline *(kosmoi)*, equipment, and zeal in two engagements against Macedonia prior to the battle of Chaeroneia, which earned them the praises of other Greeks (Dem. 18.216). In an earlier speech, he scolds the Athenians for disorderly and inefficient preparation for war against Philip by contrasting them with the civilian order, efficiency, and clear division of labor that characterized their festivals (Dem. 4.35–37; cf. 4.26). In another speech, he defends his proposals to reform Athenian military and civilian finances to enable the city to help Olynthus against Philip. The reforms "would do away with disorder *[ataxia]* and lead the city toward order *[taxis]*" (Dem. 3.33–35).

Order was also often linked to the masculine ideal of self-control and the manly responsibility of defending the Athenian moral community, including its young and female members. Aeschines, whose speech against Timarchus deals extensively with the themes of defending the city's moral order and the ideal of *sōphrosunē*, applies the concept of good order *(eukosmia)* to the wish to protect children from amorous adults, and to educating them to become useful citizens.[18] In late fourth-century Athens, elected officials called *sōphronistai* (literally, those who moderate) supervised by a *kosmētēs* (literally, orderer), watched over the education of the ephebes in the arts of order, self-control, and responsible citizenship.[19]

16. Milburn and Watman 1981, 31–33.
17. Esp. Xen, *Oec.* 8.4–8; cf. *Mem.* 3.1.17; Isoc. 12.115.
18. Order in Aes. 1: Fisher 2001, 66, 129, 205. Aeschines may have exploited the term *eukosmia* to criminalize Timarchus's indecent behavior in the Assembly (so Ford 1999, 245–47; cf. 255), but what matters for our purposes is that he was able to do so.
19. Children, self-control, and order: cf. Isoc. 7.37–39. For these offices and the moral climate that may have encouraged their creation, see *Ath. Pol.* 42.2; North 1966, 254–55; Rhodes 1993, 504–5, 535; Veligianni-Terzi 1997, 300–302; Fisher 2001, 56–66; cf. Grossmann 1950, 77–78.

Being orderly *(kosmios* for a man; *kosmia* for a woman) often meant acting decently and in conformity to men's gendered expectations. In the speeches, the conduct of an orderly woman is presented as chaste and modest; she puts things in their places in the house.[20] Sexual propriety, decorum, and orderliness make a woman's conduct predictable as well as useful, and free the male *kurios* from concern about her behavior.[21] Orderly men are likewise conforming, self-controlled, decent people (cf. Isoc. 1.15; 2.31; 3.38; 8.102). A fragment of one of Hyperides' speeches, which does not mention order by name, assesses an anonymous Athenian's sexual misconduct by asserting that nature distinguishes males from females and assigns each appropriate duties. A man who acts like a woman misuses his body and abuses nature's generosity toward males (Hyp. fr. D 16 [Burtt]).[22] Hyperides, who is perhaps referring to a male prostitute, enlists nature as part of an orderly world to validate the distinctions between the genders.

Yet the orations also reveal a deep-seated anxiety about the ability of order to withstand attacks. This is evident in litigants' attempts to deter jurors from deciding against them. The rhetorical formula is quite simple. The speaker places the jurors at the intersection of two roads: one leads to blessed order, the other to its collapse. If they judge against him, he warns, catastrophe will ensue, and then spread to the immediate audience, to other members of polis, to the city's institutions, and to the community's social and moral well-being. Offering a middle ground, or suggesting less dramatic consequences, ran counter to the Greek propensity for antithetical thinking and seemed rhetorically counterproductive.[23]

Warnings about potential doom were especially popular in public actions *(graphai),* where both parties present themselves as concerned about the public interest and safety.[24] Failure to convict Timarchus, Aeschines warns, will overturn the entire educational system (Aes.

20. Lys. 1.7; 3.6; Aes. 1.182–83; cf. [Dem.] 59.50–51; Carey 1989, 70, 75; Kapparis 1999, 269. On the orderly housewife, see also Xen, *Oec.* 8; Pomeroy 1994, esp. 285–87.

21. On attribution of lack of order and instability to women in Greek literature, see, e.g., Just 1989, 194–216; cf. Zeitlin 1996, 343–44; Ogden 1996, 366, 371; and to Persians: Isoc. 4.150.

22. The fragment has survived in a Latin translation. Cf. Aes. 1.185; Lyc. fr. E1 (Burtt); Dover 1989, 60–68; Winkler 1990a, 61–62; Fisher 2001, 48–49, 339–41. Dem. 25.15–16, a passage too unusual among the orations to be discussed here in detail, depicts nature as the chaotic reverse of orderly laws; see Allen 2000a, 181–83.

23. On antithetical perceptions: Lloyd 1966; Gordon 1981. For the following, cf. Lavency 1964, 161–62.

24. This is especially true of prosecutors: Rubinstein 2000, esp. 111–12; cf. Johnstone 1999, 52; Piepenbrink 2001, 150–66.

1.187). According to Apollodorus, a decision in Neaera's favor will un-
leash lawlessness, allowing indecent women to enjoy total freedom and
take charge of the institutions of matrimony and parenthood, obliterat-
ing traditional social, moral, and gender boundaries ([Dem.] 59.111–14;
see pp. 40–41 above). An even more apocalyptic vision can be found in
a speech attributed to Demosthenes that targets the politician Aristogeiton as a state debtor (Dem. 25.24–25; cf. 25.20).[25] Self-control, respect, and good order *(eutaxia)* are under siege, the speaker claims. Unless the jurors come to their rescue, everything will unravel and become
undone; all distinctions will be confused *(lelutai panta, aneōiktai,
sunkekhutai)* and the city given over to utmost villainy and shamelessness. Letting people imitate Aristogeiton, who has perverted the democratic notion of personal autonomy and freedom into license to do as he
pleases, means destroying public ordinances, dishonoring election results, discarding duties, laws, and discipline; if this happens, daily life
will be governed by violence, hubris, lawlessness, and slander (Dem.
25.26). Another Demosthenean speaker warns that passage of a new law
to give some latitude to state debtors will make penalties and jurors im-
potent, turn the people into the politicians' slaves, introduce oligarchy
into the system, damage the prestige of Athens, impair its military capa-
bility and finances, and bring about the overthrow of the courts, the
restoration of exiles, and the uncovering of ways to topple state institutions (Dem. 24.44, 76, 90–92, 101, 143, 152–54, 216–17; cf. 26.2).[26]
     The rhetorical purpose of these exaggerated, menacing descriptions is
clear: to scare the jurors into siding with the speaker. The unlikelihood
of their being true is equally self-evident, because they suggest that a single verdict will suffice to bring about the collapse of order or to prevent
it from occurring. Yet such depictions draw their rhetorical power from
the presumption that Athenian order rests on unsound foundations. One
misdeed, it is thought, will lead to a greater wrong, and then to the collapse of the entire system, because evildoers are waiting for an opportunity to exploit any weakness in the social order. Punishing Timarchus
will restore good order *(eukosmia)* in the city, Aeschines says, but acquitting him will inspire many to do wrong (Aes. 1.192). The prosecutor of Aristocrates argues that a verdict favorable to the defendant will

---

25. Cf. Morawetz 1999, 146–48.
26. Cf. Din. 3.21; Hunter 1997, 305, 318. According to Paulsen 1999, 522–25,
Demosthenes in Dem. 19 and Aeschines in Aes. 2 conceptualized their speeches according
to the themes of chaos and order respectively.

bestow impunity on anyone who wishes to wrong the people (Dem. 23.94). And Dinarchus, in a speech written for the prosecution of Demosthenes on the charge of bribe-taking, asserts that many are watching the trial to see if bribe-taking is legal, and whether basic assumptions and rules once considered reliable and certain are no longer so (Din. 1.46. cf. 1.3, 88, 106–7).

Other prosecutors portray the disasters as even more specific and imminent. One such danger was that the court would give wrongdoers the freedom to do as they wished. It was a fear that Aristogeiton's prosecutor (see p. 145 above) associated with a total breakdown of the political and social order but that others made less all-encompassing. Thus, a prosecutor warned that failing to punish Alcibiades the Younger for dereliction of military duty by letting him do what he wished would make laws (especially about desertion), assemblies, or elections of generals (who were supposed to enforce discipline) meaningless (Lys. 14.11). The Lysian prosecutor of grain retailers advised the jurors that if they punished the defendants, other grain retailers would be better behaved (literally, be more orderly: *kosmiōteroi)*, but if they acquitted them, grain retailers would have the freedom to do as they wished, that is, to continue to harm the citizens (Lys. 22.19–20).[27] Since the license to do as one wished was also associated with anarchic, oligarchic, and tyrannical regimes, prosecutors were making implicit appeals to jurors' anxiety about the city's political order.[28]

Other specific dangers or fears, each related to the case in point, were similarly based on the frightening prospect that a wrong decision on the jurors' part could open the door to a much greater evil. Rather than detailing every case in which the jurors were given a choice between supporting the speaker—or more accurately, law, order, and the status quo—and unleashing some kind of disorder, I shall mention only the different forms in which the latter came.

Some speakers warned that a wrong decision would undermine the functioning of and faith in the entire judicial system (Ant. 5.80; And. 1.104–5; cf. Ant. 2.4.11; Lys. 1.36; Isoc. 18.42–43). Other litigants pre-

27. Rubinstein 2000, 79–80, however, makes a case for only one defendant in this trial. Other men doing, or allowed to do, as they wish: Lys. 10.3; 30.34; Dem. 19.342; 23.67; 51.15–16; Din. 2.4; [And.] 4.36; Hyp. fr. B 17.1 (Burtt); cf. Dem. 21.91, 170; 22.56; 26.9.
28. Doing as one pleases and anarchy: Dem. 25.25–26; and oligarchy: Dem. 24.75–76; cf. Isoc. 7.7; and tyranny: Lys. 25.32–33; cf. Lys. 26.5; Hyp. fr. D 15 (Burtt). Marowetz 1999's chief interest is in how critics of democracy used the concept of the freedom to attack the demos and its powers.

dicted damage to the political system if a decision went the wrong way. An acquittal in the case of Eratosthenes, charged with responsibility for the death of his brother under the Thirty, Lysias insists, will encourage potential tyrants, embolden evildoers to think that they could act with impunity, and induce resident aliens to cease watching over Athens's interests (Lys. 12.35, 85). In his speech *On the False Embassy,* Demosthenes argues that acquittals of corrupt envoys will invite other ambassadors to serve the enemy (Dem. 19.233; cf. Din. 1.67, 113; 2.22–23). A Demosthenean speaker asserts that failure to punish a defendant charged with making an illegal proposal will turn the many into the humble slaves of evil politicians, whom he calls "animals" (Dem. 24.143).

Finally, several speakers saw dangers to vital social conventions, values, and principles of Athens. Demosthenes says that Leptines' law abolishing exemptions from civic *leitourgiai* threatens the practice of rewarding and honoring men for their services (Dem. 20.124). A man suing his business partners for an unpaid loan and breach of contract argued that the fate of the trust system, which allowed business to flourish and contracts to be made, hung in the balance (Dem. 56.48–50). Another litigant, charged with temple robbery based on information given by a slave, warned that slaves would judge by the outcome of the trial whether they would be more likely to obtain their freedom by serving their masters or by falsely testifying against them (Lys. 5.5).[29]

Although speakers frequently balanced warnings about dangers to the state with reminders about the benefits of preserving law and order, the choice they give the jurors between ushering in evil and checking it is no choice at all.[30] I also suspect that not all of the hyperbolic scenarios were meant to be taken literally. Nonetheless, they suggest an anxiety about the soundness of the legal, political, social, and moral system and about the propensity of men to falter in the hard battle between order and disorder.

By identifying a man as a danger to the system, speakers converted general anxiety into concrete fear, which the jurors could eliminate in a

---

29. See also Apollodorus's accusations against the former slave Phormio: Dem. 45.75–76; cf. 45.35. Warnings against giving citizens and politicians license to steal from the public: Lys. 27.7; 30.23; cf. Dem. 39.14.

30. Alerting the jurors that their decision would teach others a positive or negative lesson, or that they were being closely watched by others, similarly aimed to pressure them to vote in the speaker's favor. See And. 1.104; Lys. 1.47; 14.4, 12–13; 15.9; 22.19–21; 27.6; 28.17; 29.13; Dem. 19.342–43; 21.227; 22.68; 24.101, 218; 25.53; 54.43; Aes. 3.245–47; Din. 1.107; Lyc. 1.10; cf. Dem. 21.220, 59.77; Din. 1.27; 3.19; Isoc. 20.18, 21; Rubinstein 2000, 165–66; Allen 2000a, 20–21; Piepenbrink 2001, 102.

single act. Speakers depicted their adversaries as agents of disorder in the hope that the Athenians would fulfill their masculine and civic duty of guarding order by punishing them.[31] The politician Aristogeiton, the prosecutor claimed, had confounded and destroyed *(suntarattetai kai di-aphtheiretai)* anything that came under the order *(kosmos)* of the polis and the laws (Dem. 25.19; cf. 25.50, 89–90). His and other public speakers' shameful behavior had prevailed over all that was noble in the city, namely, laws, institutions, procedures, and *eukosmia* (Dem. 25.9). Other speakers added that the politicians' mutual recriminations and unruly behavior in the Assembly, probably heckling, led to slander, confusion, and disorder (Dem. *Pr.* 53.1; Aes. 3.4).[32] And litigants portray their adversaries' personal behavior as disorderly and offensive. Simon's adversary describes him as habitually disorderly man, who had struck his commander during his military service, was considered most undisciplined *(akosmotatos)* and wicked, and was the only Athenian to have been publicly dismissed from the army (Lys. 3.45). Just before he killed the adulterer Eratosthenes, Euphiletus accused him of crimes against his wife and children, rather than being a law-abiding and decent (or orderly: *kosmios*) man (Lys. 1.26). Aeschines portrays the incontinent Timarchus as contemptuous of laws and *sōphrosunē,* saying that his disorderliness *(akosmia)* revealed "a condition of his soul" (Aes. 1.189; trans. Fisher 2001, 115).

The jurors, thus, could support the polis by punishing the disorderly, but also by rewarding the orderly, namely, disciplined, decent, public-spirited, and self-controlled men. A score of speakers mention that they have served in the army, made financial contributions to the state, and lived orderly, moderate lives.[33]

In sum, speakers played on the anxiety that order was vulnerable and uncertain both to scare their audiences and to calm their concerns, as well as to depict themselves (or the jurors) as doing their masculine and civic duty to defend order. In some ways, speakers thus contributed to

31. See Aes. 3.7 urging the jurors not to desert their post of guardians *(phulakes)* of the laws and democracy.

32. See also Dem. 19.88, 187; 39.7–19; Hyp. 5.22; cf. Dem. 58.60; [And.] 4.22; Aes. 3.6, 82. Conversely, both Andocides and Demosthenes claim that they have saved the city from a crisis and its attendant turmoil and confusion: And. 1.59, 68; cf. [Lys.] 6.36; Dem. 18.168–79; Heath 1997, 234–36.

33. E.g., Is. 4.27–29; Lys. 3.47; 7.41; 12.20; 21.1–10, 16, 19; Dem. 45.77–78; 50.64; cf. Lys. 16.18; Piepenbrink 2001, 132–37. Hyp. 4.21, however, credits the decent defendant with no public contribution. For epigraphic evidence documenting honors given to Athenians for being *kosmios*: Veligianni-Terzi 1997, 204, 281; cf. 224, 300–302.

the prevailing anxiety. Their conflicting accounts of who posed a threat made it difficult for their hearers to identify whom they should trust. To assess litigants' motives—and whether they constituted a danger to the polis and its order—jurors therefore looked for patterns of behavioral consistency (seen as a virtue in itself: [Aristotle] *Rhetoric to Alexander* 38 1445b4–42) as indicated by individual records of masculine and civic character.

CONSISTENCY AND ITS RHETORIC

A passage in Demosthenes' speech *On the Chersonese* (cited pp. 144–45 above) illustrates how consistency serves as a test of character and manhood. Contrasting himself with fellow speakers, Demosthenes claims that he is more courageous *(andreioteron)* than they are, and lists the qualifications of the useful citizen and speaker: the rejection of rashness and disgrace, a willingness to face risks courageously, and a readiness to sacrifice for the public good. The courageous *(andreios)* man, he suggests, continually manifests these qualities. He "often" *(polla)* opposes the people for their own good; unlike the rash man, he says "nothing" *(mēden)* to court their favor; and he "always" *(aei)* speaks for the best (Dem. 8.68–70). The expectation of a consistent manly performance also recurs in the Athenians' national self-image. In *On the Crown,* delivered when Greece was under Macedonian control, Demosthenes justifies his calls in the past to oppose Philip's hegemonic plans by stating that Athens had always prized the quest for honor and fame and readiness to make sacrifices for the common good—mainstays of Athenian manhood— above all else. Throughout history *(ek pantos tou khronou),* the fatherland had always *(aei)* competed to be first in honor and reputation and had spent more money and men on the pursuit of honor *(philotimia)* and on conferring benefits on the Greeks than all other states together (Dem. 18.66; cf. Dem. 18.200–203; 20.25; 22.76; 24.184). Demosthenes' use of the verb "to compete" *(agōnizomai)* is telling, because the expectation that a man, leader, or even a nation be consistent was related to the Athenians' agonistic perception of manhood and character. One success was insufficient to secure manly reputation, while consistent performance, or claims to it, could validate one's manly image and confirm that one was reliable, trustworthy, and unlikely to threaten the state and its values.

Speakers accordingly claim consistency for themselves and deny it to others. They labor to harmonize good or bad performance in the family and in the private sphere with public conduct as a citizen to create a pattern of behavior across masculine roles and domains and over time. Defendants present the charges against them as incompatible with their long and unchanged record of exemplary behavior or character.[34] Conversely, Demosthenes asserts that it is well known that Meidias always treats everyone with brutality and hubris. In a speech he wrote for Ariston, Demosthenes neutralizes the effect of an oath about the veracity of his statements taken by Ariston's assailant, Conon, by advising the jurors to look at Conon's life and disposition *(tropos)* and his history of conspiratorial activity and oath breaking.[35]

Sometimes, speakers put the onus of consistency on the jury and urged them to harmonize their judgments with previous verdicts. The court's following legal precedents complemented the litigants' self-portrait as consistently good men, because each party thus contributed to the soundness of the social and judicial order, while inconsistency with previous legal decisions suggested haphazardness and fickleness, embarrassing self-contradiction, and a threat to the fairness, stability, and reliability of the judicial system. Hence, even though judicial precedents were not binding in Athens, they were considered useful for persuasive purposes.[36] Litigants accordingly addressed present and past jurors as "you," even though the odds that the same men had sat in judgment in both cases were negligible (see, e.g., Is. 5.13; Lys. 26.14; Dem. 43.6). In an earlier case, Apollodorus reminded the jurors in Neaera's trial, "you" had harshly punished a man for impiety, even though his offense was of a milder nature than that of the defendant's daughter. Would it not be awful if they failed to punish Neaera and her daughter for their acts of greater impiety ([Dem.] 59.116–17)? Hoping to constrain the jurors in the case of man accused of desertion or treason, Lycurgus surveyed the Athenians' uncompromising history of punishing traitors. He produced an old resolution as a proof that the penalties inflicted by the Athenians' ancestors on traitors were identical and in conformity with one another *(homoias kai akolouthous allēlais)* (Lyc. 1.111–20). The adopted son of Apollodorus (son of Eupolis) argued that jurors (addressed as "you") had once given Apollodorus a favorable verdict out of recognition of the

34. E.g., Lys. 5.3; 16.10–12; 19.56–58, 60–61; 21.21–24; Dem. 36.55–57; Hyp. 1.14–18; cf. Is.1.1; Lys. 12.4; Dem. 34.1, 38–39; and see pp. 145–47.

35. Meidias: Dem. 21.1, 131; Conon: Dem. 54.14, 38; cf. Dem.22.58; cf. Whitehead 2001, 133. Exposing an adversary's inconsistent behavior or statements was equally useful in court: [Aristotle] *Rhetoric to Alexander* 5 1427b15–30, 9 1430a14–21.

36. Dorjahn 1938; Todd 1993, 61; Rubinstein 2000, 80–87, 165–66. See also [Aristotle] *Rhetoric to Alexander* 11422b19–25. Consistency in Athenian law: Humphreys 1985a.

contributions of his father (i.e., the speaker's grandfather) to the polis. It would therefore be just if they honored Apollodorus's wish and gave the speaker his estate in view of the many and great services that both Apollodorus and his father had done the city. Although the speaker could not know what had moved the jurors in the past, he sought to create a history of reciprocity between the family and the state, a precedent, and an identification between former and present jurors, trying, on the basis of a dubious similarity between the cases, to oblige the jury to be consistent. Finally, a Lysian speaker put the blame for the jurors' inconsistency on his opponent. He pointed to an earlier verdict that protected his property from confiscation. His opponent, he alleged, had managed to make Athenians contradict themselves when they voted to confiscate his land. The jurors now had an opportunity to correct the wrong—and make their decisions consistent.[37]

Consistency was also desirable in politics. It identified the politician as reliable, safe, and manly. The charge of changing policy portrayed the politician as unstable, shifty, and unable to persevere as a courageous speaker and warrior should (cf. Dem. 8.68–70 above; Arist. *EN.* 3.6.2–5 1115b11–20). Contrasting Demosthenes with the general Timotheus, his prosecutor said that the latter had performed great deeds, held fast to *(diameinas)* the same policy, and never vacillated on the issues like Demosthenes (Din. 1.17). A public leader who changed his position was often suspected of taking bribes, which robbed him of his independence and loyalty to the demos (pp. 148–49 above). Among others, Demosthenes and Aeschines linked bribes to rivals' changes of policy toward Philip and pointed out the dangers of such corruption to the political order (Dem. 19.9–16, 27–28, 201–2; Aes. 2.152, 164; cf. Dem. 19.286).

In *On the Crown,* Demosthenes praises himself for displaying the same character *(ēthos)* in domestic and foreign affairs when he rejected money and chose instead to be guided by the common interests of the Athenian people or of the Greeks (Dem. 18.109). Demosthenes was responding to Aeschines' charge that he had shown the same (wicked) dis-

---

37. Apollodorus's appeal to consistency: Is. 7.37–41; Wyse 1904, 579; Millettt 198b, 239–40. Confiscation and consistency: Lys. 13.13–14. The text is problematic, although this meaning is fairly certain; see Todd 2000, 196. Cf. [And.] 4.32–34; Aes. 3.232. Complaints about or warnings against rendering different verdicts for identical crimes: Lys. 19.6; 22.18; 27.4; Dem. 21.183; 22.7; Din. 2.21; cf. Dover 1974, 219. The assertion that the jurors were deceived in a previous trial similarly relieved them from the moral obligation to conform their verdict to an earlier decision; cf. Dem. 23.95–99. Calls on the Athenians not to deviate from their ancestors' example also harp on the motif of consistency: Lys. 34.9–10; Dem. 2.24; 3.36; 22.77–78.

position *(tropos)* in private and public. Demosthenes, Aeschines said, "changed his position, but not his disposition" *(ou gar tropon, alla ton topon metēllaxen)* (Aes. 3.78). Dinarchus and Hyperides agreed that Demosthenes had been shifty toward friends and in politics, while the later biographer Plutarch, who rejected this characterization of the orator, thought Melanopus and Demades, two other fourth-century orators, more deserving of the charge.[38]

How, then, did politicians account for changes of positions? Not surprisingly, they said that they had done it for the good of the state. Melanopus and Demades are reported to have said that they changed their positions for the sake of the *politeia* (government) and the demos (Plut. *Dem.* 13.3). Changed circumstances called for a change in policy, Aeschines said in defense of having altered his stand on the peace with Philip. In his speech *On the Embassy*, he explained that he had decided to support the peace after he had seen that Athens's allies were failing to aid the city and realized that public speakers were profiting from the war (Aes. 2.79). He further exonerated himself by producing historical examples of Athens first fighting and then helping the same parties. The good adviser, he added, gives advice that best fits the circumstances, while an evil prosecutor (i.e., Demosthenes) conceals the circumstances and criticizes the (recommended) action (Aes. 2.164–65). Aeschines' change of position consistently served the public interest. Nimble in seizing opportunities, he implied, he deserved credit and his manly reputation.[39]

Consistent behavior in politics, in the courts, or in private reduced fear of unpleasant surprises and of shifty, unreliable men. It contributed to a stable order, justice, moral conduct, and trust. One does not have to be an Athenian, however, to know that it is hard to be consistent. In addition, the expectation of consistency conflicted with the need to change and be flexible. Attempting to change the jurors' minds about the extent of his wealth, a Lysian speaker asserted that "the best and the wisest are those most willing to change their minds" (Lys. 19.53). Andocides' manipulation of the balance between change and consistency was

38. Din. 1.91, 94, 97; Hyp. 5.20–21; cf. Theophrastus *FGrH* 115 F 326 = Plut. *Dem.* 13.1; Aes. 3.214. Demades and Melanopus: Plut. *Dem.* 13.1–3. Aes. 2. harps repeatedly on the theme of Demosthenes' shiftiness. Other shifty men: Dem. 23.178; Aes. 3.89–90. For the virtue of political consistency: Whitehead 2001, 425; cf. 421–23.

39. Dem. 16.14–15 cites changed circumstances and the higher cause of justice in response to objections that if Athens switches alliances as Demosthenes recommends, it will make her appear untrustworthy and inconsistent. The fault of inconsistency was at times attributed to the assembled demos, although significantly by politicians depicted as hostile to it: Dem. 19.136, 314; 58.63; cf. Isoc. 8.52; 14.44.

rather perverse. In an attempt to persuade the Athenians to let him return from the exile occasioned by his involvement in the Mysteries affair of 415, he admitted his mistake, but argued that one's body should not be blamed for errors that come from the mind. His blameless body had not changed since the affair, although his mind had; his contemporary listeners therefore had no reason to be hostile to him (And. 2.24; cf. 2.6). Andocides thus claimed to be simultaneously a changed and unchanged man, while appealing to his audience to change their minds about him. They did not—and he could not return to Athens until the amnesty of 404/3. His failure suggests that the Athenians were skeptical of the notion of a changed man.

How effective, then, was the rhetoric that appealed to the search for consistency, or that which evoked fears and anxieties about order and other concerns? I have focused on what worried Athenian men, not how worried they were, because the oratorical sources do not permit us to assess degrees of fear. The speakers were prone to manipulating their hearers' mental and emotional states and to trying to share their own fears and anxieties with their audiences. These anxieties and fears, however, were not constant but variable. Their impact depended on the context in which they were framed, the individual's personality and ranking of concerns, and other factors. My purpose has been more modest—to show principally *what* Athenian men feared.

Old Age and Manipulating Manhood

OLD MEN

We conclude with a discussion of old men and old age in the oratorical corpus.[1] The ancient Greeks normally divided adult males into youths and elders *(presbuteroi)*, the latter roughly between thirty and fifty-nine years old. Men over sixty were called "old" *(gerontes)*. However, the following discussion often conflates the elderly and the old, given that the Athenians were not particularly strict as regards age categories.[2]

In public discourse, age was associated with certain types of behavior. Like male youths, old men were judged by the standards expected of men in their prime, but with a significant difference. It was hoped that young men would grow into adults who conformed to or even exceeded masculine and civic expectations. The elderly, however, were seen as no longer capable, physically or mentally, of meeting the standards expected of younger men. They were often associated with lamentable behavioral traits. In his *Rhetoric*, Aristotle characterizes old men and those who are past their prime as skeptical and overly full of doubts. They are small-minded, miserly, suspicious, mistrustful, and pessimistic. Unlike the young, who are hot-blooded, they are cold-blooded and cowardly (cf. Amphis fr. 33.9–10 [K-A]). The more closely they approach death, the

---

1. Old age in Greece: Roussel 1951; Kirk 1971; Dover 1974, 104–6; Falkner and de Luce 1989, 1–171; Garland 1990, 242–87; Falkner 1995.
2. Kirk 1971, 124–28; Garland 1990, 242–44; Falkner 1995, 55–56.

more they cling to life. They are excessively self-centered and unmoved by virtue or nobility. While the young pity others out of *philanthropia*, the pity of the old is out of fear for themselves. They are shameless and live in the past; their desires, apart from the love of gain, and their emotions, except for short outbursts of anger, lack intensity, hence their moderate or restrained image. When they do wrong, they do it out of malice, not hubris (Arist. *Rhet.* 2.13 1389b13–1390a27).

The old thus fall short of several masculine and communal ideals. Their suspicious dispositions militate against solidarity and harmony in the city, while self-centered practices keeps them from subordinating themselves to the good of the state, fellow citizens, and the family. They lack honor and the wish to excel, and they are full of undignified fears. Their *sōphrosunē* is not the result of mastery over desires but of the weakening or disappearance of passion. Their lack of manly vigor, physical frailty (as implied in their inability to be hubristic), and chilliness feminize them.[3] Aristotle's description of the old contrasts with his more sympathetic portrayal of the young *(Rhet.* 2.12 1388b31–1389b13). For him, old age is an extremity, far less valuable than the middle.[4] Although some oratorical references resemble the philosopher's unflattering characterization, others show positive attitudes toward the old.

Aristotle's observation that old men cling to life reflects the perception that their fight against the inevitable is pathetic. It stands in stark contrast to the Lysian eulogy that describes the fallen warriors of Athens as courageous and heroic. Death is inevitable and can result from disease or old age, the speaker declares, but those who die facing danger, rather than waiting for death, are the most fortunate of men, because they have chosen the fairest of death's forms (Lys. 2.77–79; cf. Aes. 1.145).[5]

In a city where reasonable fitness was expected of adult men in their roles as warriors, men over sixty, like the disabled, women, and children,

---

3. In Aristotle's view, which was not universally accepted, women were colder than men: *Generations of Animals* 4 765b16–28, 728a19–22; Carson 1990, 138; A. Hanson 1990, 332. I could not find in the speeches a correlation between sexual and social impairments that Falkner has observed in Greek poetry: 1995, 149; cf. Scafuro 1997, 288–89.

4. Cf. Roussel 1951, 200–202; North 1966, 209; Falkner 1995, xvi–xvii; but also Byl 1970.

5. "Beautiful death" in battle: Loraux 1995, 63–74. Aeschines describes old age and poverty as the greatest of human evils: Aes. 1.88; cf. Isoc. 9.71, while a Lysian speaker depicts his adversary's old age as a divine punishment for his crimes: Lys. fr. 53 (Thalheim).

were excused from military service.[6] This exemption confirms the ancient Athenian perception of the old as pitiful, especially in the wake of military defeat. Lycurgus avails himself of this view in illustrating the desperate conditions in Athens after its defeat at Chaeroneia. He speaks of citizen women crouched, shamefully in view, at doorways, trying to find out what had happened to their men, and of old men walking around aimlessly (Lyc. 1.40). Demosthenes likewise reports that when traveling through war-devastated Delphi, he saw a land devoid of young men, with demolished houses and walls, inhabited by only few women, children, and pitiable old men (Dem. 19.65). In both accounts, the presence of old men highlights the extent of the catastrophe of the defenseless city. Their position alongside women and children also indicates their marginalization in relation to the masculine mainstream.[7]

Yet the orations also show sympathy and responsibility for the old, especially for parents and relatives. The Athenians were supposed to take care of old family members, and performing the proper rites and burial upon their deaths was a legal, familial, and moral obligation.[8] This also meant dependence on the goodwill of others and adherence to cooperative values. The old deviated from masculine ideals when they showed that they were unable to provide for themselves and had to receive rather than give aid. The speaker of the Lysian funeral oration reminds the citizens of Athens of their duty to treat the parents of fallen warriors as if they were their children. When those parents became old, weak, poor, and friendless, they became objects of pity (Lys. 2.73; cf. Dem. 60.36; Plato *Menexenus* 248d). Although meant to elicit sympathy, this portrait confirms the status of the old as under the power of others.

Other attributes, however, led the Athenians to perceive virtue and value in elderly men. They had life experience that made them wise and qualified to instruct or supervise younger men.[9] Aeschines commends the lawgiver for ordaining that men over fifty should speak first in the As-

6. Rhodes 1993, 591–93, 780; Burckhardt 1996, 21.

7. In the first part of Aristophanes' *Lysistrata*, Athens at war is populated by women and old men only. Old men, like respectable women, were supposed to be indoors: cf. Plato *Laws* 931a; Falkner 1995, 126, 289 n. 45. Yet see Lys. 2.50; [And.] 4.22; Hanson 1989, 89–95.

8. Is. 2.10–13, 20, 23, 36, 46; Dem. 24.103; Lyc. 1.144; cf. Xen. *Oec.* 7.12; Lacey 1968, 116–18, 289–91; Thompson 1981, esp. 16; Todd 1993, 223–24; Rubinstein 1993, 62–86.

9. Plato *Laws* 690a; Aristotle *Pol.* 7.8 1329a13–15; 7.13 1332b35–41; Thrasymachus fr. 1 (D-K 85); Finley 1989, 9; Hansen 1990, 223–24; 1991, 89–90. Respecting the old: Dem. 25.24; cf. Isoc. 7.49; *Letters* 4.12; Ant. 4.1.2.

sembly on account of their experience and lack of youthful rashness (Aes. 1.23–24; cf. 1.180). Although in a later speech he laments that this fine custom is no longer practiced (Aes. 3.4), both the praise and the lament illustrate the perception that older men made a significant contribution to the welfare and good order of the city.[10] Demosthenes agreed. His plan for improving the military fortunes of Athens included paying the young for their military service and the less-able elderly for managing affairs vital to the state (Dem. 3.34; cf. 13.4). Hyperides, however, reproaches Demosthenes—by then over sixty years old—for taking bribes and thus disqualifying himself from educating, criticizing, and checking the rashness of younger rhetors (Hyp. 5.21–22).

The old were perceived as distinguished by self-restraint. Old Cephalus in Plato's *Republic* (1 329b–d) recalls that Sophocles likened sexual desire to being enslaved to a mad master and says that old age has brought him peace, freedom, and contentment.[11] For Athenians who cared about conduct more than motives, a man who resisted desire could be said to have satisfied a dominant masculine expectation.

Athenian speakers thus depict the old, not only as powerless and in need of care, but also as men of authority and wisdom. The first perception is exploited by litigants to accuse their adversaries of failing to care for their elderly parents or relatives, illustrating their greed, villainy, and dereliction of duty (Dem. 24.107, 201; Aes. 1.102–4).[12] In the review *(dokimasia)* of Philon's candidacy for the Council, his accuser charges that, during the reign of the tyrannical Thirty, Philon had raided the countryside and stripped poor old men of their possessions just to make a small profit (Lys. 31.18). The speaker was less concerned about the welfare of the old men than about using their image as frail and needy to vilify the defendant (cf. Fisher 2001, 240).

Litigants also played upon the perception of the old as helpless dependents when they produced old relatives in court or described the disastrous results the latter would suffer if the speaker were convicted.[13]

---

10. Cf. Dem. *Pr.* 45.2; Isoc. *Letters* 6.6; Hyp. fr. A 14.2 (Burtt); Ford 1999, 246–45; Fisher 2001, 148–49. Similar values were probably behind making sixty the minimum age for public arbitrators in Athens: *Ath. Pol.* 53.4; cf. Hansen 1991, 89. See, however, [Aristotle] *Rhetoric to Alexander* 29 1437a 32–34.

11. Cf. Kirk 1971, 146–48; Garland 1990, 263–64, 272–73. Old men's *sōphrosunē* and lack of aggression: Democritus fr. 294 (D-K 68); North 1966, 20 and n. 67.

12. See also Aristophanes *Knights* esp. 881–83; *Clouds* esp. 1330–33, 1380–90; Plato *Rep.* 1 329a. Conversely, an Isaian speaker trumpets his and his wife's dedicated treatment of his old adoptive father (Is. 2.18).

13. Lys. 20.35; Aes. 2.179; chapter 6 n. 55.

They placed the old alongside women and children as needing protection by adult males. Prosecutors warned, however, that appeals for mercy on such grounds were deceptive ([Dem.] 53.29), or tried to evoke the jurors' ire by describing the defendant as responsible for, or unmoved by, the plight of the old and other dependents of his victims and of other men.[14]

A different use of old men was made by speakers who appealed to them as reliable sources of information about things past to validate their assertions or recommendations to the jury.[15] They did so, of course, less out of deference to the old as authority figures, or as respected repositories of memory, as to enhance and confirm their own contentions.

Yet the old did not always play a passive role in speakers' rhetorical manipulation. Several elderly speakers plead their age to elicit sympathy for themselves and their relatives. A disabled Lysian speaker, who defended his right to a disability allowance, threw himself on the Council's mercy by contrasting his frailness with their power to save or destroy him. Appealing to their sense of justice, social responsibility, and especially pity, he begged them not to take away what they had given him when he was younger and stronger now that he was old, weak, afflicted with disease, and all the attendant sufferings of an advanced age (Lys. 24.6–8).[16] In a fragment from his speech in an embezzlement case, which survived in a Latin translation, Dinarchus, by then man in his seventies, contrasts his youthful past as a public figure with his present state.[17] Then he was ambitious; now he shuns ambition. Once he assisted many; now he can barely defend and support himself. Then he fought for his country; now he can only praise its defenders. The rhetorical opposition of activity and passivity, pursuit of honor and its abandonment, giving and receiving, and acting and talking made a simultaneous claim to membership in the Athenian masculine community, based on past serv-

14. Lys. 13.44–45; Dem. 25.84; Aes. 3.157; cf. Dem. 57.58; Lyc. 1.144; Isoc. 14.48.
15. The old and recommendations to the jury: Lys. 19.45; Dem. 58.24; Aes. 3.191–192; Lyc. 1.9. Appeals to older jurors to authenticate the speaker's assertions: Is. 7.13; Dem. 20.52, 77; 57.60; 59.30; Aes. 2.150; Lyc. 1.93; Isoc. 14.56; 15.93; 16.4. The old as a source for historical events illustrating one's argument: And. 2.26; Lys. 14.39; Dem. 58.62; Din. 1.25, 72, 75; Isoc. 7.64. Cf. Lys. 23.5; Dem. 19.249, 277; *Lett.* 2.10; [Demades] 1.7; Thomas 1989, 200–201.
16. The resemblance between this self-portrait and the description of the old parents of the fallen in the Lysian funeral oration is noteworthy: Lys. 2.73 (above). For the speaker's self-characterization, see chapter 4 n. 19.
17. For the case and Dinarchus's age: Din. fr. 14.2 (Burtt); Dion. Hal. *Dinarchus* 4 (638); Worthington 1992, 3–4, 7. The year was probably 292.

ices, and to compassion for a man who could no longer be of much value
to it.[18]

Elderly litigants also labored to discredit the charges laid against them
on the grounds of their age. The Lysian speaker discussed above invoked
his age and feeble body to demonstrate that he deserved a disability allowance and to ridicule a charge of hubris directed against him (Lys.
24.8, 16; cf. Ant. 3.3.2). To refute a charge of adultery, the Athenian Ly-
cophron argued that his life was an open book; one does not start a career in adultery after fifty (Hyp. 1.15). In both cases, mature age was
used to deflect charges normally associated with younger, more vigorous,
but also less restrained, men.

Few, however, were as skilled in taking advantage of old age as
Isocrates, who was between seventy and ninety-seven when he wrote
some of his famous fictional speeches and addresses on the art of politics, philosophy, and, generally, a life of excellence.[19] To gain the goodwill and sympathy of his audience, Isocrates attributes defects in his presentation to the impairments of age, admits that his authorial voice or
speech is "softer" *(malakōteros)* and "weaker" *(katadeesteros;* also "inferior") than it used to be (Isoc. 5.149; 12.4; 15.9), acknowledges that
he is not able to imitate his youthful stylistic, literary, and rhetorical accomplishments (Isoc. 5.27–28, 83–85, 110; 12.3, 55, 232), and says that
he is too incapacitated to move about or to stand and read lengthy passages (Isoc. 15.59; *Letters* 1.1; 6.2; cf. *Letters* 2.23). Isocrates asks the
reader to be patient with his digressions, verbosity, and inability to ar-
ticulate his thoughts (Isoc. 8.141; 12.34, 88; *Letters* 3.4; 4.13). As if taking a leaf from Aristotle's depiction of old men (Arist. *Rhet.* 2.13
1389b25, 35–36), he confesses that he is concerned with petty affairs, as
well as being hard to please and querulous (Isoc. 12.8; cf. 12.16).

At the same time, Isocrates battles some of the negative perceptions
of old age and denies being senile (Isoc. 5.17–18; *Letters* 5.1). Contrary
to Aristotle's claim that old men cling to life till their last day (Arist. *Rhet.*
2.13 1389b32–35), he insists that he ranks truth above the desire to stay
alive (Isoc. 15.272). He concedes that in taking on the arduous task of
writing his speeches, he is behaving like a younger man, but he insists

---

18. See also Ant. 3.2.11; [Dem.] 49.67; Hyp. 4.3; cf. Gutmann 1977, 315–16; Falkner
1995, 18. In Demosthenes' letters to the Athenians from exile (whose authenticity is contested), the speaker uses his old age to explain his wish to leave Athens in order to avoid
imprisonment as well as to shame the Athenians for their ungrateful treatment of him: *Letters* 2.17; 3.38.

19. Too 1995, 43–48.

that he will succeed and even challenges his listeners to punish him harshly if he fails (Isoc. 5.10–12; 15.51; cf. 9.73). Despite his having availed himself of the sympathy accorded old men, Isocrates demonstrates through his output that he was able to overcome the obstacles of age and produce orations that could compete with the best of them.

Isocrates simultaneously tries to reap the benefits of the stereotypes that indulged old men's weaknesses and to show that they fail to explain his excellence. He makes rhetorical use of the stereotypes of age in several places. In his *Panathenaicus*—a fictional speech, written in his nineties, that praises the virtues of Athens and called for a pan-Hellenic expedition against Persia—he admits to an age and a state of health that would deter anyone else from writing or even listening to such a speech. If he succeeds, he says, his reputation will be enhanced; if he fails, people should take his age into account (Isoc. 12.38, 270). In a letter addressed to the children of the Thessalian tyrant Jason, he asserts that his age both qualifies him to give the best advice and is responsible for its faulty presentation (Isoc. *Letters* 6.6; cf. 5.10; 15.26). In his appeal to Philip of Macedonia to lead an all-Greek campaign into Asia, he asks the king to indulge his old age if he judges the work to be weak; but if Philip finds the work comparable to his former works, the reason is not Isocrates' age, but his divine inspiration (Isoc. 5.149). The old orator thus used, abused, and, no doubt, mocked contemporary perceptions of old age.

One episode in Isocrates' *Panathenaicus* is of particular relevance to this book, because it discusses old age and contests, an institution that often served to measure manly worth. Isocrates describes a debate between himself and his former pupil, a man skilled and experienced in speaking, on the merits of the Spartans. Isocrates won the contest convincingly, but his reaction was sharply different from that of the young listeners and spectators, who belittled the defeated pupil and praised Isocrates for speaking better and more forcefully (literally, "youthfully": *nearōterōs)* than they thought he was capable of doing. Isocrates says, however, that his former pupil went away wiser and more knowledgeable about himself, while he himself had merely showed off his debating skills. His behavior ill became his age; he had succumbed to "juvenile confusion" *(tarakhēs meirakiōdous)*. Indeed, only a few days later, he found his speech too careless, bitter, and unthoughtful (Isoc. 12.229–32). It may be that Isocrates was celebrating acquired wisdom and humility from the vantage point of an old man and denigrating youthful competitiveness and the cult of the winner in a masculine society. It is equally possible that, despite his protestations, he wished to record his victory and advertise his competency in a contest that he described so well (cf. Finley 1989, 7–8). Even his self-criticism, after all, showed his superiority to the audience.

MANIPULATING MASCULINE DISCOURSE

Isocrates' reservations about his victory, genuine or not, cannot be separated from his exploitation of cultural representations of old men. When a man was expected to win and yet be past competing, frail and marginal but also useful, worthy of honor but easily dismissed, he might as well play these ideas against each other. Whether they were young, adult, or old, Athenian men manipulated social expectations, including those related to masculinity. Rhetorical manipulation helped them not just to attain their goals but also to take their roles and gender expectations seriously without doubting their beliefs or questioning their conduct.

Athenian males were subjected to different and often contradictory perceptions, rules of behavior, and even values, related to age, social roles, status, surroundings (private or public), and other factors examined in this book. Young men were measured by adult male standards, and although they might be indulged when they failed to meet them, they might also be subject to detraction. Youths were perceived as deserving protection and nurturing but also were expected to uphold manly standards, and viewed as a potential threat to the community's manly and moral order. When Athenian males assumed their responsibilities as heads of households, kinsmen, friends, and citizens, they faced the challenge of reconciling the different expectations society had of these roles. They were supposed to harmonize the demands of the *oikos,* friendship, and the state, even if there was a conflict among these institutions, and to demonstrate solidarity with kinsmen and friends even when they quarreled with them. In private and in public, they strove to protect themselves, their families, and the state from incurring shame, and they could be praised, faulted, or indulged if they concealed shame, exposed it, or even chose other considerations (such as pragmatism and privacy) over it. When they retaliated to an insult or injury, whether using violent or nonviolent means, the action might be regarded as proper and manly but also as unseemly and excessive. If they were wealthy and wellborn, they were perceived as more (or less) capable of meeting manly expectations than the poor. If they were poor, they probably acknowledged that social standing hindered satisfying such manly values as autonomy, or the ability to right wrongs, but they may have looked down on the self-indulgent lifestyles of the wealthy. Athenians expected everyone to show up for duty when called upon for military service, but they were more tolerant of poor men who failed to report than of members of the elite. Attending a funeral for their war dead, Athenians heard themselves described in speeches as citizens of the most courageous city in Greece, but when in court or the Assembly, they learned of many fellow citizens who were shameless cowards. They were sometimes uncertain about whether an act was courageous or brazen, whether going to war was manly and good for the city or imprudent and rash. Members of the demos were told as jurors that they ranked above the litigants in freedom, power, and even moral conduct, and that they could either show them or not show them mercy, either demonstrate or not demonstrate their gratitude to them. They were informed that they were manlier and morally superior to their leaders, but also that the latter were closer than they were to fulfilling Athenian ideals. When they lost control over their appetites, others regarded them with resentment and fear, but also as sympathetic victims of human weakness. They expected everyone to adhere to the virtues of self-control and moderation but were not always sure how to recognize self-control in a man. Finally, they were concerned that other men might introduce chaos into their orderly existence and thought that they could identify them through their characters and consistent behavior. But they knew as well that assertions about one's character were self-serving. Finally, on top of all the contradictory and varied demands of masculinity, Athenian adult males learned that whatever they did would be subject to partisan, subjective interpretations.

Masculine expectations, then, were conflicting and uncertain. There were young, adult, and aged manhoods, as well as masculinities related to different social roles. And in performing manly roles, men might be called upon to exhibit either an aggressive, proactive masculinity or a pacific, quiet one. They might take their cues from the masculinity that conjured up a world full of fears and menaces, or from the one that took solidarity for granted. In sum, in thought, action, and speech, Athenian men defined and redefined adherence to masculine rules based on personality and position, interpretation of conduct, context, and the audience.[20] To an outsider, the lack of firm rules of manhood might appear confusing, but the Athenians, like us, were adept at handling cultural constructs and their contradictions.

20. See esp. Bourdieu 1977; cf. Humphreys 1985.

A common means of achieving adaptation was through manipulation of perceptions. It was a technique that, as we have seen throughout this book, was favored by speakers in the courts and the Assembly. Yet the Athenians' manipulation of masculine values was not inspired solely by the wish to achieve their own ends and outsmart and exploit social ideologies.

Men who answered the many, and often conflicting, calls of manhood were likely to feel themselves failures. Manipulation served as a refuge from, and a way to deal with, social and internal pressures. Just because Athenian adult males engaged in self-aggrandizement, denigrated other men, and toyed with social constructs, they were not necessarily cynical about manly practices. Indeed, most Athenian adult males wished to be good men and strove to live in a world filled with good and manly men. Moreover, both the praise and censure of Athenians for being good or bad, or for being good or bad at being a man (cf. Herzfeld 1985, esp. 10–11), served a functional and educational value. The anthropologist David Gilmore argues that masculinity contributes to the continuity of social systems and to the psychological integration of men into their community. Inasmuch as it facilitates individual male development and male group adaptation, gender is a problem-solving behavior (Gilmore 1990, 3–4). The concept of Athenian manhood sought through social conformity and the city's educational, political, and judicial institutions to mold young men and adults into responsible, productive community members. At the same time, Athenian masculinity disdained individuals and groups who fell outside its categories, and it thus contributed to social inequality, discord, and even oppression. In the final analysis, it was too demanding, too ambitious, too pervasive, and too ill-defined, even though Athenian men continued to try to talk their way through it.

Works Cited

Abu-Lughod, L. 1986. *Veiled Sentiments: Honor and Poetry in a Bedouin Society.* Berkeley, Calif.

Adams, C. D. 1912. Are the Political Speeches of Demosthenes to Be Regarded as Political Pamphlets? *TAPA* 43: 5–22.

Adelaye, G. 1983. The Purpose of the *Dokimasia. GRBS* 24: 295–306.

Adkins, A. W. H. 1960. *Merit and Responsibility: A Study in Greek Values.* Chicago.

———. 1972. *Moral Values and Political Behaviour in Ancient Greece.* New York.

Allen, D. S. 1997. Imprisonment in Classical Athens. *CQ* 47.1: 121–35.

———. 2000a. *The World of Prometheus: The Politics of Punishing in Democratic Athens.* Princeton, N.J.

———. 2000b. Changing the Authoritative Voice: Lycurgus' *Against Leocrates. Classical Antiquity* 19.1: 5–33.

Amit, M. 1965. *Athens and the Sea: A Study in Athenian Sea Power.* Brussels.

Arnould, D. 1990. *Le Rire et les larmes dans la littérature grecque d'Homère à Platon.* Paris.

Arthur, M. B. 1973. The Origin of Western Attitudes toward Women. *Arethusa* 6: 1–58.

Asheri, D. 1960. *L'oikos eremos* nel diritto successorio attico. *Archivo giuridico* 159: 12–24.

Aurenche, O. 1974. *Les Groupes d'Alcibiade, de Léogoras et de Teucros.* Paris.

Avramovic, S. 1991. Response to Alberto Maffi. In *Symposion 1990: Vorträge zur griechischen und hellenistischen Rechtsgeschichte,* ed. M. Gagarin, 233–37. Cologne.

Badian, E. 1995. The Ghost of Empire: Reflections on Athenian Foreign Policy in the Fourth Century B.C. In *Die athenische Demokratie im 4. Jahrhundert v. Chr.: Vollendung oder Verfall einer Verfassungsform?* ed. W. Eder, 79–106. Stuttgart.

Badian, E., and J. Heskel 1987. Aeschines 2.12–18: A Study in Rhetoric and Chronology. *Phoenix.* 41: 264–71.

Bailey, F. G. 1991. *The Prevalence of Deceit.* Ithaca, N.Y.

Balme, M. 1984. Attitudes to Work and Leisure in Ancient Greece. *G&R* 31.2: 140–52.

Balot, R. 2001. *Greed and Injustice in Classical Athens.* Princeton, N.J.

Bandy, S. J., ed. 1988. *Coroebus Triumphs: The Alliance of Sport and the Arts.* San Diego, Calif.

Barnes, J. A. 1994. *A Pack of Lies: Toward a Sociology of Lying.* Cambridge.

Bassi, K. 1995. Male Nudity and Disguise in the Discourse of Greek Histrionics. *Helios* 22.1: 3–22.

———. 1998. *Acting Like Men. Gender, Drama and Nostalgia in Ancient Greece.* Ann Arbor, Mich.

Bauman. R. A. 1990. *Political Trials in Ancient Greece.* London.

Ben-Amos, Ilana Krausman. 1994. *Adolescence and Youth in Early Modern England.* New Haven, Conn.

Beneke, T. 1997. *Proving Manhood: Reflections on Men and Sexism.* Berkeley, Calif.

Bergemann, J. 1997. *Demos und Thanatos: Untersuchungen zum Wertsystem der Polis im Spiegel der attischen Grabreliefs des 4. Jahrhunderts v. Chr. und zur Funktion der gleichzeitigen Grabbauten.* Munich.

Bernardi, B. 1985. *Age Class Systems: Social Institutions and Polities Based on Age.* Translated by D. I. Kertzer. Cambridge.

Bers, V. 1985. Dikastic Thorubos. In *Crux: Essays in Greek History Presented to G. E. M. de Ste. Croix on His 75th Birthday,* ed. P. A. Cartledge and F. D. Harvey, 1–15. London.

———. 1997. *Speech in Speech: Studies in Incorporated* Oratio Recta *in Attic Drama and Oratory.* Lanham, Md.

Beston, P. 2000. Hellenistic Military Leadership. In *War and Violence in Classical Greece,* ed. H. van Wees, 315–35. London.

Biraud, M. 1991. La Décence ou l'absence du corps: La Représentation sociale du corps dans les plaidoyers des orateurs attiques. *LEC* 59: 335–43.

Biscardi, A. 1970. La *gnome dikaiotate* et l'interprétation des lois dans la Grèce ancienne. *RIDA,* 3d ser., 17: 219–232.

Blass, F. 1887–98. *Die attische Beredsamkeit.* 4 vols. Leipzig.

Blok, J. 1987. Sexual Asymmetry: A Historiographical Essay. In *Sexual Asymmetry: Studies in Ancient Society,* ed. J. Blok and P. Mason, 1–58. Amsterdam.

Blok, J., and P. Mason, eds. 1987. *Sexual Asymmetry: Studies in Ancient Society.* Amsterdam.

Blundell, M. W. 1989. *Helping Friends and Harming Enemies: A Study in Sophocles and Greek Ethics.* Cambridge.

Blundell, S., and M. Williamson, eds. 1998. *The Sacred and the Feminine.* London.

Bobrick, E. 1997. The Tyranny of Roles: Playacting and Privilege in Aristophanes' *Thesmophoriazusae.* In *The City as Comedy: Society and Representation in Athenian Drama,* ed. G. Dobrov, 177–97. Chapel Hill, N.C.

Boedeker, D. and K. A. Raaflaub, eds. 1999. *Democracy, Empire and the Arts in Fifth-Century Athens*. Cambridge, Mass.

Boegehold, A. L. 1995. *The Lawcourts at Athens: Sites, Buildings, Equipment, Procedure, and Testimonia*. In American School of Classical Studies at Athens, The Athenian Agora, vol. 28. Princeton, N.J.

———. 1996. Group and Single Competitions at the Panathenaia. In *Worshipping Athena: Panathenaia and Parthenon*, ed. J. Neils, 95–105. Madison, Wis.

Boegehold, A. L., and A. C. Scafuro, eds. 1994. *Athenian Identity and Civic Ideology*. Baltimore.

Borthwick, E. K. 1993. Autolekythos and Lekythion in Demosthenes and Aristophanes. *LCM* 18.3: 34–37.

Bourdieu, P. 1966. The Sentiment of Honour in Kabyle Society. In *Honour and Shame: The Values of Mediterranean Society*, ed. J. G. Peristiany, 193–241. Chicago.

———. 1977. *Outline of a Theory of Practice*. Translated by R. Nice. Cambridge.

———. 1991. *Language and Symbolic Power*. Translated by G. Raymond and M. Adamson. Cambridge.

———. 1992. Rites as Acts of Institution. In *Honor and Grace in Anthropology*, ed. J. G. Peristiany and J. Pitt-Rivers, 79–89. Cambridge.

Bourriot F. 1972. La Considération accordée aux marins dans l'antiquité Grecque. *Revue d'histoire économique et sociale* 50: 7–41.

Bouwsma, W. J. 1980. Anxiety and the Formation of Early Modern Culture. In *After the Reformation: Essays in Honor of J. H. Hexter*, ed. B. C. Malament, 215–46. Philadelphia.

Bowersock, G., W. Burkert, and M. C. W. Putnam, eds. 1979. *Arctouros: Hellenic Studies Presented to Bernard M. W. Knox*. Berlin.

Bradford, A. 1994. The Duplicitous Spartan. In *The Shadow of Sparta*, ed. A. Powell and S. Hodkinson, 59–86. London.

Bremmer, J. N. 1980. An Enigmatic Indo-European Rite: Paederasty. *Arethusa* 13: 279–98.

———. 1987. The Old Women of Ancient Greece. In *Sexual Asymmetry: Studies in Ancient Society*, ed. J. Blok, and P. Mason, 191–216. Amsterdam.

———. 1991. Walking, Standing and Sitting in Ancient Greek Culture. In *A Cultural History of Gesture*, ed. J. Bremmer and H. Roodenburg, 15–35. Oxford.

Bremmer, J., and H. Roodenburg, eds. 1991. *A Cultural History of Gesture*. Oxford.

Brittan, A. 1989. *Masculinity and Power*. Oxford.

Broadbent, M. 1968. *Studies in Greek Genealogy*. Leiden.

Brockreide, W. 1972. Arguers as Lovers. *Ph&Rh* 5: 1–11.

Brod, H., and M. Kaufman, eds. 1994. *Theorizing Masculinities*. Thousand Oaks, Calif.

Brown, D. 1977. Demosthenes on Love. *Quaderni di storia* 6: 79–97.

Brown, P. G. McG. 1991. Athenian Attitudes to Rape and Seduction: The Evidence of Menander *Dyskolos* 289–93. *CQ* 41: 533–34.

———. 1993. Love and Marriage in Greek New Comedy. *CQ* 43: 189–205.

Brulé, P. 1987. *La fille d'Athènes: La Religion des filles à Athènes à l'époque classique.* Paris.

Brun, P. 1983. *Eisphora-Syntaxis-Stratiotika: Recherches sur les finances militaires d'Athènes au IVe siècle av. J.-C.* Paris.

Bruyn, Odile de. 1995. *La Compétence de l'Aréopage en matière de procès publics: Des origines de la polis athénienne à la conquête romaine de la Grèce (vers 700–146 avant J.-C.).* Stuttgart.

Bryant, J. M. 1996. *Moral Codes and Social Structure in Ancient Greece: A Sociology of Greek Ethics from Homer to the Epicureans and the Stoics.* Albany, N.Y.

Buchner, E. 1958. *Der Panegyrikos des Isokrates: Eine historisch philologische Untersuchung.* Wiesbaden.

Buffière, F. 1980. *Eros adolescent: La Pédérastie dans la Grèce antique.* Paris.

Bugh, G. R. 1988. *The Horsemen of Athens.* Princeton, N.J.

Burckhardt, L. 1995. Söldner und Bürger als Soldaten für Athen. In *Die athenische Demokratie im 4. Jahrhundert v. Chr.: Vollendung oder Verfall einer Verfassungsform?* ed. W. Eder, 105–33. Stuttgart.

———. 1996. *Bürger in Kriegwesen des 4. Jahrhunderts v. Chr.* Stuttgart.

Burke, E. M. 1972. "Character Denigration in the Attic Orators, with Particular Reference to Demosthenes and Aeschines." Ph.D. diss., Tufts University.

Burkert, W. 1983. *Homo Necans: The Anthropology of Ancient Greek Sacrificial Rituals and Myth.* Translated by P. Bing. Berkeley, Calif.

Buxton, R. G. A. 1982. *Persuasion in Greek Tragedy: The Power of Peitho.* Cambridge.

———. 1996. *Hybris,* Dishonour and Thinking Big. *JHS* 106: 1–32.

Byl, S. 1974. Platon et Aristote ont-ils professé des vues contradictoires sur la vieillesse? *LEC* 42: 113–26.

Cairns, D. L. 1993. *Aidōs: The Psychology and Ethics of Honor and Shame in Ancient Greek Literature.* Oxford.

Calame, C. 1999. *The Poetics of Eros in Ancient Greece.* Translated by J. Lloyd. Princeton, N.J.

Calhoun, G. M. 1913. *Athenian Clubs in Politics and Litigation.* Austin, Tex.

Cameron, A., and A. Kuhrt, eds. 1993. *Images of Women in Antiquity.* Detroit.

Campbell, J. K. 1964. *Honour, Family, and Patronage: A Study of Institutions and Moral Values in a Greek Mountain Community.* Oxford.

———. 1992. The Greek Hero. In *Honor and Grace in Anthropology,* ed. J. G. Peristiany and J. Pitt-Rivers, 129–49. Cambridge.

Cantarella, Eva 1990. "Neaniskoi": Classi di età e passagi di "status" nel diritto ateniese. *Mélanges de l'École française de Rome: Antiquité* 102.1: 37–51.

———. 1991. *Moicheia:* Reconsidering a Problem. In *Symposion 1990: Vorträge zur griechischen und hellenistischen Rechtsgeschichte,* ed. M. Gagarin, 289–97. Cologne.

———. 2002. *Bisexuality in the Ancient World.* Translated by C. O. Cuilleanáin. New Haven, Conn.

Carawan, E. M. 1991. *Ephetai* and Athenian Courts for Homicide in the Age of the Orators. *CP* 86: 1–16.

———. 1998. *Rhetoric and the Law of Draco.* Oxford.

Carey, C. 1989. *Lysias: Selected Speeches*. Cambridge.

———. 1990. Structure and Strategy in Lysias 24. *G & R* 37: 44–51.

———. 1991. Apollodorus' Mother: The Wives of Enfranchised Aliens in Athens. *CQ* 41: 84–89.

———. 1992. *Apollodorus against Neaira: (Demosthenes) 59*. Greek Orators, vol. 6. Warminster, Wilts., U.K.

———. 1993. Return of the Radish or Just When You Thought it Was Safe to Go Back into the Kitchen. *LCM* 18: 53–55.

———. 1994a. Legal Space in Classical Athens. *G&R* 41.2: 172–86.

———. 1994b. Rhetorical Means of Persuasion. In *Persuasion: Greek Rhetoric in Action*, ed. I. Worthington, 26–45. London.

———. 1994c. Comic Ridicule and Democracy. In *Ritual, Finance, Politics: Athenian Democratic Accounts Presented to David Lewis*, ed. R. Osborne and S. Hornblower, 69–83. Oxford.

———. 1995. Rape and Adultery in Athenian Law. *CQ* 45.2: 407–17.

———, trans. 2000.. *Aeschines*. Austin, Tex.

Carey, C., and R. A. Reid, eds. 1985. *Demosthenes' Selected Private Speeches*. Cambridge.

Carlier, P. 1990. *Démosthène*. Paris.

Carson, A. 1990. Putting her in Her Place: Women, Dirt, and Desire. In *Before Sexuality: The Construction of Erotic Experience in the Ancient World*, ed. D. M. Halperin et al., 135–70. Princeton, N.J.

Carter, L. B. 1986. *The Quiet Athenian*. Oxford.

Cartledge, P. 1981. 1987. *Agesilaos and the Crisis of Sparta*. Baltimore.

———. 1998a. Introduction: Defining a *Kosmos*. In *Kosmos: Essays in Order, Conflict and Community in Classical Athens*, ed. id. et al., 1–12. Cambridge.

———. 1998b. The *Machismo* of the Athenian Empire—or the Reign of the *Phalus*. In *When Men Were Men: Masculinity, Power and Identity in Classical Antiquity*, ed. L. Foxhall and J. Salmon, 54–67. London.

———. 2001. *Spartan Reflections*. Berkeley, Calif.

———. 2002. *The Greeks: A Portrait of Self and Others*. Oxford.

Cartledge, P. A., and F. D. Harvey, eds. 1985. *Crux: Essays in Greek History Presented to G. E. M. de Ste. Croix on His 75th Birthday*. London.

Cartledge, P., P. Millett, and S. Todd, eds. 1990. *Nomos: Essays in Athenian Law, Politics and Society*. Cambridge.

Cartledge, P., P. Millett and S. von Reden, eds. 1998. *Kosmos: Essays in Order, Conflict and Community in Classical Athens*. Cambridge.

Casson, L. 1976. The Athenian Upper Class and New Comedy. *TAPA* 106: 29–59.

———. 1991. *The Ancient Mariners*. Princeton, N.J.

Cawkwell, G. L. 1963. Demosthenes' Policy after the Peace of Philocrates. *CQ* 13: 120–38, 200–213.

———. 1984. Athenian Naval Power in the Fourth Century. *CQ* 34: 334–45.

Christ, M. 1990. Liturgy Avoidance and *Antidosis* in Classical Athens. *TAPA* 120: 147–69.

———. 1998. *The Litigious Athenian*. Baltimore.

————. 2001. Conscription of Hoplites in Classical Athens. *CQ* 51.2: 398–422.

Christiansen, J., and T. Melander, eds. *Proceedings of the 3rd Symposium on Ancient Greek and Related Pottery: Copenhagen, August 31–September 4, 1987.* Copenhagen.

Clarke, J. R. 1998. *Looking at Lovemaking: Constructions of Sexuality in Roman Art, 100 B.C. to A.D. 250.* Berkeley, Calif.

Clavaud, R., trans. 1974. *Démosthène. Discours d'apparat: Épitaphios, Éroticos.* Paris.

————. 1980. *Le Ménexène de Platon et la rhétorique de son temps.* Paris.

Cobettto Ghiggia, P., ed. and trans. 1995. *Contro Alcibiade/Andocide.* Pisa.

Cohen, D. 1983. *Theft in Athenian Law.* Munich.

————. 1984. The Athenian Law of Adultery. *RIDA* 31: 147–65.

————. 1985. A Note on Aristophanes and the Punishment of Adultery in Athenian Law. *ZSS* 102: 385–87.

————. 1989. Seclusion, Separation, and the Status of Women in Classical Athens. *G&R* 36: 3–15.

————. 1991a. Demosthenes' *Against Meidias* and Athenian litigation. In *Symposion 1990: Vorträge zur griechischen und hellenistischen Rechtsgeschichte,* ed. M. Gagarin, 155–64. Cologne.

————. 1991b. Homosexuality in Classical Athens. *Past and Present* 117: 3–21.

————. 1991c. *Law, Sexuality, and Society: The Enforcement of Morals in Classical Athens.* Cambridge.

————. 1992. Sex, Gender and Sexuality in Ancient Greece. *CP* 87: 14560.

————. 1995a. *Law, Violence and Community in Classical Athens.* Cambridge.

————. 1995b. Rule of Law and Democratic ideology in Classical Athens. In *Die athenische Demokratie im 4. Jahrhundert v. Chr.: Vollendung oder Verfall einer Verfassungsform?* ed. W. Eder, 227–44. Stuttgart.

Cohen, D., and R. Saller 1994. Sexuality in Greco-Roman Antiquity. In *Foucault and the Writing of History,* ed. J. Goldstein, 35–59. Oxford.

Cohen, E. E. 1991. Banking as a Family Business: Legal Adoptions Affecting Wives and Slaves. In *Symposion 1990: Vorträge zur griechischen und hellenistischen Rechtsgeschichte,* ed. M. Gagarin, 239–63. Cologne.

————. 1992. *Athenian Economy and Society: A Banking Perspective.* Princeton, N.J.

————. 1998. Women, Property and Status in Demosthenes 41 and 57. *Dike* 1: 53–61.

————. 2000. *The Athenian Nation.* Princeton, N.J.

Cohn-Haft, L. 1995. Divorce in Classical Athens. *JHS* 115: 1–14.

Cole, S. G. 1984. Greek Sanctions against Sexual Assaults. *CP* 79: 97–113.

————. 1996. Athenian Ritual and Male Community at Athens. In *Demokratia: A Conversation on Democracies, Ancient and Modern,* ed. J. Ober and C. Hedrick, 227–48. Princeton, N.J.

Cole, T. 1991. *The Origins of Rhetoric in Ancient Greece.* Baltimore.

Colin, G., ed. and trans. 1946. *Hypéride. Discours.* Paris.

Connor, W. R. 1971. *The New Politicians of Fifth-Century Athens.* Princeton, N.J.

———. 1988. Early Greek Land Warfare as Symbolic Expression. *Past and Present* 119: 3–27.

Conway-Long, D. 1994. Ethnographies and Masculinities. In *Theorizing Masculinities,* ed. H. Brod and M. Kaufman, 61–81.Thousand Oaks, Calif.

Corbeill, A. 1997. Dining Deviants in Roman Political Invective. In *Roman Sexualities,* ed. J. P. Hallett, and M. B. Skinner, 99–128. Princeton, N.J.

Cornwell, A., and N. Lindisfarne, eds. 1994. *Dislocating Masculinity: Comparative Ethnographies.* London.

Coulson, W. D. E., et al., eds. 1994. *The Archaeology of Athens and Attika under the Democracy.* Oxford.

Cox, C. A. 1989. Incest, Inheritance and the Political Forum in Fifth-Century Athens. *CJ* 85: 34–46.

———. 1998. *Household Interests: Property, Marriage Strategies, and Family Dynamics in Ancient Athens.* Princeton, N.J.

Craik, E. M. 1999. Mantitheus of Lysias 16: Neither Long-Haired nor Simple-Minded. *CQ* 49: 626–28.

Crane, G. 1998. *Thucydides and the Ancient Simplicity: The Limits of Political Realism.* Berkeley, Calif.

Croally, N. T. 1994. *Euripidean Polemic: The Trojan Women and the Function of Tragedy.* Cambridge.

Cronin, J. F. 1936. *The Athenian Juror and His Oath.* Chicago.

Cropp, M., E. Fantham, and S. E. Scully 1986, eds. *Greek Tragedy and Its Legacy: Essays Presented to D. J. Conacher.* Calgary.

Crowther, N. B. 1985. Male "Beauty" Contests in Greece: The Euandria and Euexia. *L'Antiquité classique.* 54: 285–91.

———. 1991. The Apobates Reconsidered. (Demosthenes lxi 23–9). *JHS* 111: 174–76.

Csapo, E. 1993. Deep Ambivalence? Notes on Greek Cockfighting. *CQ* 47: 1–28, 115–24.

Davidson, J. N. 1993. Fish, Sex and Revolution. *CQ* 43: 53–66.

———. 1997. *Courtesans & Fishcakes: The Consuming Passions of Classical Athens.* New York.

Davies, J. K. 1971. *Athenian Propertied Families, 600–300 B.C.* Oxford.

———. 1984. *Wealth and the Power of Wealth in Classical Athens.* New York.

———. 1995. The Fourth Century Crisis: What Crisis? In *Die athenische Demokratie im 4. Jahrhundert v. Chr.: Vollendung oder Verfall einer Verfassungsform?* ed. W. Eder, 29–36. Stuttgart.

Davis, J. 1977. *People of the Mediterranean.* London.

Deacy, S., and K. F. Pierce, eds. 1997. *Rape in Antiquity: Sexual Violence in the Greek and Roman Worlds.* London.

Delumeau, J. 1978. *La Peur en Occident: XIVe–XVIIIe siècles.* Paris.

Demont, P. 1990. *La Cité grecque archaïque et classique et l'idéal de tranquillité.* Paris.

de Ste. Croix, G. E. M. 1983. *The Class Struggle in the Ancient Greek World: From the Archaic Age to the Arab Conquests.* Ithaca, N.Y.

Detienne, M. 1996. *The Masters of Truth in Archaic Greece*. Translated by J. Lloyd. New York.

Detienne, M., and J.-P. Vernant. 1978. *Cunning Intelligence in Greek Culture and Society*. Translated by J. Lloyd. Hassocks, Sussex.

———, eds. 1989. *The Cuisine of Sacrifice among the Greeks*. Translated by P. Wissing. Chicago.

Di Bella, M. P. 1992. Name, Blood and Miracles: The Claims to Renown in Traditional Sicily, in *Honor and Grace in Anthropology*, ed. J. G. Peristiany, and J. Pitt-Rivers, 1992, 152–65. Cambridge.

Dobrov, G., ed. 1997. *The City as Comedy: Society and Representation in Athenian Drama*. Chapel Hill, N.C.

Dodds, E. R. 1951. *The Greeks and the Irrational*. Berkeley, Calif.

Dover, K. J. 1968. *Lysias and the Corpus Lysiacum*. Berkeley, Calif.

———. 1973. Classical Greek Attitudes to Sexual Behavior. *Arethusa* 6: 59–73. Reprinted in *Sexualität und Erotik in der Antike*, ed. A. K. Siems, Wege der Forschung 605 (Darmstadt, 1988), 264–81.

———. 1974. *Greek Popular Morality in the Age of Plato and Aristotle*. Berkeley, Calif.

———. 1989. *Greek Homosexuality*. Cambridge, Mass.

Donlan, W. 1980. *The Aristocratic Ideal in Ancient Greece: Attitudes of Superiority from Homer to the End of the Fifth Century B.C.* Lawrence, Kan.

Dorjahn, A.P. 1928. Legal Precedents in Athenian Courts. *Philological Quarterly* 7: 375–89.

Dubisch, J., ed. 1986. *Gender & Power in Rural Greece*. Princeton, N.J.

DuBois, P. 1991. *Torture and Truth*. New York.

Du Boulay, J. 1974. *Portrait of a Greek Mountain Village*. Oxford.

Dyck, A. R. 1985. The Function and Persuasive Power of Demosthenes' Portrait of Aeschines in the Speech On The Crown. *G&R* 32: 42–48.

Eadie, J. W., and J. Ober, eds. 1985. *The Craft of the Ancient Historian: Essays in Honor of Chester G. Starr*. Lanham, Md.

Easterling, P. 1999. Actors and Voices: Reading between the Lines in Aeschines and Demosthenes. In *Performance Culture and Athenian Democracy*, ed. S. Goldhill and R. Osborne, 154–66. Cambridge.

Eck, W., et al., eds. 1980. *Studien zur Antiken Sozialgeschichte: Festschrift F. Vittinghoff*. Kölner historische Abhandlungen 28. Cologne.

Eder, W. 1995a. Die athenische Demokratie im 4. Jahrhundert v. Chr.: Krise oder Vollendung? In *Die athenische Demokratie im 4. Jahrhundert v. Chr.: Vollendung oder Verfall einer Verfassungsform?* ed. W. Eder, 11–28. Stuttgart.

———, ed. 1995b. *Die athenische Demokratie im 4. Jahrhundert v. Chr.: Vollendung oder Verfall einer Verfassungsform?* Stuttgart.

Edwards, M., trans. 1995. *Andocides*. Greek Orators, vol. 4. Warminster, Wilts., U.K.

Edwards, M., and S. Usher, trans. 1985. *Antiphon & Lysias*. Greek Orators, vol. 1. Warminster, Wilts., U.K.

Ehrenberg, V. 1947. Polypragmosyne: A Study in Greek Politics. *JHS* 67: 46–67.

————. 1951. *The People of Aristophanes: A Sociology of Old Comedy*. Oxford.

Eisenstadt, S. N., ed. 1986. *The Origins and Diversity of Axial Age Civilizations*. Albany, N.Y.

Engels, J. 1993. *Studien zur politischen Biographie des Hyperides: Athens in der Epoche der lykurgischen Reformen und des makedonischen Universalreiches*. Munich.

Erffa, C. E. von. 1937. *"Aidōs" und verwandte Begriffe in ihrer Entwicklung von Homer bis Demokrit*. *Philologus*, suppl. 30.2. Leipzig.

Euben, J. P., J. R. Wallach and J. Ober, eds. 1994. *Athenian Political Thought and the Reconstruction of American Democracy*. Ithaca, N.Y.

Falkner, T. M. 1995. *The Poetics of Old Age in Greek Epic, Lyric, and Tragedy*. Norman, Okla.

Falkner, T. M., and J. de Luce, eds. 1989. *Old Age in Greek and Latin Literature*. Albany, N.Y.

Ferrari, G. 2002. *Figures of Speech: Men and Maidens in Ancient Greece*. Chicago.

Finley, M. I. 1962. Athenian Demagogues. *Past & Present* 21: 3–24.

————. 1973. *Studies in Land and Credit in Ancient Athens, 500–200 B.C.* New Brunswick, N.J.

————. 1976. The Freedom of the Citizen in the Greek World. *Talanta* 7: 1–23.

————. [1954] 1978. *The World of Odysseus*. Harmondsworth, U.K.

————. 1983a. *Economy and Society in Ancient Greece*. New York.

————. 1983b. *Politics in the Ancient World*. Cambridge.

————. 1989. The Elderly in Classical Antiquity. In *Old Age in Greek and Latin Literature*, ed. T. M. Falkner and J. de Luce, 1–20. Albany, N.Y.

Fisher, N. R. E. 1976. *Social Values in Classical Greece*. London.

————. 1992. *Hybris: A Study in the Values of Honour and Shame in Ancient Greece*. Warminster, Wilts., U.K.

————. 1998a. Gymnasia and the Democratic Values of Leisure. In *Kosmos: Essays in Order, Conflict and Community in Classical Athens*, ed. P. Cartledge et al., 84–104. Cambridge.

————. 1998b. Violence, Masculinity, and the Law in Classical Athens. In *When Men Were Men: Masculinity, Power and Identity in Classical Antiquity*, ed., L. Foxhall and J. Salmon, 68–97. London.

————. 2000. *Hybris*, Revenge and *Stasis* in the Greek City-States. In *War and Violence in Classical Greece*, ed. H. van Wees, 83–123. London.

————, ed. and trans. 2001. *Aeschines: Against Timarchus*. New York.

Foley, H. P., ed. 1981a. *Reflections of Women in Antiquity*. New York.

————. 1981b. The Concept of Women in Athenian Drama. In *Reflections of Women in Antiquity*, ed. H. P. Foley, 127–68. New York.

Föllinger, Sabina. 1996. *Differenz und Gleichheit: Das Geschlechterverhältnis in der Sicht griechischer Philosophen des 4. bis 1. Jahrhunders v. Chr.* Stuttgart.

Ford, A. 1999. Reading Homer from the Rostrum: Poems and Laws in Aeschines' *Against Timarchus*.' In *Performance Culture and Athenian Democracy*, ed. S. Goldhill and R. Osborne, 231–56. Cambridge.

Forrest, W. G. 1975. An Athenian Generation Gap. *YCS* 24: 37–52.

Foucault, M. 1978. *The History of Sexuality.* Vol. 1: *An Introduction.* Translated by R. Hurley. New York.

———. 1985. *The History of Sexuality.* Vol. 2: *The Uses of Pleasure.* Translated by R. Hurley. New York.

Fox, M. 1998. The Constrained Man. In *Thinking Men: Masculinity and Self-Representation in the Classical Tradition,* ed. L. Foxhall and J. Salmon, 6–22. London.

Foxhall, L. 1989. Household, Gender and Property in Classical Athens. *CQ* 39.1: 22–44.

———. 1991. Response to Eva Cantarella. In *Symposion 1990: Vorträge zur griechischen und hellenistischen Rechtsgeschichte,* ed. M. Gagarin, 297–303. Cologne.

———. 1996. Law and the Lady: Women and Legal Proceedings in Classical Athens. In *Greek Law in Its Political Setting: Justifications Not Justice,* ed. L. Foxhall and A. D. E. Lewis, 302–25. Oxford.

———. 1998a. The Politics of Affection: Emotional Attachments in Athenian Society. In *Kosmos: Essays in Order, Conflict and Community in Classical Athens,* ed. P. Cartledge et al., 52–67. Cambridge.

———. 1998b. Introduction. In *When Men Were Men: Masculinity, Power and Identity in Classical Antiquity,* ed. L. Foxhall and J. Salmon, 1–9. London.

———. 1998c. Natural Sex: the Attribution of Sex and Gender to Plants in Ancient Greece. In *Thinking Men: Masculinity and Self-Representation in the Classical Tradition,* ed. L. Foxhall and J. Salmon, 57–70. London.

Foxhall, L., and A. D. E. Lewis, eds. 1996. *Greek Law in Its Political Setting: Justifications Not Justice.* Oxford.

Foxhall, L., and J. Salmon, eds. 1998a. *Thinking Men: Masculinity and Self-Representation in the Classical Tradition.* London.

———, eds. 1998b. *When Men Were Men: Masculinity, Power and Identity in Classical Antiquity.* London.

Frangeskou, V. 1999. Tradition and Originality in Some Attic Funeral Orations. *CW* 92.4: 315–36.

Frontisi-Ducroux, F. 1996. Eros, Desire, and the Gaze. In *Sexuality in Ancient Art: Near East, Egypt, Greece, and Italy,* ed. N. B. Kampen, 81–100. Cambridge.

Frontisi-Ducroux, F., and F. Lissarrague 1990. From Ambiguity to Ambivalence: A Dionysiac Excursion through the "Anakreontic" Vases. In *Before Sexuality: The Construction of Erotic Experience in the Ancient World,* ed. D. M. Halperin et al., 211–56. Princeton, N.J.

Frösén, J., ed. 1997. *Early Hellenistic Athens: Symptoms of Change.* Papers and Monographs of the Finnish Institute at Athens, vol. 6. Helsinki.

Furley, W. D. 1989. Andocides IV ('Against Alcibiades'): Facts or Fiction. *Hermes* 17: 138–56.

Gabrielsen, V. 1987. The *Antidosis* Procedure in Classical Athens. *C&M* 38: 7–38.

———. 1990. Trierarchic Symmories. *C&M* 41: 89–118.

————. 1994. *Financing the Athenian Fleet: Public Taxation and Social Relations*. Baltimore.

Gagarin, M. 1979. The Athenian Law against *Hybris*. In *Arctouros: Hellenic Studies Presented to Bernard M. W. Knox,* ed. G. Bowersock, W. Burkert, and M. C. W. Putnam, 229–36. Berlin.

————, ed. 1991. *Symposion 1990: Vorträge zur griechischen und hellenistischen Rechtsgeschichte*. Cologne.

————. 1996. The Torture of Slaves in Athenian Law. *CP* 91: 1–18.

————, trans. 1997. *Antiphon. The Speeches*. Cambridge.

————. 1999. The Orality of Greek Oratory. In *Signs of Orality: The Oral Tradition and Its Influence in the Greek and Roman World,* ed. E. A. Mackay, 163–80. Leiden.

————. 2002. *Antiphon the Athenian: Oratory, Law, and Justice in the Age of the Sophists*. Austin, Tex.

Gallant, T. W. 1991. *Risk and Survival in Ancient Greece*. Stanford, Calif.

Gardiner, E. N. 1910. *Greek Athletic Sports and Festivals*. London.

Gardner, J. 1989. Aristophanes and Male Anxiety: The Defense of the *Oikos*. *G&R* 36: 31–62.

Garlan, Y. 1975. *War in the Ancient World: A Social History*. Translated by J. Lloyd. New York.

————. 1980. Le Travail libre en Grèce ancienne. In *Non-Slave Labour in the Greco-Roman World,* ed. P. Garnsey, 6–22. Cambridge.

Garland, R. 1990. *The Greek Way of Life: From Conception to Old Age*. Ithaca, N.Y.

Garner, R. 1987. *Law and Society in Classical Athens*. New York.

Garnsey, P., ed. 1980. *Non-Slave Labour in the Greco-Roman World*. Cambridge.

Gauthier P. 1976. *Un Commentaire historique des Poroi de Xénophon*. Geneva.

Gazzano, F., ed. and trans. 1999. *Contro Alcibiade Pseudo-Andocide*. Genoa.

Geddes, A. G. 1987. Rags and Riches: The Costume of Athenian Men in the Fifth Century. *CQ* 37.2: 307–31.

Gellner, E. 1988. Trust, Cohesion, and the Social Order. In *Trust: Making and Breaking Cooperative Relations,* ed. D. Gambetta, 142–57. New York.

Gernet, L., trans. 1954–60. *Démosthène: Plaidoyers civiles*. Vols. 1–4. Paris.

————. 1955. *Droit et société dans la Grèce ancienne*. Paris.

Gill, C. 1998. Altruism and Reciprocity in Greek Ethical Philosophy? In *Reciprocity in Ancient Greece,* ed. id. et al., 303–28. Oxford.

Gill, C., N. Postlethwaite, and R. Seaford, eds. 1998. *Reciprocity in Ancient Greece*. Oxford.

Gilmore, D., ed. 1987a. *Honor and Shame and the Unity of the Mediterranean*. Washington, D.C.

————. 1987b. Introduction: The Shame of Dishonor. In *Honor and Shame and the Unity of the Mediterranean,* ed. id., 2–21. Washington, D.C.

————. 1990. *Manhood in the Making: Cultural Concepts of Masculinity*. New Haven, Conn.

Gleason, M. W. 1990. The Semiotics of Gender: Physiognomy and Self-Fashioning in the Second Century C.E. In *Before Sexuality: The Construction of Erotic Experience in the Ancient World,* ed. D. M. Halperin et al., 389–416. Princeton, N.J.

———. 1995. *Making Men: Sophists and Self-Presentation in Ancient Rome.* Princeton, N.J.

Gold, B. K. 1977. Eukosmia in Euripides' Bacchae. *AJP* 98: 3–15.

Goldberg, S. 1993. *Why Men Rule: A Theory of Male Dominance.* Chicago.

Golden, M. 1984. Slavery and Homosexuality. *Phoenix* 38: 308–24.

———. 1985. Pais, Child and Slave. *AC* 54: 91–104.

———. 1990. *Children and Childhood in Classical Athens.* Baltimore.

———. 1991. Thirteen Years of Homosexuality (and Other Recent Works on Sex, Gender and the Body in Ancient Greece). *Échos du monde classique / Classical Views* 10: 327–40.

———. 1997. Equestrian Competition in Ancient Greece. *Phoenix* 51.3–4: 327–44.

———. 1998. *Sport and Society in Ancient Greece.* Cambridge.

Golden, M., and P. Toohey, eds. 1997. *Inventing Ancient Culture: Historicism, Periodization, and the Ancient World.* London.

———. eds. 2003. *Sex and Difference in Ancient Greece and Rome.* Edinburgh.

Goldhill, S. 1986. *Reading Greek Tragedy.* Cambridge.

———. 1990. The Great Dionysia and Civic Ideology. In *Nothing to Do with Dionysos? Athenian Drama in Its Social Context,* ed. J. J. Winkler and F. I. Zeitlin, 97–129. Princeton, N.J.

———. 1994. Representing Democracy: Women at the Great Dionysia. In *Ritual, Finance, Politics: Athenian Democratic Accounts Presented to David Lewis,* ed. R. Osborne and S. Hornblower, 347–69. Oxford.

———. 1998. Seductions of the Gaze: Socrates and His Girlfriends. In *Kosmos: Essays in Order, Conflict and Community in Classical Athens,* ed. P. Cartledge et al., 105–24. Cambridge.

Goldhill, S., and R. Osborne, eds. 1994. *Art and Text in Ancient Greek Culture.* Cambridge.

———, eds. 1999. *Performance Culture and Athenian Democracy.* Cambridge.

Goldstein, J., ed. 1994. *Foucault and the Writing of History.* Oxford.

Gordon, R. L. 1981. *Myth, Religion, and Society: Structuralist Essays by M. Detienne, L. Gernet, J.-P. Vernant and P. Vidal-Naquet.* Cambridge.

Gosling, J. C. B., and C. C. P. Taylor 1982. *The Greeks on Pleasure.* Oxford.

Gould, J. 1980. Law, Custom and Myth: Aspects of the Social Position of Women in Classical Athens. *JHS* 100: 38–59.

Gouldner, A. 1965. *Enter Plato: Classical Greece and the Origins of Social Theory.* New York.

Gribble, D. 1997. Rhetoric and History in [Andocides] 4. *CQ* 47.2: 367–91.

———. *Alcibiades and Athens: A Study in Literary Representation.* Oxford.

Grossmann, G. 1950. Politische Schlagwörter aus der Zeit des peloponnesichen Krieges. Diss. Zurich.

Gutmann, D. 1977. The Cross-Cultural Perspective: Notes Toward a Comparative Psychology of Aging. In *Handbook of the Psychology of Aging,* ed. J. Birren and K. Schaie, 302–26. New York.

Hakkarainen, M. 1997. Private Wealth in the Athenian Public Sphere during the

Late Classical and Early Hellenistic Period. In *Early Hellenistic Athens: Symptoms of Change,* ed. J. Frösén, 1–32. Helsinki.

Hall, E. 1995. Lawcourt Drama: The Power of Performance in Greek Forensic Oratory. *BICS* 40: 39–58.

Hallett, J. P., and M. B. Skinner, eds. 1997. *Roman Sexualities*. Princeton, N.J.

Halliwell, S. 1991a. Comic Satire and Freedom of Speech in Classical Athens. *JHS* 111: 48–70.

———. 1991b. The Use of Laughter in Greek Culture. *CQ* 41.2: 279–96.

Halpern, B., and D. W. Hobson, eds. 1993. *Law, Politics and Society in the Ancient Mediterranean World*. Sheffield, U.K.

Halperin, D. M. 1990. *One Hundred Years of Homosexuality and Other Essays on Greek Love*. New York.

Halperin, D. M., J. J. Winkler, and F. I. Zeitlin, eds. 1990. *Before Sexuality: The Construction of Erotic Experience in the Ancient World*. Princeton, N.J.

Hamel, D. 1998. *Athenian Generals: Military Authority in the Classical Period*. London.

Hands, A. R. 1968. *Charities and Social Aid in Greece and Rome*. Ithaca, N.Y.

Hansen, M. H. 1975. *Eisangelia: The Sovereignty of the People's Court in Athens in the Fourth Century B.C. and the Impeachment of Generals and Politicians*. Odense, Denmark.

———. 1976. *Apagoge, Endeixis and Ephegesis against Kakourgoi, Atimoi, and Pheugontes*. Odense University Classical Studies, vol. 6. Odense, Denmark.

———. 1985. *Demography and Democracy: The Number of Athenian Citizens in the Fourth Century B.C.* Herning, Denmark.

———. 1987. *The Athenian Assembly in the Age of Demosthenes*. Oxford.

———. 1989a. *The Athenian Ecclesia, II: A Collection of Articles, 1983–89*. Copenhagen.

———. 1990. The Political Powers of the People's Court in Fourth-Century Athens. In *The Greek City from Homer to Alexander,* ed. O. Murray and S. Price, 215–43. Oxford.

———. 1991. *The Athenian Democracy in the Age of Demosthenes: Structure, Principles and Ideology*. Translated by J. A. Crook. Oxford.

———, ed. 1993. *The Ancient Greek City State*. Copenhagen.

Hanson, A. E. 1990. The Medical Writers' Woman. In *Before Sexuality: The Construction of Erotic Experience in the Ancient World,* ed. D. M. Halperin et al., 309–37. Princeton, N.J.

Hanson, V. D. 1989. *The Western Way of War*. Oxford.

———, ed. 1991. *Hoplites: The Classical Greek Battle Experience*. London.

———. 1995. *The Other Greeks: The Family Farm and the Agrarian Roots of Western Civilization*. New York.

———. 1996. Hoplites into Democrats: The Changing Ideology of Athenian Infantry. In *Demokratia: A Conversation on Democracies, Ancient and Modern,* ed. J. Ober and C. Hedrick, 289–312. Princeton, N.J.

———. 2000. Hoplite Battle as Ancient Greek Warfare: When, Where, and Why? In *War and Violence in Classical Greece* ed. H. van Wees, 201–32. London.

Harding, P. 1973. The Purpose of Isokrates' *Archidamus* and *On the Peace*. *CSCA* 6: 137–149.

————. 1981. In Search of a Polypragmatist. In *Classical Contributions: Studies in Honor of M. F. McGregor,* ed. G. Shrimpton and D. J. McCargar, 41–50. New York.

————. 1987. Rhetoric and Politics in Fourth-Century Athens. *Phoenix* 41: 25–39.

————. 1994. Comedy and Rhetoric. in *Persuasion: Greek Rhetoric in Action,* ed. I. Worthington, 196–221. London.

Harris, E. M. 1989. Demosthenes' Speech against Meidias. *HSCPh* 92: 117–36.

————. 1990. Did the Athenians Regard Seduction as a Worse Crime Than Rape? *CQ* 40: 370–77.

————. 1994. Law and Oratory. In *Persuasion: Greek Rhetoric in Action,* ed. I. Worthington, 130–50. London.

————. 1995. *Aeschines and Athenian Politics.* New York.

————. 1996. Demosthenes and the Theoric Fund. In *Transitions to Empire. Essays in Greco-Roman History 360–146 B.C.,* in Honor of E. Badian, ed. R. W. Wallace and E. M. Harris, 57–76. Norman, Okla.

Harris, W. V. 1997. Athenian Beliefs about Revenge. *CQ* 47.2: 363–66.

Harrison, A. R. W. 1968–71. *The Law of Athens.* Vol. 1: *The Family and Property.* Vol. 2: *Procedure.* Oxford.

Harvey, F. D. 1985. *Dona Ferentes:* Some Aspects of Bribery in Greek Politics. In *Crux: Essays in Greek History Presented to G. E. M. de Ste. Croix on His 75th Birthday,* ed. P. A. Cartledge and F. D. Harvey, 76–117. London.

————. 1990. The Sykophant and Sykophancy: Vexatious Redefinition? In *Nomos: Essays in Athenian Law, Politics and Society,* ed. P. Cartledge et al., 103–21. Cambridge.

Hawley, R. 1998. The Male Body as Spectacle in Attic Drama. In *Thinking Men: Masculinity and Self-Representation in the Classical Tradition,* ed. L. Foxhall and J. Salmon 1998, 83–99. London.

Heap, A. 1998. Understanding the Men in Menander. In *Thinking Men: Masculinity and Self-Representation in the Classical Tradition,* ed. L. Foxhall and J. Salmon, 1998, 115–29. London.

Hearn, J., and D. L. Collinson 1994. Theorizing Unities and Differences between Men and between Masculinities. In *Theorizing Masculinities,* ed. H. Brod and M. Kaufman, 97–118. Thousand Oaks, Calif.

Heath, M. 1997. Aristophanes and the Discourse of Politics. In *The City as Comedy: Society and Representation in Athenian Drama,* ed. G. Dobrov, 230–49. Chapel Hill, N.C.

Henderson, Jeffrey 1990. The *Demos* and the Comic Competition. In *Nothing to Do with Dionysos? Athenian Drama in Its Social Context,* ed. J. J. Winkler and F. I. Zeitlin, 271–313. Princeton, N.J.

————. 1991a. *The Maculate Muse: Obscene Language in Attic Comedy.* Oxford.

————. 1991b. Women and the Athenian Dramatic Festivals. *TAPA* 121: 133–47.

————. 1998. Attic Old Comedy, Frank Speech, and Democracy. In *Democracy,*

Empire and the Arts in Fifth-Century Athens, ed. D. Boedeker and K. A. Raaflaub, 255–73. Cambridge, Mass.

Henderson, John. 1994. *Timeo Danaos:* Amazons in Early Greek Art and Pottery. In *Art and Text in Ancient Greek Culture,* ed. S. Goldhill and R. Osborne, 85–137. Cambridge.

Herman, G. 1987. *Ritualised Friendship and the Greek City.* Cambridge

———. 1993. Tribal and Civic Codes of Behaviour in Lysias 1. *CQ* 43: 406–19.

———. 1994. How Violent was Athenian Society? In *Ritual, Finance, Politics: Athenian Democratic Accounts Presented to David Lewis,* ed. R. Osborne and S. Hornblower, 99–117. Oxford.

———. 1995. Honour, Revenge and the State in Fourth-Century Athens. In *Die athenische Demokratie im 4. Jahrhundert v. Chr.: Vollendung oder Verfall einer Verfassungsform?* ed. W. Eder, 43–60. Stuttgart.

———. 1996. Ancient Athens and the Values of Mediterranean Society. *Mediterranean Historical Review* 11: 5–36.

———. 1998. Reciprocity, Altruism, and the Prisoner's Dilemma: The Special Case of Classical Athens. In *Reciprocity in Ancient Greece,* ed. C. Gill et al., 199–225. Oxford.

Herzfeld, M. 1985. *The Poetics of Manhood: Contest and Identity in a Cretan Mountain Village.* Princeton, N.J.

———. 1986. Within and Without: The Category of Female in the Ethnography of Modern Greece. In *Gender & Power in Rural Greece,* ed. J. Dubisch, 215–34. Princeton, N.J.

Hesk, J. 2000. *Deception and Democracy in Classical Athens.* Cambridge.

Hexter, R., and D. Selden, eds. 1992. *Innovations of Antiquity.* New York.

Hillgruber, M. 1988. *Die zehnte Rede des Lysias: Einleitung, Text und Kommentar mit einem Anhang über die Gesetzesinterpretationen bei den attischen Rednern.* Berlin.

Hobbs, A. 2000. *Plato and the Hero: Courage, Manliness and the Impersonal Good.* Cambridge.

Hollein, H. G. 1988. *Bürgerbild und Bildwelt der attischen Demokratie auf den rotfigurigen Vasen des 6.-4. Jh. v. Chr.* Frankfurt a/M.

Holt, F. N. 1992. Love's Body Anatomized: The Ancient Erotic Handbooks and the Rhetoric of Sexuality. In *Pornography and Representation in Greece and Rome,* ed. A. Richlin, 90–111. New York.

Hopkins, K., P. Garnesy, and C. R. Whittaker, eds. 1983. *Trade and Politics in the Ancient Economy.* Berkeley, Calif.

Hornblower, S. 1991–96. *A Commentary on Thucydides.* 2 vols. Oxford.

Huart, P. 1973. *Gnōmē chez Thucydide et ses contemporains.* Paris.

Hubbard, T. K. 1991. *The Mask of Comedy: Aristophanes and the Intertextual Parabasis.* Ithaca, N.Y.

———. 1998. Popular Perceptions of Elite Homosexuality in Classical Athens. *Arion* 6.1: 48–78.

———. ed. 2003. *Homosexuality in Greece and Rome.* Berkeley, Calif.

Humphreys, S. C. 1985a. Law as Discourse. *History and Anthropology* 1: 241–65.

———. 1985b. Lycurgus of Butadae: An Athenian Aristocrat. In *The Craft of the*

Ancient Historian: Essays in Honor of Chester G. Starr, ed. J. W. Eadie and
J. Ober, 199–252. Lanham, Md.

———. 1985c. Social Relations on Stage: Witnesses in Classical Athens. *History
and Anthropology* 1: 313–69.

———. 1986a. Dynamics of the Greek Breakthrough: The Dialogue between
Philosophy and Religion. In *The Origins and Diversity of Axial Age Civilizations,* ed. S. N. Eisenstadt, 92–110. Albany, N.Y.

———. 1986b. Kinship Patterns in the Athenian Courts. *GRBS* 27: 57–91.

———. 1989. Family Quarrels. *JHS* 109: 182–85.

———. 1993. *The Family, Women and Death.* Ann Arbor.

———. 1995. Women's Stories. In *Pandora: Women in Classical Greece,* ed.
E. D. Reeder, 102–10. Baltimore.

———. 1997. Fragments, Fetishes, and Philosophies: Towards a History of
Greek Historiography after Thucydides. In *Collecting Fragments: Fragmente
sammeln,* ed. G. W. Most, 207–24. Göttingen.

Hunt, P. 1998. *Slaves, Warfare, and Ideology in the Greek Historians.* Cambridge.

Hunter, V. J. 1973. *Thucydides the Artful Reporter.* Toronto.

———. 1989a. The Athenian Widow and Her Kin. *Journal of Family History*
14: 291–311.

———. 1989b. Women's Authority in Classical Athens: The Example of
Kleoboule and Her Son (Dem. 27–29.) *Échos du monde classique / Classical
Views* 8: 39–48.

———. 1993. Agnatic Kinship in Athenian Law and Athenian Family Practice:
Its Implications for Women. In *Law, Politics and Society in the Ancient
Mediterranean World,* ed. B. Halpern and D. W. Hobson, 100–121. Sheffield,
U.K.

———. 1994. *Policing Athens: Social Control in the Attic Lawsuits, 420–320
B.C.* Princeton, N.J.

———. 1997. The Prison of Athens. *Phoenix* 51: 298–326.

Hunter, V. J., and J. Edmonson, eds. 2000. *Law and Social Status in Classical
Athens.* Oxford.

Hupperts, C. A. M. 1988. Greek Love: Homosexuality or Pederasty? Greek
Love in Black Figure Vase-Paintings. In *Proceedings of the 3rd Symposium on
Ancient Greek and Related Pottery,* ed. J. Christiansen and T. Melander,
255–65. Copenhagen.

Hutter, H. 1978. *Politics as Friendship: The Origins of Classical Notions of Politics in Theory and Practice of Friendship.* Waterloo, Ont.

Isager, S. 1981. The Marriage Pattern in Classical Athens: Men and Women in
Isaeus. *C&M* 33: 81–96.

Isager, S., and M. H. Hansen 1975. *Aspects of Athenian Society in the Fourth
Century B.C.: A Historical Introduction to and Commentary on the* Para-
graphē-*Speeches and the Speech* Against Dionysodorus *in the* Corpus Demos-
thenicum. Odense, Denmark.

Jackson, A. H. 1991. Hoplites and the Gods: The Dedication of Captured Arms
and Armour. In *Hoplites: The Classical Greek Battle Experience,* ed. V. D.
Hanson, 228–49. London.

Jaeger, W. 1945. *Paideia: The Ideals of Greek Culture*. Translated by G. Highet. 3 vols. New York.

Jameson, M. 1990. Private Space in the Greek City. In *The Greek City from Homer to Alexander*, ed. O. Murray and S. Price, 171–95. Oxford.

Johnston, C. L., ed. 1996. *Theory, Text, Context: Issues in Greek Rhetoric and Oratory*. Albany, N.Y.

Johnstone, S. 1999. *Disputes and Democracy: The Consequences of Litigation in Ancient Athens*. Austin, Tex.

Jones, A. H. M. 1960. *Athenian Democracy*. Oxford.

Jones, N. F. 1999. *The Associations of Classical Athens: The Response to Democracy*. New York.

Jordan, B. 1975. *The Athenian Navy in the Classical Period: A Study of Athenian Naval Administration and Military Organization in the Fifth and Fourth Centuries B.C.* Berkeley, Calif.

Jost, K. 1936. *Das Beispiel und Vorbild der Vorfahren bei den Attischen Rednern und Geschichtsschreibern bis Demosthenes*. Paderborn, Ger.

Just, R. 1985. Freedom, Slavery and the Female Psyche. In *Crux: Essays in Greek History Presented to G. E. M. de Ste. Croix on His 75th Birthday*, ed. P. A. Cartledge and F. D. Harvey, 169–88. London.

———. 1989. *Women in Athenian Law and Life*. London.

Kallet-Marx, L. 1994. Money Talks: Rhetor, Demos and the Resources of the Athenian Empire. in *Ritual, Finance, Politics: Athenian Democratic Accounts Presented to David Lewis*, ed. R. Osborne and S. Hornblower, 227–51. Oxford.

Kampen, N. B., ed. 1996. *Sexuality in Ancient Art: Near East, Egypt, Greece, and Italy*. Cambridge.

Kapferer, B., ed. 1976. *Transaction and Meaning: Directions in the Anthropology of Exchange and Symbolic Behavior*. Philadelphia.

Kapparis, K. A. 1995. When Were the Athenian Adultery Laws Introduced? *RIDA* 42: 97–122.

———. 1996. Humiliating the Adulterer: The Law and the Practice in Classical Athens *RIDA* 43: 63–77.

———, ed. and trans. 1999. [Apollodoros] *Against Neaira [D. 59]*. New York.

Kely, W., Jr. 1973. Rhetoric as Seduction. *Rh&Ph* 6: 69–80.

Kennedy, G. A. 1963. *The Art of Persuasion in Greece*. Princeton, N.J.

Kerschensteiner, J. 1962. *Kosmos: Quellenkritische Untersuchungen zu den Vorsokratikern*. Zetemata, vol. 30. Munich.

Keuls, E. C. 1985. *The Reign of the Phallus: Sexual Politics in Ancient Athens*. Berkeley, Calif.

Kilmer, M. 1993. *Greek Erotica on Attic Red-Figured Vases*. London.

———. 1997 Painters and Pederasts: Ancient Art, Sexuality, and Social History. In *Inventing Ancient Culture: Historicism, Periodization, and the Ancient World*. ed. M. Golden and P. Toohey, 36–49. London.

Kimmel, M. S. 1994. Masculinity as Homophobia. In *Theorizing Masculinities*, ed. H. Brod and M. Kaufman, 119–41. Thousand Oaks, Calif.

Kirk, G. S. 1971. Old Age and Maturity in Ancient Greece. *Eranos Jahrbuch* 40: 23–58.

Kleijwegt, M. 1991. *Ancient Youth: The Ambiguity of Youth and the Absence of Adolescence in Greco-Roman Society.* Amsterdam.

Knox, R. A. 1985. "So Mischievous a Beast?" The Athenian *demos* and Its Treatment of Its Politicians. *G&R* 32: 132–61.

Koch-Harnack, G. 1983. *Knabenliebe und Tiergeschenke: Ihre Bedeutung in päderastischen Erziehungssystem Athens.* Berlin.

Konstan, D. 1989. Between Courtesan and Wife: A Study of Menander's "Perikeiromene." *Phoenix* 41: 121–39.

———. 1994. Premarital Sex, Illegitimacy, and Male Anxiety in Menander and Athens. In *Athenian Ideology and Civic Ideology,* ed. A. L. Boegehold and A. C. Scafuro, 217–36. Baltimore.

———. 1995. Patrons and Friends. *CPh* 90.4: 328–42.

———. 1997. *Friendship in the Classical World.* Cambridge.

———. 1998. Reciprocity and Friendship. In *Reciprocity in Ancient Greece,* ed. C. Gill et al., 279–302. Oxford.

———. 2000. *Oikia d' esti tis philia:* Love and the Greek Family. *Syllecta Classica* 11: 106–26.

———. 2001. *Pity Transformed.* London

Krentz, P. 2000. Deception in Archaic and Clasical Greeek Warfare. In *War and Violence in Classical Greece,* ed. H. van Wees, 167–200. London.

———. 2002. Fighting by the Rules: The Invention of the Hoplite *Agōn. Hesperia* 71.1: 23–39.

Kulesza, R. 1995. *Die Bestechung im politischen Leben Athens im 5. und 4. Jahrhundert v. Chr.* Constance, Ger.

Kurke, L. 199. *The Traffic in Praise: Pindar and the Poetics of Social Economy.* Ithaca, N.Y.

Kyle, D. G. 1987. *Athletics in Ancient Athens.* Leiden.

Lacey, W. K. 1968. *The Family in Classical Greece.* Ithaca, N.Y.

Lambert, S. D. 1998. *The Phratries of Attica.* Ann Arbor, Mich.

Lane, M. S. 1998. *Method and Politics in Plato's Statesman.* Cambridge.

Lane Fox, R. 1985. Aspects of Inheritance in the Greek World. In *Crux: Essays in Greek History Presented to G. E. M. de Ste. Croix on His 75th Birthday,* ed. P. A. Cartledge and F. D. Harvey, 208–32. London.

———. 1994. Aeschines and Athenian Democracy. In *Ritual, Finance, Politics: Athenian Democratic Accounts Presented to David Lewis,* ed. R. Osborne and S. Hornblower, 135–55. Oxford.

———. 1997. Demosthenes, Dionysius and the Dating of Six Early Speeches. *C & M.* 48: 167–203.

Lanni, M. A. 1997. Spectator Sport or Serious Politics? *Oi Periestēkotes* and the Athenian Lawcourts. *JHS* 127: 183–89.

Laqueur, T. 1990. *Making Sex: Body and Gender from the Greeks to Freud.* Cambridge, Mass.

Larmour, D. H. J., P. A. Miller, and C. Platter, eds. 1997. *Rethinking Sexuality: Foucault and Classical Antiquity.* Princeton, N.J.

Lateiner, D. 1982. "The Man Who Does Not Meddle in Politics": A Topos in Lysias. *CW* 76: 1–12.

Lavency, M. 1964. *Aspects de la logographie judiciaire attique.* Louvain.

Lazenby, J. 1991. The Killing Zone. In *Hoplites: The Classical Greek Battle Experience,* ed. V. D. Hanson, 87–109. London.

Lefkowitz, M. R. 1986. *Women in Greek Myth.* Baltimore.

Lefkowitz, M. R., and M. B. Fant, eds. 1982. *Women's Life in Greece and Rome.* Baltimore.

Lentz, T. M. 1983. Spoken versus Written: Inartistic Proof in Athenian Courts. *Philosophy and Rhetoric* 16: 242–61.

Leisi, E. 1908. *Der Zeuge im attischen Recht.* Frauenfeld, Switz.

Lengauer W. 1979. *Greek Commanders in the 5th and 4th Centuries B.C.: Politics and Ideology. A Study of Militarism.* Translated by M. Paczynska and L. Piatek. Warsaw.

Leppin, H. 1995. Die Verwaltung öffentlicher Gelder im Athens des 4. Jahrhunderts v. Chr. In *Die athenische Demokratie im 4. Jahrhundert v. Chr.: Vollendung oder Verfall einer Verfassungsform?* ed. W. Eder, 557–71. Stuttgart.

Leutsch, E. L., and F. G. Schneidewin, eds. 1958. *Corpus Paroemiographorum Graecorum.* 2 vols. Hildesheim, Ger.

Lévy, E. 1976. *Athènes devant la défaite de 404: Histoire d'une crise idéologique.* Paris.

Lewis, N. 1960. *Leitourgia* and Related Terms. *GRBS* 3: 175–84.

Lindisfarne, N. 1994. Variant Masculinities, Variant Virginities: Rethinking "Honor and Shame." In *Dislocating Masculinity: Comparative Ethnographies,* ed. A. Cornwell and N. Lindisfarne, 82–96. London.

Lissarrague, F. 1990a. *The Aesthetics of the Greek Banquet.* Princeton, N.J.

———. 1990b. *L'Autre Guerrier: Archers, peltastes, cavaliers dans l'imagerie attique.* Paris.

Littman, R. J. 1979. Kinship in Athens. *Ancient Society* 10: 5–31.

Lloyd, A. B., ed. 1996. *Battle in Antiquity.* London.

Lloyd, G. E. R. 1966. *Polarity and Analogy: Two Types of Argumentation.* Cambridge.

———. 1983. *Science, Folklore and Ideology.* Cambridge.

———. 1984. *The Man of Reason: "'Male" and "'Female" in Western Philosophy.* London.

Lohmann, H. 1995. Die Chora im 4. Jahrhundert v. Chr. Festungswesen, Bergbau and Siedlungen. In *Die athenische Demokratie im 4. Jahrhundert v. Chr.: Vollendung oder Verfall einer Verfassungsform?* ed. W. Eder, 514–33. Stuttgart.

Loizos, P., and E. Papataxiarchis, eds. 1991. *Contested Identities: Gender and Kinship in Modern Greece.* Princeton, N.J.

Longo, C. P. 1971. *Eterie e gruppi politici nell'Atene del IV sec. a.C.* Florence.

Loraux, N. 1975. *Hēbē* et *andreia:* Deux versions de la mort du combattant athénien. *Ancient Society* 6: 1–31.

———. 1986. *The Invention of Athens: The Funeral Oration in the Classical City.* Translated by A. Sheridan. Cambridge, Mass.

———. 1993. *The Children of Athens: Athenian Ideas about Citizenship and the Division between the Sexes.* Translated by C. Levine. Princeton, N.J.

———. 1995. *The Experiences of Tiresias: The Feminine and Greek Man.* Translated by P. Wissing. Princeton, N.J.

————. 1998. *Mothers in Mourning.* Translated by C. Pache. Ithaca, N.Y.

MacCormack, C. P. 1980. Nature, Culture, and Gender: A Critique. In *Nature, Culture and Gender,* ed. id. and M. Strathern, 1–24. London.

MacCormack, C. P., and M. Strathern, eds. 1980. *Nature, Culture and Gender.* London.

MacDowell, D. M., ed. 1962. Andocides. *On the Mysteries.* Oxford.

————. 1978. *The Law in Classical Athens.* Ithaca, N.Y.

————. 1983. Athenian Laws about Bribery. *RIDA* 30: 57–78.

————. 1989a. Athenian Laws about Choruses. In *Symposion 1982: Vorträge zur griechischen und hellenistischen Rechtsgeschichte,* ed. F. J. Fernández Nieto 1989, 65–77. Cologne.

————. 1989b. The *Oikos* in Athenian law. *CQ* 39: 10–21.

————, trans. and ed. 1990. *Demosthenes: Against Meidias (Oration 21).* Oxford.

————, trans. and ed. 2000. *Demosthenes: On the False Embassy (Oration 19).* Oxford.

MacKay, E. A., ed. 1999. *Signs of Orality: The Oral Tradition and Its Influence in the Greek and Roman World.* Leiden.

Maffi, A. 1991. Adozione e strategie successori a Gortina e ad Atene. In *Symposion 1990: Vorträge zur griechischen und hellenistischen Rechtsgeschichte,* ed. M. Gagarin, 205–31. Cologne.

Malament, B. C., ed. 1980. *After the Reformation: Essays in Honor of J. H. Hexter.* Philadelphia.

Manville, P. B. 1990. *The Origins of Citizenship in Ancient Athens.* Princeton, N.J.

Markle, M. M. 1976. Support of Athenian Intellectuals for Philip: A Study of Isocrates' *Philippus* and Speusippus' *Letter to Philip. JHS* 96: 80–99.

————. 1985. Jury Pay and Assembly Pay at Athens. In *Crux: Essays in Greek History Presented to G. E. M. de Ste. Croix on His 75th Birthday,* ed. P. A. Cartledge and F. D. Harvey, 265–97. London.

McCabe, D. F. 1981. *The Prose-rhythm of Demosthenes.* New York.

McCann, D. R., and B. S. Strauss, eds. 2001. *War and Democracy: A Comparative Study of the Korean War and the Peloponnesian War.* Armonk, N.Y.

McKinlay, A. P. 1951. Attic Temperance. *QJSA* 12: 61–102.

Meier, C. 1990. *The Greek Discovery of Politics.* Translated by D. McLintock. Cambridge.

Milburn, T. W., and K. H. Watman 1981. *On the Nature of Threat.* New York.

Miller, W. I. 1995. *Humiliation and Other Essays on Honor, Social Discomfort, and Violence.* Ithaca, N.Y.

Millett, P. 1983. Maritime Loans and the Structure of Credit in Fourth-Century Athens. In *Trade and Politics in the Ancient Economy,* ed. K. Hopkins, P. Garnsey, and C. R. Whittaker 1983, 36–52. Berkeley, Calif.

————. 1990. Sale, Credit and Exchange in Athenian Law and Society. In *Nomos: Essays in Athenian Law, Politics and Society,* ed. P. Cartledge et al., 167–94. Cambridge.

————. 1991. *Lending and Borrowing in Ancient Athens.* Cambridge.

————. 1993. Warfare, Economy, and Democracy in Classical Athens. In *War and Society in the Greek World,* ed. J. Rich and G. Shipley, 176–96. London.

———. 1998a. Encounters in the Agora. In *Kosmos: Essays in Order, Conflict and Community in Classical Athens,* ed. P. Cartledge et al., 203–28. Cambridge.

———. 1998b. The Rhetoric of Reciprocity in Classical Athens. In *Reciprocity in Ancient Greece,* ed. C. Gill et al., 229–53. Oxford.

Mills, S. 1997. *Theseus, Tragedy and the Athenian Empire.* Oxford.

Miner, J. 2003. Courtesan, Concubine, Whore: Apollodorus' Deliberate Use of Terms for Prostitutes. *AJP* 124: 19–37.

Mirhady, D. C. 1991. The Oath-Challenge in Athens. *CQ* 41: 78–83.

———. 1996. Torture and Rhetoric in Athens. *JHS* 116: 119–31.

———. 2000. Demosthenes as Advocate: The Private Speeches. In *Persuasion: Greek Rhetoric in Action,* ed. I. Worthington, 181–204. London.

Missiou, A. 1992. *The Subversive Oratory of Andocides: Politics, Ideology, and Decision-Making in Democratic Athens.* Cambridge.

———. 1998. Foreign Affairs of Fifth-Century Athens and Sparta. In *Reciprocity in Ancient Greece,* ed. C. Gill et al., 181–98. Oxford.

Mitchell, L. G. 1997. *Greeks Bearing Gifts. The Public Use of Private Relationship in the Greek World, 453–323 B.C.* Cambridge.

Mitchell L. G. and P. Rhodes. 1996. Friends and Enemies in Athenian Politics. *G&R* 43.1: 11–30.

Monoson, S. S. 1994a. Citizen as Erastes: Erotic Imagery and the Idea of Reciprocity in the Periclean Funeral Oration. *Political Theory* 22: 253–76.

———. 1994b. Frank Speech, Democracy, and Philosophy: Plato's Debt to a Democratic Strategy of Civic Discourse. In *Athenian Political Thought and the Reconstruction of American Democracy,* ed. J. P. Euben et al., 172–197. Ithaca, N.Y.

Montgomery, H. 1983. *The Way to Chaeroneia: Foreign Policy, Decision-Making and Political Influence in Demosthenes' Speeches.* Bergen, Norway.

———. 1986. "Merchants Fond of Corn": Citizens and Foreigners in the Athenian Grain Trade. *OS* 61: 43–61.

Morawetz, T. 2000. *Der Demos als Tyrann und Banause.* Frankfurt a/M.

Morgan, D. H. J. 1994. Theater of War. Combat, the Military, and Masculinities. In *Theorizing Masculinities,* ed. H. Brod and M. Kaufman, 165–82. Thousand Oaks, Calif.

Morris, I. 1994. Everyman's Grave. In *Athenian Identity and Civic Ideology,* ed. A. L. Boegehold and A. C. Scafuro, 67–101. Baltimore.

———. 1996. The Strong Principle of Equality and the Archaic Origins of Greek Democracy. In *Demokratia: A Conversation on Democracies, Ancient and Modern,* ed. J. Ober and C. Hedrick, 19–48. Princeton, N.J.

———. 1999. Beyond Democracy and Empire: Athenian Art in Context. In *Democracy, Empire and the Arts in Fifth-Century Athens,* ed. D. Boedeker and K. A. Raaflaub, 59–86. Cambridge, Mass.

Morrison, J. S. 1984. Hyperesia in Naval Contexts in the Fifth and Fourth Centuries B.C. *JHS* 104: 48–59.

Mossé C. 1983. The "World of the Emporium" in the Private Speeches of

Demosthenes. In *Trade and Politics in the Ancient Economy,* ed. K. Hopkins, P. Garnsey, and C. R. Whittaker, 53–63. Berkeley, Calif.

———. 1984. *Politeuomenoi* et *idiotai:* L'Affirmation d'une classe politique à Athènes au IVe siècle. *Revue des études anciennes* 86: 193–200.

———. 1987. Égalité démocratique et inégalités sociales: Le Débat à Athènes au IVème siècle. *Metis* 2: 165–76, 195–206.

———. 1991. La Place de la *pallakē* dans la famille athénienne. In *Symposion 1990: Vorträge zur griechischen und hellenistischen Rechtsgeschichte,* ed. M. Gagarin, 273–79. Cologne.

———. 1994. *Démosthène, ou les ambiguïtés de la politique.* Paris.

———. 1995. *Politique et société en Grèce ancienne: Le Modèle athénien.* Paris.

Most, G. W., ed. 1997. *Collecting Fragments: Fragmente sammeln.* Göttingen.

Moysey, R. A. 1982. Isokrates' *On the Peace:* Rhetorical Exercise or Political Advice. *AJAH* 7: 118–27.

Murray, O., ed. 1990a. *Sympotica: A Symposium on the Symposion.* Oxford.

———. 1990b. The Affair of the Mysteries: Democracy and the Drinking Group. In *Sympotica: A Symposium on the Symposion,* ed. O. Murray, 149–61. Oxford.

———. 1990c. Sympotic History. In *Sympotica: A Symposium on the Symposion,* ed. O. Murray, 3–13. Oxford.

———. 1990d. The Solonian Law of *Hubris.* in *Nomos: Essays in Athenian Law, Politics and Society,* ed. P. Cartledge et al., 139–45. Cambridge.

Murray, O., and S. Price, eds. 1990. *The Greek City from Homer to Alexander.* Oxford.

Murray O., and M. Tecusan, eds. 1995. *In Vino Veritas.* London.

Naphy, W. G., and P. Roberts, eds. 1997a. *Fear in Early Modern Society.* Manchester, U.K.

———. 1997b. Introduction. In *Fear in Early Modern Society,* ed. W. G. Naphy and P. Roberts, 1–8. Manchester, U.K.

Nash, L. 1978. Concepts of Existence: Greek Origins of Generational Thought. *Daedalus* 107: 1–21.

Neils, J. 1994. The Panathenaia and Kleisthenic Ideology. In *The Archaeology of Athens and Attika under the Democracy,* ed. W. D. E. Coulson et al., 151–60. Oxford.

———, ed. 1996. *Worshipping Athena: Panathenaia and Parthenon.* Madison, Wis.

Nevett, L. C. 1995a. Gender Relations in the Classical Greek Household: The Archaeological Evidence. *BSA* 90: 363–81.

———. 1995b. The Organization of Space in Classical and Hellenistic Houses from Mainland Greece and the Western Colonies. In *Time, Tradition and Society in Greek Archaeology: Bridging the Great Divide,* ed. N. Spencer, 89–108. London.

Nieto, F. J. Fernández, ed. 1989. *Symposion 1982: Vorträge zur griechischen und hellenistischen Rechtsgeschichte (Santander, 1.-4. September 1982).* Cologne.

Nill. M. 1985. *Morality and Self-Interest in Protagoras, Antiphon, and Democritus.* Philosophia Antiqua 43. Leiden.

Norlin, G., trans. 1928. *Isocrates*. 3 vols. Cambridge.

North, H. 1966. *Sophrosyne: Self-knowledge and Self-restraint in Greek Literature*. Ithaca, N.Y.

Nouhaud, M. 1982. *L'Utilisation de l'histoire par les orateurs attiques*. Paris.

Oakley, J. H. and R. H. Sinos. 1993. *The Wedding in Ancient Athens*. Madison, Wis.

Ober, J. 1989. *Mass and Elite in Democratic Athens: Rhetoric, Ideology, and the Power of the People*. Princeton, N.J.

———. 1991. Hoplites and Obstacles. In *Hoplites: The Classical Greek Battle Experience*, ed. V. D. Hanson, 173–96. London

———. 1993. The *Polis* as a Society: Aristotle, John Rawls and the Athenian Social Contract. In *The Ancient Greek City State*, ed. M. H. Hansen, 129–60. Copenhagen.

———. 1994a. How to Criticize Democracy in Late Fifth- and Fourth-Century Athens. In *Athenian Political Thought and the Reconstruction of American Democracy*, ed. J. P. Euben et al., 149–71. Ithaca, N.Y.

———. 1994b. Power and Oratory in Democratic Athens: Demosthenes 21, *Against Meidias*. In *Persuasion: Greek Rhetoric in Action*, ed. I. Worthington, 85–108. London.

———. 1996. *The Athenian Revolution. Essays on Ancient Greek Democracy and Political Theory*. Princeton, N.J.

———. 1998. *Political Dissent in Democratic Athens. Intellectual Critics of Popular Rule*. Princeton, N.J.

Ober J., and B. S. Strauss. 1990. Drama, Political Theory, and the Discourse of Athenian Democracy. In *Nothing to Do with Dionysos? Athenian Drama in Its Social Context*, ed. J. J. Winkler and F. I. Zeitlin, 237–70. Princeton, N.J.

Ober, J. and C. Hedrick, eds. 1996. *Demokratia: A Conversation on Democracies, Ancient and Modern*. Princeton, N.J.

O'Brien, J. M. 1980. Alexander and Dionysus: The Invisible Enemy. *Annals of Scholarship* 1: 83–105.

Ochs, D. J. 1996. Demosthenes: Superior Artist and Victorious Monomachist. In *Theory, Text, Context: Issues in Greek Rhetoric and Oratory*, ed. C. L. Johnston, 129–46. Albany, N.Y.

Oeri, H. G. 1948. *Der Typ der komischen Alten in der griechischen Komödie*. Basel.

Ogden, D. 1996a. *Greek Bastardy in the Classical and the Hellenistic Periods*. Oxford.

———. 1996b. Homosexuality and Warfare in Ancient Greece. In *Battle in Antiquity*, ed. A. B. Lloyd, 107–68. London.

Oliensis, E. 1997. The Erotic of *Amicitia*: Readings in Tibullus, Propertius, and Horace. In *Roman Sexualities*, ed. J. P. Hallett and M. B. Skinner, 151–71. Princeton, N.J.

Ollier, F. 1973. *Le Mirage spartiate*. Paris.

Osborne, M. J. 1981–83. *Naturalization in Athens*. 4 vols. Brussels.

Osborne, R. 1985a. Demos: *The Discovery of Classical Attika*. Cambridge.

———. 1985b. Law in Action in Classical Athens. *JHS* 105: 40–58.

———. 1990. Vexatious Litigation in Classical Athens: Sykophancy and the

Sykophant. In *Nomos: Essays in Athenian Law, Politics and Society,* ed. P. Cartledge et al., 83–102. Cambridge.

———. 1993. Competitive Festivals and the Polis: A Context for Dramatic Festivals at Athens. In *Tragedy, Comedy and the Polis,* ed. A. H. Sommerstein et al., 21–38. Bari, Italy.

———. 1996. Desiring Women on Athenian Pottery. In *Sexuality in Ancient Art: Near East, Egypt, Greece, and Italy,* ed. N. B. Kampen, 65–80. Cambridge.

———. 1997. Men without Clothes: Heroic Nakedness and Greek Art. *Gender & History* 9.3: 504–28.

———. 1998a. Inter-Personal Relations on Athenian Pots. In *Kosmos: Essays in Order, Conflict and Community in Classical Athens,* ed. P. Cartledge et al., 13–36. Cambridge.

———. 1998b. Sculptured Men of Athens: Masculinity and Power in the Field of Vision. In *Thinking Men: Masculinity and Self-Representation in the Classical Tradition,* ed. L. Foxhall and J. Salmon, 23–42. London.

Osborne, R. and S. Hornblower, eds. 1994. *Ritual, Finance, Politics: Athenian Democratic Accounts Presented to David Lewis.* Oxford.

Ostwald, M. 1955. The Athenian Legislation against Tyranny and Subversion. *TAPA* 86: 103–28.

———. 1986. *From Popular Sovereignty to the Sovereignty of the Law: Law, Society and Politics in Fifth-Century Athens.* Berkeley, Calif.

———. 1996. Shares and Rights: "Citizenship" Greek Style and American Style. In *Demokratia: A Conversation on Democracies, Ancient and Modern,* ed. J. Ober and C. Hedrick, 49–62. Princeton, N.J.

Page, D. 1981. *Further Greek Epigrams.* Cambridge.

Papataxiarchis, E. 1991. Friends of Heart: Male Commensal Solidarity, Gender, and Kinship in Aegean Greece. In *Contested Identities: Gender and Kinship in Modern Greece,* ed. P. Loizos and E. Papataxiarchis, 156–79. Princeton, N.J.

Papillon, T. L. 1998. *Rhetorical Studies in the Aristocratea of Demosthenes.* New York.

Patterson, C. 1986. *Hai Attikai:* The Other Athenians. *Helios* 13: 49–67.

———. 1990. Those Athenian Bastards. *CA* 9: 40–72.

———. 1991a. Marriage and the Married Woman in Athenian Law. In *Women's History and Ancient History,* ed. S. B. Pomeroy, 48–72. Chapel Hill, N.C.

———. 1991b. Response to Claude Mossé. In *Symposion 1990: Vorträge zur griechischen und hellenistischen Rechtsgeschichte,* ed. M. Gagarin, 281–87. Cologne.

———. 1994. The Case against Neaira. In *Athenian Identity and Civic Ideology,* ed. A. Boegehold and A. C. Scafuro, 199–216. Baltimore.

———. 1998. *The Family in Greek History.* Cambridge, Mass.

Patterson, O. 1982. *Slavery and Social Death.* Cambridge, Mass.

Patteson, A. J. 1978. Commentary on [Demosthenes] LIX: Against Neaera. Ph.D. diss., University of Pennsylvania.

Paulsen, T. 1999. *Die Parapresbeia-Reden des Demosthenes und des Aeschines. Kommentar und Interpretationen zu Demosthenes, Or. XIX, und Aechines, Or. II.* Trier, Ger.

Pearson, L. 1962. *Popular Ethics in Ancient Greece.* Stanford, Calif.

———. 1981. *The Art of Demosthenes.* Chico, Calif.

Pélékidis, C. 1962. *Histoire de l'éphébie attique des origines à 31 av. J-C.* Paris.

Pelling, C., ed. 1990. *Characterization and Individuality in Greek Literature.* Oxford.

Percy, W. A., III. 1996. *Pederasty and Pedagogy in Archaic Greece.* Urbana, Ill.

Peristiany, J. G. 1966a. Honour and Shame in a Cypriote Highland Village. In *Honour and Shame: The Values of Mediterranean Society,* ed. J. G. Peristiany, 173–90. Chicago.

———, ed. 1966b. *Honour and Shame: The Values of Mediterranean Society.* Chicago.

———. 1992. The *Sophron*—a Secular Saint? Wisdom and the Wise in a Cypriot Community. In *Honor and Grace in Anthropology,* ed. J. G. Peristiany and J. Pitt-Rivers, 103–27. Cambridge.

Peristiany, J. G., and J. Pitt-Rivers, eds. 1992a. *Honor and Grace in Anthropology.* Cambridge.

———. 1992b. Introduction. In *Honor and Grace in Anthropology,* ed. J. G. Peristiany and J. Pitt-Rivers, 1–17. Cambridge.

Perlman, S. 1961. The Historical Example: Its Use and Importance as Political Propaganda in the Attic Orators. *SHI* 7: 150–66.

———. 1976. On Bribing Athenian Ambassadors. *GRBS* 17: 223–33.

Piepenbrink, K. 2001. *Politische Ordnungskonzeptionen in der attischen Demokratie des Vierten Jahrhunderts V. Chr.* Stuttgart.

Pierce, K. F. 1998. Ideals of Masculinity in New Comedy. In *Thinking Men: Masculinity and Self-Representation in the Classical Tradition,* ed. L. Foxhall and J. Salmon, 130–47. London.

Pitt-Rivers, J. 1966. Honour and Social Status, In *Honour and Shame: The Values of Mediterranean Society,* ed. J. G. Peristiany, 19–77. Chicago.

———. 1992a. Introduction. In *Honor and Grace in Anthropology,* ed. J. G. Peristiany and J. Pitt-Rivers, 1–17. Cambridge.

———. 1992b. Postscript: The Place of Grace in Anthropology. In *Honor and Grace in Anthropology,* ed. J. G. Peristiany and J. Pitt-Rivers, 242. Cambridge.

Podlecki, A. J. 1990. Could Women Attend the Theatre in Ancient Athens? A Collection of Testimonia. *Ancient World.* 21: 27–43.

Poliakoff, M. B. 1987. *Combat Sports in the Ancient World: Competition, Violence, and Culture.* New Haven, Conn.

Pohlenz, M. 1966. *Freedom in Greek Life and Thought.* Translated by C. Lofmark. Dordrecht, Neth.

Pomeroy, S. B. 1975. *Goddesses, Whores, Wives and Slaves.* Chicago.

———, ed. 1991. *Women's History and Ancient History.* Chapel Hill, N.C.

———. 1994. *Xenophon Oeconomicus: A Social and Historical Commentary.* Oxford.

———. 1997. *Families in Classical and Hellenistic Greece: Representations and Realities.* Oxford.

Porter, J. 1997. Adultery by the Book: Lysias 1 *(On the Murder of Eratosthenes)* and Comic Diegesis. *Échos du monde classique / Classical Views* 16: 422–53.

———, ed. 1999. *Constructions of the Classical Body.* Ann Arbor, Mich.

Powell, A., ed. 1990. *Euripides, Women, and Sexuality.* London.

Powell. A., and S. Hodkinson, eds. 1994. *The Shadow of Sparta.* London.

Pritchett, W. K. 1971–91. *The Greek State at War.* 5 vols. Berkeley, Calif.

Pucci, P. 1980. *The Violence of Pity in Euripides'* Medea. Ithaca, N.Y.

———. 1987. *Odysseus Polutropos: Intertextual Readings in the* Odyssey *and the* Iliad. Ithaca, N.Y.

Raaflaub, K. A. 1980. Des freien Bürgers Recht der freien Rede: Ein Beitrag zur Begriffs- und Sozialgeschicthe der athenischen Demokratie. In *Studien zur Antiken Sozialgeschichte: Festschrift F. Vittinghoff,* ed. W. Eck et al., 7–57. Cologne.

———. 1981. Zum Freiheitsbegriff der Griechen. In *Soziale Typenbegriffe im alten Griechenland und ihr Fortleben in den Sprachen der Welt,* vol. 4, ed. C. E. Welskopf, 180–405. Berlin.

———. 1983. Democracy, Oligarchy, and the Concept of the "Free Citizen" in Late Fifth-Century Athens. *Political Theory* 11: 517–44.

———. 1985. *Die Entdeckung der Freiheit: Zur historischen Semantik und Gesellschaftsgeschichte eines politischen Grundbegriffes der Griechen.* Vestigia 37. Munich.

———. 1994. Democracy, Power, and Imperialism in Fifth-Century Athens. In *Athenian Political Thought and the Reconstruction of American Democracy,* ed. J. P. Euben et al., 103–46. Ithaca, N.Y.

———. 1996. Athens: Equalities and Inequalities in Athenian Democracy. In *Demokratia: A Conversation on Democracies, Ancient and Modern,* ed. J. Ober and C. Hedrick 1996, 139–74. Princeton, N.J.

———. 2001. Father of All, Destroyer of All: War in Late Fifth-Century Athenian Discourse and Ideology. In *War and Democracy: A Comparative Study of the Korean War and the Peloponnesian War,* ed. D. R. McCann, and B. S. Strauss, 307–56. Armonk, N.Y.

Raepsaet, G. 1981. Sentiments conjugaux à Athènes aux Vᵉ aux IVᵉ siècles avant notre ère. *L'Antiquité classique* 50: 677–84.

Raubitschek, A. E. 1948. The Case against Alcibiades (Andocides IV). *TAPA* 79: 191–210.

Rawlings, L. 2000. Alternative Agonies: Hoplitic Martial and Combat Experiences beyond the Phalanx. In *War and Violence in Classical Greece,* ed. H. van Wees, 233–59. London.

Rawson, B., and P. Weaver, eds. 1997. *The Roman Family in Italy: Status, Sentiment, Space.* Oxford.

Reden, S. von. 1995. *Exchange in Ancient Greece.* London.

———. 1998. The Commodification of Symbols: Reciprocity and Its Perversions in Menander. In *Reciprocity in Ancient Greece,* ed. C. Gill et al., 255–78. Oxford.

Reden, S. von, and S. Goldhill. 1999. Professional Performance and the Democratic Polis. In *Performance Culture and Athenian Democracy,* ed. S. Goldhill and R. Osborne, 257–89. Cambridge.

Reeder, E. D., ed. 1995. *Pandora: Women in Classical Greece.* Baltimore.

Reinmuth, O. 1971. *The Ephebic Inscriptions.* Leiden.

Reinsberg, C. 1989. *Ehe, Hetärentum und Knabenliebe in antike Griechenland.* Munich.

Rehm, R. 1994. *The Conflation of Wedding and Funeral Rituals in Greek Tragedy.* Princeton, N.J.

Rhodes, P. J. 1979. *Eisangelia* in Athens. *JHS* 99: 103–14.

——. 1985. *The Athenian Boule.* Oxford.

——. 1993. *A Commentary on the Aristotelian Athēnaiōn Politeia.* Oxford.

——. 1995. Judicial Procedures in Fourth-Century Athens: Improvement or Simply Change? In *Die athenische Demokratie im 4. Jahrhundert v. Chr.: Vollendung oder Verfall einer Verfassungsform?* ed. W. Eder, 303–19.

——. 1998. Enmity in Fourth-Century Athens. In *Kosmos: Essays in Order, Conflict and Community in Classical Athens,* ed. P. Cartledge et al., 144–61. Cambridge.

Rich, J., and G. Shipley, eds. 1993. *War and Society in the Greek World.* London.

Richlin, A., ed. 1992. *Pornography and Representation in Greece and Rome.* New York.

Ridley, R. T. 1979. The Hoplite as Citizen: Athenian Military Institutions in their Social Context. *AC* 48: 508–48.

Roberts, J. T. 1982. *Accountability in Athenian Government.* Madison, Wis.

——. 1994. *Athens on Trial: The Antidemocratic Tradition in Western Thought.* Princeton, N.J.

——. 1996. Athenian Equality: A Constant Surrounded by Flux. In *Demokratia: A Conversation on Democracies, Ancient and Modern,* ed. J. Ober and C. Hedrick, 187–202. Princeton, N.J.

Robertson, B. G. 2000. The Scrutiny of New Citizens at Athens. In *Law and Social Status in Classical Athens,* ed. V. J. Hunter and J. Edmonson, 149–74. Oxford.

Roisman, J. 1999. How Can an Agamemnon Be an Achilles? Drama in Athenian Courts. *AHB* 13.4: 157–61.

——. 2003. The Rhetoric of Courage in the Athenian Orators. In *Andreia: Studies in Manliness and Courage in Classical Antiquity,* ed. R. Rosen and I. Sluiter, 127–43. Leiden.

——. 2004. Speaker-Audience Interaction at Athens: A Power Struggle. In *Free Speech in Classical Antiquity,* ed. I. Sluiter and R. Rosen, 261–78. Leiden.

Romilly, Jacqueline de. 1956. La Crainte dans l'oeuvre de Thucydide. *C&M* 17: 119–27.

——. 1975. *Magic and Rhetoric in Ancient Greece.* Cambridge.

——. 1979. *La Douceur dans la pensée grecque.* Paris.

——. 1980. Réflexions sur le courage chez Thucydide et chez Platon. *REG* 93: 307–23.

Ronnet, G. 1951. *Étude sur le style de Démosthène dans les discours politiques.* Paris.

Roper, M., and J. Tosh, eds. 1991. *Manful Assertions: Masculinities in Britain since 1800.* London.

Rosen, R. 1997. The Gendered Polis in Eupolis' *Cities.* In *The City as Comedy:*

Society and Representation in Athenian Drama, ed. G. Dobrov, 149–76. Chapel Hill, N.C.

Rosen, R., and I. Sluiter, eds. 2003. *Andreia: Studies in Manliness and Courage in Classical Antiquity.* Leiden: 127–43.

Rosivach, V. J. 1984. *Aphaeresis* and *apoleipsis:* A Study of the Sources. *Revue internationale des droits de l'antiquité,* 3d ser., 31: 193–230.

———. 1985 [1992]. Manning the Athenian Fleet: 433–426 B.C. *American Journal of Ancient History* 10.1: 41–66.

———. 1991. Some Athenian Presuppositions about "the Poor." *G&R* 38: 189–98.

———. 1999. Enslaving *Barbaroi* and the Athenian Ideology of Slavery. *Historia* 48: 129–75.

Rothwell, K. S., Jr. 1990. *Politics and Persuasion in Aristophanes' Ecclesiazusae.* Leiden.

Roussel, M. P. 1951. Étude sur le principe de l'ancienneté dans le monde hellénique du Ve siècle av. J.-C. à l'époque romaine. *Mémoires de l'Institut national de France, Académie des Inscriptions et Belles-Lettres* 43.2: 123–227.

Rowe, G. O. 1966. The Portrait of Aeschines in the Oration *On the Crown. TAPA* 97: 397–406.

———. 1968. Demosthenes' First Philippic: The Satiric Mode. *TAPA* 99: 361–74.

———. 1993. The Many Facets of *hubris* in Dem. *Against Meidias. AJP* 114.3: 397–406.

Roy, J. 1991. Traditional Jokes about the Punishment of Adulterers in Ancient Greek Literature. *LCM* 16: 73–76.

———. 1999. *Polis* and *Oikos* in Classical Athens. *G&R* 46.1: 1–17.

Rubinstein, L. 1993. *Adoption in IV. Century Athens.* Opuscula Graecolatina 34. Copenhagen.

———. 1998. The Athenian Political Perception of the *Idiotes.* In *Kosmos: Essays in Order, Conflict and Community in Classical Athens,* ed. P. Cartledge et al., 125–43. Cambridge.

———. 2000. *Litigation and Cooperation: Supporting Speakers in the Courts of Classical Athens.* Stuttgart.

Rudhardt, J. 1962. La Reconnaissance de la paternité, sa nature et sa portée dans la société athénienne. *MH* 19: 39–61.

Ruschenbush, E. 1957. *Dikastērion pantōn kurion. Historia* 6: 257–74.

Russell, D. A. 1990. Ethos in Oratory and Rhetoric. In *Characterization and Individuality in Greek Literature,* ed. C. Pelling, 197–212. Oxford.

Sahlins, M. 1972. *Stone Age Economics.* London.

Saller, R. 1997. Roman Kinship: Structure and Sentiment. In *The Roman Family in Italy: Status, Sentiment, Space,* ed. B. Rawson and P. Weaver, 7–34. Oxford.

Sampaix, J. 1937. Le Comique, l'ironie dans la Ière Philippique de Démosthène: Essais de traductions, commentaires, notes. *Nova et Vetera* (B): 309–23.

Santoro L'Hoir, F. 1992. *The Rhetoric of Gender Terms: "Man", "Women", and Portrayal of Characters in Latin Prose.* Mnemosyne Supplement 120. Leiden.

Sartori, F. 1957. *Le eterie nella vita politica ateniese del VI e V secolo a.C.* Rome.

Saunders, T. J. 1991. *Plato's Penal Code.* Oxford.

Scafuro, A. 1994. Witnessing and False Witnessing: Proving Citizenship and Kin Identity in Fourth-Century Athens. In *Athenian Identity and Civic Ideology,* ed. A. L. Boegehold and A. C. Scafuro, 159–98. Baltimore.

———. 1997. *The Forensic Stage: Settling Disputes in Greco-Roman New Comedy.* Cambridge.

Scanlon, T. F. 1988. Combat and Contest: Athletic Metaphors for Warfare in Greek Literature. In *Coroebus Triumphs: The Alliance of Sport and the Arts,* ed. S. J.Bandy, 230–44. San Diego, Calif.

Schaefer, A. 1885–87. *Demosthenes und seine Zeit.* 3 vols. Leipzig.

Schaps, D. M. 1977. The Women Least Mentioned: Etiquette and Women's Names. *CQ* 27: 323–31.

———. 1979. *The Economic Rights of Women in Ancient Greece.* Edinburgh.

———. 1998. What Was Free about a Free Athenian Woman? *TAPA* 128: 161–88.

Schmitt-Pantel, P. 1992. *Le Cité au banquet: Histoire des repas publics dans les cités grecques.* Rome.

Schmitz, T. 2000. Plausibility in The Attic Orators. *AJP* 121.1: 47–77.

Schneider, J. 1971. Of Vigilance and Virgins. *Ethnology* 9: 1–24.

Schofield, M. 1998. Political Friendship. In *Kosmos: Essays in Order, Conflict and Community in Classical Athens,* ed. P. Cartledge et al., 37–51. Cambridge.

Schuller, W., ed. 1982. *Korruption im Altertum.* Munich.

Schwertfeger, T. 1982. Der Schild des Archilochos. *Chiron* 12: 253–80.

Seaford, R. S. 1990. The Structural Problems of Marriage in Euripides. In *Euripides, Women, and Sexuality,* ed. A. Powell, 151–76. London.

———. 1994. *Reciprocity and Ritual: Homer and Tragedy in the Developing City-State.* Oxford.

Seager, R. 1966. Lysias against the Corndealers. *Historia* 15: 172–84.

Sealey, R. 1967. Pseudo-Demosthenes XIII and XXV. *Revue des études grecques* 80: 250–55.

———. 1984. On Lawful Concubinage in Athens. *CA* 3: 111–33.

———. 1990. *Women and Law in Classical Greece.* Chapel Hill, N.C.

———. 1993. *Demosthenes and His Time: A Study in Defeat.* New York.

Segal, C. 1982. *Dionysiac Poetics and Euripides' Bacchae.* Princeton, N.J.

Sekunda, N. V. 1990. IG II² 1250: A Decree Concerning the *Lampadephoroi* of the Tribe Aiantis. *ZPE* 83: 149–82.

Shapiro, H. A. 1992. Eros in Love: Pederasty and Pornography in Greece. In *Pornography and Representation in Greece and Rome,* ed. A. Richlin, 53–72. New York.

Shipton, K. M. W. 1997. Private Banks in Fourth-Century Athens. *CQ* 47.2: 396–422.

Shrimpton, G., and D. J. McCargar, eds. 1981. *Classical Contributions: Studies in Honor of M. F. McGregor.* New York.

Siems, A. K., ed. 1988. *Sexualität und Erotik in der Antike.* Wege der Forschung 605. Darmstadt.

Siewert, P. 1977. The Ephebic Oath in Fifth Century Athens. *JHS* 97: 102–11.

Silk, M. S., ed. 1996. *Tragedy and the Tragic: Greek Theater and Beyond*. Oxford.

Sinclair, R. K. 1988. *Democracy and Participation in Athens*. Cambridge.

Sissa, G. 1999. Sexual Bodybuilding: Aeschines against Timarchus. In *Constructions of the Classical Body*, ed. J. Porter, 147–68. Ann Arbor, Mich.

Slater, P. 1968. *The Glory of Hera*. Boston.

Sluiter, I., and R. Rosen, eds. 2004. *Free Speech in Classical Antiquity*. Leiden.

Smoes, É. 1995. *Le Courage chez les Grecs, d'Homère à Aristote*. Cahiers de philosophie ancienne 12. Brussels.

Sommerstein, A. H. 1986. The Decree of Syrakosios. *CQ* 36: 101–8.

———. 1998. Rape and Young Manhood in Athenian Comedy. In *Thinking Men: Masculinity and Self-Representation in the Classical Tradition*, ed. L. Foxhall and J. Salmon, 100–114. London.

Sommerstein, A. H., S. Halliwell, J. Henderson, and B. Zimmermann, eds. 1993. *Tragedy, Comedy and the Polis*. Bari, Italy.

Sourvinou-Inwood, C. 1995. Male and Female, Public and Private, Ancient and Modern. In *Pandora: Women in Classical Greece*, ed. E. D. Reeder, 111–20. Baltimore.

Spence, I. G. 1993. *The Cavalry of Classical Greece: A Social and Military History with Particular References to Athens*. Oxford.

Spencer, N., ed. 1995. *Time, Tradition and Society in Greek Archaeology: Bridging the Great Divide*. London.

Stadter, P. A. 1989. *A Commentary on Plutarch's Pericles*. Chapel Hill, N.C.

Stafford, E. J. 1998. Masculine Values, Feminine Forms: On the Gender of Personified Abstractions. In *Thinking Men: Masculinity and Self-Representation in the Classical Tradition*, ed. L. Foxhall and J. Salmon, 43–56. London.

Stears, K. 1998. Death Becomes Her: Gender and Athenian Death Ritual. In *The Sacred and the Feminine*, ed. S. Blundell and M. Williamson, 113–27. London.

Stechler, G. 1987. Gender and the Self: Developmental Aspects. *Annual of Psychoanalysis* 14: 345–55.

Stechler, G., and S. Kaplan 1980. The Development of the Self: A Psychoanalytic Perspective. *Psychoanalytic Study of the Child* 35: 85–105.

Stehele, E. 1997. *Performance and Gender in Ancient Greece: Non-Dramatic Poetry in Its Setting*. Princeton, N.J.

Stewart, A. 1995. Rape? In *Pandora: Women in Classical Greece*, ed. E. D. Reeder, 74–90. Baltimore.

———. 1997. *Art, Desire, and the Body in Ancient Greece*. Cambridge.

Stewart, F. H. 1994. *Honor*. Chicago.

Storey, I. 1989. The "Blameless Shield" of Kleonymos. *RhM* 132: 247–61.

Strasburger, H. 1954. Der Einzelne und die Gemeinschaft im Denken der Griechen, *Historische Zeitschrift* 177: 227–48.

Strauss, B. S. 1985. The Cultural Significance of Bribery and Embezzlement in Athenian Politics. *Ancient World* 11: 67–74.

———. 1986. *Athens after the Peloponnesian War: Class, Faction and Policy 403–386 B.C.* London.

————. 1993. *Fathers and Sons in Athens: Ideology and Society in the Era of the Peloponnesian War.* Princeton, N.J.

————. 1994. The Melting Pot, the Mosaic, and the Agora. In *Athenian Political Thought and the Reconstruction of American Democracy,* ed. J. P. Euben et al., 252–64. Ithaca, N.Y.

————. 1996. The Athenian Trireme, School of Democracy. In *Demokratia: A Conversation on Democracies, Ancient and Modern,* ed. J. Ober and C. Hedrick, 313–25. Princeton, N.J.

————. 2000. Perspectives on the Death of Fifth-century Athenian Seamen. In *War and Violence in Classical Greece,* ed. H. van Wees, 261–83. London.

Süss, W. 1910. *Ethos: Studien zu älteren griechischen Rhetorik.* Leipzig.

Svenbro, J. 1993. *Phrasikleia. An Anthropology of Reading in Ancient Greece.* Translated by J. Lloyd. Ithaca, N.Y.

Tacon, J. 2001. Ecclesiastic *Thorubos:* Interventions, Interruptions, and Popular Involvement in the Athenian Assembly. *G&R* 48.2: 173–92.

Taylor, C. 2001a. Bribery in Athenian Politics Part I: Accusations, Allegations, and Slander. *G&R* 48.1: 53–62

————. 2001b. Bribery in Athenian Politics Part II: Ancient Reactions and Perceptions. *G&R* 48.2: 154–72.

Thomas, R. 1989. *Oral Tradition and Written Record in Classical Athens.* Cambridge Studies in Oral and Literate Culture 18. Cambridge.

————. 1994. Law and Lawgiver in Athenian Democracy. In *Ritual, Finance, Politics: Athenian Democratic Accounts Presented to David Lewis,* ed. R. Osborne and S. Hornblower, 119–34. Oxford.

Thompson, W. E. 1967. The Marriage of First-Cousins in Athenian Society. *Phoenix* 21: 273–82.

————. 1972. Athenian Marriage Patterns: Remarriage. *CSCA* 5: 211–26.

————. 1981. Athenian Attitudes toward Wills. *Prudentia* 13: 13–23.

————. 1987. Athenian Ideologies. *Prudentia* 19: 22–33.

Thomsen. R. 1977. War Taxes in Classical Athens. In *Armées et fiscalité dans le monde antique: Paris, 14–16 octobre 1976,* 135–47. Colloques nationaux du Centre nationale de la recherche scientifique, no. 936. Paris.

Thornton, B. S. 1997. *Eros: The Myth of Ancient Greek Sexuality.* Boulder, Colo.

Thür, G. 1977. *Beweisführung vor den Schwürgerichtshöfen Athens: Die Proklesis zur Basanos.* Vienna.

————, ed. 1994. *Symposion 1993: Vorträge zur griechischen und hellenistischen Rechtsgeschichte.* Cologne.

————. 1995. Die athenischen Geschworengerichte-eine Sackgasse? In *Die athenische Demokratie im 4. Jahrhundert v. Chr.: Vollendung oder Verfall einer Verfassungsform?* ed. W. Eder, 321–31. Stuttgart.

Tod, M. N. 1946–48. *Greek Historical Inscriptions.* 2 vols. Oxford.

Todd, S. C. 1990a. *Lady Chatterley's Lover* and the Attic Orators: The Social Composition of the Athenian Jury. *JHS* 110: 146–73.

————. 1990b. The Purpose of Evidence in Athenian Courts. In *Nomos: Essays in Athenian Law, Politics and Society,* ed. P. Cartledge et al., 19–40. Cambridge.

———. 1990c. The Use and Abuse of the Attic Orators. *G&R* 37: 159–78.

———. 1993. *The Shape of Athenian Law.* Oxford.

———. 1996. Lysias against Nikomachos: The Fate of the Expert in Athenian Law. In *Greek Law in Its Political Setting: Justifications Not Justice,* ed. L. Foxhall and A. D. E. Lewis, 101–31. Oxford.

———. 1998. The Rhetoric of Enmity in the Attic Orators. In *Kosmos: Essays in Order, Conflict and Community in Classical Athens,* ed. P. Cartledge et al., 162–69. Cambridge.

———, trans. 2000. *Lysias.* Austin, Tex.

Tomaselli S., and R. Porter, eds. 1986. *Rape.* Oxford.

Too, Yun Lee 1995. *The Rhetoric of Identity in Isocrates: Text, Power, Pedagogy.* Cambridge.

Trédé, Monique. 1992. *Kairos, l'à-propos et l'occasion: Le Mot et la notion, d'Homère à la fin du IVe siècle.* Paris.

Treu, K. 1991. Rede als Kommunikation: Der attischen Redner und sein Publikum. *Philologus* 135.1: 124–30.

Trevett, J. 1992. *Apollodoros the Son of Pasion.* Oxford.

———. 1994. Demosthenes' Speech on Organization (Dem. 13). *GRBS* 35: 179–93.

Tsitsiridis, S. 1998. *Platons Menexenos: Einleitung, Text, und Kommentar.* Stuttgart.

Tuplin, C. J. 1985. Imperial Tyranny. In *Crux: Essays in Greek History Presented to G. E. M. de Ste. Croix on His 75th Birthday,* ed. P. A. Cartledge and F. D. Harvey, 348–75. London

Tyrrell, W. B. and F. S. Brown 1991. *Athenian Myth and Institutions.* Oxford.

Usher. S. 1976. Lysias and His Clients. *GRBS* 17: 31–40.

———, trans. 1990. *Isocrates: Panegyricus and To Nicocles.* Greek Orators, vol. 3. Warminster, Wilts., U.K.

———, trans. 1993. *Demosthenes:. On the Crown.* Greek Orators, vol. 5. Warminster, Wilts., U.K.

———. *Greek Oratory: Tradition and Originality.* Oxford.

Van Northwick, T. 1998. *Oedipus: The Meaning of Masculine Life.* Norman, Okla.

van Wees, H. 1998a. Reciprocity in Anthropological Theory. In *Reciprocity in Ancient Greece,* ed. C. Gill et al., 13–49. Oxford.

———. 1998b. A Brief History of Tears: Gender Differentiation in Archaic Greece. In *When Men Were Men: Masculinity, Power and Identity in Classical Antiquity,* ed. L. Foxhall and J. Salmon, 10–53. London.

———. ed. 2000. *War and Violence in Classical Greece.* London.

———. 2000. The Development of the Hoplite Phalanx. In *War and Violence in Classical Greece,* ed. H. Van Wees, 125–66. London.

Veligianni-Terzi, C. 1977. *Wertbegriffe in den attischen Ehrendekreten der Klassischen Zeit.* Heidelberger althistorische Beiträge und epigraphische Studien, vol. 25. Stuttgart.

Vernant, J.-P. 1989. At Man's Table: Hesiod's Foundation Myth of Sacrifice. In *The Cuisine of Sacrifice among the Greeks,* ed. M. Detienne and J.-P. Vernant, trans. P. Wissing, 57–68. Chicago.

————. 1990. One . . . Two . . . Three: *Erōs*. In *Before Sexuality: The Construction of Erotic Experience in the Ancient World*, ed. D. M. Halperin et al., 417–64. Princeton, N.J.

Vernant, J.-P., and P. Vidal-Naquet. 1988. *Myth and Tragedy in Ancient Greece*. Translated by J. Lloyd. New York.

Versnel, H. S. 1987. Wife and Helpmate. Women of Ancient Athens in Anthropological Perspective. In *Sexual Asymmetry: Studies in Ancient Society*, ed. J. Blok and P. Mason, 59–86. Amsterdam.

Vidal-Naquet, P. 1986a. *The Black Hunter: Forms of Thought and Forms of Society in the Greek World*. Translated by A. Szegedy-Maszak. Baltimore.

————. 1986b. The Black Hunter Revisited. *PCPhS* 212, n.s., 32: 126–44.

Visser, M. 1986. Medea: Daughter, Wife and Mother: Natal Family versus Conjugal Family in Greek and Roman Myths about Women. In *Greek Tragedy and Its Legacy: Essays Presented to D. J. Conacher*, ed. M. Cropp et al., 149–65. Calgary.

Vogt, J. 1974. *Ancient Slavery and the Ideal of Man*. Translated by T. Wiedemann. Oxford.

Walker, S. 1993. Women and Housing in Classical Greece: The Archaeological Evidence. In *Images of Women in Antiquity*, ed. A. Cameron and A. Kuhrt, 81–91. London.

Wallace, R. W. 1989. *The Areopagos Council to 307 B.C.* Baltimore.

————. 1994. The Athenian Laws against Slander. In *Symposion 1993: Vorträge zur griechischen und hellenistischen Rechtsgeschichte*, ed. G. Thür, 109–24. Cologne.

Wallace, R. W., and E. M. Harris, eds. 1996. *Transitions to Empire: Essays in Greco-Roman History 360–146 B.C., in Honor of E. Badian*. Norman, Okla.

Wankel, H., ed. and trans. 1976. *Demosthenes, Rede für Ktesiphon über den Kranz*. 2 vols. Heidelberg.

————. 1982. Die Korruption in der rednerischen Topik und in der Realität des klassichen Athens. In *Korruption im Altertum*, ed. W. Schuller, 29–47. Munich.

Weissenberger, M. 1987. *Die Dokimasiereden des Lysias (Or. 16, 25, 26, 31)*. Beiträge zur klassische Philologie 182. Frankfurt a/M.

Weiler, I. 1974. *Der Agon in Mythus: Zur Einstelung der Griechen zum Wettkampf*. Darmstadt.

Welskopf, E. C., ed. 1981. *Soziale Typenbegriffe im alten Griechenland und ihr Fortleben in den Sprachen der Welt*. Vol. 4. Berlin.

Welwei, K-W. 1974–77. *Unfreie im antiken Kriegsdienst*. 2 vols. Wiesbaden.

Wheeler, E. L. 1991. The General as Hoplite. In *Hoplites: The Classical Greek Battle Experience*, ed. V. D. Hanson, 121–70. London.

Whitehead, D. 1977. *The Ideology of the Athenian Metic*. Cambridge Philological Society, suppl. 4. Cambridge.

————. 1983. Competitive Outlay and Community Profit: *Philotimia* in Democratic Athens. *CM* 34: 55–74.

————. 1986. *The Demes of Attica, 508/7–ca. 250 B.C.* Princeton, N.J.

————. 1990. *Aeneas the Tactician: How to Survive under Siege*. Oxford.

———. 1993. Cardinal Virtues: The Language of Public Approbation in Democratic Athens. *C&M* 44: 37–75.

———. 2000. *Hypereides: The Forensic Speeches.* Oxford.

Wilson, P. J. 1991. Demosthenes 21 *(Against Meidias)*: Democratic Abuse. *PCPhS* 37: 164–95.

———. 1996. Tragic Rhetoric: The Use of Tragedy and the Tragic in the Fourth Century. In *Tragedy and the Tragic: Greek Theater and Beyond,* ed. M. S. Silk, 310–31. Oxford.

Winkler, J. J. 1990a. *The Constraints of Desire: The Anthropology of Sex and Gender in Ancient Greece.* New York.

———. 1990b. The Ephebes' Song: *Tragodia* and *Polis.* In *Nothing to Do with Dionysos? Athenian Drama in Its Social Context,* ed. J. J. Winkler and F. I. Zeitlin, 20–62. Princeton, N.J.

Winkler, J. J. and F. I. Zeitlin, eds. 1990. *Nothing to Do with Dionysos? Athenian Drama in Its Social Context.* Princeton, N.J.

Wohl, V. 1998. *Intimate Commerce: Exchange, Gender, and Subjectivity in Greek Tragedy.* Austin, Tx.

———. 2002. *Love among the Ruins: The Erotics of Democracy in Classical Athens.* Princeton, N.J.

Wolff, H. J. 1944. Marriage Law and Family Organization in Ancient Athens, *Traditio* 2: 43–95.

Wolpert, A. 2002. *Remembering Defeat: Civil War and Civil Memory in Ancient Athens.* Baltimore.

Wood, E. M. 1988. *Peasant-Citizen and Slave: The Foundations of Athenian Democracy.* London.

———. 1996. Demos versus "We the People": Freedom and Democracy Ancient and Modern. In *Demokratia: A Conversation on Democracies, Ancient and Modern,* ed. J. Ober and C. Hedrick, 121–37. Princeton, N.J.

Worthington, I. 1991. Greek Oratory, Revision of Speeches and the Problem of Historical Reliability. *C&M* 42: 55–74.

———. 1992. *A Historical Commentary on Dinarchus: Rhetoric and Conspiracy in Later Fourth-Century Athens.* Ann Arbor, Mich.

———. 1994a. History and Oratorical Exploitation. In *Persuasion: Greek Rhetoric in Action,* ed. I. Worthington, 109–29. London.

———, ed. 1994b. *Persuasion: Greek Rhetoric in Action.* London.

Wyse, W. 1904. *The Speeches of Isaeus with Critical and Explanatory Notes.* Cambridge.

Younger, W. 1966. *Gods, Men, Wine.* Cleveland.

Yunis, H. 1996. *Taming Democracy: Models of Political Rhetoric in Classical Athens.* Ithaca, N.Y.

Zanker, G. 1998. Beyond Reciprocity: The Akhilleus and Priam Scene in *Iliad* 24. In *Reciprocity in Ancient Greece,* ed. C. Gill et al., 73–92. Oxford.

Zeitlin, F. I. 1982. Cultic Models of the Female: Rites of Dionysus and Demeter. *Arethusa* 15: 129–55.

———. 1986. Configurations of Rape in Greek Myth. In *Rape,* ed. S. Tomaselli and R. Porter, 112–51. Oxford.

————. 1992. The Politics of Eros in the Danaid Trilogy of Aeschylus. In *Innovations of Antiquity*, ed. R. Hexter and D. Selden, 203–52. New York.

————. 1996. *Playing the Other: Gender and Society in Greek Classical Literature.* Chicago.

Ziolkowski, J. E. 1981. *Thucydides and the Tradition of Funeral Speeches in the Classical City.* New York.

General Index

Index Locorum

Compositor:	Binghamton Valley Composition, LLC
Text:	10/13 Sabon
Display:	Sabon
Printer and binder:	Maple-Vail Manufacturing Group